Imperial Bayonets

Imperial Bayonets

Tactics of the Napoleonic Battery, Battalion and Brigade as Found in Contemporary Regulations

George Nafziger

Greenhill Books, London
Stackpole Books, Pennsylvania

Greenhill Books

Imperial Bayonets
First published 1996 by Greenhill Books, Lionel Leventhal Limited,
Park House, 1 Russell Gardens, London NW11 9NN
and
Stackpole Books, 5067 Ritter Road, Mechanicsburg, PA 17055, USA

British Library Cataloguing in Publication Data
Nafziger, George
Imperial bayonets : tactics of the Napoleonic battery, battalion and
brigade as found in contemporary regulations
1. France. Armee – Drill and tactics – History
2. Tactics – History – 19th century
3. Military maneuvers – History – 19th century
4. Drill and minor tactics – History – 19th century
I. Title
355.4'2'09034

ISBN 1-85367-250-5

Library of Congress Cataloging-in-Publication Data
Nafziger, George F.
Imperial bayonets : tactics of the Napoleonic Battery, Battalion, and
Brigade as found in contempoary regulations / George Nafziger.
320p. 24cm.
Originally published: A guide to Napoleonic warfare. G.F. Nafziger
Includes bibliographical references and index.
ISBN 1-85367-250-5
1. Drill and minor tactics—History—18th century.   2. Drill and
minor tactics—History—19th century.   3. Europe—History—1789–
1815.   I. Title.
U164.N34   1996
355.5'094'09033—dc20   96-32212
                                                      CIP

Publishing History
Imperial Bayonets is the first trade publication of 'A Guide to Napoleonic Warfare' by G. F. Nafziger, which was privately published by the
author in 1995.

Printed and bound in Great Britain

This work is dedicated to the memory
of a dear friend and kindred spirit,
whose life was cut far too short:

Grover C. Cox

Contents

List of Illustrations

Figures

9

Tables

Charts

Imperial Bayonets

Foreword

The system of warfare used between 1792 and 1815 was unique in many senses. It was the logical evolution from systems used during the Seven Years War, and provided the basis for the evolution of warfare for years to come. Even as late as 1914 the campaigns of Napoleon were seriously studied at the various national military academies. Two Napoleonic generals, Clausewitz and Jomini, acted as the disciples and preachers of Napoleon's system of warfare, spreading it throughout the world. Napoleon's system was as innovative as had been Frederick the Great's, and warfare would never be the same again after he had put his mark on it. It is because of the historical significance of this period that I have felt an obligation to document how its wars were fought.

The aim of this study of Napoleonic tactics is to push through the mountain of misconceptions held by modern readers of military history, and provide them with a clear understanding of what actually transpired on the battlefield. Attempts by 'armchair generals' to interpret events in the light of their personal military experiences, or to confirm their own pet theories, have led to the publication of inaccurate accounts of the manoeuvres employed. Unfortunately, very few people today have the time, the inclination, or the ability to judge the accuracy of these documents, and as a result, when the average reader finds an inaccurate document in his hands, he accepts it as gospel.

Because of the dearth of accurate data to be found in print, I have made every effort to clearly identify the sources of the various manoeuvres and tactics discussed, though they are included in the text rather than lost in a page of otherwise tedious and generally unread footnotes. As many primary source documents as possible were used in an effort to ascertain the truth. The use of secondary sources has been carefully limited to those which have special significance and were written by reputable historians, contemporary military students, or philosophers of note.

It is worth noting that this period had more than its fair share of military students, who wrote copious numbers of books of the 'how to' type. Most notable among them were Dundas, Rothemberg, Cooper, Barber, Smirke, and Dedon. The identity of many others remains a mystery. The work of these men occasionally received official endorsement, while some reflect little more than wishful thinking. A few such books, no doubt, record events as they actually happened, but, being written outside of an 'official' environment, this cannot always be determined. Despite this, where their ideas can be compared to the regulations or to documented facts they are included.

This work contains much that is my own analysis and original thought, and the sources and logic used to arrive at every conclusion are carefully presented so that the reader can follow my train of thought. It is my interpretation of what transpired, based on written evidence, not personal experience.

I am obliged to acknowledge, with deepest gratitude, the special help provided over the years by two friends, Hans-Karl Weiss and Peter Hofschröer, both of whom tracked down copies of a multitude of obscure and rare drill regulations, without which this analysis would not have been possible. I would also like to acknowledge the assistance of Alan Croft, John Cook, Nigel Ashcroft, and Warren Worley, in the preparation of this study.

Note on German spelling

Some difficulties were experienced with the consistency of spelling found in the drill regulations of the various German-speaking nations, and between these and modern German. Though some of the more 'unusual' spellings have been revised to their modern equivalents, some have not. In addition, inconsistencies in many source documents have resulted in some other spelling variations in the text – for example, *chevauxleger/chevauxléger/chevauléger*, and *echequer/echiquier*. My apologies to those who will be confused or distressed by this.

Introduction

In order to understand the tactics of the Napoleonic Wars it is necessary to under-stand both those that preceded them and the structure and inter-relationship of the three combat arms: infantry, cavalry, and artillery.

The evolutionary history of Napoleonic tactics really begins in the 15th century, when the pike and the ancestor of the musket first made their appearance. In the mediaeval period heavily-armoured cavalry, being the dominant combat arm, merrily rode over the peasant militias, scattering them like chaff before the wind. However, when the Swiss introduced disciplined bodies of pike-armed infantry, the cavalry of the period found their prickly hedgehogs more than it could handle.

Early firearms, though cumbersome, were found superior to the bow and crossbow for several reasons. The skill to use a longbow required years of training. Also, the physical strength necessary to use it suffered dramatically during the privations of a long campaign. Though using a crossbow did not require the same strength as for a longbow, it still required considerable training. By contrast the arquebus, and its suc-cessor, the musket, required no more strength than that necessary to lug it about, and anyone could be trained to fire, as accurately as such weapons could fire, within a day. The inevitable marriage subsequently occurred, where pike and shot formations oper-ated together. The arquebusiers sheltered under the protective quills of the pike for-mation and shot down those cavalry impudent enough to close within range.

It gradually became apparent that the dense formations of pikemen were a waste of manpower that might more effectively be used as arquebusiers. In addition, the advent of the tactical use of artillery on the battlefield, which found the dense masses of pikemen irresistible targets, encouraged the abandonment of such formations.

The initial ratio of several pikemen to a single arquebusier (or, later, musketeer) shrank until the pike had all but vanished, and it finally disappeared with the introduc-tion of the plug bayonet, which converted the musket itself into a short pike. The musketeer could now protect himself from cavalry. However, the plug bayonet had a disadvantage, in that it was thrust into the muzzle of the musket and prevented it from being used as a firearm. The socket bayonet which subsequently replaced it al-lowed the musket to still be fired, being attached by means of a ring which slipped around the muzzle instead.

With this evolution in weaponry there was also a steady decline in the density of infantry formations. Pike formations had originally been extremely dense, usually deeper than they were wide. The theory was that the rear ranks would provide both weight and replacements for casualties once the pike formation was locked in a 'push-of-pike' (a shoving contest, where weight counted most), which determined who won the en-gagement.

With the disappearance of the pike, the push-of-pike was no longer a tactical consideration. The principal considerations were: 1) the density of formation necessary to repel a cavalry attack; 2) the maximum density of infantry that could safely discharge their weapons; and 3) the method of firing used by formed infantry.

Musketeer formations had started out six-deep. The first three ranks fired with the first rank kneeling, and the second and third ranks standing. The fourth, fifth and sixth ranks loaded and, when the first three ranks had fired, rotated forward to assume the firing position. This six-rank formation was also a vestige of the earlier idea that a thick formation was ideal for defending against cavalry.

The number of ranks was reduced to three when it was found that the rate of fire could be improved when the rear ranks did not have to walk forward through the front three. Simultaneously, the first three ranks were closed up so that the soldiers stood elbow to elbow, increasing the number of musket discharges per linear foot of frontage. This change in density did not immediately effect some of the formations in use. The square, a formation used to repel cavalry, continued to be formed up six-deep by many nations into the Napoleonic era.

Cavalry itself underwent a change, abandoning the use of *l'arme blanche*, or cold steel. The clash of sword on helm all but died. Heavy cavalry was replaced by *reiters*, whose principal weapon was the wheellock or matchlock pistol. Their tactic was the *caracole*, in which a cavalry regiment would walk up to the formation selected as its target. As each rank rode up, it would discharge its pistols into the mass of infantry or cavalry, wheel away, and reload as the next rank rode up and fired. This system almost completely supplanted the use of the sword until Gustavus Adolphus revived it by demonstrating the effectiveness of charging heavy cavalry into other cavalry. However, the impact of either tactic on a mass of pikemen was still minimal.

The cavalry did not undergo much evolution beyond this. By the French Revolution almost all of Europe's cavalry was armed with both a sword and a variety of firearms. The *caracole* had disappeared, and the principal battlefield tactic of cavalry was, once again, shock. The use of body-armour had come close to disappearing. In the French army, for instance, only one of more than 20 heavy cavalry regiments – the Cuirassier Regiment – continued to wear body-armour. The British army had abandoned it entirely, and a similar trend existed in the rest of Europe. However, this was subsequently reversed, and by the end of the Napoleonic Wars there were cuirassiers in the armies of most of the major European powers.

The evolution of the tactical use of artillery was closely tied to its technological evolution. Early artillery was heavy, relatively unmanoeuvrable, and very slow firing. Initially, it was used exclusively as a siege weapon, but this changed. Metallurgy improved the strength and reduced the weight of gun-barrels, allowing an increased rate of fire and longer ranges. Improved carriage designs, coupled with lower barrel weights, made the guns more manoeuvrable.

Once the guns could be manoeuvred with some rapidity and could fire more than a few times a day it was found that masses of pikemen and cavalry provided ideal targets. Even as the pike formations vanished, improvements in the rate of fire and manoeuvrability of artillery secured its own place on the battlefield. Its tactical use did not vary once it arrived, and even today its role remains that of destroying any enemy formation within range.

Chapter 1

The Basics of Napoleonic Infantry

In 1792 there were two basic types of infantry: line and light. The term 'heavy infantry' is not appropriate for this period and had long since disappeared from use. Infantry units carried several different names, depending on the nation which raised them, but generally line infantry consisted of any infantry formation known as *infanterie de ligne*, infantry, musketeers, grenadiers or guards. Light infantry consisted of any formation known as *chasseurs, jägers, freiwilliger jägers, pandors, schützen, infanterie légère* or light infantry. The term 'fusilier', unfortunately, can denote either. There were some exceptions. The British fusilier regiments were not light infantry, while many nations had light infantry as part of their guard formations. It should be clearly understood that there are almost always exceptions to any rule one might establish for this period.

The distinction between line and light infantry was that the light infantry was trained to operate in skirmish formations, and the line infantry was trained to stand in the 'line of battle'. The skirmish formation was a loose line of infantry, in which they operated relatively free of rigid control. They operated in pairs and several paces apart. They hid behind rocks and bushes when they fought, and were used to harass the enemy line infantry as well as to screen their own. Light infantry could, if required, operate as line infantry and, depending on the nation, did so to greater or lesser degrees.

The line infantry operated under very strict discipline. They stood elbow to elbow, marched in step to the cadence of drums, fired controlled volleys, and used all the various manoeuvres and formations that will be discussed later. In contrast to the free-spirited skirmishers, the line infantry were often beaten and held in formation by their officers and NCOs.

In the armies of some nations there were some minor equipment differences between the light and the line infantry. The uniforms would often vary, with green being the most common colour for elite light infantry. Many armies issued rifles to their light infantry, but it was rare for an entire light battalion to be totally thus equipped. The British were one of the few nations to do this, with the 5/60th and 95th Rifles being equipped with rifles since their formation, while as the wars progressed the KGL light battalions steadily increased the number of rifles in their ranks until every man carried one. However, British light infantry regiments rarely carried rifles. The many German states equipped only one-third of their light infantry with rifles, and in the French army only the sergeants in the *voltigeur* companies of the light infantry battalions carried rifles. Some German states also issued rifles to men in the light companies of their line regiments. Those men who were not issued rifles usually carried the same musket as the line infantry.

If a rifle was carried the light infantry would either have a different bayonet or no bayonet at all. Aside from these minor differences of uniform, weapon, and bayonet, the light infantryman was fundamentally a line infantryman who was taught to fight in skirmish formation.

Line infantry

In order to fully understand line infantry and its operations it is necessary to examine its basic formation, manoeuvring techniques, firing systems, and other significant characteristics. The line infantry was the summation of these characteristics and without a good understanding of them it is impossible to understand why things were done as they were.

When infantry formed up it was a universal practice that this was done in three ranks. The British two-rank exception (and a French exception) will be discussed later, but it should be noted that even their regulations, right through to 1815, specified that they be formed up in a three-deep formation. In all armies the tallest men were placed in the front rank. They were ranked from right to left in most armies, but the British ranked them from the flank to the centre. The next tallest were placed in the third rank and the shortest were in the middle or second rank.

This might seem illogical, because it would have short men trying to fire over the heads of taller men, but this was not the case. In this period very tall hats were worn, and the fire was between the front rank's soldiers, not over their heads. By placing the shorter men behind them the muskets of the second rank would be as far as possible from the ears of the taller front rank men. The idea of having a musket detonate right next to one's ear is enough to cause one to flinch with anticipated pain, so logic would suggest that if the men were not to suffer ear damage, and if they were to hear the commands of their officers, the noise of the firing needed to be kept as far away from their ears as possible.

Each man was allocated an interval of 22 inches in the British army and 26 inches in the French army. The infantry was always closed up, so that the elbows of each soldier touched those of the man beside him. The theoretical spacing allocated to each man and the distance between the ranks were closely prescribed. The actual spacing, of course, was left to the men in the ranks to sort out, so long as each man's elbows touched those of the man next to him. Table 1 provides a quick review of some of these theoretical spacings.

The manner in which the interval between the ranks was defined is not always clear. Only the French *Réglement de 1791* clearly states that it is measured from the

Table 1. Space allocated for a man in ranks and between ranks.		
	Width per man	*Interval between ranks*
Austrian	Unknown	2 paces (49.8 ins)
British	22 ins	1 pace
French	26 ins	13 ins
Prussian	Unknown	26 ins
Russian	27 ins	14 ins

Figure 1. Positioning of the ranks.

a) Front.   b) Flank.   c) Position when marching.

d) Spacing of companies, closed (*serré*), file closers not shown.

   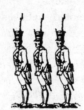

front rank's back, or the back of their packs, to the chest of the man in the rear rank. It is unknown if this is a consistent manner of defining the interval between ranks. No other regulation that was reviewed was so specific in defining this aspect of the formation. Figure 1 provides a graphic illustration of how the ranks were formed and demonstrates the dimensions provided in Table 1.

The company was an administrative formation within the battalion. The principal tactical component found in the battalion was the 'division'. The division was divided into smaller manoeuvring elements. The company was the smallest administrative unit. It is critical that it be understood that the administrative company and the tactical division – depending on the national definition of that unit – do not have an exactly analogous nature. Because of differences in organising the battalion, the division was either the tactical equivalent of the company (Prussia and Russia) or the equivalent of two companies (the rest of Europe).

Today the difference between the company and the division or *peloton* has ceased to exist, but it is critical in the period 1792–1815. As a result, when tactics are discussed the term *peloton* or division will be used. Though the names might change between armies, this practice of subdividing the division into smaller elements was universal. The ultimate unit was the file, which consisted of three men, one from the first rank, one from the second rank, and one from the third rank. It was the number of files that was used to size the next larger manoeuvring element and to control the frontages of every formation the infantry used.

The number of files per division cannot easily be provided because the organisational strengths of the divisions varied repeatedly for these armies during the period 1792–1815. Every reorganisation either increased or decreased the number of files, and a compilation of those relationships is beyond the scope of this work.

Table 2. Breakdown of divisions at full strength.

Austrians	1 division = 2 *Compagnies* = 4 *Halb-compagnies* = 8 *Züge*.
Bavarians	1 division = 2 *Compagnies* (or 2 *Halbdivision*) = 4 *Züge* = 8 sections = 16 *Halbsection*.
British	1 division = 2 platoons (companies) = 4 sub-divisions = 8 sections.
French	1 division = 2 *pelotons* (companies) = 4 sections.
Prussians	1 division (*Compagnie*) = 2 *Pelotons* = 4 *Züge* = 32 sections.
Russians	1 division (company) = 2 platoons = 4 half-platoons = 12 sections.
Saxons	1 division = 2 *Halbdivision* (2 companies) = 4 *Pelotons* = 8 sections.

The size of the sub-divisions, sections, etc., were critical. They had to be of equal size, because if they were not the formation would be both ragged and might well not work as desired.

All of the regulations laid down a maximum and a minimum number of files for each of these manoeuvring elements. When casualties occurred, men were drawn from the third rank and placed into the second rank to maintain the 'critical' minimum frontage of the manoeuvring element. If casualties were high enough the third rank would disappear completely. Some regulations even allow for the second rank to be totally depleted and used to fill out the first rank. Furthermore, if one *peloton* suffered heavy casualties, men from other companies could be drawn into it to flesh it out and maintain its frontage at the length required by regulation.

Should casualties be high enough the division could eliminate one of its larger manoeuvring elements and use the men to flesh out the remaining elements. It would then simply operate with a smaller frontage, but the number of files in the sections had to remain relatively constant. The 1804 British *Manual of Platoon Exercises* states: 'The companies [meaning platoons] may be equalised in point of numbers at all times when the battalion is formed for field movement and could the battalions of a line also

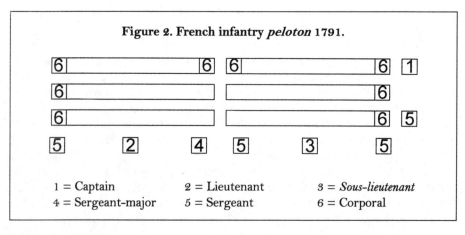

Figure 2. French infantry *peloton* 1791.

1 = Captain   2 = Lieutenant   3 = *Sous-lieutenant*
4 = Sergeant-major   5 = Sergeant   6 = Corporal

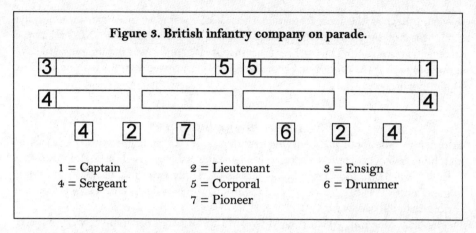

Figure 3. British infantry company on parade.

1 = Captain   2 = Lieutenant   3 = Ensign
4 = Sergeant   5 = Corporal   6 = Drummer
              7 = Pioneer

be equalised, the greatest advantages would arise.' This would even indicate that battalions might transfer personnel to equalise their strengths, though this seems unlikely. This practice leads to a very interesting analysis of the reasons for the two-rank firing method used by the British, which the rest of Europe did not adopt. The reasons for this will be addressed in Chapter 2.

The formations shown in Figures 2 and 3 are typical of the various nations' infantry *peloton* formations of the period 1791–1815. Though there were some national variations the company invariably consisted of three ranks of infantry, with officers and NCOs interspersed within their ranks, and a rank of officers and NCOs positioned behind them, known variously as 'file closers' or 'supernumeraries'. This rank stood at various intervals behind the third rank. In the French and post-1809 Prussian armies it was two paces, in the British army it was three paces, and in the 1792 Prussian army it was four paces.

The 'file closers' or 'supernumeraries' were part of the command and control structure. Their function was to maintain the discipline of the formation. They did this by ensuring that no-one in the *peloton* broke ranks and ran away through its rear. They did this by means of blows with their canes and halberds initially, and later with their muskets and the flats of their swords as the former two implements were discarded. In most armies this function could be brutal, to the point of shooting anyone trying to break ranks. In the French army, especially during the Revolution when officers and NCOs were elected by popular vote, this disciplinary action was not so brutal. Indeed, in the *fédérés*, a Revolutionary formation of great notoriety, any officer or NCO having the temerity to be too aggressive stood an excellent chance of being lynched by his own men. However, once the Napoleonic reforms of the army took place the elections ceased and the conscripts were driven back into formation by the flat of a sword. This was, basically, the function of the file closers' rank.

The officers and NCOs posted within the *peloton* were placed on the ends of the various manoeuvring elements so that they might serve as 'guides'. The function of the NCO or officer acting as a guide was to provide a reference point on which the line of infantry might 'dress'. This meant that they would form so that, if the 'guide' was standing on a line that ran perpendicular to the direction in which he was facing, everyone else in the manoeuvring element would align themselves so that they too were standing on that line and facing in the same direction. This ensured the 'dress', or straightness, of the linear formation. Because of the importance of maintaining the straightness of the front rank in particular, it would usually have more NCOs than the second and third ranks. During Frederick the Great's time it was not unknown to have surveyors with transits checking that the lines were dressed exactly, with no-one out of alignment.

Manoeuvring techniques

In order to talk about manoeuvring techniques one must begin with the basics of marching: cadences. There were three fundamental cadences used throughout Europe: 1) slow; 2) medium; and 3) fast. Some nations used only two rates, but when speaking in generalities it is best to categorise them into three basic speeds. Table 3 lists the various national cadences.

The slow cadences, which ranged from 75 to 80 paces per minute, were initially used in the field, but eventually abandoned. They had lovely nicknames such as the 'Saldern Waddle', the name by which the Prussian 75 paces per minute cadence was known. The medium cadences ranged from 100 to 120 paces per minute and were in general use throughout the period 1792–1815. Their names often betray their older origins and the concept that they were exceptionally fast, e.g. *Geschwindschritt* or 'quick pace'. These were the cadences generally used for manoeuvres on the battlefield.

Fast cadences were just that, fast. Some of them were so fast that the infantry was nearly running, and must have been very difficult for the drummers, who had to march with a snare drum in front of their legs. These paces did not exist in every army and were used with various frequencies. Though the Russians shared a regulated 'fast cadence' with the French, their goose-stepping march prohibited its frequent use. In general this fast cadence was entirely the province of the French.

		Paces per minute	Feet per minute
Table 3. Comparison of marching cadences.			
Austrian	*Ordinairschritt*	90–95	188–98
	Geschwindschritt	105	219
	Doublirschritt	120	250
French	*Pas ordinaire*	76	165
	Pas de route	85–90	184–95
	Pas accéléré	100	217
	Pas de manoeuvre	120	260
	Pas de charge	120	260
	Pas de course	250	542
Prussian	*Ordinaire schritt*	75	156
	Geschwindschritt	108	225
English	Ordinary pace	75	188
	Quick pace	108	270
Russian	*Tchyi szag*	60–70	150–75
	Skoryi szag	100–10	250–75
	Udwonyi szag	140–60	350–400

Probably the most significant factor is not the actual cadence, but the velocity of the various nations' infantry. Slow cadences with long paces provided the Russians with one of the fastest marches, and change the impression that one might get if one looked only at the number of paces taken per minute. The French nevertheless maintain their position as the fasting-moving infantry.

There were problems associated with the various marching cadences. These related directly to the formation of the marching unit and were integral to the national military philosophy prevailing at the time. In the case of the Russians, a goose-step marching technique was used, and any attempt to march in this manner at high speed would quickly exhaust the troops. Also, green troops would have more trouble maintaining the cadence and performing their manoeuvres at the faster cadences.

As a point of comparison, the French and Prussians marched with a locked knee (see Figure 1c) where the foot was thrust straight forward as if to kick the back of the leg of the man in the next forward rank. The kick was relatively low and required absolute faith on the part of everyone involved that it would be simultaneous. If it was not, the closeness of the ranks guaranteed that chaos would reign.

When manoeuvring in lines, in the manner of Frederick the Great's armies, it was necessary to march at a very slow pace. Any attempt to march a long line of infantry quickly for any length of time would result in the loss of its alignment. The military philosophy of Frederick's day was that a nice, straight line was best. It allowed better fire and it was more rigid. If it wavered and became serpentine in shape it would break if struck. As a result the 75 paces per minute rate was commonly used during this period. The slower rates were also used to train new soldiers, and in the French army the slowest was referred to as the *pas d'école* or 'school cadence'.

A column, with its smaller frontage, is not restrained by this problem quite as much. Indeed, because of its density and the pressure from the rear ranks it is far easier to march a column at very high speeds and still have it maintain sufficient alignment.

The use of columns and lines caused a tremendous philosophical debate in French military circles immediately before the French Revolution. There were two factions. Mesnil-Durand was an advocate of fast-moving columnar formations modelled after the Macedonian phalanx, that would crash into the enemy. His philosophical opponent, Guibert, advocated a mixture of columns and lines. He supported linear firing techniques, while columns were to be employed solely as a method of moving quickly to the site of the fire fight. Guibert won the argument and authored the famous Regulation of 1 August 1791.

The system generated by Guibert was a military philosophical revolution, on the magnitude of that imposed by Frederick the Great in his day. It used fast-moving columns that marched from position to position. Once there, the columns would deploy into line and resume the old system of combat. This system enabled the French to successfully use the faster marching cadences.

When it is said that Guibert fathered the use of columns and lines it does not mean that he created a new system, or that he worked in a total vacuum. Many of the manoeuvres in his Regulation are identical to the Prussian manoeuvres illustrated in *La Tactique Prussienne* of 1789, most significantly the conversions from column to line and vice versa. What Guibert did was to build on existing methods of manoeuvring and develop an overall philosophy of how to employ them once on the battlefield that was entirely different.

In addition – and though not the principal factor it is certainly one worthy of serious examination – the adoption of columns was also suited to the personnel revolution that took place in the French army between 1792 and 1796. The French officer corps, before the mass emigration of the French nobility that resulted from the Revolution, consisted predominantly of noblemen. There was a small percentage of junior officers who were not nobles and had risen through the ranks, but they were not a significant factor. When the nobility fled, the officers who took their places were not as experienced in manoeuvring their *pelotons* as their predecessors. In addition, thousands of new recruits, volunteers and conscripts, flooded the ranks, and there was insufficient time to drill them into proficiency in the rigid linear tactics of the day. As a result, the ease and manoeuvrability of the column made it the preferable manoeuvring system.

There were also problems instituting the discipline required for linear formations. Early in the Revolution all officers and NCOs were elected, and consequently the position of an officer or NCO was not strong. Denunciations were common, and the result of a denunciation for anti-Revolutionary activities was generally execution. The use of a column made it easier for the file closers to keep their men in position, because anyone attempting to flee would have to run through several successive ranks of their fellows. In addition, a higher cadence speed gave them less time to think about what was awaiting them.

The other European armies did not have this problem and followed the successful formulas of Frederick the Great. They tended to rely on linear formations, even after the French showed them the power of the column. It would, however, be untrue to suggest that those nations did not eventually modify their procedures to accommodate the use of the column after the fashion of the French.

The second basic manoeuvring technique that needs to be examined is the pivot. There were two types of pivot, fixed and floating. The fixed pivot is illustrated in Figure 4. As can be seen, the *peloton* marches until it arrives at the point where it is to pivot. Assuming this is a left pivot, as illustrated in Figure 4, the left flank practically

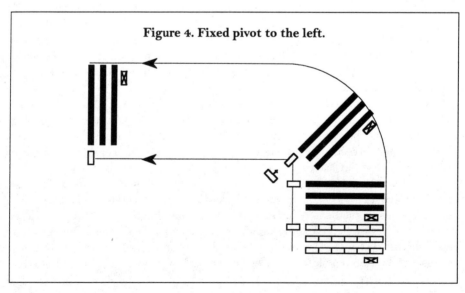

Figure 4. Fixed pivot to the left.

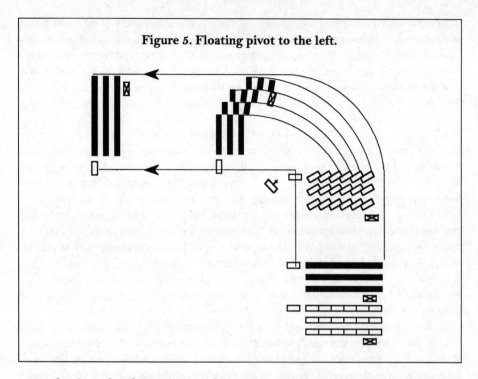

Figure 5. Floating pivot to the left.

stops when it reaches the pivot point while everyone to the right marches with a slightly longer stride until the outermost soldier is practically running in order to maintain the alignment of the *peloton*.

Figure 5 illustrates the floating pivot. As can be seen, the *peloton* breaks up into a number of segments, each of which marches in a direct line to its final destination maintaining the cadence without any serious strain.

The simple mathematics of these two systems show that the floating pivot is more direct and faster. It also prevents a traffic-jam of *pelotons* building up behind the pivot-

Table 4. National use of types of pivots after 1791.

	Type of pivot	Year adopted or in use
Austrians	Fixed	Pre-1791, still used by militia in 1808
	Floating	In use by 1807
French	Fixed	Pre-1791
	Floating	1791
British	Fixed	Pre-1791
	Floating	In use in 1804 but fixed pivot seems more prevalent
Russians	Fixed	Pre-1791
	Floating	Unknown
Prussians	Fixed	1788
	Floating	1812

ing *peloton* because the pivoting soldier on the left flank clears the pivot point before the next *peloton* arrives and begins its own pivot. With a fixed pivot, the rear *peloton* must stop and mark time (march in place) until the pivoting *peloton* has cleared the pivot point. If it advances, it will collide with its predecessor and, in addition, it will lose the established interval between the two manoeuvring *pelotons*.

Firing systems

The fundamentals of musketry tactics were directly influenced by the weapon and its limitations. The muskets were heavy and clumsy devices of very limited accuracy. They were smoothbore weapons, which means that they had no rifling to spin the bullet and thereby make it more accurate. In contrast to modern weapons which have high rates of fire, use self-contained cartridges, automatic loading and chambering, and a multitude of other technological innovations, the 19th century musket was crude and slow. Its charge consisted of black powder, a lead ball, and wadding. The powder charge was ignited by means of a powder train that transmitted fire from the pan through a touch-hole to the main charge. The powder in the pan was ignited by a spring-loaded mechanism that caused a flint to strike a steel, generating sparks and igniting the powder.

The ball was not tightly fitted to the bore of the musket and the wadding was used to form the necessary gas seal. The ball rattled down the bore and came out the muzzle at no generally predictable angle. Gun sights were almost unknown, whilst aiming or target practice was, in most armies, an annual affair where three or four rounds were fired so the soldier could learn not to be afraid of the tremendous kick of his musket.

The line infantry was not taught to aim, but simply to point their muskets in the general direction of the enemy. Problems arose when firing from raised parapets or a slope: because they were not trained to aim they were known to fire straight ahead, over the heads of the advancing enemy.

When loading and firing a musket the infantryman was required to remember up to 17 separate steps (the actual number varied from army to army). Failure to execute these steps properly could result in a misfire of the musket. One common error, usually executed by green troops, was to forget to replace the ramrod in its holder. The troops would fire the musket with the ramrod still in the barrel, sending it flying off in the direction of the enemy and leaving the soldier without the means to reload his weapon.

Short cuts evolved, but they were dangerous. Because of the looseness of the fit between the bullet and the bore soldiers found they could simply put the wadding and ball in the mouth of the musket. They would then slam the butt of the musket on the ground a couple of times and cause the wadding and ball to fall down the barrel. However, this would only work if the ground was dry and hard, while it could also cause the musket to discharge if the trigger mechanism was sensitive to such shocks.

Another trick was not to reverse the ramrod to use its blunt end to shove the round home, but to pull it straight out of the stock and shove the narrow end down the barrel. The problem with this was that the ramrod could get wedged in the barrel. The goal of both tricks was to increase the rate of fire. On average, trained troops could fire about two rounds per minute, but in practice this rate steadily slowed because the quality of the powder was not up to modern standards and quickly fouled the bore.

After about 50 rounds it was necessary to clean the bore. In addition, the flint would have to be periodically changed or adjusted to ensure that it continued to operate satisfactorily.

Because of these inherent mechanical problems with 19th century muskets misfires were common. The term 'flash in the pan' derives from one such mishap. Here the trigger mechanism functioned properly and ignited the powder in the pan, with the attendant 'flash', but the main charge was not ignited. This required the soldier to re-prime the pan and fire again. As hard as it might seem to believe, and despite the terrific kick of these weapons, when a musket misfired in the heat of battle some soldiers would not notice the misfire and would ram home a second round on top of the first. When these superimposed charges were finally ignited the results could be deadly to the soldier and his neighbors. During the American Civil War a similar smoothbore musket was found at Vicksburg with seven unfired loads in the barrel.

The formations used were heavily influenced by the shortcomings of these weapons. Because the muskets were such notoriously inaccurate weapons the best method of ensuring a hit was to mass fire and point it in the general direction of the enemy. Little if any effort was ever made to aim the musket at the enemy as there was little hope of an aimed round hitting its intended target. It was generally acknowledged that anyone hit by an aimed round at 200 paces was a terribly unlucky person.

Accuracy of musketry

The question of the accuracy and effectiveness of musketry from the Seven Years War to the American Civil War has been the subject of considerable debate for years. There is, however, little empirical data upon which to work. Period descriptions of 'massive' casualties inflicted by a single volley are seldom if ever supported by a precise 'body count', and have generally resulted in rather wild speculation as to the actual impact of a single volley of musketry fired by a formed body of infantry. There is, however, a small amount of period data that can be used for the purpose of developing some idea of what might have been the true impact of such a volley, which can minimise subjective arguments.

The first data to consider is that from the notorious Prussian musketry trials. The Prussian General Scharnhorst ran a series of trials around 1810 in which he formed a company of grenadiers and blazed away at a canvas sheet at varying distances. The target approximated the size of a company of 'enemy' infantry. In performing this test the Prussians used six different types of musket.

The Prussians found that hits on small targets by rifles compared two to one with hits made by muskets at a range of 160 yards, and compared four to one on targets at a range of 240 yards. On large targets the ratio of rifle to musket hits was four to three at 160 yards and two to one at 300 yards. The relatively better performance of the musket on the larger target can be explained by the reduction of the musket's large cone of fire when firing on large targets.

The times needed to load and fire a rifle, compared to a musket, at a range of 160 yards was five to two, and at 240 yards, five to one. Scharnhorst concluded that the 'rifle and musket have about the same effect in the same period of time, but the musket needs three to four times as much ammunition as the rifle. Furthermore, under enemy fire the *jäger* [light infantryman] is more liable to aim than an ordinary infantryman because he is convinced that without aiming he never hits at all, and he has been trained and is accustomed to aim from youth on.'

In a combat situation where the tactics did not rely mainly on massed, unaimed fire, the rifleman was at least as effective as the musketeer. However, he was at a disadvantage where heavy small-arms fire was necessary to repel a charge.

Tables 5 and 6 provide the details of the test run on large targets, approximating the size of a formed infantry *peloton*, and small targets, probably the size of a single man. For the purposes of this study the first set of data will be analysed. Table 7 converts the raw data into an 'average' accuracy figure that will permit a single line of 'best fit' to be developed.

Two artificial data points have been added. The first is based on the assumption that at point blank range (0 yards) none of the 200 shots would have missed. The second is that 450 yards is beyond the effective range of the period musket and none of the hits, if any occurred, would have been sufficient, on average, to cause any serious damage. These points were necessary from a mathematical perspective and permit the preparation of a curvilinear regression analysis of the average results of a company firing under ideal conditions. Chart 1 is the result of that test plotted with the line of 'best fit' for comparison with the original test data.

A regression analysis, using the SAS procedure NLIN, generated the following formula from the Prussian test data:

$$\text{Percentage of hits} = 100 \left(1 - \text{Distance}/450\right)^{1.50 \pm 0.23}$$

The uncertainty quoted in the formula is the standard error. Using this formula, and rounding the exponential to 1.5, the percentage of hits generated is shown in Table 8.

Table 5. Hits obtained out of 200 rounds fired at a large target.

Musket	Range in yards			
	80	160	240	320
'Old Prussian' 1782 musket	92	64	64	42
'Old Prussian' with angled butt	150	100	68	42
Nothardt musket 1805	145	97	56	67
'New Prussian' musket 1809	153	113	70	42
French Charville 1777	151	99	53	55
British musket	94	116	75	55

Table 6. Hits obtained out of 100 rounds fired at a small target.

	Range in yards		
	120	160	240
Prussian rifle using plaster bullets	68	49	21
Prussian rifle using cartridges	51	26	–
Prussian 1809 musket	–	21	4

Table 7. Average accuracy figures.

	Range in yards					
	0	*80*	*160*	*240*	*320*	*450*
Number of hits	200	92	64	64	42	0
	200	150	100	68	42	0
	200	145	97	56	67	0
	200	153	113	70	42	0
	200	151	99	53	55	0
	200	94	116[1]	75	55	0
Total hits	1200	785	589	386	303	0
Percentage of shots hitting target	100%	65%	49%	32%	25%	0%

Table 8. Percentage of hits generated.

Range (yds)	*Percentage of hits*	*Range (yds)*	*Percentage of hits*	*Range (yds)*	*Percentage of hits*	*Range (yds)*	*Percentage of hits*
0	100%	125	61%	250	30%	375	7%
25	92%	150	54%	275	24%	400	4%
50	84%	175	48%	300	19%	425	1%
75	75%	200	41%	325	15%	450	0%
100	69%	225	35%	350	10%		

However, this table is based on a volley being fired by a steady line of infantry, not under fire or in combat and suffering the attendant 'jitters'. They are firing clean weapons, and their target is a sheet. It needs to be remembered that a hit on the sheet is not necessarily a hit on a man.

The second step is to make some modification from these ideal test figures that will permit them to relate to battlefield conditions. Such information is not common but does exist for one volley fired at the Battle of Göhrde. This battle was fought in northern Germany on 16 September 1813, between Wallmoden's Corps and a brigade under General Pécheux. The Bremen-Verden Battalion, a Hanoverian militia unit, took a single volley from 66 muskets at a range of 60–80 paces[2] and suffered 27 casualties.[3] The casualty reports indicate that a total of 30 casualties were suffered, and a second volley was reportedly fired at the battalion as it collapsed. This adds some doubt to the

[1] Various documents on firing muskets in this period have indicated that it was necessary to point a musket at the feet of a target at close ranges because the kick of the musket threw the barrel up, causing the ball to arc up, which would, if the barrel was not aimed lower, cause the ball to pass over the target.

This increase in the number of hits at a longer range clearly indicates that the muskets were pointed, not aimed, and that the kick of the musket threw the balls up in an arc whose optimum effectiveness, when fired with the musket level to the ground at a man-sized target, was somewhere between 80 and 160 yards. That of the other muskets was somewhere below 80 yards.

[2] For all calculations the average estimated range of 70 yards will be used.

[3] von Quistorp, B. *Die Kaiserlich Russisch-Deutsch Legion*, p.99.

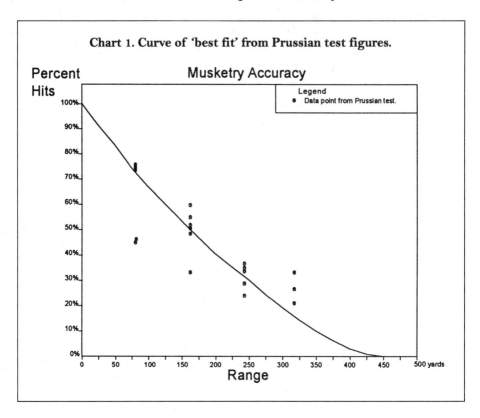

Chart 1. Curve of 'best fit' from Prussian test figures.

validity of the casualty count of the first volley, but then that number is far lower than what the Prussian test indicates they should have been.

The French were conscripts with several months service, but this was their first engagement of any note. Though not hardened veterans, they were certainly well trained and drilled in the use of their muskets. An initial volley was fired at a range of approximately 70 yards with a second volley being fired at a closer, unspecified range. This indicates a reasonable level of discipline.

The result is that there are historical records indicating that the actual number of hits was 27, or 41%. The Prussian tests would have indicated a 75–81% hit ratio – about twice the field returns.

It is desirable to have more such 'real' examples of the effectiveness of firepower, but, alas, they do not exist or are not available. Efforts to repeat the mathematical analysis done on the Prussian tests by correcting all data points using this ratio did not prove satisfactory, so instead it was decided that it was preferable to use the three data points 100% @ 0 yards, 41% @ 70 yards and 0% @ 450 yards, and allow the computer's curve smoothing process to generate an approximation of musketry effectiveness under battle conditions. That curve is shown in Chart 2.

The third step in the process is to march a battalion against the firing line, firing 2–2½ volleys every minute (to a maximum of 30, which was the normal allowance of ammunition), assuming the attacking infantry was marching at its 'charge pace' through the field of fire. For a variety of reasons, including a desire to get a moderate hit figure, a rate of fire of two rounds per minute will be used hereafter.

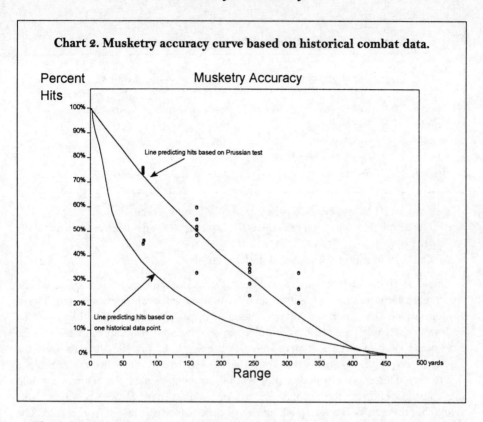

Chart 2. Musketry accuracy curve based on historical combat data.

Musketry Accuracy

Percent Hits

Line predicting hits based on Prussian test

Line predicting hits based on one historical data point

Range

The various 'charge paces' for the principal combatants in the period are shown in Table 9.

Combining the percentage of hits and the rate of advance with the rate of fire a table can be generated that will predict the number of casualties that could be inflicted by a line of infantry on an advancing column of attacking infantry. It should be noted that only two-thirds (80 men) of the unit could fire. The only thing that remains to be determined is the distance at which the defending infantry would begin its fire. Valentini states: '*Geschlossene Infanterie muss nie weiter als auf dreihundert Schritt feuern*' ('Closed [formed] infantry must never fire at distances greater than 300 paces').[4] Assuming that a period general officer is about as good a source as one could hope to find, the analysis will start with the first volley being fired at that distance. It is assumed that a pace will equate to a yard, allowing for the inability of an officer to precisely estimate with his eyes a distance of 300 paces.

Using the Göhrde curve, and manually reading the percentage hits at a given range, we arrive at the following table of casualties to be inflicted by a line of infantry firing on an attacking line of infantry. The following assumptions were made in producing Table 10:

1) Two rounds per minute are fired.
2) The attacking infantry marches exactly at its regulated rate.

[4] von Valentini, Generalmajor Freiherr *Abhandlung über den Kleinen Krieg und über den Gebrauch der leichten Truppen*, p.67.

	Name of pace	Paces per minute	Rate of advance (feet per minute)
Austria	Geschwindschritt	90–5	188–98
France	Pas de charge	120	260
Britain	Quick pace	108	270
Prussia	Geschwindschritt	108	225
Russia	Skoryi szag	100–10	250–75

Table 9. Charge paces.

3) The results of the Göhrde volley are typical and average.
4) The first volley was fired exactly as the attacker arrived within 300 yards of the defender.
5) The terrain is perfectly flat and without cover.

The first thing that this chart indicates is that the slow marching speed of the Austrians guarantees that a higher level of casualties will be inflicted on them. That a slower unit would suffer more volleys is not a surprise. The Austrians will receive four volleys to the three received by the other nations. It is, however, questionable if the Prussians would receive that fourth volley, as the length of time for them to cover the distance from the third volley is exactly that required to load and fire the muskets a fourth time. One could argue that they would receive it because the defenders would move faster and faster the closer the attacking column came. However, one can also argue that the attackers might push harder to close before that last volley arrived. The deciding factor would be if the attacking unit was 'staggered' by the various volleys. However, it would appear that there are more variables that favour a fourth volley being delivered.

The truly significant results of this table are that in every instance, theoretically, a defending line of infantry should be able to completely obliterate any equal force of attacking infantry. Yet we know historically that this did not occur. Indeed, it would appear that infantry was regularly able to close and bring to melee enemy infantry that stood and supposedly fired volley after volley into (or probably over) the charging unit.

What, therefore, was the effectiveness of early 19th century musketry? First, one must recognise that the variability of musketry was incredibly wide. There is, obviously, a band of results, rather than a single line. The single Göhrde volley that broke the first line of advancing Hanoverians would appear to be in a region that one might term the 'upper limit' of the anticipated results of a good volley. On the other hand, similar volleys were delivered that inflicted so few hits that the attacking infantry ignored them and closed with bayonets.

The second consideration is a combination of ammunition supplies and knowledge of the lack of effectiveness of musketry by the officers controlling the fire. It is known that the defending officers would conserve their fire to save their limited supply of ammunition and that they would also try to hold their volleys to the point where they would be most effective.

In the same Battle of Göhrde a second French battalion allowed the Bennigsen Battalion to advance to within 10 paces before they fired. It would appear, however,

Table 10. Musketry hits based on Göhrde curve.		
	Range of volley (yds)	*Projected casualties*
English column under fire	30	61%
	120	28%
	210	14%
	300	8%
	Total	111%
French or Russian column under fire	39	53%
	126	26%
	213	13%
	300	8%
	Total	100%
Prussian column under fire	75	40%
	150	22%
	225	12%
	300	8%
	Total	82%
Austrian column under fire	44	50%
	100	33%
	175	17%
	235	11%
	300	8%
	Total	119%

that many of the front rank of the French lost their nerve, threw down their guns, and pushed back through their line. The French battalion collapsed and turned to the rear, withdrawing. The Bennigsen Battalion did not break and lost only 16 men during the battle. It is not clear if they lost them in this single volley, however broken, or if they were cumulative.

All this suggests that it may have been the general practice to fire one volley, or at most two volleys, at an attacking infantry formation. The remainder of the infantry fire would, therefore, appear to have been between lines of infantry blasting away ineffectively at longer ranges and stationary targets.

This does not, however, resolve the question of musketry accuracy and effectiveness under combat conditions. Nor can it reasonably be predicted by test results or a single battlefield incident. There are simply too many unknowns and too many variables. As a result, and climbing out on a limb, I would suggest that Chart 3 reasonably defines the effectiveness of period musketry.

Zone A is that area between the curve produced by the Prussian tests and an artificially drawn mid-point line between the Prussian test results and the Göhrde volley. The Göhrde volley was selected as a lower limit because the troops were conscripts with less than six months of service, firing under ideal conditions. Zone A would describe the 'perfect conditions zone' (crack troops, clean muskets, no fear, and no enemy fire to unsettle them). The probability of a volley occurring in Zone A under battlefield conditions must be considered an act of divine intervention.

Zone B is a region in which one would expect to find the normal results of veteran troops firing their first volley on a battlefield. Successive volleys would, necessarily, decline in effectiveness as the weapons fouled.

Zone C is an artificial zone, drawn by eyeball estimate more than anything, of the region where the effectiveness of most battlefield musketry would *probably* lie over the course of a prolonged battle.

Zone D is that region where the musket, as a piece of equipment, ceases to be the determining factor in effectiveness. It is where the morale, or the lack thereof, on the part of the attacker or defender plays a greater role in the effectiveness of the volley.

One might wonder why rifles were not common on the battlefield. There were several reasons. First, they were significantly more expensive. In addition they were slower to fire, as shown by Scharnhorst's study. They often required a mallet to pound the ball into firing position, they usually required better grades of powder, required custom-manufactured balls, and fouled too easily. Also, there was a tremendous amount of bureaucratic resistance to such innovations in many of the armies. As a result the musket prevailed, and because of its inherent inaccuracies linear formations had to be used.

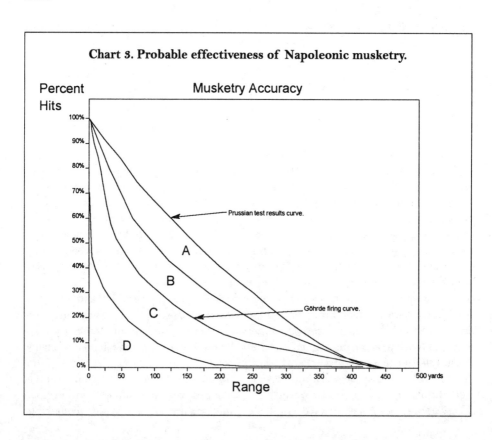

Chart 3. Probable effectiveness of Napoleonic musketry.

It is worth noting that there was an evolution of thought on aimed fire and the ranges at which it was used. The Austrian 1808 *Landwehr* regulation actually speaks of aimed fire at 400 yards' range. It is highly unlikely that this was rifle fire, as generally the *Landwehr* generally was the last force armed and the worst equipment available was generally issued to them.

Types of volleys

The use of a formal firing line led to several types of fire. The easiest manner to review the fire systems is to examine those used by the French, the Prussians, and the British, which represent those most commonly used.

The French army battalion executed fire by *pelotons*, by divisions, by *demi-rang* (half-rank) and by *bataillon* (battalion). Fire by *peloton* was regulated by odd divisions. The *pelotons* fired successively in the order of their numbers: 1st, 3rd, 5th, 7th, or 2nd, 4th, 6th, and 8th. The *peloton* pairs executed their fire by the half division, alternating their fire. Only the grenadiers (in amalgamated battalions) fired by the entire division. The fire by division was executed in the following sequence: 1st, 3rd, 2nd, 4th and grenadiers. *Demi-rang* fire was started from the right. Fire by battalion started with the first battalion, and the second battalion fired only as the first reloaded their weapons.

The *Réglement de 1764* established a firing system based on three ranks. The *Réglement de 1791* modified this and established a two rank voluntary firing system. This was because it was found that the third rank's fire was inefficient and at times dangerous to the men in the first two ranks. In this system the third rank did not fire, but loaded the muskets of those in the first two ranks, passing loaded muskets forward.

The danger to the first two ranks was proven in 1813. Concern over the number of seemingly self-inflicted wounds caused a study to be made. It was found that the new recruits in the third rank often got excited and wanted to fire as well. The result was the head being blown off someone in the front rank.

Again, the infantry was taught to fire by *peloton*, by *demi-bataillon* and by *bataillon*. They were taught an advancing fire system where the *peloton* would advance, halt and fire, and advance again *en échequer* with other *pelotons* which fired when they advanced. In the advancing fire the front rank would kneel and all three ranks fired.

Fire by ranks was a second type of fire that was executed by all three ranks. It was executed by having the third rank move six and a half inches to the right and fire through the gap between the front two ranks. This fire was executed across the front of the unit by each rank, the other two ranks holding their fire. The third rank fired first, then the second and finally the first rank. The ranks were never permitted to fire out of sequence. This type of fire was especially useful against cavalry, where fire erupted from the entire front of the *peloton* with each volley.

This system permitted a reserve firing capability for the *peloton*, so as to protect it against a surprise attack by cavalry. This did not always work and various nations developed cavalry tactics in an effort to tease a battalion into discharging its weapons so they could close into sabre range before the infantry was able to reload.

The British fired by battalions, wings and 'grand divisions'. This fire was executed by all three ranks. The first rank stood and fired in place, the second rank took one half step to the right and fired between the ranks, and the third rank took a full step to the right and fired through the ranks. As each rank fired it would begin loading immediately. In this system the front rank could fire either from a standing position or from a kneeling position. The firing of every rank was closely controlled and executed on order so fire was essentially the same as the French 'fire by rank'.

The British also used a system of firing by files. The file was three men, one from each rank. When these men fired they moved into firing position as indicated before and fired. When they had fired, the file next to them fired, and the fire swept down the line. As each file fired it automatically reloaded and fired again 'without waiting for any word of command.' The fire of a company was independent of the fire of any other company. In general 'all fire began in the centre and not on the flanks.'

As a variation the British were trained to fire two ranks from a kneeling position. When given the order to present 'each man slowly and independently levelling at the particular object which his eye has fixed upon; and as soon as he has covered his object, each man fires of his own accord, without waiting for any word of command.'

When firing wings by companies each wing carried on its fire independently, without regard to the other wing. It could fire from the centre to the flanks or the flanks to the centre as it chose. If there were five companies in the wing, two pauses were made between the fire of each, and if there were only four companies three pauses were made. This was done to allow the first firing company sufficient time to reload. When firing by grand divisions three pauses were made between the fire of each division, again to allow the division which had fired sufficient time to reload and maintain a smooth rate of fire.

All armies appear to have had a universal type of fire known as oblique fire, which allowed the firing unit to project its musket fire in a direction other than straight ahead. It was performed using the systems described above, but if the third rank was to fire the first rank would probably have had to kneel. Unfortunately, the regulations make no mention of this.

There were some different systems of fire. The Prussian army of 1792 used several different firing techniques. When a battalion was formed by *Halb-compagnien* (half-companies or *pelotons*) in line, fire was executed by the alternate firing of half-companies. The three ranks fired simultaneously. The first rank knelt, while the second and third stood upright. The fire began from the right.

A second form of fire used by the Prussians was by half-companies with the third rank taking a half turn to the right. This fire was executed when the battalion made a half-turn to the right, but with the line not moving from its original position. The rest of the action was the same as firing by half-companies.

The third form of Prussian fire was the advancing fire. Here the half-companies marched towards the enemy. The right half-company stopped and fired first. Upon the signal of their officer, and without reloading, the right hand half-company shouldered arms and advanced. The next half-company would stop and fire when the first half-company caught up with the slowly retreating line, and so on down the line of the battalion.

The fourth method of fire was retreating fire. When advancing directly away from the enemy the first half-company (formerly on the left, now the right) would stop, turn about, and fire. When the fire was executed, the soldiers would shoulder their arms, about face and resume the retreat, catching up with the battalion. Each successive half-company would act in the same manner as the preceding half-company caught up with the retiring battalion. Again, there is no indication of stopping to reload.

There were also three types of an unusual firing method known as 'hedge' (sniper) fire. The first of these was a withdrawing fire where pairs of files would turn about and fire on pursuing hussars or skirmishers. This was intended as just enough fire to keep the harassing forces away. The second type of hedge fire was used when facing small groups of enemy infantry which were not sufficient to justify a battalion volley, but were sufficiently annoying to merit some response. In this latter instance pairs of files would advance eight paces in front of the battalion, form in two ranks, fire, re-form in three ranks, and return to the battalion. The purpose and use of this fire will become more obvious when light infantry is discussed later.

The third form of 'hedge' fire was exactly the same as the second type, but the pair of files did an about face, advanced out of the rear of the battalion and fired to the rear. All other actions were the same.

The bayonet

As mentioned in the introduction to this book, the bayonet was the evolutionary successor of the pike, and in its use many of the pike's tactics were inherited. Its principal use was to convert the infantry formation into a prickly hedgehog that was safe from cavalry. Its secondary use was the bayonet attack. The bayonet had generally supplanted the sword as the infantryman's close-quarters weapon and, though a few formations in various armies retained infantry swords, the bayonet was the only universal edged weapon.

Its use varied tremendously. The Russian general Souvarov is noted for his famous quote: 'The bayonet is a fine fellow, but the musket is a lazy fellow.' He far preferred the bayonet attack to exchanges of musketry. One might assume that the bayonet was a major weapon on the battlefield, but it was not. Larrey, Napoleon's Surgeon General of the *Grande Armée*, did a battlefield study of wounds after the battles of 1807 and found that most were caused by artillery and musketry. Only about 2% of the wounds he examined were caused by bayonets.

Bayonet charges were a frequent tool of the French. During the Revolutionary period they were usually executed in line and against an enemy who had already been broken by fire. This is the Frederickan use of the bayonet and represents the way the Allied powers generally used the bayonet during the entire period 1792–1815. During the Napoleonic era the French bayonet charge was usually executed by a battalion formed in column. It became a major weapon that struck at the morale of the enemy. However, in this instance the French had generally softened up their enemies with concentrated artillery fire, not musketry.

There is also a misconception about the frequency of bayonet charges executed against cavalry. It is reputed that there were only three such charges in history: 1) by the Prussian Bernberg Infantry Regiment attacking Austrian cavalry at Liegnitz in 1760; 2) by the Russian Lithuanian Guard Infantry Regiment attacking the French cavalry at Borodino; and 3) by the British 5th Foot Regiment attacking French cavalry at El Bodon in 1811. In fact, there appear to have been more. During the Seven Years War British infantry appears to have charged French cavalry during the Battle of Minden. One more such attack is reported in a letter from *Général de division* Baron de Lorencz to *Maréchal* Oudinot. It occurred on 18 May 1813 in a battle near Neukirchen when the French 52nd and 137th Line Regiments formed square to repulse a Russian cavalry attack, and after repulsing two attacks, reformed into column and advanced more than once against the cavalry at the *pas de charge*.

In the battles around Katzbach on 26 August 1813 the 4/34th Line Regiment found a force of Prussian Uhlans had charged into and captured the park of the French XI Corps. When only about one-sixth of their muskets would fire because of the day long rain the 4/34th charged, in a battalion mass, against the cavalry, drove it away, and recaptured the XI Corps park. They do not appear to have suffered any appreciable losses.

At the Battle of Vauchamps, fought on 13 February, two companies of the Silesian *Schützen* found themselves with a squadron of French cavalry sitting on their line of escape from the disaster that was befalling their brigade. The two companies, totalling about 230 men, formed column, fixed their bayonets, and charged forward, cutting their way through the French cavalry. They suffered *no* casualties. In fact, the casualty report lists a few lost shakos and bayonets as the result of some actual physical contact with the French cavalry.

On 25 March 1814, during the Battle of La Fère-Champenoise, Delord's brigade of national guardsmen, part of Pacthod's Division, formed itself into attack columns and advanced at the *pas de charge* against two Russian cavalry regiments, forcing them to withdraw. This charge was executed with almost no casualties, though later events in the battle resulted in the total destruction of Pacthod's division.

The last such attack in history appears to have occurred on 27 April 1920, when the Russian 7th Rifle Division executed a bayonet attack against a Polish cavalry brigade near Malin. In contrast to the other such reported incidents, the casualty figures for this clash are not totally unknown. It appears that the Russians lost 40% of their strength! This was, no doubt, because the Poles had machine-guns with them, but it is more than enough to discourage any but the most desperate from attempting such an act, at least in the 20th century.

However, there are so many instances of it occurring in the early 19th century that it cannot be denied as a valid, yet still desperate tactic. This was made particulary clear in every instance reviewed.

Chapter 2

Infantry Tactics

Both line and light infantry used the same drill regulations for their basic manoeuvres. However, the light infantry often had supplementary manuals issued to cover its specialised duties of pickets and skirmishing. As a result, there were three basic types of formations that were used by both types of infantry: line, column and square.

The line

The line is probably the simplest of the formations used by the armies of this period. It consisted of anything from the smallest manoeuvring element greater than the file, to a battalion or a complete regiment deployed in 'line of battle'. This meant that the formation was organised so that it was three ranks deep and as wide as it could possibly be with the standard intervals allowed between the soldiers and the various manoeuvring elements. Table 11 lists the dimensions of the various nations' companies and battalions formed in line. Because of organisational changes these dimensions are listed by date and are based on the theoretical full organisational strength.

Two versus three ranks

A great deal of controversy surrounds the use of the third rank in the French army, as well as other Continental armies, after the showing of the British army and the 'superior utilisation of available firepower' its two-rank system permitted. There is a great

---

Table 11. Dimensions of line infantry in line of battle.
All figures are at full theoretical strength.

	Year	Company length (ft)	Battalion length (ft)
Austrian	1807	114–27	684–762
British	1792	64	640
French	1791	70	560
	1808	80	480
Prussian	1792	90	360
	1799	79	316
	1808	86	344
Russian	1802	92	368
Saxon	1792	94	376
	1810	92	368

---

deal to be considered from the French perspective, and it probably reflects the philosophies of the other European nations which also used the three-rank system.

The two-rank system was first introduced by the Prince von Anhalt in the Prussian
army during the Seven Years War. The intent was to bring more muskets to bear.
However, it was found that light cavalry could savage such a formation and its actual
adoption was delayed until 1778.

The French instructions of 20 May 1775 allowed a two-rank formation, and it
continued until 1776 when it was removed, only to be reinstated in 1788. The French
general Schauenbourg also put it into his divisional orders during Year VI. The
Réglement de 1791 directed a three-rank formation, but also directed that when the
number of files in the *peloton* fell below 12 it was to form in two ranks. Similar statements can be found in the Saxon, Prussian and British regulations.

In 1813, Napoleon issued plans for the elimination of the third rank to make up for
the lack of recruits. His comments with regard to the worth of the third rank are
quite telling, in that he says very specifically that the 'bayonets of the third rank are of
no use.' Generally, this third rank was used primarily as a reserve to replace casualties
and to provide some weight to the formation. It had some disadvantages, not the least
of which was that the fire delivered by the third rank could and did cause casualties in
the first rank. It was found that, in their enthusiasm to fire on the enemy, the third
rank was merely pointing its weapons in their general direction and blasting away.

Gouvion-Saint-Cyr is quoted in Colin's *La Tactique et La Discipline* on this topic as
saying:

> It is no exaggeration that the third rank wounded as many as a quarter of the men who are
> wounded in an affair; this evaluation is not higher if it is a troop of recruits, as those which
> fought at Lützen and at Bautzen. Napoleon was astonished at the high number of men wounded
> between the hand and the elbow, from which he imagined that a great number of these con-
> scripts had shot themselves in an effort to evade service. He proposed to make a severe exam-
> ple of some of them, but he quickly learned that a very large number had been wounded by
> men in the third rank, be it in ramming their gun, or when they turned the ramrod. He then
> resolved to fight only with troops in two ranks.

True, the third rank was not intended to fire, but only to load muskets and to pass
them forward. This did not, however, always happen and the overexcited recruit would
often feel an irrepressible urge to shoot as well. Indeed, if the third rank were to fire
through the first two ranks, by passing the barrel of their gun over the shoulder of
the second rank, the muzzle of their weapon would be about eight inches behind the
back of the first rank. It is therefore little wonder that when they fired the first rank
suffered casualties.

In earlier firing systems the front rank was to kneel and then the rear two ranks
could both fire over their heads. However, it was found that if the front rank knelt it
was nearly impossible to get them back on their feet so that they could advance again.

The problems with the three rank system, however, went further than simply musketry. When executing a bayonet attack the third rank was still a threat to men in the
first and second ranks. The first two ranks could see the terrain over which they were
advancing, but the third rank was obliged to blunder forward blindly. If the battlefield
was littered with corpses or other rough terrain they would stumble and often fall.

To avoid this dangerous situation, the first two ranks advanced with bayonets lowered and the third followed carrying their weapons at port arms. When the line reached

the ground occupied by the enemy, it was to fire without moving from the position of the bayonet charge. The third rank was then to deploy as skirmishers to support the continuing charge. If the enemy withstood the charge the third rank was not to deploy as skirmishers, but to lower their bayonets and support the charge.

When charged by cavalry the third rank was valuable in providing depth to the infantry square. This thick formation provided a hedgehog of bayonets, and with the third rank behind them the men in the front ranks felt more secure.

Despite the present controversy over the reasons for this third rank, it persisted in use with the various Continental armies into the period of the Crimean War. There must have been many well-placed advocates of this formation who had, for what they perceived as good reasons, allowed it to survive for so long. A few such advocates as Okounef and Meunier felt that the third rank made the formation more solid, and that fire discipline could be imposed on the third rank to prevent it inflicting casualties on the front two. One has to wonder what the file closers behind the third rank were doing if they did not notice the third rank was firing. It would seem reasonable to suppose that either they didn't care or they weren't paying attention. It is also possible, since most of the casualty comments relate to 1813, that the French cadres were so poor that they didn't know any better. That, however, is unsupported speculation.

The British use of the two-deep line may or may not have been the result of an enlightened general wishing to increase his firepower. No reputable, historical statements to that effect were found when this manuscript was prepared. However, another equally sound reason for the practice can be found in the British infantry drill regulations.

The British regulations, like those of every other European nation, specifically directed that the infantry be organised in three ranks. All of these regulations also directed that if the company strength fell below a specific strength the third rank was to be incorporated into the front rank to maintain its frontage. These two regulation requirements alone are sufficient to explain why the British universally used a two-deep formation. An analysis of the strength of the British battalions deployed in Spain and Flanders (Table 12) shows that the minimum frontage requirements would have obliged the terribly understrength British battalions to form up in two-deep ranks.

A British battalion theoretically had a strength of 1000 men. Assuming a company strength of 100 rank and file, the frontage in three ranks would have been 33 men. The minimum frontage of a platoon is set at five files by regulation, which would give a company two platoons, each with a frontage of 10 men, a total of 60 men in all three ranks. This means that a battalion with 660 men could meet the requirements of the minimum frontage of 20 files per company and three full ranks. By the same analysis, if the strength fell to 400 men the battalion would absolutely have to be in two ranks if it were to maintain the minimum frontage.

As can be seen in Table 12, the vast majority of the British battalions were understrength enough that to maintain the normal full company frontage they would have to be in two ranks. It also shows that 21% of the army was so understrength that it was required, by the regulations on frontage, to be in two ranks. It is, therefore, highly debatable if the British chose the two-deep formation for the avowed purposes of increasing fire power.

Amazingly, this chart clearly shows that the average British battalion had no superiority in firepower per man than did the French battalion or the battalion of any

Table 12. Battalion strengths in the Peninsula and Netherlands under Wellington.[5]			
	Battalions with over 660 men	*Battalions with 400–660 men*	*Battalions with under 400 men*
Salamanca	9	33	12
15 September 1811	9	25	9
Waterloo	10	20	7
Total	28	78	28
Percentage	21%	58%	21%

other Continental power using the three-deep system. This is because they were so understrength their two-deep line had a frontage equal to that of the three-deep French formation.

Columns

There were three types of columns used by the French army during this period. The principal one was the battalion column, which had many different forms, all of which were carefully regulated by the *Réglement de 1791*. The second form of column was the brigade, division or corps column, which was composed of numerous battalions and will be discussed later. The third type was the road column, which was used solely to permit the transit of the unit from one position to another. It was not a battle formation, but merely a vehicle for transiting long distances. The armies of other nations used the battalion and road columns, but the division or corps column was used solely by the French.

French battalion columns existed in three principal forms: the *colonne par division* (column by division), the *colonne par peloton* (column by *peloton*), and the *colonne par section* (column by section). These varied within each category with the interval between each sub-section of the column. These intervals were the widths of the principal frontage unit or the width of any and all component elements of the principal frontage unit. That is to say that a *colonne par division* could have its divisions formed at intervals equal to the length of the division, the *peloton*, the section or the minimum distance (*colonne serrée*). In the same sense the *colonne par peloton* could be formed only at the *distance de peloton*, *distance de section* and *serrée*.

Figure 6, illustrating column and line formations for *colonne par division*, shows each division formed from two *pelotons*. The distance between each division at full interval is sufficient for the *peloton* to wheel and just come into contact with the division behind it. This clearly illustrates the relationship between the frontage of the unit and the interval.

In practical use the *colonne par division* was formed either as a *colonne serrée par division* (column of division closed up) or a *colonne par division à distance de section* (column of division at a section's or half interval). The *colonnes serrées par peloton* were

---

[5] The figures for this chart were averaged from a review of the orders of battle for these battles found in Oman's *History of the War in the Peninsula*. The 1815 data is drawn from Gurwood's *Wellington's Dispatches*.

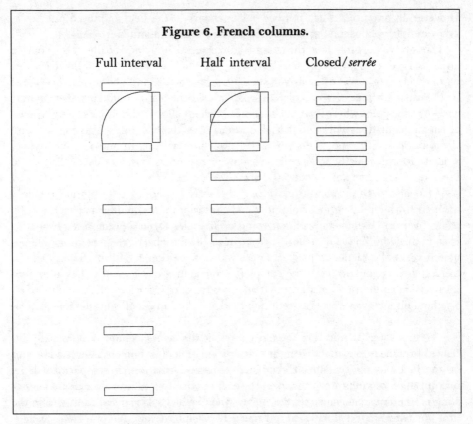

Figure 6. French columns.

Full interval   Half interval   Closed/*serrée*

generally referred to as *colonnes serrées en masse* (columns closed up in mass), *colonnes en masse*, or *masses*. The *colonnes par peloton* were generally at full interval and were referred to as being *ouvert* or open. This was also referred to as being at *distance entière*. When formed at a half-interval columns were referred to as being at *demi-distance*. The *colonne serrée* was a very dense formation where the interval was three paces between the elements of the column. That is to say, in a *colonne serrée par division* the distance between the successive divisions was three paces.

Having discussed the different types of French columns it is necessary to discuss the philosophies surrounding their use and the arguments between the advocates of the *ordre mince* (linear formations) and those of the *ordre profound* (columnar formations). The advocates of the linear or the Prussian system directed the manner in which tactical evolutions occurred. The infantry formed and manoeuvred in lines, but the problems of maintaining alignment limited their mobility. To resolve this problem columns were adopted as the proper formation to manoeuvre the unit into battle. However, because the column was the ideal manoeuvre formation, Mesnil-Durand became enamoured with it and mistook it for the Macedonian phalanx which, in its day, had been invincible. He erroneously believed that it could both defend itself with fire and annihilate its enemies with shock.

This philosophy can be found in the *Réglement de 1791*, where it has nevertheless been modified by Guibert, who blended the ideas of linear formations with those of columnar tactics to evolve a reasonable mixture of what were two extreme viewpoints.

However, in practice French military commanders in the field employed practically every military philosophy of this period in one battle or another.

Though Guibert intended the column as a means of moving rapidly to the point of attack, where it would deploy into line to engage the enemy with fire, followed with a bayonet advance, it was often driven straight at the enemy line. The enemy, threatened by the rapid advance of a column covered with skirmishers, would have their morale shaken to the point where it would break. This eventually led to columns being thrown at enemy formations with the probable intent of actually coming into contact with them, but casualty reports do not corroborate this with large numbers of bayonet wounds. Morale usually broke and the enemy formation ran away, or enemy fire would break up the column and a counter-charge would force it to flee.

It has also been proposed that during the early days of the Revolution the only manner in which the various volunteer and conscript units could be managed was by using them in column, the column being a far easier formation for raw recruits to master than the line. The true Prussian linear evolutions were something that required years of practice to master. There was not the time for Revolutionary volunteers and conscripts to learn the complete programme; consequently they were manoeuvred in columns, often straight at and into the enemy for lack of the ability to do anything else. However, this assumption has been the subject of considerable historical debate.

There is some justification for the view that the attack column was actually intended to come into contact with the enemy formation. The *ordre mixte* was a mixture of the line and the column; it combined a linear formation, which permitted the maximisation of firepower to weaken the enemy, with two columns, formed on either wing of the line, to advance on the enemy when he had suffered sufficiently from the fire. The *ordre mixte* is illustrated in Figure 97 (Chapter 6).

Other nations manoeuvred in columns for much the same reasons as the French, but their use of the column does not seem to have attracted the same attention as has its use by the French. No doubt this is largely due to the fact that they tended to be on the defensive, with the French army attacking them as they stood on their chosen ground. At Borodino the Russian Guard and grenadiers were formed in columns and, exposed to the French artillery fire, were cut down in swathes. At Ligny the Prussians suffered a similar fate. Only the British seem to have consistently been deployed in line on their chosen defensive ground.

The basics of the columns used by other nations are fundamentally the same as the French. They formed them with frontages as large as the division and as small as the smallest manoeuvring unit larger than the file. They also formed them with full intervals, closed up, or at all the manoeuvring element intervals between.

The square

The square was the universal anti-cavalry formation. Each nation formed it according to the requirements of its battalion organisation. During the period of the Seven Years War the square was generally formed with six ranks per face; however, by 1792 some nations had abandoned this. The French *Réglement de 1791* set the formation of the square with three ranks on each face. Forming square was done by divisions, and a column was formed at the *distance de peloton*, or length of a *peloton* formed in line. The

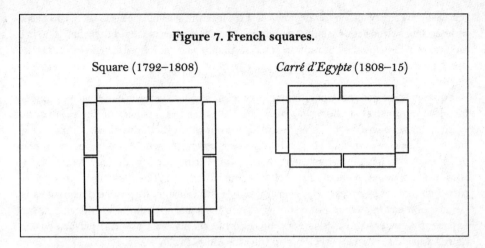

Figure 7. French squares.

Square (1792–1808)   *Carré d'Egypte* (1808–15)

first division did not move, the last division did an about face, and the centre *pelotons* swung out to the right or left to form those faces of the square.

There was a second French square known as the *carré d'Egypte*. There was no official revision of the formation of the French square after the issuance of the *Réglement de 1791*, but the 1808 reorganisation required some modification in how it was formed. Later editions of the *Réglement* have footnotes speaking of differences in the square formation but do not address it in detail. The *carré d'Egypte* was more or less formally recognised in the *Manuel d'infanterie ou resumé de tous les règlements, décrets, usages, et renseignements propos aux sous-officiers de cette armée*, which was published in Paris in 1813. It principally differed from the other squares employed by the French army in being rectangular rather than square.

When forming a *carré d'Egypte*, the first action of the infantry battalion was to form a column of *pelotons* at the *demi-distance de division* or half-distance of a division, which was half the length of the division (or the length of a *peloton*) when deployed in line. The column was oriented parallel to the direction desired for the longest face of the rectangular square. The *pelotons* then wheeled out and marched forward to assume their positions. Figure 7 illustrates the two French forms of the battalion square.

In addition to these, the French also formed regimental squares, large and more complex affairs that provided a maximisation of fire while retaining the integrity of a square formation. These regimental squares were used at Lützen, Borodino and Weissenfels. The fusiliers formed independent squares that were linked by the elite companies. However, these formations were probably not made in immediate response to an attack by cavalry, but were, at least in the case of Lützen and Weissenfels, the formations in which the French marched onto the battlefield. (See Figures 85 and 86, Chapter 5.)

Experience had shown the necessity of placing a reserve in the centre of any square, but this reserve was never more than one-twelfth of the total strength of the unit forming the square. The officer commanding a square was required to be attentive and observe the sustained effect of enemy attacks. Any disorder resulting from these attacks, artillery fire or other causes could weaken the square and cause disaster for all.

While in square the infantry was always to fire by rank or by file. Fire by file commenced from the right with the target at a maximum of 150 paces. Each file fired with increasing rapidity as the cavalry closed. Fire by rank was only executed at 100 paces or less. Ranks fired sequentially; as one rank fired the other two held their fire. The fire would then be rotated from rank to rank, so that as one rank fired, one loaded and the other held its loaded weapons ready. This form of fire was the most effective against cavalry.

Squares were generally positioned in echelon so that they were mutually support-ing. The regimental artillery was placed in the outermost corners of the regimental square checkerboard to provide greater firepower at these, the weakest points of the square. These corners could be, and often were, strengthened by placing caissons and other train and baggage equipment there and covering them with a few skirmishers, who were to keep the enemy from clambering over them. The gaps between squares were habitually 120 paces and, generally, filled with caissons, forges, field baggage and such equipment that could not be dragged into the square. Though this might seem to expose this material to damage and provide the enemy with cover, it performed the more valuable service of breaking up the attacking cavalry's formations.

However, the square was not the only formation for receiving cavalry. General Scherer made the following statement:

> To permit infantry to resist the shock of the cavalry it is necessary to present the cavalry with a formation which joins the double advantage of the *ordre mince* and the *ordre profond*. The best formation is the column at a *demi-distance* [half a *peloton* interval between *pelotons*], which permits the infantry to not fear the charge of cavalry and to overthrow the best infantry solely by impulse.

This is nearly the same formation that Marshal Ney advocated if inadequate time was available for a unit to form into a proper square. Ney described in his *Memoirs* what was known as the *masse*, where the column closed up and the three files on either flank of the column would face outwards and the rear division would face about form-

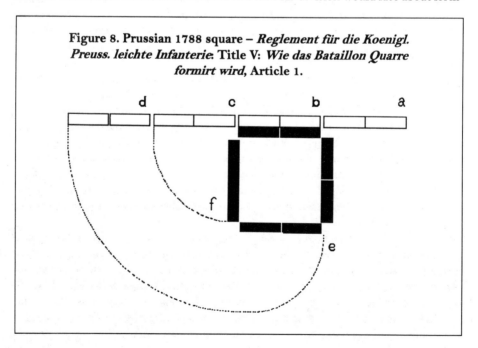

Figure 8. Prussian 1788 square – *Reglement für die Koenigl. Preuss. leichte Infanterie.* Title V: *Wie das Bataillon Quarre formirt wird*, Article 1.

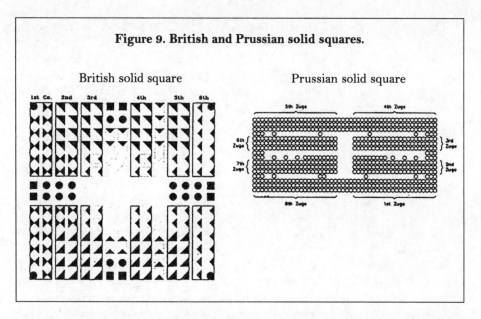

Figure 9. British and Prussian solid squares.

British solid square

Prussian solid square

ing the rear of the dense formation. In doing so, the companies closed up until they were *serré*, or closed up to an interval of three paces. The principal difference was that Scherer's formation was far more open than that of Marshal Ney. There are, however, very few battle accounts of these formations being employed. In one instance, which occurred at the end of the Battle of Salamanca, the French battalion which formed this 'closed column' was smashed by the British cavalry that struck it. The battalion square was used by the other European nations without exception. The method of forming it, however, varied, usually for two reasons: 1) because of the number of manoeuvring elements in the battalion; and 2) because of the type of pivot employed.

The Prussian 1788 Regulation prescribed a square formed by great wheeling movements (see Figure 8). The British and Russians used a number of methods, one being like that of the French and another being like that of the Prussians.

Though the French knew, and occasionally used, the *masse* it was more common among some of the other nations. The Austrians used two formations known as the *Bataillonsmasse* and the *Divisionsmasse.* They were dense formations formed either by division or by battalion. Smirke's *Review of a Battalion of Infantry* shows that the British were trained to use one similar formation, and in 1812 the Prussians adopted another. The Prussian 1812 Regulation shows this as the only approved anti-cavalry formation – the great wheeling formation of the 1788 Regulation has vanished. Figure 9 is a copy of the illustrations of these formations drawn from the British and Prussian source manuscripts.

However, campaign and battle accounts do not provide any accounts of the British using the formation shown in Smirke. Indeed, accounts of the Battles of Quatre-Bras and Waterloo are very precise in their descriptions of the squares, leaving no doubt that a *masse* was not being used. At Quatre-Bras a Highland regiment in the process of swinging closed actually trapped some French cavalry inside the square. This indicates that even in instances where the cavalry surprised the infantry the square was preferred to the *masse*.

There are several reasons for this. In the case of the British, they usually began the battle in a defensive posture, formed in line. The *masse* was formed quickest from a column, where the square formed more easily from a line. The *masse* minimised the firepower of a battalion, while the square was the optimum formation for fire in defence against cavalry. In addition, the performance and steady nature of the British infantry made the square as solid as the *masse* would have been. These considerations probably caused the British to prefer the square over the *masse*.

In the case of the Prussians there was an overriding consideration. In 1812 their army consisted almost entirely of drafts and reservists. There were very few battle-hardened veterans. Only a handful of them had accompanied the *Grande Armée* into Russia, and nothing significant remained from the pre-1806 army. Having a green army, therefore, the Prussians were more concerned that their battalions survived the battle than how many Frenchmen they killed. The thick formation of the *masse* was very difficult for enemy cavalry to break and required far less discipline to execute than the square.

No doubt the Austrians adopted their *masse* formations because of similar considerations. They seemed to be continually rebuilding their army every few years, with massive injections of new recruits between 1799 and 1810. The Austrian *Divisionsmasse* was formed so that each division of the battalion acted as a separate tactical entity and divided into its *Züge*. These *Züge* then formed themselves into a column on the centre *Züge* so that the new formation was one *Züge* wide and eight deep. The men closed up the ranks and the file closers moved outwards to fill in the gaps between the *Züge*. The men then faced outwards, forming a compact mass that bristled with bayonets. The *Bataillonsmasse* was formed in a similar manner, except the battalion divided itself into half-companies and formed in a similar manner to the *Divisionsmasse*.

The advantage of forming the *Divisionsmasse* from line was that, compared to the *Bataillonsmasse*, the soldiers had a shorter distance to go before the formation was complete. However, if the unit was deployed in a battalion column of companies or half-companies the *Bataillonsmasse* was quicker to form.

Because the principal threat which forced infantry to change formation into a square was fast-moving cavalry, the speed at which the formation change occurred was critical. The faster the formation could be formed the safer the infantry was, and the less likely to be caught out of formation.

One of the many current misconceptions of the square is that it was a fixed formation, barely able to move. This is not true. When the Prussians retreated off the field after their defeat at Jena-Auerstädt, their rearguard was a Saxon grenadier battalion in square. It out-marched the pursuing French infantry and held the French cavalry at bay. In his memoirs Baron Seruzier, commander of the artillery of General Morand's Division, III Corps (Davout), states that at the Battle of Jena: '*J'en étais là, quand notre division, formée en carrés d'infanterie marchant au pas de charge, parvint à notre hauteur.*' This passage states very clearly that he witnessed his division formed in square, marching at the *pas de charge* (120 paces per minute). Such a passage is rare because it specifies the march rate and the formation, but it clearly shows that the square was as mobile as any other formation. In 1813, due to the lack of cavalry to protect them, many units of the French army marched onto the battlefield at Lützen in square. How slow could the square have truly been, if it was used on a divisional scale by manoeuvring armies?

One reason that the square might have gained a reputation for moving slowly would be if the infantry forming it was poorly trained and could not maintain formation at a higher speed. It is also possible that when moving faster it moved in a loose square, that tightened up and set itself when cavalry approached. If cavalry was too near the square might well not move very quickly, so as to prevent its ranks from opening up as a result of the 'accordion effect' (discussed later). It would be possible, under such circumstances, for a formed square to be broken if cavalry could dash in upon it quickly enough before it had closed all the gaps.

Chapter 3

Manoeuvring the Battalion

In order to understand the tactical systems used by the various nations involved in the Napoleonic Wars it is necessary to review in detail the methods by which they manoeuvred. This examination also provides considerable insight into the fundamental differences between the armies of most of the major combatants during this period. The tactical manoeuvres of France, Britain, Prussia and Russia will be examined on the basis of how their regulations stated they were to manoeuvre.

In order to do this it is necessary that the battalion of each nation be examined on a uniform basis. As a result, some artificial, universal assumptions must be made. The first is that the human body either conformed to the regulated width, or that it was of a consistent and uniform width. Obviously it is not, but if one assumes the regulated widths are reasonable averages the impact of this should not significantly bias the analysis. The second assumption is that people are capable of marching like machines, with an absolutely standardised pace. In the short term this is not true, but long term, with an eye to the statistical mean of all normally distributed events, the marching will distill down to an average probably very close to the regulated cadence and length of pace. The third assumption is that the condition of the terrain being marched over is smooth and uniform. This is absolutely unrealistic, but it is necessary in order to provide a uniform comparison between the systems. In battle there would be bodies, ploughed fields, ditches and a thousand other impediments to slow down any given manoeuvre, but there would also be some motivational aspects to combat, such as live shot whirling overhead to add wings to men's feet. Unfortunately, none of this is easily quantifiable and must be ignored.

Figure 10. Formation of a company in line of battle – *Réglement de 1791: Formation en Ordre de Bataille,* Part I, Plate I.

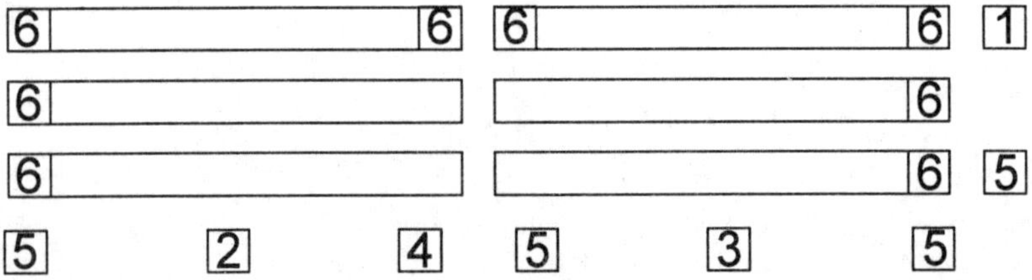

1 = Captain	2 = Lieutenant	3 = *Sous-lieutenant*
4 = Sergeant-major	5 = Sergeant	6 = Corporal

Table 13. French paces.[6]		
Pace	*Length of pace*	
Petit pas	1/3 metre	= 13 ins
Pas de deux pieds	2/3 metre	= 26 ins
Pas elongé	5/6 metre	= 32.5 ins
Grand pas	1 metre	= 39.5 ins

Any attempt to consider the influence of these aspects of the battlefield would not assist in an uniform and even analysis of the tactical systems and has been eliminated. The goal is to provide a uniform analysis. It should be assumed that under actual combat situations anything could happen, but it would also be reasonable to presume that any relationships established in this study would be relatively unchanged.

France 1800–8

Organisation

The first point that must be addressed in any study of tactics is marching distance. The distances involved are directly determined by the formation the infantry has assumed. The French *peloton*, or manoeuvring element, is shown in Figure 10 as it was formed for manoeuvres.

The French battalion established in 1791 was organised with one grenadier and eight fusilier companies. However, the grenadier companies were often stripped off and formed into converged grenadier battalions. These grenadier battalions will not be considered and the battalion with eight fusilier companies will be used for all calculations for French infantry between 1800 and 1808.

Dimensions and speeds

A fusilier *peloton* had a frontage of 38 files. The distance allocated to a single soldier by the *Réglement* is two French *pieds*, or 26 inches; however, other sources (P. Escalle, *Des marches dans les Armées de Napoléon*) indicate that a distance of 22 inches would be a more appropriate interval. For the purposes of this study, therefore, the 22-inch interval will be used. This will have the effect of slightly speeding up the manoeuvres discussed, but with the high probability of a unit being below the standard establishment strength, this compromise is in the direction of increased faithfulness to reality in the field. The 22-inch interval means that a fusilier *peloton* at full strength had a length of about 70 ft. This is what was known as the *distance entière*, or the *peloton*'s full interval.

The second factor that must be established is the infantry's velocity. Velocity consists of two elements: the length of the individual pace or step of the soldier, and the number of paces per minute. The length of the French pace was strictly regulated and established as shown in Table 13.

According to the *Réglement* and the *Manuel d'infanterie* (an official 1813 compilation of all changes made to the *Réglement*, but not an official replacement for it) the most

[6] *Manuel d'infanterie*, p. 90.

Table 14. French cadences.

Cadence	Paces per minute	Year instituted
Pas ordinaire	60	1766
Pas redouble	120	1766
Pas d'ecole	60	1776
Pas ordinaire	70	1776
Pas de manoeuvre	120	1776
Pas de route	90–100	1776
Pas ordinaire	76	1791
Pas de route	85–90	1791
Pas accéléré	100	1791
Pas de charge	120	1791
Pas de course	200–50	Unknown

commonly used pace was the *pas de deux pieds,* or 26 inches. This is the pace that will be used for all calculations of French manoeuvres. There were also several marching cadences established by three regulations. These rates are shown in Table 14.

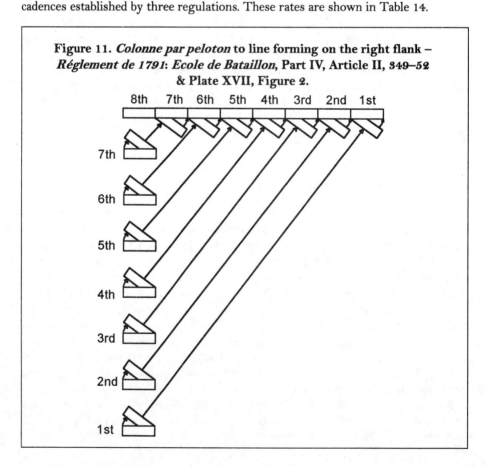

Figure 11. *Colonne par peloton* to line forming on the right flank – *Réglement de 1791: Ecole de Bataillon,* Part IV, Article II, 349–52 & Plate XVII, Figure 2.

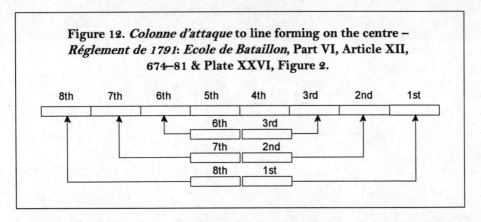

Figure 12. *Colonne d'attaque* to line forming on the centre –
Réglement de 1791: Ecole de Bataillon, Part VI, Article XII,
674–81 & Plate XXVI, Figure 2.

The *Manuel d'infanterie* and the *Réglement de 1791* both clearly state that all manoeuvres were executed at the *pas de charge*, 120 paces per minute. It is also noteworthy that the 1776 *pas de manoeuvre* or manoeuvre pace was also 120 paces per minute. Using this cadence and the 26-inch pace the march rate, or speed of manoeuvre, was 260 ft per minute.

Column and line evolutions

The first manoeuvre is the deployment from a *colonne par peloton* to a line forming to one flank. This is illustrated in Figure 11 and is the slowest method of deploying. Each *peloton* wheeled 45 degrees and advanced in line directly towards its final destination. Once there they performed another 45 degree turn and fell into line. Figure 12 illustrates the fastest method of deploying, that of forming a line from the *colonne d'attaque* on the centre. In all the following examples columns are at a full *peloton* interval, though the illustrations may not always clearly indicate it.

The following calculations are made with the assumption that a facing manoeuvre, an 'about face' or a 'left/right' face, takes only a couple of seconds and is not worth taking into consideration when performing calculations. In the case of Figure 11, the 1st fusilier *peloton* must move further than any other. It executes a 45 degree turn which requires it to travel 55 ft. Being at full distance, the 1st *peloton* travels 10 *peloton* intervals. The time is then determined by the *peloton* performing two wheels, at 55 ft each, and advancing 10 *peloton* intervals. The total distance is 810 ft. If they advanced at 260 ft per minute it would take them 3.1 minutes to cover that distance.

In the manoeuvre shown in Figure 12 the 1st and 8th fusilier *pelotons* move the greatest distances, three *peloton* intervals to the flank and three forward, plus one for 'accordion effect'. This accordion effect occurs when a line faces to one flank and advances. The soldiers will naturally assume the proper interval between them so as to not step on the heels of the man in front. This effectively doubles the length of the line, which, allowing for this accordion effect, means that the 1st and 8th *pelotons* must travel seven intervals (490 ft), requiring a total of 1.9 minutes.

When a line ployed[7] from line into column it could do so in two ways. It could form on the end or on the centre of the line. In either instance the column could be formed

---

[7] In French 'deploy' means to move from a column out into a line, while 'ploy' means to collapse a line into a column. The latter term has been adopted throughout this book.

Figure 13. Line forming *colonne par peloton* on the left flank –
Réglement de 1791: *Evolutions de Ligne*, Article I, 24–34.

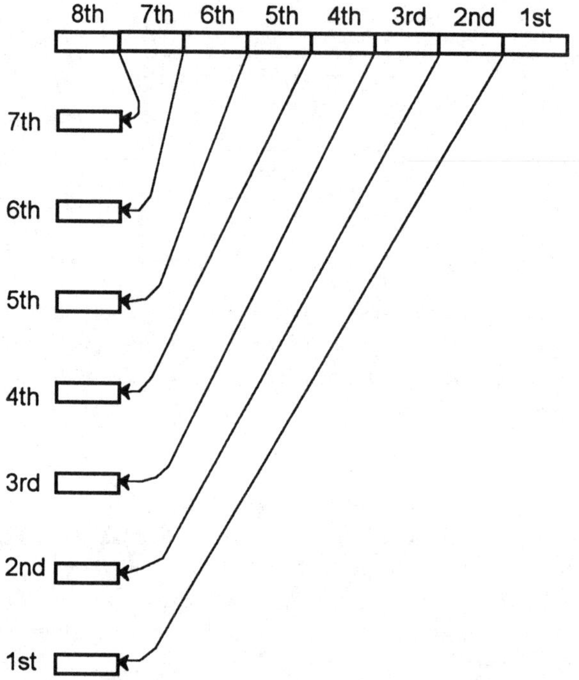

8th   7th   6th   5th   4th   3rd   2nd   1st

7th

6th

5th

4th

3rd

2nd

1st

Figure 14. Line forming *colonne d'attaque* on the centre –
Réglement de 1791: *Ecole de Bataillon*, Part VI, Article XIII, 663–73
& Plate XXVI, Figure 1.

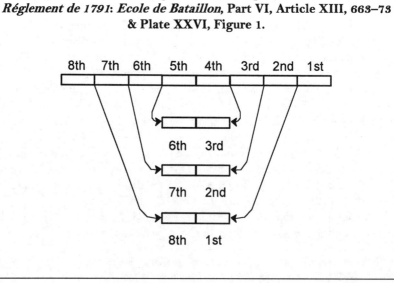

8th   7th   6th   5th   4th   3rd   2nd   1st

6th   3rd

7th   2nd

8th   1st

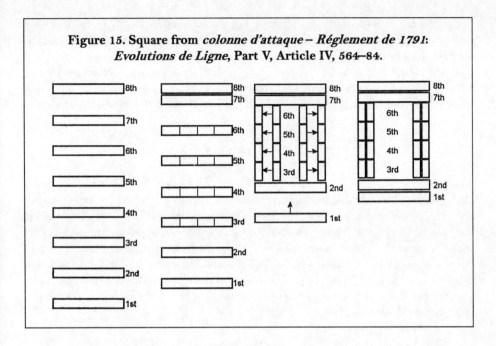

**Figure 15. Square from *colonne d'attaque – Réglement de 1791*:
Evolutions de Ligne, Part V, Article IV, 564–84.**

with its head, rear, or middle on the line. These manoeuvres were always done by marching to the flank directly towards the *pelotons'* final destination, rather than by a squared manoeuvre. Figures 13 and 14 show these manoeuvres, executed by flank movements that march directly to their final positions.

The manoeuvre shown in Figure 13 required the 1st *peloton* to move a total of 11.2 *peloton* intervals and would take three minutes. The timing of the manoeuvre shown in Figure 14 is determined by the distance moved by the division formed by the 1st and 8th *pelotons*. They move a total of 4.8 *peloton* intervals in 1.3 minutes.

The square

The next formation change to be examined is the square. Here time is a very critical element: being slow to form square could have some very nasty results.

Figure 15 shows the evolution of forming square from the *colonne par peloton*, depicting each *peloton* and its two sections. This was the principal manoeuvre in the process of forming square. If the *colonne par peloton* was at full interval it first closed up to a quarter-interval. Next the 7th and 8th *pelotons* closed up until the interval between them disappeared. The other *pelotons* advanced the same quarter-interval and then the 6th, 5th, 4th and 3rd *pelotons* broke up by half-sections and the half-sections wheeled outwards from the centre of the battalion and doubled up on the flanks facing outward. The 1st and 2nd *pelotons* then closed up and completed the square. The *Réglement* speaks only of a column of several battalions performing this manoeuvre. In the account provided here the same manoeuvre has been performed, except with a single battalion and its sub-elements.

This manoeuvre required the battalion to close up so that the first two *pelotons* were at a closed interval (*serré*) and the rest of the *pelotons* were at a quarter-interval. This effectively reduced the depth of the formation from seven intervals to 1.5. This reduction of 5.5 intervals required 1.5 minutes. For the internal half-sections to advance a quarter-interval and wheel required a total of 0.17 minutes. The total manoeuvre required 1.7 minutes.

If the battalion was in line it would simply form a column of *pelotons* (see Figure 13) and then execute the manoeuvre shown in Figure 15. The time to perform this manoeuvre would then be the total of both individual manoeuvres, or 4.7 minutes.

France 1808–15
Organisation

The company or *peloton* established by the Decree of 18 February 1808 had 140 men. Each battalion was established with six companies. The fusilier, grenadier and voltigeur companies did vary slightly in the positioning of some individuals when the battalion was formed,[8] but these differences did not affect the size of the *peloton's* interval. Likewise, the interval between the ranks was changed from one *pied* (13 ins) to 0.33 metres (13 ins +). This had no real impact. The illustration shown in Figure 10 remains accurate enough for our purposes. There was no basic or fundamental change, other than the expansion to 140 men and a decrease in the number of companies, that would affect these calculations.

The third rank

The debate regarding the use of two-rank formations in the British army almost invariably involves comparisons with the French use of three ranks. It is, as a result, of great interest, to note a letter from Napoleon to Murat, dated 14 October 1813, in which he orders that the infantry of Marmont's corps should be placed in two ranks 'because the fire and the bayonet of the third rank are insignificant. One of the advantages of this new disposition would be to cause the enemy to believe that the army is one-third stronger than it is in reality.' This reorganisation may or may not have occurred. The French regulations, like the British, did allow for a minimum number of files, so the French would have normally moved to a two-deep line. However, the French were only a few days from the Battle of Leipzig at the time, and in the midst of a serious campaign. If Marmont's corps was deliberately reorganised in accordance with this instruction, there probably wasn't enough of it left after Leipzig for this 'change of theory' to continue.

The 1814 campaign probably saw the French operating in two ranks. This, however, would have occurred because of the requirement for a minimum frontage for the *peloton*. Title III, *Ecole de Peloton,* of the *Réglement de 1791* states that 'when the number of files shall be below 12, the *peloton* shall be formed in two ranks.' This would mean that if the battalion fell below a strength of 198 men it would form in two ranks. A review of the archival listing of the French VI Corps on 21 January 1814 shows that 29 of 30 regiments in the corps must have been in two ranks. On 28 January the V Corps had 20 battalions, all under 198 men; the VI Corps had now improved to only 16 of 42 battalions under 198; and the XI Corps had 11 battalions under 198 men. On 5 March the VII Corps had 10 of 27 battalions under 198 men. On 12 March, by contrast, of the 53 battalions in the II and VI Corps there was only one with more than

---

[8] See revisions to *Ecole du Soldat et de Peloton – Manual d'Infanterie*, pp.437–47.

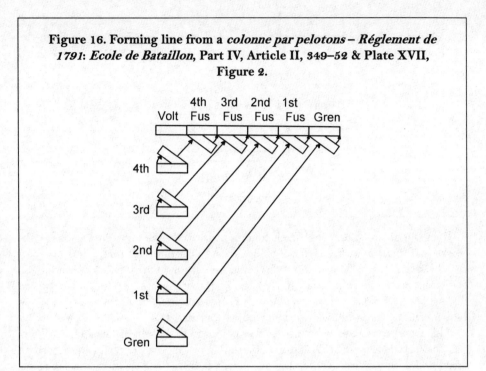

Figure 16. Forming line from a *colonne par pelotons* – *Réglement de 1791: Ecole de Bataillon*, Part IV, Article II, 349–52 & Plate XVII, Figure 2.

198 men. It is, therefore, highly likely that in 1814 the bulk of the French army was in two ranks.

Dimensions and speeds

The new *peloton* decreed in 1808 would have had a frontage of 44 files. The 22-inch interval means that its length at full strength was 80 ft. Marching at the *pas de charge* it would cover this distance in about 0.3 minutes. It could wheel 90 degrees, a distance of 126 ft, in about 0.5 minutes.

Column and line evolutions

The first manoeuvre is the deployment from a *colonne par peloton* to a line forming to one flank. This is illustrated in Figure 16 and was the slowest method of deploying. Figure 17 shows the deployment of a *colonne d'attaque* to a line, forming on the centre, which was the quickest method of forming a line from a column.

Assuming that the facing manoeuvre, a right/left face or an about face, takes an insignificant amount of time, it is deleted from the time calculations. In Figure 16 the grenadier *peloton* to the extreme right determines the time necessary to form line. It performs two 45 degree wheels covering a distance of 125 ft. Then it advances to its final position, a further 7.1 intervals (568 ft). The grenadiers move a total distance is 693 ft and at 260 ft per minute in 2.62 minutes.

In the manoeuvre shown in Figure 17 the grenadier and voltigeur *pelotons* make the longest move. This manoeuvre requires them to move two intervals forward and two to the flank. Adding in the accordion effect, they would move five intervals and take 1.5 minutes.

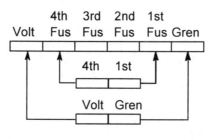

Figure 17. Forming line from a *colonne d'attaque* – *Réglement de 1791*:
***Ecole de Bataillon,* Part VI, Article XII, 674–81 & Plate XXVI, Figure 2.**

It should be noted that the attack column had exactly the same dimensions as the *colonne par divisions* at the distance of a section. That is to say that it was approximately square in its shape and its sides could vary from 20 to 60 paces, depending on the strength of the companies. If a *peloton* had a strength of 16 files, as most had during 1793, the square *colonne d'attaque* was approximately 30 paces to a side. When ploying from column to line the same method was used as before 1808.

This manoeuvre required the grenadier company to move a distance of 5.7 intervals to reach the corner of the formation. Adding one more interval for the accordion effect and a further interval for the movement into its final position, the grenadier *peloton* must move a total of 616 ft. At a rate of advance of 260 ft per minute it would take 2.4 minutes.

Figure 18. Line forming *colonne par peloton* on the right flank –
***Réglement de 1791*: *Evolutions de Ligne*, Article I, 24–34.**

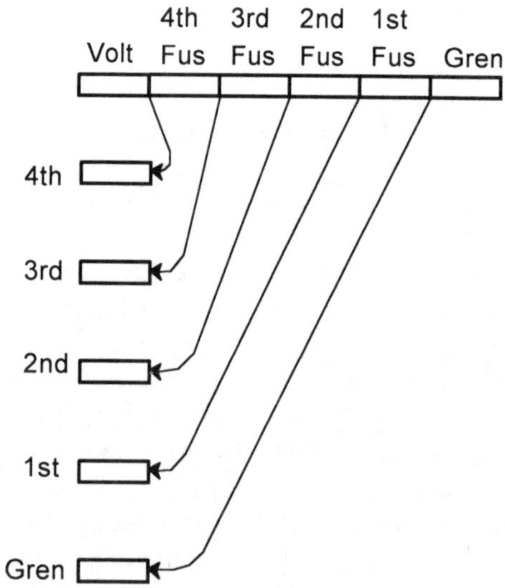

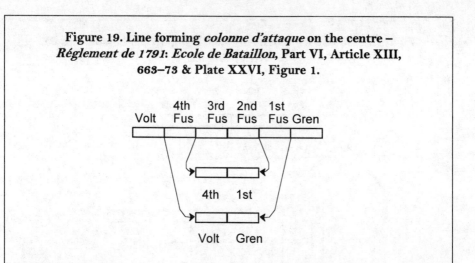

Figure 19. Line forming *colonne d'attaque* on the centre –
Réglement de 1791: Ecole de Bataillon, Part VI, Article XIII,
663–73 & Plate XXVI, Figure 1.

The manoeuvre shown in Figure 19 required the grenadier company to advance 2.8 intervals to the corner of the formation, plus one for the accordion effect and one more to take its position. This required covering a total of 4.8 intervals at 260 ft per minute, or 2.3 minutes.

The square

After 1808 this formation became a rectangle with two faces formed with two *pelotons* and two faces formed by one *peloton*. Again, no matter what the formation of the infantry, it always formed square by passing through the intermediary formation of a column at a *peloton* interval. The *Manual d'Infanterie* shows this clearly.[9] Figure 20 shows the transformation from line to square as illustrated in that work.

The manoeuvre is thoroughly illustrated in Figure 20. The 1st fusilier *peloton* and the grenadier *pelotons* remain stationary as the other *pelotons* wheel into a *colonne par peloton*. Once the wheel is completed the four manoeuvring *pelotons* advance until the 2nd fusilier *peloton* is at the far end of the grenadier *peloton*. It halts, and the 4th and 3rd fusilier *pelotons* wheel to the right. They form the back of the square while the voltigeur *peloton* closes the flank of the square. The voltigeur *peloton* does not move the greatest distance. Instead the distance moved by the 1st and 2nd fusilier *pelotons* is greater because of the two wheels. They advance two *peloton* intervals and wheel twice. The two wheels require one minute and the time to cover the two intervals is 0.62 minutes, making a total of 1.6 minutes to form square. This particular manoeuvre is the longest way of converting from line to square. If the square was formed on centre companies the time required would be 1.1 minutes. If the battalion was in *colonne d'attaque* the manoeuvre was carried out as shown in Figure 21.

In forming a square this way the governing manoeuvre was the wheel of the 1st and 4th fusilier *pelotons*, which required 0.5 minutes. The voltigeur and grenadier *pelotons* merely advanced one interval, which only required 0.3 minutes. In essence, this formation change required 0.5 minutes, for by the time the two flank fusilier companies were in place the two elite *pelotons* would also be in place.

---

[9] *Manual d'Infanterie*, pp.51–6.

Figure 20. Square from line – *Manual d'Infanterie,* **Lesson Fifteen, Article 76–82.**

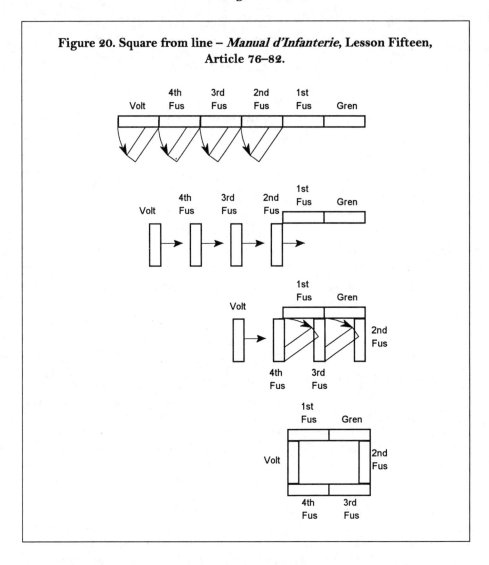

Observations and conclusions

The major point to note is that the change in the internal organisation of the battalion which occurred on 18 February 1808 was not whimsical, but was a change which produced some very decided improvements in the French military system. With the sole exception of the conversion of a line to *colonne d'attaque,* every manoeuvre was speeded up significantly. Even in this one exception it is worth noting that the loss in speed amounted to only 0.2 minutes, or 12 seconds, which is not significant.

There was a reduction in the number of fusiliers and corporals, the principal constituents of the company, from 896 to 774, a total of 112 men. The impact of this had a negative effect on the battalion by diluting its command cadre. The number of companies was reduced from eight to six. Of these two companies, 112 fusiliers and corporals were eliminated. This represents one company. The other company was absorbed into the remaining six as fusiliers. This meant that the existing officer and NCO cadre

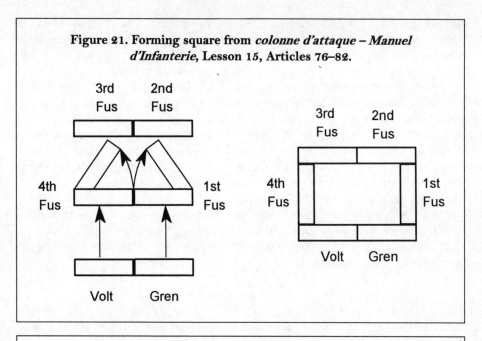

Figure 21. Forming square from *colonne d'attaque* – *Manuel d'Infanterie*, Lesson 15, Articles 76–82.

Table 15. Summary of French manoeuvring speeds.

	Starting formation	Ending formation	Time required (minutes)		Change (minutes)	
			Low	*High*	*Low*	*High*
1800–8	Column	Line	1.9	3.1	–	–
	Column	Square	1.7	–	–	–
	Line	Column	1.3	3.0	–	–
	Line	Square	4.7	–	–	–
1808–15	Column	Line	1.5	2.7	-0.4	-0.4
	Column	Square	0.5	1.6	-1.2	–
	Line	Column	1.5	2.4	+0.2	-0.6
	Line	Square	1.6	–	-3.1	–

now had to supervise a larger number of fusiliers, 121 as against 104. This could indicate either a recognition of the troops' greater martial skills, which seems dubious, or a decision to increase the size of the companies to cope with a reduction in the availability of, or an increased demand for, trained, experienced cadres.

Britain 1795–1815

Regulations

The regulations used by the British during the Napoleonic Wars were written by Sir David Dundas. His drill system, first published in 1788 and officially adopted by the British in 1792, was the first system universally adopted by the British army. It was developed and hung upon the pivot, which resulted in his nickname, 'Old Pivot'. Dundas had seen action during the American War of Independence in 1783, as well as in operations in the Caribbean and India. He brought his experiences in those campaigns together as he forged his new drill regulations.

After the Seven years War, in 1763, the British military was broken into two schools of thought, the 'American' and the 'German'. The German school was steeped in rigid, close-ordered drill suited to the open plains of Europe and large forces of strong, well-drilled cavalry. The American school was characterised by open formations, fast marching, and light infantry tactics suited to the woodlands of North America. Dundas, despite his experiences in the New World, was a disciple of the German school and wrote his regulations in that style, with precise evolutions and precision marching. They were written for a three-rank formation.

Despite official adoption of the Dundas system, it was not proven until the British campaign in Egypt, when General Abercromby, who had taken great pains to train his expeditionary force, was the first British general to employ the new regulations in the field. Though they were in place, the Duke of York had not used them during the disastrous Dutch campaign.

Organisation

The question of British organisation is a very ticklish subject. The British did not have a single standard company organisation. Between 1803 and 1815 as many as 20 different battalion strengths can be found if official records are examined. Secondly, there is a serious discrepancy between the regulated company structure, which called for a three-deep formation, and a wide variety of sources which report the regular employment of the 'thin red line', or two-rank formation.

Researches done for this and other projects have turned up no standard company establishment beyond the cadre of officers and non-commissioned officers. The cadre consisted of a captain, two lieutenants, an ensign, a paymaster sergeant, three sergeants, three corporals, a drummer and a fifer. The number of privates appears to have been regulated by the regiment's ability to draw recruits and other unknown factors. Britain did not have a draft (conscription system) to fill out its regiments, but instead used some very unsavoury ruses that ranged up to what amounted to kidnapping.

Indications are that it was intended that there should be approximately 100 privates, but since the average battalion in the field seems to have had a strength between 500 and 700, a figure of 54 privates is going to be used. This gives a company strength of 66 and a battalion strength of 660.

There is a great deal of mixed evidence on whether or not the British used two- or three-deep formations. Because of this controversy, the figures presented in Chapter 1 concerning the average strengths oblige the use of a two-rank formation with a minimum frontage. As a result, the company used in this analysis will be at full interval, but in two ranks.

The British company was organised into four sections, each with a minimum of five files. This gave the company a minimum frontage of 20 men, though allowances were made for a company with only three sections if its strength were to fall so far as to necessitate it. If such a minimum company was organised in two ranks it would have six officers and NCOs and 34 privates. If it was organised with three ranks it would require six officers and NCOs and 54 privates. However, the company to be used in this analysis will have six officers and 60 privates. The British company organised in

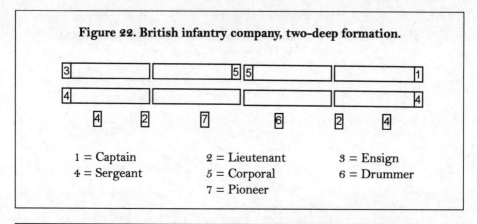

Figure 22. British infantry company, two-deep formation.

1 = Captain   2 = Lieutenant   3 = Ensign
4 = Sergeant   5 = Corporal   6 = Drummer
                     7 = Pioneer

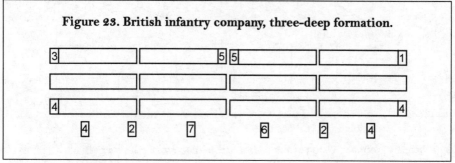

Figure 23. British infantry company, three-deep formation.

two ranks is shown in Figure 22, and the three-deep formation is shown in Figure 23 for the period 1795–1815.

One other organisational fact remains to be considered. That is the number of companies in a British battalion. This was very specifically set at 10. However, it was not unusual for a British battalion to detach its light and grenadier companies. There were also instances where the battalion was formed with less than eight fusilier companies, and the Foot Guards and other oversized battalions often added additional grenadier or light companies. However, for purposes of this study, the battalion will be considered to have all 10 companies.

Dimensions and speeds

An interval of 22 inches was allocated for each man. They were formed with their hands touching, and though Figures 22 and 23 show intervals between the sections there were none. This gave the company a width of 37 ft, while the company shown in Figure 22 would have a width of 55 ft. Only the formation shown in Figure 22 will be used for calculations.

Regulations established the basic British pace at 30 inches. This is 14% longer than the French 26 inch pace. Regulations also set the 'ordinary pace' at 75 paces per minute and the 'quick step' at 108. This means that at the ordinary pace the British advanced at 188 ft per minute, and when marching at the quick step they moved 270 ft per minute. Both figures were calculated because the British used both rates of march during some manoeuvres. The use of these two rates and a 33-inch pace in pivots

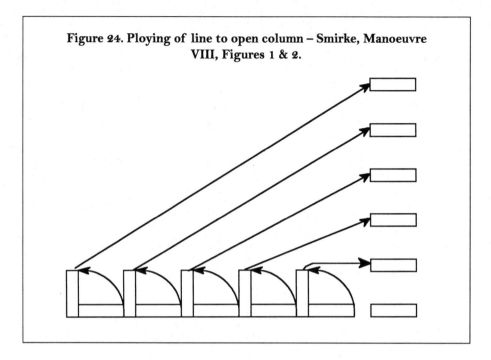

Figure 24. Ploying of line to open column – Smirke, Manoeuvre VIII, Figures 1 & 2.

significantly complicates the evaluation of the manoeuvres. However, thanks to Smirke's work the situations where each different rate was used are clearly stated and the problems are minimised.

Column to line evolutions

When the British changed from line into an open column, a column formed at full interval, they did so as illustrated in Figure 24.

As can be seen, the first action was for the companies to wheel backwards 90 degrees at a quick step. The man at the end of the company lengthened his pace to 33 inches, increasing his rate of march from 270 ft per minute to 297 ft per minute. A company took 0.3 minutes to wheel. The company would then face to the left, and in a filing motion at the quick pace file directly to its new position. The facing manoeuvre is considered to take no significant time to execute and is, therefore, ignored. Since this occurred by a flank march it was subject to the accordion effect, which adds one interval to the march time. The farthest company would, as a result, march a distance defined by nine intervals to the right and eight to the rear, plus one to move into the column. That comes to a distance of 13 intervals, or 715 ft. They took 2.6 minutes to complete this manoeuvre.

If forming on a centre company, with half of the battalion ploying forward of the centre company and the remainder forming behind it, a line could be formed in the shortest time. This is shown in Figure 25.

Ignoring the time of the facing manoeuvre, the outermost company had a flank march direct to the new position. This is a distance of 6.4 intervals, plus one for the accordion effect and one more for moving into the column. This 8.4 interval manoeuvre would take the company 1.7 minutes.

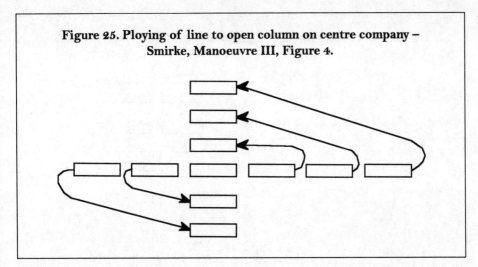

**Figure 25. Ploying of line to open column on centre company –
Smirke, Manoeuvre III, Figure 4.**

When the British converted from line to column they used the system illustrated in Figure 25. However, this shows the manoeuvre being to closed column. Because the calculations for the French were made from a full interval column a full interval or open column will be used for all of the British manoeuvres to permit an accurate comparison.

Performing this manoeuvre to form a column of grand divisions, the equivalent of the French *colonne d'attaque*, does not appear to have been possible. Smirke's Manoeuvre I and II, figures 7 and 8, show the divisions moving in tandem, not splitting into companies and swinging out to either side as separate manoeuvring elements as the French did when they converted from this formation to line. As a result, the time for the manoeuvre from an open column will be the same as if the manoeuvre was made from a column of companies.

Again, we use the 10-company battalion and presume the column forms on the flank company, which would be the slowest method of forming line. This would require the rear-most company to move nine company intervals in a flank march (plus one for the accordion effect), halt, face forward and march forward nine intervals. This is a total manoeuvre of 19 company intervals, which, executed at the quick step, would take 3.9 minutes.

Figure 26 shows the method of forming a line from column of grand divisions. This is a variation on the other column formations and requires no explanation.

The square

The various regulations consulted showed a number of varieties of hollow squares, the variation being, principally, in the number of companies used to form them. It was, however, quite a surprise to find Smirke providing instructions for and illustrations of a solid square along the lines of those used by the Austrians (*Bataillonsmasse*) and the Prussians. Figure 27 depicts the type of square described in the various British regulations, which show six- and 10-company battalions forming square. For purposes of the time study, the 10-company battalion and manoeuvre will be used.

As can be seen, in the 10-company manoeuvre the company on the right flank of the battalion had the furthest march. It would advance to the corner of the formation,

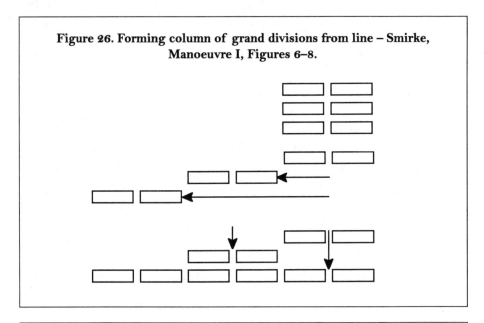

Figure 26. Forming column of grand divisions from line – Smirke, Manoeuvre I, Figures 6–8.

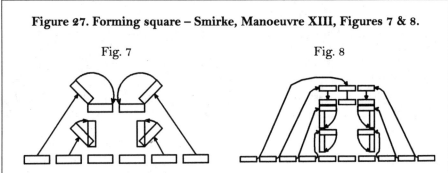

Figure 27. Forming square – Smirke, Manoeuvre XIII, Figures 7 & 8.

Fig. 7   Fig. 8

approximately 3.5 company intervals, face forward, march one more company interval and closes the square. The first portion of the manoeuvre would take 4.6 company intervals, plus one for the accordion effect. The second portion would take 2.1 intervals and the third portion one further interval. The total manoeuvre required the right flank company to move 8.7 company intervals (478.5 ft). The entire manoeuvre would be done at the quick pace and required 1.8 minutes.

A solid square is shown by Smirke in his Manoeuvre VII. When forming it from an open column of divisions, a precautionary command was given and the battalion closed up on the head. Then the first company moved back, closing with the second company, while the last two companies closed up with the rest. The central companies did not move, but faced outwards and detached four individuals to move into the intervals and fall in behind the file closers (NCOs and officers). (For illustration see Figure 9, Chapter 2.) When closed up the ranks were one pace apart. As a result, five divisions closed up had a depth of 25 paces, or approximately 60 ft.

If formed from a column of divisions, the rear division advanced 160 ft. Moving at the quick pace this took 0.6 minutes. The movement of the central files to fill in the

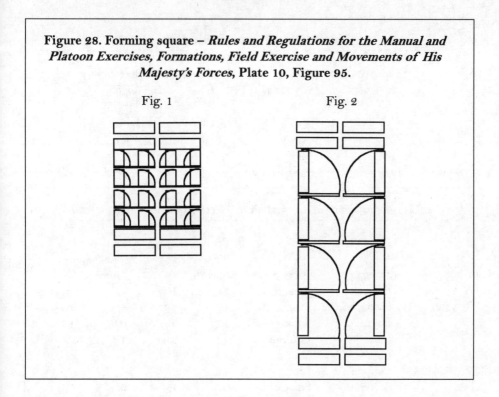

Figure 28. Forming square – *Rules and Regulations for the Manual and Platoon Exercises, Formations, Field Exercise and Movements of His Majesty's Forces*, Plate 10, Figure 95.

Fig. 1   Fig. 2

gaps between the companies took time, but certainly took no more than 0.1 minutes. The entire manoeuvre then took 0.7 minutes.

It should be noted that the first two ranks of this solid square were to kneel and slope their arms. The second two ranks stood and delivered the usual fire by file. After they had discharged their muskets the two kneeling ranks stood and fired their weapons and the others reloaded. A third volley could be delivered in quick order, but no provisions are made in Smirke for the reloading of the two kneeling ranks.

The 1808 regulations show a slightly a different method of forming square, which is shown in Figure 28.

The battalion would close from the full interval to a half-interval. The 2nd to 8th (centre) companies would remain stationary. The front and rear companies moved backwards (or forwards) until they had closed with the nearest company. The 3rd to 7th companies them broke into platoons, which wheeled outward to close the formation. This is nearly identical to the manoeuvre shown in the French *Réglement de 1791* for a multiple battalion square. The initial closing from a full to a partial interval required a reduction of the column's length from 550 to 225 ft. Being done at a quick pace this would take 0.8 minutes. The outward wheeling would take 0.3 minutes, and the entire manoeuvre 1.1 minutes.

Summary

Tables 16 and 17 provide a summarisation of the manoeuvring times of a British 10-company battalion with a strength of 660 men and its companies formed in two ranks. Table 16 simply lists the times for each manoeuvre, while Table 17 compares those

Table 16. British manoeuvring speeds.

Starting formation	Ending formation	Time required (minutes) Low	High
Column	Line	–	3.9
Column	Square	0.6	1.1
Line	Column	1.7	2.6
Line	Square	1.8	–

Table 17. Comparison of British and French manoeuvring speeds.

	Starting formation	Ending formation	French Time required (minutes) Low	High	British Time required (minutes) Low	High
1800–8	Column	Line	1.9	3.1	–	3.9
	Column	Square	1.7	–	0.6	1.1
	Line	Column	1.3	3.0	1.7	2.6
	Line	Square	4.7	–	1.8	–
1808–15	Column	Line	1.5	2.7	–	3.9
	Column	Square	0.5	1.6	0.6	1.1
	Line	Column	1.5	2.4	1.7	2.6
	Line	Square	1.6	–	1.8	–

times to the French manoeuvring system. Because of the reorganisation of the French in 1808, Table 17 is broken into two parts.

Observations and conclusions

Before the 1808 reorganisation the French conversion from column to line was significantly faster than the British. This was not due to their manoeuvring technique, as the British quick pace (270 ft per minute) covered 10 ft per minute more than the French *pas de charge* (260 ft per minute). Instead, it was due to the smaller size of the French battalions. There were no significant differences in the speeds of manoeuvring from line to column or column to square. However, the British system displayed a significant advantage when it came to converting a line to a square. After the 1808 reorganisation the differences between the British and the French manoeuvring systems fundamentally disappeared. The only major disadvantage the British had was forming from column into line.

The only conclusion that can be drawn is a tentative one. With the superior ability of the French to change from column to line one could logically suspect there might be a preference by the French to move in column and quickly deploy into line. Similarly, the British showed a preference to operate in line. This should not be interpreted to mean that there were no other reasons for these two preferred formations, but that the differences in manoeuvring times provide additional justification for Wellington's preference for forming his units in position and awaiting the French advance.

It might well also indicate why the French figured they would have time to deploy from column into line and engage the British in a fire-fight. History showed they couldn't, but they kept on trying.

Prussia 1788–99

Organisation

The Prussian infantry company of 1788 was established with four officers, 12 non-commissioned officers, three drummers, 10 *schützen* and 140 soldiers. When the musketeers and grenadiers were formed they were in three ranks; however, the fusiliers were formed only in two ranks. This meant that a musketeer or grenadier company had a frontage of 49 files and a fusilier company had a frontage of 73 files. Figures 29 and 30 illustrate how these companies were formed.

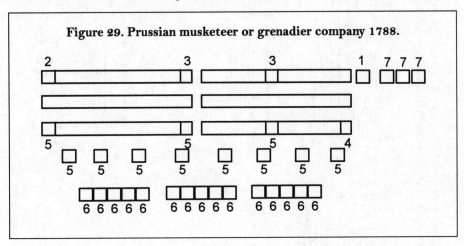

Figure 29. Prussian musketeer or grenadier company 1788.

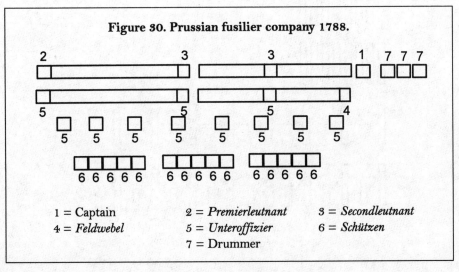

Figure 30. Prussian fusilier company 1788.

1 = Captain	2 = *Premierleutnant*	3 = *Secondleutnant*
4 = *Feldwebel*	5 = *Unteroffizier*	6 = *Schützen*
	7 = Drummer	

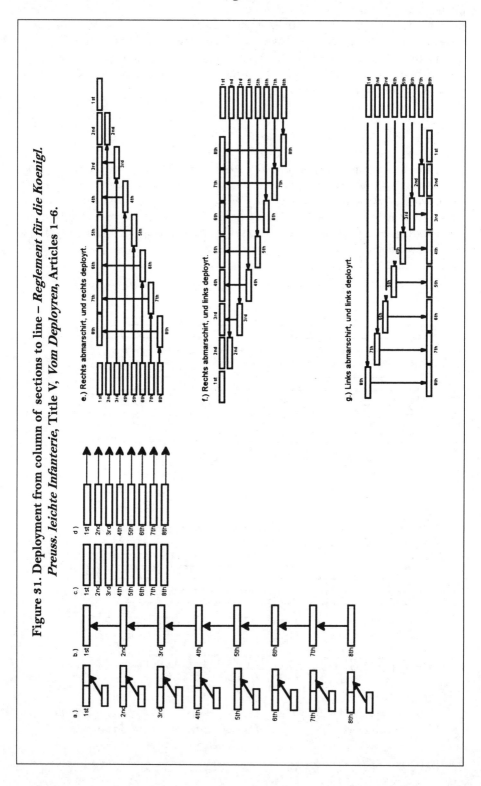

Figure 31. Deployment from column of sections to line – *Reglement für die Koenigl. Preuss. leichte Infanterie*, Title V, *Vom Deployren*, Articles 1–6.

Dimensions and speeds

In contrast to the French Regulation of 1791, the Prussian 1788 Regulation does not clearly state the frontage allocated to a soldier in the ranks, nor does it provide the length of his step or the rate of his march. Two rates of march are known to have been used: the *Ordinairschritt* of 75 and the *Geschwindschritt* of 108 paces per minute. However, von der Goltz indicates clearly that the rate of march for all manoeuvres was 75 paces per minute and speaks of it as the 'Saldern Waddle'.

Though no concise statement of interval is allocated to a soldier, an analysis of the 1759 translation of Frederick the Great's Prussian drill regulation supports the 22-inch interval used in the French study. Consequently a musketeer or grenadier company would have had a frontage of approximately 90 ft and the fusilier company a frontage of approximately 134 ft. This is the Prussian equivalent of the *distance entière* used in the French analysis, though the actual lengths are different.

The Prussian regulations do not provide a specific statement as to the width of the Prussian pace, though it was found that the pace was two Rhenish paces, or about 25 inches. At the *Ordinairschritt* the rate of advance was 156 ft per minute, or 1.74 musketeer company intervals. The *Geschwindschritt* advanced 225 ft per minute, or 2.5 musketeer company intervals.

Column to line evolutions

When the pre-1799 Prussian battalion moved in column it was a half-*Zug* column. There were four methods of deploying from this formation into line: 1) *Rechts abmarschirt, und rechts deployiert* (forming on right, deploying on the right); 2) *Rechts abmarschirt, und links deployiert* (forming on right, deploying on the left); 3) *Links abmarschirt, und rechts deployiert* (forming on left, deploying on the right); and 4) *Links abmarschirt, und links deployiert* (forming on left, deploying on the left).

The first action was to take the column of half-*Zug* and form a column of *Züge* (plural form of *Zug*) at full interval – see Figure 31. This could be done either to the right or the left. Figure 31a shows it being done to the right. This was executed by the second half-*Zug*, designated as the manoeuvring *Zug*, facing to the right (or left) and marching forward until it was clear of the other half-*Zug*. It would then halt, turn to face forward and march forward until it fell into place alongside the first half-*Zug*. Once this was done the *Züge* closed up until each was at a distance of two paces from the *Zug* in front. Figures 31b and c show this. Once this dense or closed-up column of *Züge* was formed the direction of the next action had to be decided. Again, it was a choice of deploying to the right or left.

In the *rechts abmarschirt* form of deployment the column would form line to the right of the 1st *Zug*. In the *rechts abmarschirt und rechts deployiert* the column would face right, with the exception of the 8th *Zug*, which remained facing forward. The first seven *Züge* then began to march forward (see Figure 31d). As soon as the 7th *Zug* cleared the 8th it would halt, face left and begin marching forward. Similarly, each successive *Zug*, as it cleared the *Zug* behind it, halted, faced left and began marching forward. This is illustrated in Figure 31e.

In the case of a *links abmarschirt* (Figure 31f) a similar procedure was followed; however, the 8th *Zug* remained fixed and the other *Züge* fell in on it in the *links deployiert* or shifted to the right, and the 1st *Zug* occupied its original position in the *rechts deployiert*. For the purpose of a time and motion study all four methods were equally fast.

Manoeuvring time

In deploying from the column of sections to a line using the *rechts abmarschirt, rechts deployiert,* the first evolution was to convert the column of sections into a column of *Züge.* This evolution would take 0.4 minutes. The second step was to collapse the column to a close interval and then to convert the column of *Züge* to a line. The accordion effect would occur in the flank march, and would increase the time by one additional interval. The total manoeuvre covered a maximum of 15.75 company intervals, requiring a total of seven minutes to cover at the 75 paces per minute rate of the *Ordinairschritt.*

The square

According to the *Reglement für die Koenigl. Preuss. leichte Infanterie,* published in 1788, the square was always formed from a line. The first act was for the battalion to compress towards the centre (where the 4th and 5th *Züge* met), filling in all of the empty files. The *Züge* then split into halves, the first half of each *Zug* moving behind the second half, effectively doubling the thickness of the formation and halving its length.

The 3rd and 4th *Züge* formed what became the front of the square. The 1st and 2nd *Züge* performed an about face and wheeled about the juncture of the 2nd and 3rd *Züge* in a large, fixed pivot until they were perpendicular to the 3rd *Zug.* In a similar fashion the 5th, 6th, 7th and 8th *Züge* pivoted about the juncture of the 4th and 5th in a massive fixed pivot wheel until they too were perpendicular to the 3rd *Zug.* At that time the 5th and 6th *Züge* stopped and the 7th and 8th continued to pivot about the juncture of the 6th and 7th until they closed the back of the square and the 8th *Zug* touched the 1st. Figure 32 demonstrates this manoeuvre.

Manoeuvring time

Because of the method of forming square, a grenadier or musketeer battalion required 3.8 minutes to form square. This is established by the wheel of the longest arm that forms both the right and rear of the square.

Prussia 1799–1806

In 1799 there was a reorganisation of the Prussian infantry. The fusiliers appear to have been exempted from this, but the musketeers and grenadiers had their battalion and company structures changed. There were now five companies – one grenadier and four musketeer – per battalion. These new grenadier companies were formed by breaking up the old grenadier battalions and incorporating two into each of the musketeer battalions. The other two companies were left as independent grenadier companies assigned to the regiment. They were stripped off and used to form amalgamated grenadier battalions.

The battalion had 22–23 officers, 60 *unteroffiziere,* 50 *schützen,* 15 drummers and 600 men. Each of the 10 companies had 120 men. A company had a total of 43 files.

The musketeer company had a total of 41 files. The other major change was the adoption of the *Geschwindschritt,* 108 paces per minute, for all tactical manoeuvres. The increase in the number of companies and slight reduction in their size had no effect on how the manoeuvres were executed, except for the square. The 1799 reorganisation was not accompanied by the issuance of a new regulation. Since many of

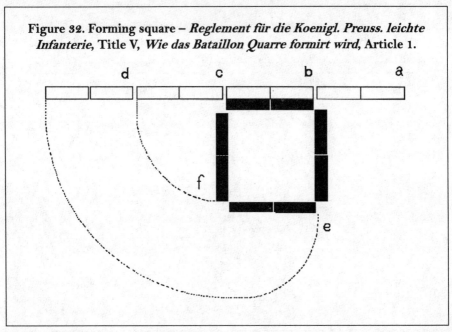

Figure 32. Forming square – *Reglement für die Koenigl. Preuss. leichte Infanterie*, Title V, *Wie das Bataillon Quarre formirt wird*, Article 1.

the manoeuvres of the 1788 Regulation are repeated in the 1812 Regulation it can be presumed that they were used between 1799 and 1806.

The conversion of the marching column to a line is fundamentally the same. The entire manoeuvre consists of the conversion of a column of sections to a column of *Züge* – 1.5 intervals. As there are now 10 sections, the furthest marching company moves nine intervals, plus one for the accordion effect, giving us a total manoeuvre of 11.5 intervals. This takes 3.9 minutes. The principal change in the time results from the increased speed of manoeuvre, not the increased number of companies nor the slightly reduced company size.

The only indication of how the Prussians now formed a square is found in a footnote to Jany's work, *Urkundliche Beiträge und Forschungen zur Geschichte des Preussischen*

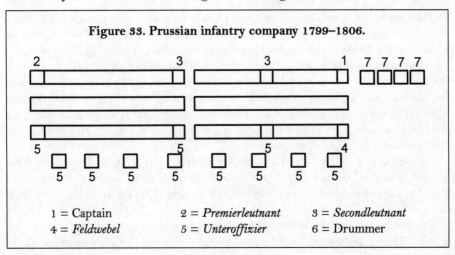

Figure 33. Prussian infantry company 1799–1806.

| 1 = Captain | 2 = Premierleutnant | 3 = Secondleutnant |
| 4 = Feldwebel | 5 = Unteroffizier | 6 = Drummer |

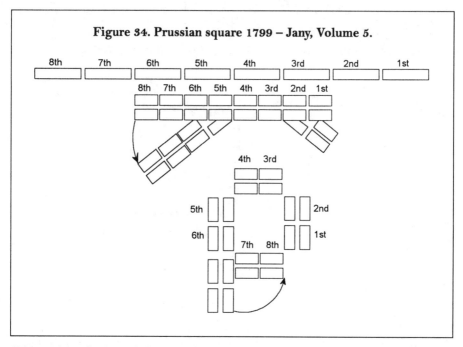

Figure 34. Prussian square 1799 – Jany, Volume 5.

Heeres, volume five: *Die Gefechtsausbildung der Preussischen Infanterie von 1806*. Jany states that it was formed from a column of companies. The lead company would stop. The remaining companies would close up to the interval of the *Züge*. The middle three companies would split by *Züge*, and the *Züge* would swing outwards to form the flanks of the square (three *Züge* to a flank) and the rear company would close up the rear.

This manoeuvre was quite quick. The closing of the ranks required the fifth company to advance 2.5 intervals. To close up it would advance another half-interval. Assuming that the middle companies had been wheeling while the fifth company advanced and were in place when it closed the rear of the square, this manoeuvre required a marching time of 0.9 minutes. Opening up into column should require about the same time. Figure 34 illustrates this.

How the manoeuvre was executed from line is an unanswered question. There are two methods by which the conversion to line could have occurred. The first was by collapsing the line into column via the *rechts abmarschirt, und rechts deployiert* or one of the other three methods for deploying. From that column this method of forming square would be used. The total time for this manoeuvre would, therefore, have been 4.8 minutes. Unfortunately, there is no indication whether the earlier system of an inward folding line was still used or if it had been abandoned. If this system was used, the line could not have doubled up as shown in the earlier 1788 Regulation. It is impossible to form a square with five equal sides.

As Jany's discussion provides for a square with a depth of three files we can force the collapsing line into a rectangular formation if we use *Züge* rather than companies as the manoeuvring elements. This speculative manoeuvre is shown in Figures 35 and 36.

Depending on the orientation of this square there are two possible speeds of formation. The square formed with a two-*Züge* front oriented along the direction of the

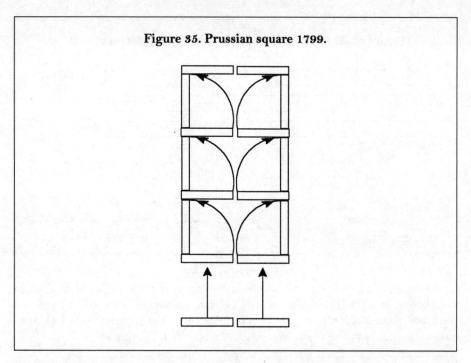

Figure 35. Prussian square 1799.

original line is the fastest. Figure 35 shows this manoeuvre. To execute this would require 10.99 intervals of movement, while the other square would require 12.56 intervals. The speeds of execution would be 3.8 and 4.4 minutes respectively.

Prussia 1806–15

Organisation

In 1808 the Prussians reorganised their infantry and this was followed by the *Exerzir Reglement für die Infanterie der Königlich Preussischen Armee* of 1812. An infantry company now had five officers, one *feldwebel,* one *portepeefähnrich,* three sergeants, seven *unteroffiziere,* 20 *gefreite* and 115 soldiers. The company was formed as shown in Figure 37.

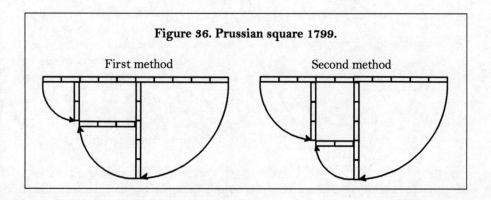

Figure 36. Prussian square 1799.

First method   Second method

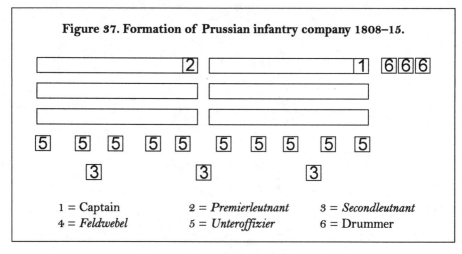

Figure 37. Formation of Prussian infantry company 1808–15.

1 = Captain   2 = *Premierleutnant*   3 = *Secondleutnant*
4 = *Feldwebel*   5 = *Unteroffizier*   6 = Drummer

Dimensions and speeds

This reorganisation gave the post-1808 infantry company a frontage of 45 files, which translates into 86 ft. The *Ordinairschritt* and *Geschwindschritt* were still 75 and 108 paces per minute. This meant that at the *Ordinairschritt* the company covered its interval in 0.6 minutes and at the *Geschwindschritt* it required 0.4 minutes.

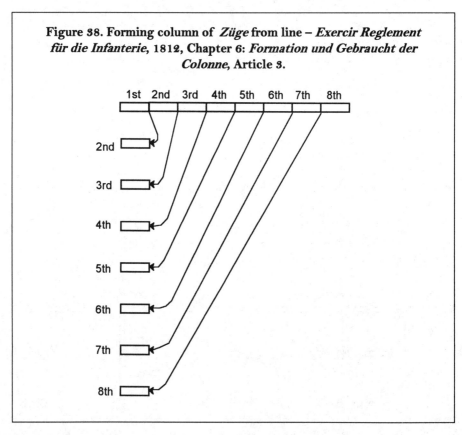

Figure 38. Forming column of *Züge* from line – *Exercir Reglement für die Infanterie*, 1812, Chapter 6: *Formation und Gebraucht der Colonne*, Article 3.

Line and column evolutions

As in 1788, the post-1812 Prussian infantry manoeuvred in the *Zug* column and executed many of its manoeuvres from this formation. The *rechts (links) abmarschirt, und rechts (links) deployiert* manoeuvres were executed in an identical manner; however, when ploying back into column they used a direct march identical to that used by the French when ploying. As in 1799, these manoeuvres were all executed at the *Geschwindschritt* of 108 paces per minute.

Line to column and column to line

The manner of forming line from column of *Züge* was the same as shown in Figure 31. The only difference was the speed at which the manoeuvre was executed. When the line ployed back into column the 1st *Zug* remained stationary and the seven remaining *Züge* marched directly to their positions, at half-*Zug* intervals, behind the 1st *Zug* in numerical sequence. Figure 38 illustrates the manner in which the battalion ployed into column.

Manoeuvring time

The *rechts (links) abmarschirt, rechts (links) deployiert* manoeuvres were executed at the *Geschwindschritt.* The calculations are the same as described before except for this fact, and the manoeuvre required 3.5 minutes. In ploying from line to column the longest march is made by the 8th *Zug.* The *Züge* advance directly to the corner of the formation, a total of 9.2 *Zug* intervals. In addition, due to the accordion effect and the last portion of the manoeuvre, an additional company interval must be added. The total distance moved is, therefore, 5.1 company intervals. This requires 2.0 minutes.

Column and line evolutions from the attack column

The attack column or *Angriffscolonne* was formed as a double column of *Züge*, or as a column of *pelotons.* It was generally formed closed up, which meant that there was an

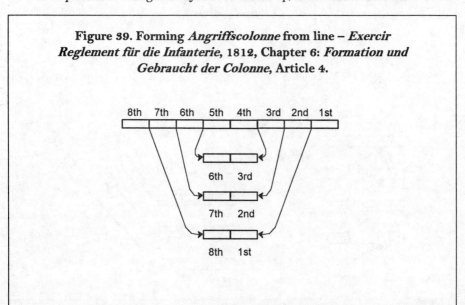

Figure 39. Forming *Angriffscolonne* from line – *Exercir Reglement für die Infanterie*, 1812, Chapter 6: *Formation und Gebraucht der Colonne*, Article 4.

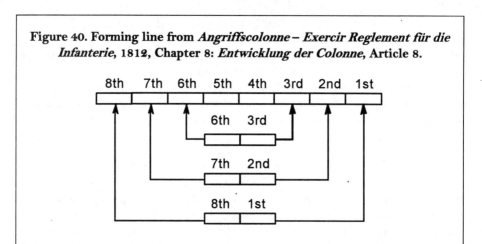

Figure 40. Forming line from *Angriffscolonne – Exercir Reglement für die Infanterie*, 1812, Chapter 8: *Entwicklung der Colonne*, Article 8.

interval of two *Füsse* (two feet, approximately 25 ins) between the first *Zug* and the first rank of the *Züge* immediately behind it. This was tactically the same as the French *colonne d'attaque*, which it closely resembled. When forming from line the 4th and 5th *Züge* remained stationary and the three flank *Züge* on either side faced to the centre and proceeded to march to their final positions at the *Geschwindschritt.* Figure 39 illustrates how this was done.

When the *Angriffscolonne* deployed into line it used a system more similar to that used before 1806 for deploying into line. Figure 40 illustrates the method by which this manoeuvre was executed. Please note that this is exactly identical to Figure 12

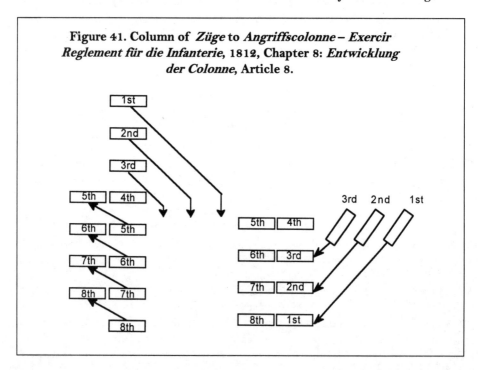

Figure 41. Column of *Züge* to *Angriffscolonne – Exercir Reglement für die Infanterie*, 1812, Chapter 8: *Entwicklung der Colonne*, Article 8.

(the French *colonne d'attaque* to line forming on the centre, drawn from the *Réglement de 1791*).

When the Prussian infantry marched to the battlefield it still marched in the *Züge colonne*. When it changed into the *Angriffscolonne* the 4th *Zug* remained stationary. The 5th, 6th, 7th, and 8th *Züge* marched to the left one interval and advanced until the 4th and 5th *Züge* were lined up. The other *Züge* closed in behind them at the proper interval. The 1st, 2nd and 3rd marched quickly to the rear of the 4th *Zug* and fell in in reverse order so that the 3rd *Zug* was just behind the 4th, followed by the 2nd and 1st *Züge*. The 1st *Zug* travelled the greatest distance and set the speed of the manoeuvre. Figure 41 illustrates this.

Manoeuvring times

When the *Angriffscolonne* or attack column was formed from a line the longest manoeuvre was made by the two flank *Züge*. The distance travelled was 3.6 *Zug* intervals, plus one for accordion effect and one more to enter their final position. The total manoeuvre covered 4.6 *Zug* intervals. At the *Geschwindschritt* this required 0.7 minutes.

When the attack column formed line the 1st and 8th *Züge* again moved the greatest distance. However, since this was a squared movement, they advanced three *Zug* intervals to the flank, 1.5 forward and one more for the accordion effect. These seven *Zug* intervals took 1.4 minutes at the *Geschwindschritt*.

When changing from *Zug* column to attack column the longest manoeuvre was made by the 1st *Zug*. However, a precise calculation is more difficult because it marched more or less directly, but had to manoeuvre outwards to avoid contacting the other two *Züge* preceding it around the 4th *Zug*. The 1st *Zug* moves backwards six *Zug* intervals. One must be added for the accordion effect and a further half-*Zug* to allow for the distance to the right that the *Zug* must go to avoid the other two manoeuvring *Züge*. This 3.5 company interval manoeuvre required 1.4 minutes

The square

The 1812 Regulation eliminated the hollow square formation in favour of a dense column formed from the *Angriffscolonne*. This formation is very closely related to the French *colonne serré* and the Austrian *Bataillonsmasse*. Again, it was executed at the *Geschwindschritt*. The attack column simply closed its ranks until there was a standard file interval between the file closers' rank of the first *peloton* (4th and 5th *Züge*) and the second *peloton* (6th and 3rd *Züge*). This was repeated with the other two *pelotons*. The formation that resulted was 30 *Füsse* deep. Figure 42 illustrates the final formation.

Manoeuvring time

Because the formation described by the Prussians as a *Quarre*, or square, was approximately one *Zug* in thickness, the 4th *peloton* was required to advance only two company intervals. At the *Geschwindschritt* this took 0.8 minutes.

Observations and conclusions

Because the French system was not studied before 1800, when their organisation settled down into something approaching regularity, an accurate comparison is not possible. However, a quick comparison shows that the French were dramatically faster,

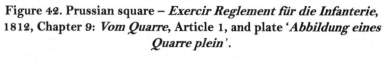

Figure 42. Prussian square – *Exercir Reglement für die Infanterie,* 1812, Chapter 9: *Vom Quarre,* Article 1, and plate '*Abbildung eines Quarre plein*'.

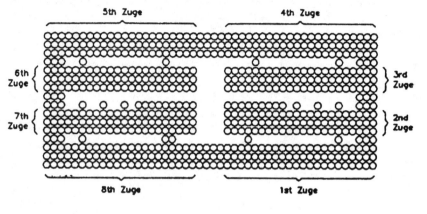

which probably provoked the Prussians into making some serious revisions to their own system. Indeed, these differences may well be what prompted the 1799 reorganisation.

It is also interesting to notice that the Prussian system of changing a column to a square was, with an allowance for the different number of companies per battalion,

Table 18. French and Prussian manoeuvring speeds 1788–98.

Starting formation	Ending formation	Prussia 1788–99 (minutes)	France 1800–8 (minutes)
Column	Line	7.0	1.9
Column	Square	10.8	1.7
Line	Column	7.0	1.3
Line	Square	3.8	4.7

Table 19. French and Prussian manoeuvring speeds 1799–1806.

Starting formation	Ending formation	Prussia 1799–1806 (minutes)	France 1800–8 (minutes)	French speed advantage
Column	Line	3.9	1.9	205% faster
Column	Square	0.8	1.7	53% slower
Line	Column	3.9	1.3	297% faster
Line	Square	3.8–4.8	4.7	19% slower

identical to the system provided by the French Regulation of 1791. It is quite possible that in their clashes with the French Revolutionary army the Prussians decided they needed to pull out of the war in order to institute some systemic changes as well as to overcome financial problems. With the institution of the 1799 reorganisation and the resulting changes in manoeuvre speeds we find a new relationship evolved. Table 19 shows the relationship that existed between 1799 and 1806.

Table 19 clearly shows us that the French had a tremendous advantage in converting line to column and column to line. The Prussians, in adopting the French system of forming square and altering their battalion organisation, had only succeeded in obtaining an advantage when forming square. This is unusual, because records show very few instances of the Prussians employing squares during the 1806 campaign. The French advantage in converting from column to line, and vice versa, still implies that they would be far faster in the advance as well as in offensive and defensive deployment of reserves.

With the institution of the 1812 Regulation these speed differences diminished significantly. Much of this must be attributed to the Prussian reorganisation of 1808–12. It is obvious that the military commission established by the Prussian General Staff carried out some serious studies and recognised the deficiencies of their old system vis-a-vis that of the French. Table 20 shows the new relationships.

Table 21 provides a comparison of how the Prussians improved their speed of manoeuvre by the adoption of the 1812 Regulation and the abandonment of their Frederician linear tactical system. It shows that they significantly improved their system and that the gains they made were significantly greater than the improvements

Table 20. French and Prussian manoeuvring speeds 1808–15.

Starting formation	Ending formation	Prussia 1799–1806 (minutes)		France 1800–8 (minutes)		French speed disadvantage
		Low	High	Low	High	
Column	Line	1.1	2.1	1.5	2.7	27% slower
Column	Square	0.3	–	0.5	1.6	40% slower
Line	Column	0.7	1.3	1.5	2.4	54% slower
Line	Square	1.0	1.3	1.6	–	38% slower

Table 21. Prussian improvements 1788–1812.

Starting formation	Ending formation	1788 (minutes)	1799 (minutes)	1808 (minutes)	
				Low	High
Column	Line	7.0	3.9	1.4	3.5
Column	Square	10.8	0.9	0.8	–
Line	Column	7.0	3.9	0.7	2.0
Line	Square	3.8	3.8	1.0	1.4

made to the French system by the organisational changes resulting from Napoleon's Decree of 18 February 1808.

The best conclusion that can be drawn from this study, as well as from the history of the period, is that the Prussians were no longer the innovators, but they knew a good system when they saw one. They adopted the French system of forming square in 1799, but went one step further and picked up an anti-cavalry formation modelled on the Austrian *Batallionsmasse* and the British solid square. This new square formation sacrificed firepower for speed of formation. No doubt the Prussians felt that their own cavalry would drive off the French cavalry and the infantry had only to survive the initial assault.

There is absolutely no doubt that the Prussian *Angriffscolonne* was modelled after the French *colonne d'attaque*. Indeed, the abandonment of the five-company battalion and adoption of a four-company battalion supports this. The method of manoeuvres was a perfect imitation of the eight-company system used in the French Regulation of 1791.

The Prussians made significant improvements in their system. As their army was severely reduced by the treaty ending the 1806 campaign, they were obliged to increase the quality of their army as much as possible. By adopting the best of the enemy's tactics as well as making a few modifications of their own the Prussians appear to have developed a superior system.

Russia

Documentation on the Russians is very scarce and as a result the 1837 *Russian Infantry Drill Regulation, School of the Battalion*, was used as the basis for analysis of Russian battalion manoeuvres. It clearly shows that the Russians followed the linear tactics of Frederick the Great as well as eventually adopting many French manoeuvres from the Regulation of 1791.

Warfare did not evolve significantly between 1800 and 1837 (indeed, the Crimean War was to be the last war fought using truly Napoleonic tactics), and the tactics shown in the Russian 1837 Regulation are decidedly Napoleonic. It cannot be stated specifically when these were adopted. When a date is given for the use of a formation it is based on the evidence of other documents which mention it. At best, these dates are a guess.

Indications of battalion-level tactics in military histories are generally poor and very little evidence was found to support or refute the assumption that there were few fundamental changes in the 1837 Regulation over its predecessor. What follows is assumed to be a reasonable representation of what the Russians probably did during the Napoleonic Wars based on an analysis of what they definitely did in 1837.

Organisation

Though there were some changes in the organisation of Russian infantry battalions between 1802 and 1815, the fundamental structure remained unaltered. Each company had three officers, a cadet, seven non-commissioned officers, three drummers and 141 soldiers. This meant that the company had a total of 50 files. When used as a manoeuvring formation the company was redesignated as a division. Figure 43 shows the formation of a Russian infantry company or division.

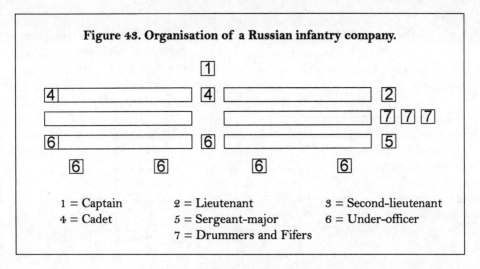

Figure 43. Organisation of a Russian infantry company.

1 = Captain　　　2 = Lieutenant　　　3 = Second-lieutenant
4 = Cadet　　　5 = Sergeant-major　　　6 = Under-officer
7 = Drummers and Fifers

Dimensions and speeds

No source was found that provided the interval allocated to the Russian infantryman, so the standard 22-inch interval was used in all calculations. A division had a total of 50 files, giving it a standard distance of 92 ft.

The Russians had three march paces: 1) the *tchyi szag*, 60–70 paces per minute; 2) the *skoryi szag*, 100–110 paces per minute; and 3) the *udwonyi szag*, 140–160 paces per minute. The *udwonyi szag* was a later development and definitely not used for manoeuvring. Source documents do not explicitly state which of the other two paces was used, but enough indication is given to suggest that the *skoryi szag* of 100–110 paces per minute is the rate that was used. Authoritative sources indicate that the standard pace of the Russian infantryman was slightly over two *archine* (an *archine* was 14 inches) or approximately 30 inches long. Using this pace the *skoryi szag* (105 paces per minute average) advanced at a rate of 262.5 ft per minute and could cover the division interval in 0.3 minutes.

Russian column formations

Figures 44 to 48 show the various types of columns used by the Russians in 1837. Historical documentation indicates that all of these columns were employed during the Napoleonic Wars (1800–15). In these illustrations the first unit is the staff and standard bearers. The second is either the over-complement or a separate force of skirmishers drawn from the battalion. I believe this second group was a post-Napoleonic evolution and it is best ignored.

Figure 44, the attack column, is a column of divisions at a half-platoon interval. It was the second most common column formation. Figure 45 is the close column of divisions, which was formed so that the interval between the divisions was the same as between the ranks of the formed division. This formation was used, but not as frequently as the attack column because it restricted the ability of the column to deploy. It should be noted that the standard bearers and staff are formed on the right. Figure 46 is a variation on Figure 45, with the staff formed in the middle of the first division.

Figures 47 and 48 are columns of divisions. Though they are shown at a close interval, they operated at half-platoon and full platoon intervals under normal field

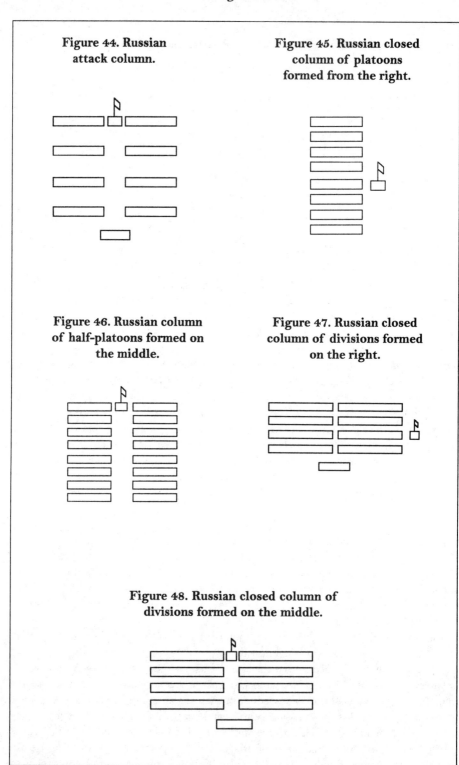

Figure 44. Russian attack column.

Figure 45. Russian closed column of platoons formed from the right.

Figure 46. Russian column of half-platoons formed on the middle.

Figure 47. Russian closed column of divisions formed on the right.

Figure 48. Russian closed column of divisions formed on the middle.

conditions. These illustrations have been compressed for the purpose of illustration only. The principal difference is the position of the standard bearers and staff. They are positioned in the same manner as in Figures 45 and 46. The column of platoons appears to have been the principal manoeuvring formation. The position of the staff, though it varies, is a minor consideration in the study of manoeuvres that follows.

Column and line manoeuvres

Figure 49a is identical to the illustration used earlier in the discussion of Prussian manoeuvres from column to line. As this system occurs in the Russian 1837 Regulation and was in use by the Prussians in 1788 it is highly probable that the Russians were using it by at least 1800.

There is considerable evidence in the 1837 drill regulation that the Russians manoeuvred in half-platoons, but there is nothing to indicate if the Russians used a column of half-platoons or smaller for general manoeuvres as the 1788 Prussians did. As a result all of the manoeuvres that follow are made from a column of platoons or divisions.

Deployment of columns to line

In Figure 49a we have a column of platoons converting into a line by the Prussian 1788 system of manoeuvre. The 8th platoon has the longest march. It must move to the flank seven platoon intervals and then it must advance seven intervals. In addition, during the flank march we must add one interval for the accordion effect. This brings the total manoeuvre to 15 platoon intervals, or 7.5 division intervals. This converts to a manoeuvre time of 2.6 minutes.

Figure 49b shows an alternative method of executing the manoeuvre. It is not likely that this was used during the Napoleonic period. However, for the purpose of consistency and completeness, it will be examined. The time required for this manoeuvre was again controlled by the movement of the 8th platoon. It moved three intervals to the left, plus one for the accordion effect. It would then move forward approximately one full platoon interval. Figure 49b shows that the line was formed somewhat in advance of the original position of the head of the column. As this forward movement is not absolutely necessary, and as the final distance in front of the original column cannot be determined, it is safest to assume that it formed on the head of the old column and there was no advance beyond that position. This would limit the total manoeuvre to five platoon intervals, requiring 0.9 minutes to execute.

Whenever it was adopted, the Russian attack column (Figure 44) was identical to that adopted by the Prussians in their 1812 drill regulation. There are sufficient historical accounts to suggest that this formation was used as early as 1800 and firm evidence that it was used during the 1812 campaign. Attack column frontage was always a division, but the interval between divisions could vary considerably according to the 1837 Regulation. Indications are that it was most frequently formed at a half-division interval. As a result, all manoeuvres in the following analysis will be based on that, except for one form of the square.

Figure 49c shows the method of converting the attack column into a line. The system shown in the 1837 Regulation is identical to the French system of converting the *colonne d'attaque* to a line. The rear platoons must flank march three platoon intervals and then march forward a further 0.75 intervals (the column is at quarter-platoon

Figure 49. Russian column of platoons deploying into line.

a) Deployment to line from column of platoons right, keeping the 1st platoon stationary.

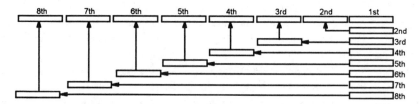

b) Deployment to line from column of platoons by advancing the 5th platoon.

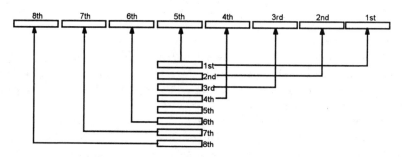

c) Deployment to line from attack column, on the centre.

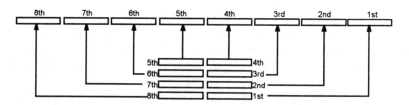

d) Deployment to line from column of half-platoons, on the centre.

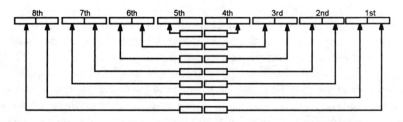

intervals). If we add one interval for the accordion effect we have a total manoeuvre of 4.75 platoon intervals, or 2.375 division intervals. This equates to 0.83 minutes.

Figure 49d shows the method employed to convert a column of platoons into a line. The rear-most platoons controlled the time of manoeuvre. They advance by a flank march a total of seven half-platoon intervals, plus one for the accordion effect. They then advanced a full platoon interval. The manoeuvre would take nine half-platoon intervals, or 2.25 division intervals, requiring 0.78 minutes.

Ploying from line to column

Figure 50a shows a system for advancing the line and converting it into an attack column. It is unlikely that this was used during the Napoleonic period. The time required to ploy into the attack column would be regulated by the outermost platoons. They advance a total of 4.3 platoon intervals, or 2.15 division intervals, equating to a time of manoeuvre of 0.8 minutes.

Figures 50b and c show other methods for converting a line into an attack column. In Figure 50b the two platoons on the right flank would move the furthest distance. They would march a distance of 2.1 platoon intervals, to which we must add one for the accordion effect and a further two for the movement into place along the front of the column. This comes to a total of 2.6 division intervals or 1.9 minutes. In Figure 50c the method employed is identical to that used by the French to convert a line to an attack column, from which, no doubt, it was copied. In this manoeuvre the flank platoons would advance the greatest distance, a total of 4.3 platoon intervals, 2.15 division intervals or 0.8 minutes.

Figure 50d shows the manoeuvre converting a line into a column of platoons by half-platoons. In this manoeuvre the flank half-platoon would move the furthest. They would march 9.2 half-platoon intervals, plus one for the accordion effect and one further to assume their final position. This is a total of 2.5 division intervals. This translates to 0.9 minutes. There is no reason to assume that this manoeuvre was used early in the Napoleonic period. Indeed, it is probable that it was not used until after 1810.

In Figure 50e we have a line of platoons converting into a column of platoons using the French 1791/Prussian 1812 system of manoeuvre. The 8th platoon had the longest march, moving a total of 9.2 platoon lengths. We must then add one for the accordion effect and one more to put them in their final position. This gives a total of 11.5 total platoon lengths, or 5.8 division lengths. This manoeuvre, as a result, would take two minutes to execute.

The square

There were three principal types of square used by the Russians. The first form of square, Figure 51a, was formed with division faces of a single rank. Figure 51b shows the method used to deploy from this square to line; however, this manoeuvre is not one that has been explored earlier in connection with the other nations, so will not be explored here.

Figure 51c is the second method of forming this square. It is best described as a 'follow-the-leader' square. The 3rd (or 6th) platoon faced inward and marched forward, tracing the sides of the square to be formed until it was in its final position on the reverse side of the square. It had to march three platoon intervals, which is not significant. However, the accordion effect would significantly effect this very long for-

Figure 50. Russian conversions from column into line.

a) Ployment to attack column by the forward movement of the 4th and 5th platoons.

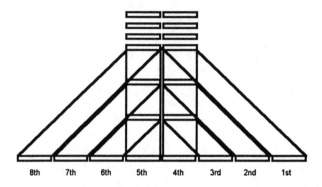

8th   7th   6th   5th   4th   3rd   2nd   1st

b) Ployment to a closed column of divisions to the right on the 3rd division.

c) Ployment to attack column on the 4th and 5th platoons.

8th   7th   6th   5th   4th   3rd   2nd   1st

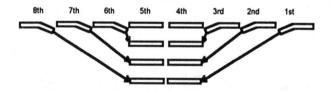

d) Ployment to column of half-platoons on the middle.

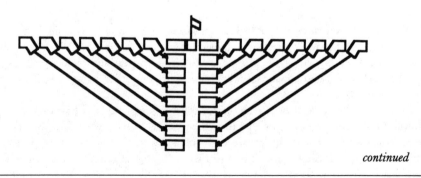

continued

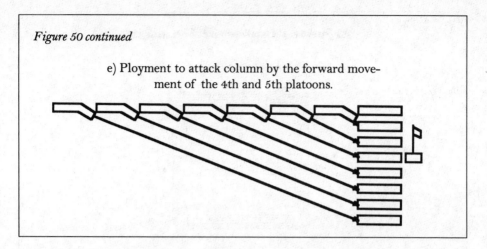

Figure 50 continued

e) Ployment to attack column by the forward movement of the 4th and 5th platoons.

mation. Each platoon will double its length and the last platoons to move (the 1st and 8th) will not move until the 3rd (and 6th) are already in their final position.

The process is best explained in this manner. As each platoon moved out it stretched to a division length. When the head of the 3rd platoon was at its final position its tail would still be a full division interval behind it. The 2nd platoon would also be at a full division interval. This means that the 2nd and 3rd platoons would be four platoons long when the head of the 3rd platoon was in its final position. If you count platoon intervals backwards from the final position of the 3rd platoon, you will find that the head of the 1st platoon is still two platoon intervals from its final position. Not only must the head of the platoon march two further intervals, but the rear of the 1st platoon must march one further interval. This means that the manoeuvre required seven platoon intervals of movement, taking 1.2 minutes.

Figure 51d shows the second method of forming this square. In this the 2nd and 3rd platoons would wheel and march directly backwards until they were perpendicular to the original line. The longest advance would be made by the 1st platoon, which proceeded via a flank march directly to its final position. The total manoeuvre required 4.8 platoon intervals, or 2.4 division intervals, and 0.8 minutes.

When the Russian battalion was in an attack column and wished to form square there were two methods of doing so. Figure 52a shows the first of these in reverse, *ie* ploying into column. The second square formed from an attack column is shown in 52c. It was formed from the attack column at a close interval and was very similar to the post-1812 Prussian square.

The square in Figure 51a was formed from an attack column at half-platoon interval. When it was to form square, the second and third divisions broke into quarters. These half-platoons would wheel outward towards the nearest flank and double up, forming the flanks of the square. The rear division would simply advance and close in the rear of the square.

The longest manoeuvre was made by the half-platoons in the centre of the column, which wheeled 0.39 division intervals and then advanced 0.25 division intervals. The total manoeuvre was 0.64 division intervals. The 4th division only had to advance 0.25 division intervals. The manoeuvres of the innermost half-platoons required 0.2 minutes.

Figure 51. Russian square formations.

a) Square formed with deployed fronts.

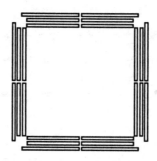

b) Forming line from a square with deployed fronts.

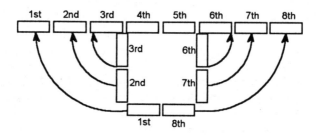

c) Forming square by moving the 4th and 5th platoons in front.

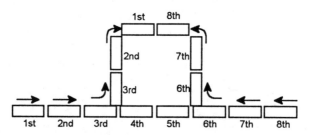

d) Forming square, keeping the 4th and 5th platoons stationary.

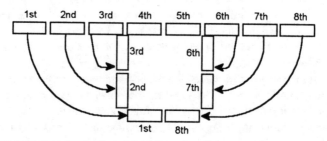

Figure 52. Russian conversions from square into column.

a) Forming attack column
from square.

b) Square formed from
attack column.

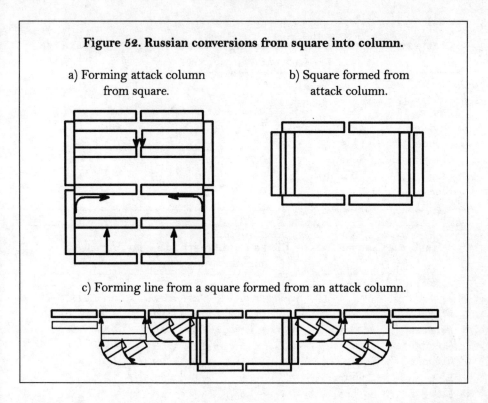

c) Forming line from a square formed from an attack column.

Very clear evidence exists to support this form of square being in use in 1810 during the wars with the Turks. Against the Turks this formation and manoeuvre would be worthwhile; however, against a European army it had serious handicaps. If threatened from the flank it could only form square. It would be unable to form a line perpendicular to the column head without an extensive and complicated manoeuvre. As a result, it does not appear to have been in particularly common use against the French.

In this method of forming square the central divisions again broke into half-platoons. The outermost or flank half-platoons marched forward just sufficient to clear the innermost half-platoons. Once clear, the innermost half-platoons marched directly to the flank. In its final form it is nearly identical to the 1812 Prussian square formation. However, unlike the Russians, the Prussians did not form this square from a column of divisions at close interval. As the facing movement of the inner half-platoons and the advance of the flank half-platoons should take about the same time and are not of a very significant time interval, the real time would be taken by the innermost half-platoons' flank march. As with the Prussian square, only the first three files really have to be in place for the square to be effective, so the accordion effect is irrelevant. The total manoeuvre, then, requires 0.25 division intervals or 0.09 minutes.

For the sake of comparison and because no hard data was found that states the actual rate of manoeuvre the Russians used, the figures calculated for them at the *skoryi szag* (105 paces per minute) are recalculated at the *tchyi szag* rate (65 paces per minute). This comparison is shown in Table 22. Table 23 provides a summary and comparison of the Russian and French manoeuvring systems.

Table 22. Comparison of manoeuvring speeds at the *skoryi szag* and the *tchyi szag* in minutes.

Starting formation	Ending formation	Skoryi szag Time required Low	High	Tchyi szag Time required Low	High
Column	Line	0.8	2.6	1.3	4.2
Column	Square	0.9	1.5	1.5	2.4
Line	Column	0.8	2.0	1.3	3.2
Line	Square	0.2	1.5	0.3	2.4

Table 23. Comparisons of Russian and French manoeuvring speeds in minutes.

Starting formation	Ending formation	Skoryi szag Time required Low	High	Tchyi szag Time required Low	High	France 1800–8 Time required Low	High
Column	Line	0.8	2.6	1.3	4.2	1.9	3.1
Column	Square	0.9	1.5	1.5	2.4	1.7	–
Line	Column	0.8	2.0	1.3	3.2	1.3	3.0
Line	Square	0.2	1.5	0.3	2.4	4.7	–

Starting formation	Ending formation	Skoryi szag Time required Low	High	Tchyi szag Time required Low	High	France 1808–15 Time required Low	High
Column	Line	0.8	2.6	1.3	4.2	1.5	2.7
Column	Square	0.9	1.5	1.5	2.4	0.5	1.6
Line	Column	0.8	2.0	1.3	3.2	1.5	2.4
Line	Square	0.2	1.5	0.3	2.4	1.6	–

The square described in Figures 52a to c has not been included in Table 23, not because it was not used during this period, but because according to historical sources it was used solely against the Turks.

The sole surprise in this comparison is that the Russian system of forming square shown in Figure 52a is faster than the French system. Other than that it shows the anticipated slower speed of Russian manoeuvres.

Conclusion

Assuming the manoeuvres illustrated in the 1837 Regulation correctly reflect those used by the Russians during the Napoleonic Wars, we find that if the Russians used their slow pace, *tchyi szag*, their manoeuvres are very comparable to those of the French. This results, in the most part, from their longer pace and similar system of manoeuvres offsetting the increased size of their manoeuvring elements. If the *skoryi szag* is used we find that the Russians manoeuvred significantly faster than the French. There are accounts which confirm this, and the Souvarovian love of the bayonet would suggest that they might well wish to move as quickly as possible.

The compensating consideration is that the Russians used a high, goose-stepping march that would both wear out the soldiers and cause them to lose their organisational integrity if they marched too fast for too long. It is, therefore, reasonable to assume that the Russians used both cadences and that if there was no real need to march quickly the slower *tchyi szag* was used.

Austria

The only complete regulations available when this analysis was prepared were the Austrian 1807 Regulation and the 1806 *Abrichtungs Reglement.* Though these regulations were in effect considerably after 1815, they provide no certain insight into the 1805 reforms of Mack or anything that preceded them. However, Mack's reforms apparently never really took hold, and his loss at Ulm finished them. In addition, according to Wagner, in his work *Von Austerlitz bis Königgratz, Osterreichische Kampftaktic im Spiegel der Reglmenets 1805–1814,* the only differences between these two regulations and Lacy's regulations of 1769 were the sections on skirmishing and *massen.* If Wagner is correct, one can reasonably assume that all other portions of this review are appropriate for the entire period from 1792 to 1815.

Organisation

The Austrians had three basic infantry formations: German infantry regiments, Hungarian infantry regiments, and grenadier battalions. There were significant size differences between these. However, the cadre of each company was standardised, with one *Hauptman* or *Capitain-Lieutenant,* one *Oberleutnant,* one *Unterleutnant,* one *Fähnrich* (cadet), one *Feldwebel* (sergeant-major), six corporals, seven vice-corporals, two drummers and a sapper. The German fusilier companies had 160 men, the Hungarian fusilier companies had 180, and the grenadier companies had 120. The company was not divided evenly and the number of files in each *Zug* varied. Figure 53 shows the formation of an Austrian company. It is interesting to note that though a captain was assigned to each company, he was not positioned within the company structure, but within the division structure.

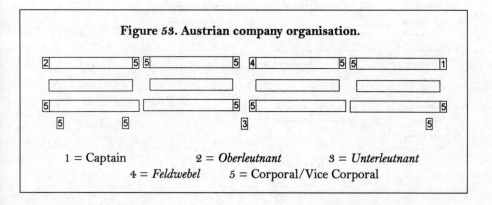

Figure 53. Austrian company organisation.

1 = Captain   2 = *Oberleutnant*   3 = *Unterleutnant*
4 = *Feldwebel*   5 = Corporal/Vice Corporal

Table 24. Numbers of files per Austrian company and *Zug*.				
	Total files	*Middle Zug*	*Wing Zug*	*Company length*
German	54	14	13	114 ft
Hungarian	61	16	15	127 ft
Grenadier	38	10	9	85 ft

Dimensions and speeds

Table 24 shows the breakdown of *Züge* and the company widths. As the Austrian Regulation doesn't specify a width per man it is necessary to once again use the 22-inch average.

The Austrians used three marching cadences, the *Ordinairschritt* (95 paces per minute), the *Geschwindschritt* (105 paces per minute) and the *Doublirschritt* (120 paces per minute). According to the *Abrichtungs Reglement* of 1806 the *Doublirschritt* was to be used for all formation conversions. It was considered 'essential to the assault, the attack, or fast evolution of the column through deploying, or deploying-march of the *masse*, over short distances and time so as not to exhaust the strength of the soldiers.' However,

Figure 54. Austrian column formations.

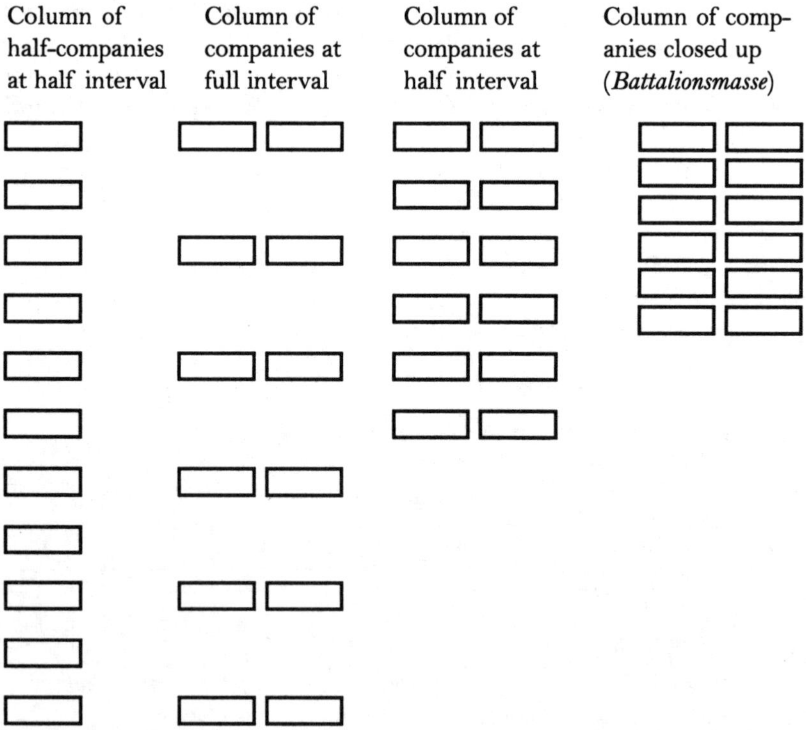

Dr Rothenberg states that the *Doublirschritt* was, in fact, rarely used, because it tended to cause the ranks to become disordered if used for very long.

The Austrian pace was 2.5 *Schuh* (shoes) or *Füsse* (feet) long, which comes to approximately 30 inches. Because there is some uncertainty as to which is the proper rate to use all calculations have been performed using both the *Geschwindschritt* and the *Doublirschritt* and both speeds are provided in the tables. So, at 105 paces (218 ft) per minute, this means that marching a German company interval takes 0.52 minutes, a Hungarian interval takes 0.58 minutes, and a grenadier interval takes 0.4 minutes. At 120 paces (300 ft) per minute, this means that marching a German company interval takes 0.38 minutes, a Hungarian interval 0.42, and a grenadier interval 0.28.

Column formations

The Austrians had four basic column formations. They were quite similar to those of other nations and were defined by their intervals as well as by their widths. There were columns formed by *Zug*, half-companies, half-divisions (companies) or divisions. The intervals were *masse* (close), half and full intervals. Though the regulations are not specific as to which form of column was preferable, the plates concentrate on manoeuvres by company and half-company. Those by half-company seem to predominate, indicating it was the most commonly used formation. This assumption is reinforced by the *Divisionsmasse* being formed with a half-company frontage. As a result, all columnar calculations will be made principally for the half-company column, with a comparison for the full company column

Deployment of column into line and line into column

Figure 55 shows a column of companies deploying to the right into line. This is approximately the same system as was used by the French and the Prussians, except

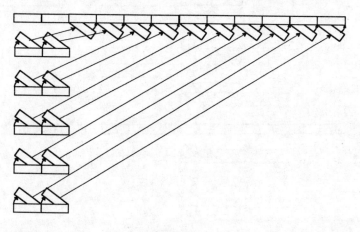

Figure 55. Conversions from column into line on the head to the left flank – *Exercir Reglement für die K.u.K. Infanterie*, Vienna, 1807, 2nd *Hauptschnitt*, 3rd *Abschnitt*, 2nd paragraph, *Brechung durch die Schwenkung und Abthielung*, pp.84–5 & Plate 23.

Table 25. Conversion of column of companies and half-companies to line on the head to one flank.

Geschwindschritt	Column of companies (minutes)	Column of half-companies (minutes)
German	3.9	4.2
Hungarian	4.3	5.0
Grenadier	3.0	3.1
Doublirschritt	Column of companies (minutes)	Column of half-companies (minutes)
German	2.8	3.1
Hungarian	3.1	3.7
Grenadier	2.2	2.3

there is a quarter-pivot performed by the company. Once completed the company marches to its final position and quarter pivots into place. The same system was used for a column of half-companies. The Regulation indicates that this method was used both to deploy and to ploy. The speeds required for this manoeuvre were as shown in Table 25.

Apparently the Austrians also deployed from column into line of battle using an oblique marching step. This oblique step is found in all armies, but almost never used. Though it is a crab-like side-stepping process, in practice it is as if every soldier faced

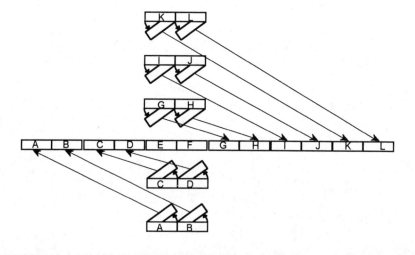

Figure 56. Conversions from column to line on the middle – *Exercir Reglement für die K.u.K. Infanterie*, Vienna, 1807, 2nd *Haupschnitt*, 3rd *Abschnitt*, 3rd paragraph, *Ausschwenken in des Alignement der Colonne*, p.867 & Plate 24.

Table 26. Column into line on the middle.		
Geschwindschritt	*Column of companies (minutes)*	*Column of half-companies (minutes)*
German	2.4	2.3
Hungarian	3.0	2.8
Grenadier	1.9	1.8
Doublirschritt	*Column of companies (minutes)*	*Column of half-companies (minutes)*
German	1.8	1.7
Hungarian	2.2	2.0
Grenadier	1.4	1.3

half-right or left (45 degrees) and the companies or *Züge* marched directly to their final position in line. Because of the awkwardness of the process, designed to keep the soldiers facing the enemy at all times, and there being no clear and sure method of calculating the rate of advance in this marching style, it does not seem appropriate to speculate as to the length of time necessary to make the conversion in this manner. A guess would suggest that, again because of the awkward marching process, it was at least as long as using the wheel, and possibly longer.

Figure 56 shows the formation of a line on the centre of a column of companies. The manoeuvre from a column of half-companies would have been performed in the same manner. As before, the units perform a half-pivot at both ends of the manoeuvre. Table 26 shows the time requirements.

The square

The Austrians used two anti-cavalry formations. The first was the traditional square. Though its methods of formation were different, the Austrians did use it extensively. The second was the *masse*. This formation is similar to the *colonne serré* or the Prussian post-1812 square discussed earlier. It had the advantage of being quick to form, but it had the disadvantage of being a far more tempting artillery target. The other disadvantage of the *masse* was that it enabled fewer men to fire on the attacking cavalry.

An Austrian battalion formed in a French *carré d'Egypte* would be able to fire a total of 648 muskets (not considering any fire from NCOs or officers) in all four directions. It would be able to fire 216 forwards or backwards. To each flank it would be able to fire 108 muskets. However, in the *Battalionsmasse*, the frontage of which was a single company, it could fire only 108 muskets forward and 36 to either flank.

The Austrian battalion square had a similar problem. It could fire only 108 muskets to the front or rear, and on the flanks it could fire only 48. It is apparent that the Austrians felt it was more important to form square quickly and survive the impact of the cavalry charge than it was to shoot the cavalry as it attacked. This may well be the result of their years of combat with the Turks and the type of terrain in which they fought. The *masse* would cut down the enemy's chances of surprise and would minimise the impact of their cavalry on the Austrian infantry. Also, as the Turks did not

Figure 57. Dimensional relationships between '*Battalionsmasse*', column and line – *Exercir Reglement für die K.u.K. Infanterie*, Vienna, 1807, 2nd *Haupschnitt*, 3rd *Abschnitt*, 5th paragraph, *Deploirung*, pp.89–92 & Plate 27.

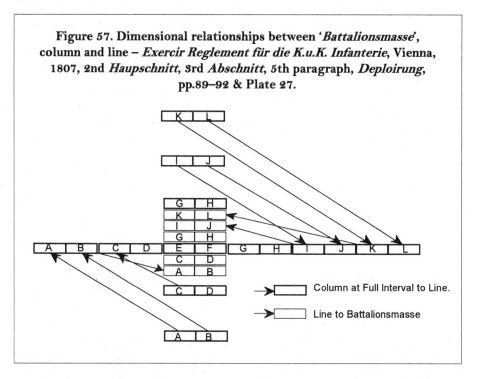

have a significant field-artillery establishment it would mean that they could pose no real threat to the heavy blocks of Austrian infantry formed in *masse*.

Figure 57 shows the relationships between the column of companies, the line and the *Battalionsmasse* (a *masse* formed from a battalion). The purpose of this diagram is not to indicate that a column would deploy into line and then into *masse* if attacked, but simply to show the manoeuvres to and from each formation and to give an idea of the relative sizes of the formations.

The conversion from line into *Bataillonsmasse* as shown in Figure 57 requires that we consider the thickness of the company. The distance between the ranks, heel to heel, was 2.5 *Schuh*, or 2.5 ft. As in *masse* the file closers' rank vanished, this gives the distance from the heels of the first rank of the first company to the heels of the first rank of the second company as 7.5 *Schuh* or 7.5 ft. The furthest company would move three company intervals and be 31.2 ft offset from the original line of the battalion. The total distance covered for a German company would be 299 ft, taking 1.6 minutes.

Table 27. Forming *Battalionsmasse* from line.

	Geschwindschritt (minutes)	*Doublirschritt (minutes)*
German	1.6	1.2
Hungarian	1.8	1.3
Grenadier	1.3	1.0

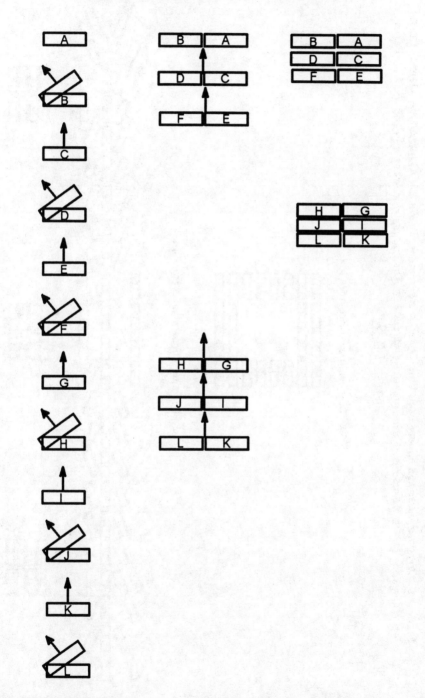

Figure 58. *Divisionsmasse* from column of *Züge – Exercir Reglement für die K.u.K. Infanterie*, Vienna, 1807, Plate 60.

Figure 59. *Divisionsmasse* and square from line – *Exercir Reglement für die K.u.K. Infanterie, Vienna, 1807, 4th Haupschnitt, 4th Abschnitt, Formirung des Quarres und Anwendung der Massen gegen die Kavallerie,* pp.208–21 & Plates 48 & 58.

a) Forming square from line.

b) Forming *Divisionsmasse* from line.

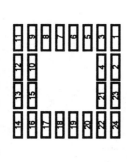
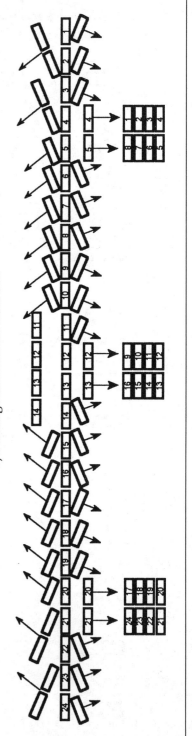

Table 28. Forming *Divisionsmasse* from column of *Züge*.

	Geschwindschritt (minutes)	Doublirschritt (minutes)
German	0.90	0.70
Hungarian	1.00	0.73
Grenadier	0.69	0.50

Table 29. Forming *Divisionsmasse* from column of half-companies.

	Geschwindschritt (minutes)	Doublirschritt (minutes)
German	0.62	0.42
Hungarian	0.69	0.50
Grenadier	0.50	0.37

Table 30. Forming *Divisionsmasse* from line.

	Geschwindschritt (minutes)	Doublirschritt (minutes)
German	0.54	0.39
Hungarian	0.60	0.44
Grenadier	0.41	0.30

When closing up from column of *Züge* to *Divisionsmasse*, as shown in Figure 58, the 6th *Zug* marched the greatest distance. It performed a half-wheel to the left and then a half-wheel to the right. From there it advanced four *Zug* intervals less the thickness of the 1st and 2nd *Züge*. A German *Zug* was 24.75 ft wide. A half-wheel was 39 ft long and the two half-wheels would take 78 ft. It then advanced three *Zug* intervals ($3 \times 24.75 = 74.25$ ft) and, in closing up, moved another 18.9 ft. The total distance covered was 171 ft and required 0.57 minutes.

The *Divisionsmasse* could also be formed from a column of half-companies and the manoeuvre was quite simple. The half-companies closed up on the lead half-company in groups of four. There was no need for any deployment or manoeuvring other than simply marching forward into *masse*. A German company would march forward two full intervals and and close up. The total manoeuvre required 0.42 minutes.

Divisionsmasse could also be formed directly from a line, as indicated in Figure 59b. In this manoeuvre the central two *Züge* marched forwards far enough to allow the other *Züge* to close into position behind them. It could also be formed as shown in the Russian manoeuvre represented in Figure 59a. According to the regulations the outside *Züge* manoeuvred as if forming a column on the middle. This entailed a half-pivot to face inwards, a forward march until they were behind the central two *Züge*,

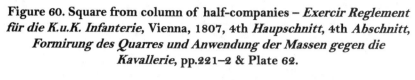

Figure 60. Square from column of half-companies – *Exercir Reglement für die K.u.K. Infanterie,* **Vienna, 1807, 4th** *Haupschnitt,* **4th** *Abschnitt, Formirung des Quarres und Anwendung der Massen gegen die Kavallerie,* **pp.221–2 & Plate 62.**

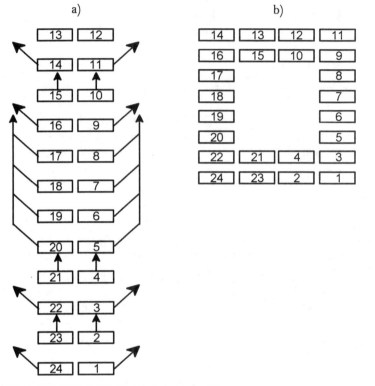

and a half-wheel to the left, followed by a forward march until they closed up behind the other *Zug.*

When the *Battalionsmasse* or *Divisionsmasse* was attacked by cavalry it knew it was safe. In the *Battalionsmasse* the staff officers and their horses were pulled into the centre of the formation. Against cavalry it was quite secure, but against artillery it had problems. These dense formations offered artillery an ideal target upon which they would inflict heavy casualties. The response was not to have a number of *masses* in close proximity to one another, but to disperse them.

The Austrians formed square from either line or column. Figure 59a shows the method of forming square from line. The central four *Züge* marched directly backwards. The other *Züge* did a half-right (or left) and marched towards the centre, and then did a half-left (or right) and marched into their final position. The outermost or wing *Züge* marched the greatest distance. It marched nine *Zug* intervals and did two half-wheels. That manoeuvre required 1.16 minutes for a German company.

If the square was to be formed from a column of half-companies (Figures 60a and b), or double column of *Züge,* the column would form square by *Züge.* The two leading

Table 31. Forming square from line.		
	Geschwindschritt (minutes)	*Doublirschritt* (minutes)
German	1.59	1.15
Hungarian	1.42	1.04
Grenadier	0.98	0.72

Table 32. Forming square from column of half-companies.		
	Geschwindschritt (minutes)	*Doublirschritt* (minutes)
German	1.59	0.95
Hungarian	1.42	1.04
Grenadier	0.98	0.72

Züge stopped in place and those immediately to their rear pivoted outwards, then forward, and fell in on the first two *Züge*'s outer flanks. This gave the front of the square a frontage of a full company (four *Züge*). The third row *Züge* marched straight forward and took position immediately behind the two lead *Züge*. The fourth row of *Züge* split in half, wheeled outwards, and marched forward immediately behind the outermost two *Züge*. The next four pairs wheeled outwards, then wheeled forwards, and marched forward, closing up into *masse* with the double row of *Züge* now forming the front two ranks of the square. The remaining four pairs of *Züge* performed the same manoeuvre as that performed by the first four pairs and closed up. This means that the rear two *Züge* had the longest march. They performed two half-wheels, advanced six full *Zug* intervals and closed up with the mass before them. The total manoeuvre took a German company 0.95 minutes to perform.

The Austrian squares defended themselves with fire by ranks. The first rank stood with its weapons lowered and saved its fire until the moment of closing. The second rank started firing when the charging cavalry was 300 paces from them and the third rank loaded muskets and passed them forward to the second rank.

The Austrian was quite unique amongst European systems. Its square did not closely resemble those of any nation except the Russians, who copied that particular square from the Austrians. Its cadences were within the range of those used by the rest of Europe, but with Austria's shorter pace its actual manoeuvring rates were the slowest in Europe. Fortunately, this was offset by their manoeuvring system. There is truly not much that can be said for this system without comparison to that in use earlier, other than that it seems to have learned nothing from the French system.

Conclusion

The preceding sections have analysed the manoeuvres of the various armies from one formation to another. A review of the systems prior to 1809 shows the Russian and Austrian systems to have been surprisingly quick in responding to a cavalry threat. It

Table 33. Summarisation of Austrian manoeuvres.

Manoeuvre	Geschwindschritt (min.)			Doublirschritt (min.)		
	Ger.	Hung.	Gren.	Ger.	Hung.	Gren.
Column of companies to line on the flank	3.9	4.3	3.0	2.9	3.1	2.2
Column of half-companies to line on the flank	4.2	5.0	3.1	3.1	3.7	2.3
Column of companies to line on the middle	2.4	3.0	1.9	1.8	2.2	1.4
Column of half-companies on the middle	2.3	2.8	1.8	1.8	2.0	1.3
Battalionsmasse from line	1.6	1.8	1.3	1.2	1.3	1.0
Divisionsmasse from line	0.54	0.60	0.43	0.4	0.4	0.3
Divisionsmasse from column of *Züge*	0.90	1.00	0.69	0.7	0.7	0.5
Divisionsmasse from column of half-companies	0.62	0.69	0.48	0.5	0.5	0.4
Square from line	1.60	1.77	1.23	1.2	1.3	0.9
Square from column of half-companies	1.27	1.42	0.98	0.9	1.0	0.7

Table 34. Comparative analysis of minimum times of manoeuvre in minutes, 1800–8.

Manoeuvre	France	Britain	Prussia	Russia	Austria Geschwind-schritt	Doublir-schritt
Column to line	1.9	3.9	3.9	0.8–1.3	2.0	1.5
Column to square	1.7	1.1	0.8	0.9–1.5	1.3	1.0
Line to column	1.3	1.7	3.9	0.8–1.3	2.3	1.7
Line to square	4.7	1.8	3.8	0.2–0.3	1.6	1.2

Table 35. Comparative analysis of minimum times of manoeuvre in minutes, 1809–15.

Manoeuvre	France	Britain	Prussia	Russia	Austria Geschwind-schritt	Doublir-schritt
Column to line	1.5	3.9	1.1	0.8–1.3	2.3	1.5
Column to square	0.5	0.6	0.3	0.9–1.5	1.3	1.0
Line to column	1.5	1.7	0.7	0.8–1.3	2.3	1.7
Line to square	1.6	1.8	1.0	0.2–0.3	1.6	1.2

is surprising to note that if the Russians did indeed use the faster *skoryi szag* (first figure in the Russian column of Table 34) they were the quickest manoeuvring army in Europe prior to 1808. Even if they used the *tchyi szag* (second figure), most of their manoeuvres were still faster. On the other side of the coin, the Austrians were the slowest.

The potential Russian superiority of marching remains after 1808, but again it is assumed that the Russians did indeed manoeuvre at the *skoryi szag*. If the *tchyi szag* was used many of their speed advantages are lost.

Though the other nations improved their speeds and manoeuvres over the last part of the period in question, the British seem to have become the slowest manoeuvring army in Europe. This is, no doubt, due to their failure to revise their regulations and accept the new manoeuvring reality.

Chapter 4

Light Infantry

History of light infantry

In the Middle Ages, and earlier, light infantry was generally the missile element of an army. Its function was to engage the enemy with its missile fire rather than in hand-to-hand combat. If it did involve itself in close combat, it would quickly perish. When the pike and musket were adopted light infantry began to rapidly disappear from the battlefield and remained a thing of the past, with a few exceptions, until Frederick the Great encountered it in Bohemia. Here the Austrian light infantry and cavalry proved to be so annoying, yet so elusive, that he was forced to withdraw his forces rather than let them be chewed up. His reaction was to raise his own light infantry; but he never returned to Bohemia.

The British were taught the effectiveness of light infantry and skirmishers when they went to America in 1775 to put the colonials back in their place, though they had some experience with light infantry during the Seven Years War in Europe. Despite the hard lessons that they learned in the American War of Independence, Britain disbanded all but a very few of its light infantry formations until the need for them arose again in 1792. By the outbreak of the French Revolutionary Wars, however, they had lost their expertise at skirmishing and had to start all over again.

There are a multitude of reasons why the French plunged headlong into the use of skirmishers in 1792. Not having sufficient time to train their conscript army in the finer points of the line of battle, they instead adopted the column, which required some training, and the skirmish line, which required only loyalty. As the French were long on loyalty in their early volunteer armies, they could trust most of their infantry not to desert, even though, as skirmishers, they were operating under fire without the tight control of the officer cadre one finds in a formed company.

The desertion problem was so great in Frederick the Great's army that if he deployed any of his line battalions in a skirmish line it was guaranteed that much of it would desert before the battle was over. Despite this, he did have a few specialised light infantry formations, *ie* the *Freikorps*. As the other European powers modelled their armies on his system they paid little attention to raising and training light infantry. Only the Austrians, with the continual state of unrest along their border with the Ottoman Empire, maintained a large body of trained light infantry.

Until the French Revolution this state of affairs remained relatively unchanged. Then France's political and social problems obliged it to adopt the column and the skirmish line as its principal battle formations. It was in the Battle of Jemappes that the French first deployed entire battalions into skirmish formation and used light cavalry to support them. This battle was very successful for the French and the tactics were subsequently emulated elsewhere.

In reaction to the increased use of light infantry by the French the Austrians expanded their own light infantry by using men from line formations, but this proved to be not very successful. From then on the French employed more and more skirmishers until on occasion entire divisions were employed in skirmish formations.

Skirmishers

As mentioned earlier, the fundamental trait of light infantry that distinguished them from line infantry was their training and general usage as skirmishers. The function of skirmishing was the process by which a number of men broke from their rigid formation and deployed into a loose line, positioning themselves between the enemy and their own lines. Once deployed in this manner they would fire on any enemy formation that stood before them. The advantage of a skirmish line over a formed line was that it often did not present a target sufficiently large for a line unit to justify firing a volley at it.

From the perspective of the enemy line it was very much like trying to hit a fly with a table. If the volley hit any of the skirmishers they would be dead, but with the notoriously poor accuracy of the musket and the fact that skirmishers would hide behind rocks, trees, walls, etc, the return for the expenditure of the volley did not justify its use. Also, once the line had fired it was vulnerable to a quick rush by cavalry. The risk of perhaps killing a few skirmishers just didn't offset the chance of the line being hit by cavalry whilst its weapons were unloaded. This is why the 1792 Prussian army had a specialised type of fire known as *heckenfeuer* or 'hedge' (sniper) fire.

From the perspective of the skirmisher it was very different. His musket was as poor as that of the line infantryman, but it didn't matter. When he shot it was like trying to hit a barn from the inside. His target was so big that he almost couldn't miss. His goal was to position himself so that he could get in a good shot at his target, yet remain under some sort of cover.

Skirmishers had two goals. The first was to engage the enemy's formed units and pepper away at them until their morale was so shaken by the continual effect of seeing people falling around them that they would break when attacked by formed infantry. The second was to deliberately kill the officers and non-commissioned officers of the opponent's infantry. Indeed, the morale impact of the deaths of the soldiers standing around them was compounded by the deliberate policy of French skirmishers to aim at the officers and NCOs. Though no published French Regulation states that this was official policy, it is obvious from the comments of the Prussians after Jena-Auerstädt that this was how French skirmishers fought. The Prussians reported taking heavy casualties on the flanks of their companies. Figure 61 illustrates this point, showing that officers and NCOs were customarily posted on the flanks of a company. Even with inaccurate musket shots, the statistical concentration of hits will still be in the area where the firing soldier has been aiming.

By eliminating those individuals in the formed unit charged with maintaining order as well as controlling the manoeuvres of the unit, the skirmishers forced replacements to be drawn from the file closers' rank. When these men were drawn forward into the ranks they were unable to perform as file closers, and the ability of men to break ranks and flee the scene of battle increased. Eventually, the file closers' rank would be so depleted that it could not keep men from breaking ranks and running away. Once the company was no longer able to prevent desertions, and found itself threatened by a charging enemy, it was doomed to break.

That this was deliberately done is confirmed in a memoir of the period by Nadezhda Durova, a Russian cavalry officer. Durova's work, *The Cavalry Maiden*, contains the following passage:

> I asked the captain for permission not to remount; he agreed, and we went on talking. 'Explain to me, Captain, why so many of our officers are being wounded. There is such a dense mass of soldiers that it would be easier to kill more of them. Are they really aiming on purpose at the officers?'
>
> 'Of course,' answered Podjampolsky. 'That is the most effective way of disrupting and weakening enemy forces.'
>
> 'Why is that?'
>
> 'Why? Because one brave, competent officer can do the enemy more harm with his knowledge, sagacity, and skill in using both the advantages of the landscape and the mistakes of the opposing side — particularly when he is an officer endowed with the lofty sense of honour which makes him face death dauntlessly and act coolly no matter how great the danger — such an officer, I repeat, can do more harm to the enemy than a thousand soldiers with nobody to command them.'

The functioning of the skirmisher and his fire on the enemy seems to have had two effects. First, they seem to have locked the enemy formation in place, causing it to direct its attention at the skirmishers who were harassing it and distracting it from the formed units that were advancing behind the skirmishing line. In addition, the formed enemy would not be willing to manoeuvre so as to expose its flanks to the skirmishers. This would permit the forces advancing behind the skirmishers to manoeuvre at will so as to take advantage of the terrain without the enemy being able to react to those manoeuvres. Various sources indicate that the French skirmishers were quite adept at penetrating larger holes in the enemy battle formation and positioning themselves so that they could fire on the flanks of the forward units.

The second function of a skirmish screen was to protect friendly forces from the fire of the enemy's own skirmishers. This they did by engaging the enemy skirmishers and physically preventing them from approaching the friendly lines.

Tactical use of light infantry

As mentioned earlier, there are very few documents of any type and almost no regulations that speak of the employment and operations of light infantry in battle. Most documents that speak of light infantry tactics dwell on pickets, vedettes or the operations of raiding parties. The following is a compilation of what little information is available on the topic of skirmisher tactics.

French skirmishers

In a Prussian regulation translated for use by the French in 1794 we find the following:

> When the corps of troops is formed in line of battle, or when it must deploy, one ordinarily directs that several detachments be made to cover the wings and front of the troops during the execution of its movement. The officer destined to fill this operation should move forward with his troop, with regards to the part of the formation he is to defend. He should advance himself more or less according to the proximity of the enemy and the advantages provided by the terrain. He shall detach from his flanks *tirailleurs* who will mask the manoeuvres of the

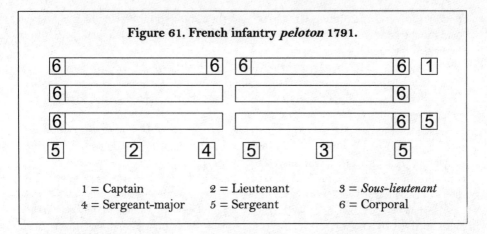

Figure 61. French infantry *peloton* 1791.

1 = Captain	2 = Lieutenant	3 = *Sous-lieutenant*
4 = Sergeant-major	5 = Sergeant	6 = Corporal

formation he is charged to protect. He shall support his *tirailleurs* according to the circumstances and the strength of his detachment by small troops, each commanded by an officer or *sous-officer*.

The duty of the *tirailleurs* is to hold the enemy at a distance by means of their continual fire. If pressed too hard, the *tirailleurs* shall rally on the small troops destined to support them, while those small detachments attempt to drive back the advancing enemy.

While the *tirailleurs* are engaged, the officer in charge shall continually watch the enemy and the force he is to cover. He shall pay particular attention to the unit he is defending so that he may coordinate the movements of his forces and to take successive positions, which favour the formation of the line. When he hears or perceives the recall signal from the commander of the line he should promptly reassemble his detachment and assure that it resumes its position in the line. If the detached officer was charged with covering a body of cavalry he should not move until the force he was masking is formed, then he should move to the most uncovered or the closest wing. He shall join the attack, covering the flank, and may charge or envelope the enemy as he chooses. If he succeeds in throwing back the enemy he should pursue the enemy rapidly so as to prevent him from rallying and attempt to push him into a rout. Those involved in the pursuit should not advance so far that they can no longer be supported by the troop from which they are detached. They should not run the risk of being enveloped asa result of their advancing too far.

J. Colin, in *La Tactique et la Discipline*, spends some time discussing Revolutionary skirmish tactics. It would appear that the various battalions detached skirmishers in groups of 30, 50, and 100, depending on the situation. The notorious third rank of each company is specifically called out as being the source of the skirmishers drawn from Revolutionary infantry battalions. He also states that the newest recruits, those who had absolutely no training in manoeuvres were simply thrown forward in a skirmish cloud to act as they will. This would indicate that there two qualities of French skirmisher in the early Revolutionary wars – good, and very bad.

It is interesting to note that Colin contends that Austrian skirmishers significantly outnumbered French in the early Revolutionary period, and he states that the Prussians only detached 12 men per company to act as skirmishers.

Colin also provides an interesting few paragraphs of discussion on how skirmishers were deployed. He states that a *peloton* or two would be detached to form a skirmish line. Upon the order to assume a skirmish formation, these would move so that there was a 10, 15, or 20 pace space between each man, alignment being maintained by eye. When the skirmishers were to clear the front of their parent formation, be it to allow the passage of a column or the fire of a battery, they would be ordered to rally on the flanks of their own columns. If threatened they were to move behind their parent formation, which would form into line. Here they would rally and defend the flanks of the parent formation.

Colin quotes de Laubépin as saying that the 'great bands of skirmishers were not destined to manoeuvre symmetrically as the lines of battle, the columns or the *masses*.' Their march resembled a loosely organised hunt. If they acted with too much prudence they would be timid and unsuccessful.

In 1811, Marshal Davout issued instructions that provide a great deal of insight into the actual employment of skirmishers by the French. Davout felt that it was preferable to deploy entire companies as skirmishers rather than subsections of the company. In contrast, many German states, Russia, and other countries regularly drew men out of the third ranks of each company to act as skirmishers.

Marshal Davout directed that skirmish lines be formed approximately 100 to 200 paces in front of the formed infantry they were screening. The skirmish formation was organised into three sections. The first and second ranks of the two wing sections deployed immediately by files at intervals of 15 paces and formed a semi-circle of skirmishers 100 paces in front of their parent unit. In each of the deployed sections, the third rank, the sergeant, the corporals and the drummer or bugler were held in reserve with an officer, a lieutenant or *sous-lieutenant*. The captain remained in the middle of this formation with the sergeant-major and the centre section. From here he directed the skirmish line. The centre section acted as the principal reserve for the skirmish screen.

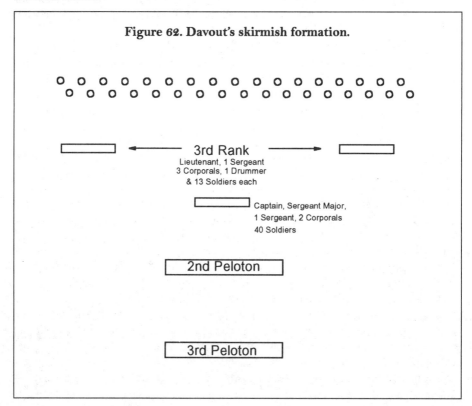

Figure 62. Davout's skirmish formation.

The reserves were to furnish replacements for the line, to reinforce points where the line was attacked, and to provide escorts for officers. This reserve also formed a rallying point, and guided withdrawals. The reserve was generally no less than six men. If a non-commissioned officer was detached to carry orders to the skirmishers he was escorted by a fusilier drawn from the reserve.

The skirmishers were taught to operate in pairs. One of the two always kept his musket loaded so that he could defend his partner. When the skirmishers protected a retreating line they formed parallel to that line and withdrew in such a way that their captain could maintain visual contact with the line and his skirmishers. Communications were maintained by using non-commissioned officers as runners.

The skirmishers were trained to operate at the *pas ordinaire* (76 paces per minute) but they also operated at the *pas de course* (250 paces per minute – a run). This was because they were often obliged to move quickly when covering changes of direction or charges by the parent formation. In the case of a cavalry attack the skirmishers theoretically would retire to their parent unit at the *pas de course* according to regulation, but it is not likely that they overly worried about maintaining a specific rate of movement. If they were unable to return to their parent unit, they would find whatever cover they could, hiding behind obstacles of any sort and continuing to fire on the attacking cavalry. There was also a 'quick' or 'rally' square that could be formed. The Austrian equivalent of this formation was the *Klumpen*, which means 'clump'. In this situation, a sergeant or other individual would stand, calling the men to him, and they would form around him in a tight knot, all facing outwards. This formation was not capable of significant movement or much fire, but it formed a hedgehog bristling with bayonets that would provide safety for those men that had sought shelter in it.

When advancing, the skirmishers remained silent and attempted to hold the enemy far enough away from their parent unit that enemy fire would not strike it. When operating in broken terrain, it was the mission of the skirmishers to search through all the cover that might conceal a possible ambush.

Marshal Davout's instructions provide considerable insight into the practical employment of skirmishers. If they were to traverse a village the captain would march in the rear, with his reserve, and take an advantageous position that would allow the occupation of the principal avenues, as the skirmishers searched through the village, and provide a strategically located rallying point. If the skirmishers were clearing a wood or passing through terrain broken up by trenches, hedges, etc, they were to advance cautiously and place themselves so that if they encountered the enemy they would be able to profit from the enemy's errors and force him from his position, the objective being to expose and turn any ambushes. To do this some individuals were expected to seek high points and expose themselves to the enemy, thereby causing the enemy to think that his position was turned.

Because of the system of control, and the tactical ability of the skirmishers to profit from the various terrain features, they were able to quickly reinforce a threatened position or deploy so as to take advantage of errors on the part of the enemy. The system that evolved was one where the skirmishers would endeavour to tie the enemy down and allow the formed troops to strike at his weak point. They succeeded in this by screening the advance of the formed troops, not in the sense that the line wasn't visible, but so that the galling effect of the skirmish fire locked the attention of the enemy on the skirmishers, not on what was happening behind them.

British skirmishers

British skirmish tactics had their roots in the Seven Years War and the American War of Independence, but they chopped themselves off from those roots when they disbanded nearly every light unit after the latter conflict ended. In 1798 a work by Rottemberg known as the *Regulations for the Exercise and Conduct of Rifles and Light Infantry on Parade and in the Field* was published. These regulations formed the basis for all English light infantry operations into the late 19th century. They drew from earlier experience, but when they were issued in 1798 the French Revolutionary Wars were already six years old.

Chapter 4 of Rottemberg's book addresses firing in extended order and skirmishing. He directs that the skirmishers should not have their bayonets fixed when firing in extended order. He also indicates that their movements are controlled by bugles. He also directs that skirmishers operate in pairs, with one always retaining a loaded weapon. It is stated that if a light infantry company is sent forward to skirmish, each platoon will deploy half of its strength in extended order and engage in skirmish fire. The second half-platoon will remain formed behind the skirmish line. He does, however, allow that a company may completely deploy into skirmish order without retaining a formed reserve.

Rottemberg also speaks of forming a 'chain'. This was a line of light troops designed to scour a piece of terrain for enemy forces. If a light infantry company were to form a chain, one fourth of it, a platoon or a section, would remain formed. The remainder would deploy into extended order 50 paces in front of this reserve. The chain marched at the ordinary time, taking care to preserve distance and alignment. The reserve followed at a distance of 50 paces. When the chain stopped to fire, it used an unusual firing system. The right wingman of each division would take three paces forward and fire, fall back and load. The next three men would perform the same action singly, and the fire would be kept up until the order to cease fire. If obliged to manoeuvre to a different front the line was to march at quick time.

When forming an advanced guard the company broke into four half-platoons or sections. The first half-platoon moved to 500 paces in front of the main body; at night or in hazy weather this was reduced to 300 paces. The second section was 200 paces in front of the first and a party consisting of a sergeant and six men was pushed forward a further 100 paces. The third and fourth half-platoons were placed 300 paces to the right and left of the first, and in alignment with it, taking care to preserve their distance from it. They detached a non-commissioned officer and six men 100 paces out at an oblique angle from their front, to act as a picket.

The duty of the advanced guard was to scour the country ahead of the main body, penetrating woods and enclosures and searching villages. If the patrol met with an enemy, the officer commanding the half-platoons was to inform the company captain who, in turn, sent a messenger back to the battalion commander. The advanced guard commanding officer was to have been given instructions prior to contact on what his action was to be in such an event. He could attack, withdraw, or merely 'amuse' the enemy with his skirmishers. If he were to withdraw he was to do so at an oblique, so as to draw the enemy skirmishers away from the front of his battalion and to clear both himself and the enemy skirmishers away from its front and give it a clear field ahead.

When ordered to close, the outer sections and the detachments closed on the central section. What actions were to be taken then are not specified, but it is presumed that the skirmishers would return to their parent battalion. Unfortunately, no comment is made about actions to be taken in the event of attack by cavalry when in skirmish formation.

Captain Cooper's work provides a summarisation of the skirmish tactics in use by the English in 1806. Among the many details he provides, there are some unique notes on the differences in intervals in the 'formed' line. I say 'formed' because the process he describes moves it from the tightly compressed line to a skirmish line in a very regulated manner. Cooper first discusses 'loose files', which occurred when an infantry company opened its ranks so that there was a six-inch gap between each man. Open order he defines as having further widened this gap between men to a distance of two feet. The largest interval, extended order, he defines as being two paces between men.

At this point it is worth pausing for a historical digression and some analysis. When formed in line, the average infantryman occupied about 22 inches. If one assumes two paces as being approximately six feet, a line of infantry going into extended order would increase its length by about 300%, but its density would not appear as thin as a French skirmish line. Indeed, it might well appear to be a formed line if not examined too carefully. In his introduction, Cooper says that 'in the open plain, they can act as a compact body', which suggests that they were likely to be in 'extended order', but could also be a reference to the use of light infantry in the traditional linear mode. This is, of course, substantiated by Rottemberg's work, which clearly states that they were in extended order.

As mentioned in Chapter 2, British battalions were notoriously understrength. A full-strength battalion (1000 men), deployed in a two-deep line, would form a line 916 ft long. The average battalion had something less than 660 men, which would give it an interval of 605 ft. A 100-man company, the standard detachment of skirmishers for the British, would occupy an interval of 189 ft in open order. It is, therefore, quite likely that the French might well perceive a British skirmish line in extended order as a formed line.

This takes several steps towards explaining why, in Spain, the French often thought that they had broken the first British line when, in fact, they had only pierced the British skirmish line. Though it does not provide much insight into Oman's theories on the effect of the line on the attacking column, it does begin to suggest someting of what was actually occurring.

Cooper points out that in open order the officers were in front of the company, and in extended order the officers and NCOs were behind the line. In extended order the British skirmishers still apparently could and did fire volleys. They operated in pairs, one holding his fire while the other reloaded.

Though Cooper does not provide a reserve of 'regulated' strength such as was employed by the French and other nations, he does clearly state that a 'considerable portion of their force should at all times be kept in reserve.' He also states that the men deployed in the skirmish line were to be supported by 'small parties a little to their rear; and these again should depend upon, and communicate with stronger bodies, further removed from the point of attack.' He does, however, diverge from the French in that he says that these reserves should be concealed from the enemy.

In contrast to Cooper's rather vague statement, Barber's 1804 treatise on skirmishing states that 'it is a rule that one half of the company remains formed as a reserve; but when acting under the support of another corps, the whole may skirmish.' Barber adds some interesting notes on the system the British skirmishers used in the event of a cavalry attack. All of the soldiers apparently fired, and 'every man makes the best of his way round the flanks [of the battalion] to the rear or through any opening in the line.' It sounds like a rather uncoordinated scramble to the rear.

In stark contrast to Cooper's wild scramble away from attacking cavalry, Barber speaks of a hollow square. The reserve closed with the skirmishers: 'they, being the second section, form front as quickly as possible, and the remaining sections complete the square.' Though very brief, this sounds very much like the system described by Major-General Winfield Scott in his manual of infantry tactics.

As in Davout's instructions, Barber and Cooper both allow that British skirmishers could and should take advantage of any cover, and that they should be able to fire standing, kneeling or lying down.

In actual execution in the field in Spain, the British drew the light companies from their line battalions, in every division. They then combined these light companies with companies of the 5/60th Regiment of Foot and the Brunswick Oels, forming *ad hoc* light battalions that deployed ahead of the line infantry. Thus, the battalions of light infantry spoken of by Barber and Cooper were formed and ready to function.

Figure 63. British skirmish screen formation – Captain Barber, *Instructions for Volunteer Sharpshooters*: 'The Formation & Disposition of a Company of Sharpshooters or Light Infantry which is to form an Advanced Guard', Plate 3.

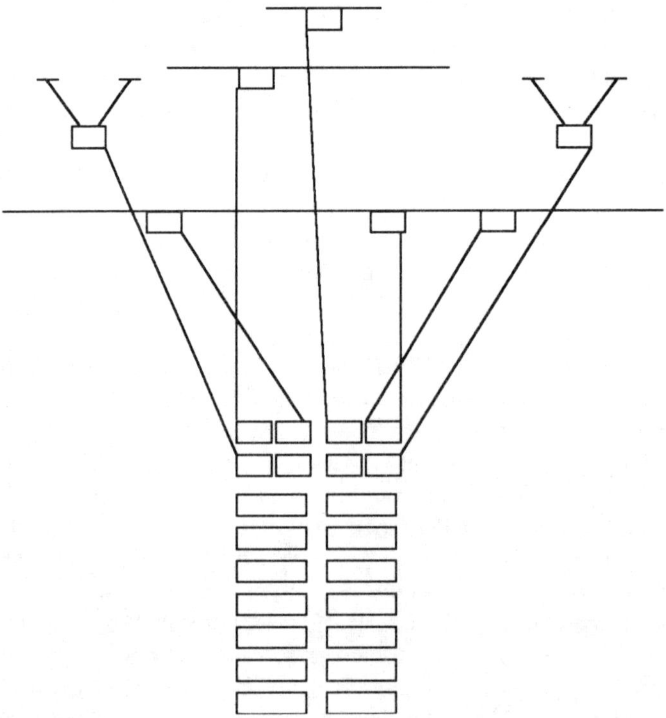

Austrian skirmishers

In a post-Napoleonic work by Valentini, an Austrian officer, many of the skirmish techniques used during the Napoleonic period are repeated and a few additional points made which were, no doubt, valid for the manner in which skirmish warfare was conducted during the Napoleonic Wars.

Valentini states that the officers charged with coordinating a skirmish line should establish a rally point at which their men could pull together and reorganise if they were pushed back. The skirmish line was always to be supported by a formed reserve. Skirmishers were always to be 100 paces in front of the infantry they were covering. They could begin their fire on an enemy at ranges up to 300 paces. When attacked by formed infantry they were to manoeuvre so as to attack uncovered flanks. If unable to do this, they were to withdraw slowly and hinder the attack of the enemy by their fire. When covering the charge of their own infantry the skirmishers were to advance and attempt to keep the front of the charging infantry clear of enemy skirmishers. They could keep up with the advance because they were not formed and the terrain problems would not affect them.

The Austrian 1807 Infantry Regulation is one of the few official sources that goes into skirmishing in any depth. This Regulation lists the situations in which skirmishers were to be used: 1) when in a defensive position. to keep the enemy skirmishers away; 2) to mask or screen the fronts and flanks of advancing formed infantry; 3) to cover the withdrawal of formed troops from enemy skirmishers; and 4) to mask the flank march of a column of formed infantry from enemy skirmishers. These conditions were principally used in open terrain, where formed troops were exposed to the attentions of enemy skirmishers.

The Austrian 1807 Regulation clearly states that it was the third rank of the infantry company that was detached for this duty. Whether or not the entire third rank was deployed depended on how broken the terrain was, the level of fatigue of the skirmishers, or if the skirmish line had taken heavy casualties. It was estimated that 60–80 skirmishers were sufficient to support a battalion.

When the third rank was deployed as skirmishers these were drawn from the first and, if necessary, second *Züge* of the right and left flank companies. The *Züge* doubled up so that there were two ranks, and pairs of skirmishers were formed. The line arranged itself so that there was a non-commissioned officer on each flank of a given *Zug* of skirmishers and a third non-commissioned officer was in the middle of the *Zug* skirmish line. The skirmishers moved at the *Doublirschritt* and opened up until they were at six-pace intervals. The skirmish screen established itself 300 paces in front of the battalion. About 80–100 paces behind the screen a *Zug* stood in closed order to act as a reserve and quick support for the skirmish screen. A further 100 paces back the captain stood with the two remaining *Züge* of the company as yet a further reserve. Figure 64 shows the generalised skirmish formation drawn from the Austrian 1807 Regulation.

Skirmishers alternated firing and loading so that one skirmisher in every pair was always loaded. This is quite typical of the period. However, one variation was that every manoeuvre was controlled by drum signals, in contrast to the bugles and voice commands used by the French. If able to react in time, the pairs of skirmishers were taught to form 'hasty squares' known as *Klumpen*. When forming a *Klumpen*, two to four pairs of skirmishers would rush together, form a knot and face outwards with

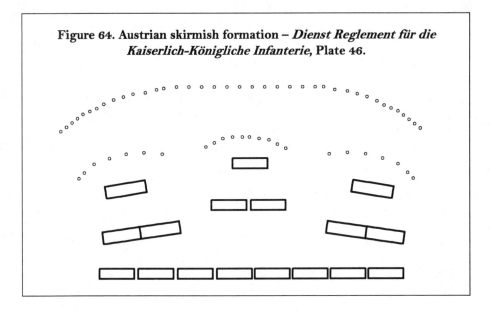

Figure 64. Austrian skirmish formation – *Dienst Reglement für die Kaiserlich-Königliche Infanterie*, Plate 46.

bayonets lowered. They were also taught how to deal with a cavalry threat while in extended order, when they were to get to the left side of the cavalry to make it more difficult for the latter to use their sabres or pistols against them. They were also to use their bayonets against the breasts of the cavalrymen's horses. If under attack while in *Klumpen*, when the attack subsided sufficiently these were to move towards the reserves and, eventually, back to the main battalion.

Russian skirmishers

Russian skirmish tactics are not a common topic and only one source of hard data was found to be available. This is Zweguintzov's work on the Russian army, which provides the following details of Russian skirmishing before and during the Napoleonic era.

Zweguintzov speaks of a work entitled *Notes Relative to the Service in the Infantry in General and in the Light Infantry in Particular*, which was written by Kutusov for the Bougski (Bug) *Jager* Corps in 1786. This work served in 1789 as general guidance for the employment of skirmishers and eventually became the equivalent of a regulation for that service.

The *jagers* were armed with a special fusil (musket) designated for their use, as well as a pistol. After 1777 the NCOs had a rifled carbine. According to Zweguintzov the *jagers* were trained in marksmanship, though there is some strong evidence to suggest that it was only 'enlightened' regimental commanders who encouraged such practice. *Jagers* were to serve as the advanced and flank guards during marches, as well as in combat, when they were placed on the wings in the order of battle or on the back flanks of a square, to cover the guns and to occupy the important points.

The *Notes* described the following as the *Jagers*' duties: 'To reconnoiter and protect the march of the army or the corps in a terrain where cavalry cannot perform that task.' They were to occupy defiles with small numbers of men, so that the enemy might not delay the army's passage. They were to reconnoitre forests and brushy areas, to 'rake' them clean, to defend a wood, with or without *chevaux de frise*, and to prevent the enemy from penetrating them. The procedures called for during the re-connaissance and sweeping of a forest applied, with appropriate modifications, to clear-ing villages, cemeteries and all other places, notably terrain that was rugged or broken with forests. The *jagers* occasionally deployed in dispersed order before formed infan-try and protected them with skirmish fire during those times when the line infantry were deploying in order of battle or traversing broken terrain where it was suscepti-ble to disorder.

In operating in concert with infantry, the battalions of *jagers* formed themselves in three ranks like the line infantry, but operated independently. After 1765 they operated in two ranks. A *jager* battalion was divided into four 'divisions', each of two 'demi-divisions', and each demi-division contained two *pelotons*. When operating in closed order in line or in column the normal cadence of the *jagers* was 80 paces per minute. When they deployed for combat, and when manoeuvring on the field of battle ('to execute the decisive blow against the adversary') they used the 'redoubled cadence' of 120 paces per minute. Kutusov directed the use of the *pas de course*[10] for all cases where the *jagers* did not advance in closed order.

Kutusov's *Notes* foreshadowed the 'march by *pelotons*', the 'march by files', the 'march in dense column' (by entire divisions, where the interval defaulted to 'demi-divisions', by *pelotons*, or finally by files of four), and four 'manoeuvres proper for *jagers*'. The following are specific manoeuvres from Kutusov's *Notes*:

First manoeuvre

During manoeuvres in lightly-wooded terrain, inhabited localities and cemeteries, the skirmishers' line was combined with a formed reserve in two lines. They advanced at the redoubled cadence, firing on order or signal, using natural cover, and advancing by bounds. On the order '*pelotons* advance in skirmish order', the even-numbered *pelotons* went 60 paces forward at the run and deployed themselves as skirmishers (the men of the second rank manoeuvred so as to place themselves to the left of those in the first rank); the *pelotons* of the wing divisions covered the flanks of their skirmish line. This formation advanced (the odd-numbered *pelotons* followed behind the skirmish line at a distance of 60 paces) until the moment when the commander ordered the men to either commence fire on a target or to take cover.

When arriving at difficult terrain that must be traversed, the commander passed the formed infantry through the skirmishers and reformed them after they had tra-versed the terrain, and covered the manoeuvre with *peloton* fire. During this time the even-numbered *pelotons* regrouped and ran to place themselves in formation between the intervals of the odd *pelotons*.

In the case of a retreat by line infantry which was unable to hold off the enemy, the odd-numbered *pelotons* which had placed themselves before the skirmish line withdrew through the line at the *pas de course* and, once 60 paces behind it, reformed to face the enemy. During this time the skirmishers were to maintain a constant fire on the enemy. Then the men of the second rank, which found itself in the skirmish line, withdrew 30 paces at the run. The odd-numbered *pelotons* then deployed as skirmishers, while the men of the first rank of the even *pelotons*, which had stood before those of the second rank while it withdrew, themselves withdrew at the *pas de course* behind the odd-num-

---

[10] The term *pas de course* is French and is a march cadence of 250 paces per minute. Zweguintzov uses this term and it may have been that the actual pace used was the Russian equivalent, the *udwonyi szag*.

bered *pelotons* deployed as skirmishers, and reformed 60 paces behind them in two ranks.

Second manoeuvre

This was used when visibility was 60 paces or less. On the order 'a *peloton* by twos forward', the even-numbered *pelotons* advanced at the *pas de course* and deployed as two lines of skirmishers, instead of just one, the first at 60 paces from the main body. The second line formed at 30 paces ahead of the reserve *pelotons*. The two skirmisher lines then advanced with or without firing. When the first line fired, the second line passed through it at the *pas de course*, stopped 30 paces ahead of the first line and, after giving the first line time to reload, fired in turn. After this the two lines resumed their advance and fired, each line in its turn. When the commander recalled his skirmish lines to the rear, they moved at the *pas de course* until they were 10 paces behind the formed reserves, where they reformed anew as two lines of skirmishers 30 and 60 paces behind those reserves. The reserve *pelotons* then withdrew at the *pas de course* and reformed in two ranks behind them.

Third manoeuvre

This was used in wooded terrain as well as in street fighting when it was not possible to deploy as skirmishers. One *peloton* in two placed itself in Indian file, by the first rank and then the second rank. If it encountered the enemy, where deployment was not possible, the leading skirmishers fired and turned to the right, the following skirmishers advanced and fired, stepping to the side, and eventually every soldier in the line rotated forward and fired in a caracole by *pelotons*. If space allowed, the *peloton* deployed in one or two skirmish lines according to conditions. When the edge of a wood was occupied the reserve *pelotons* were to pass through the skirmish line and form ahead of them.

Fourth manoeuvre

When traversing a narrow file, the *pelotons* formed in two ranks and formed a column by fours. To do this the two halves of the battalion made a demi-turn to the centre and the column moved forward from this point. When the column stopped, the soldiers made a facing to the right and then to the left, reforming their two ranks towards each side. The column square was formed with the *pelotons* of the head of the column moving to the right and left to become the front face of the square, the following *pelotons* facing towards the right and left, to form the lateral flanks, and the rear *pelotons* running by files to form the rear face of the square, always moving by files to occupy their places. In lieu of a square, the column could also form a circle. In approaching a wood which was to be swept the commander stopped the column and the men of every other *peloton* advanced at the *pas de course* to form a skirmish line 60 metres in front of the column so that the extremities of the line were pulled back to cover the flanks of the battalion; the other *pelotons* remained as a reserve. The column could, on signal, deploy in a line across natural obstacles. If it was necessary to open fire instantly, the best shots of the two ranks advanced and occupied the enemy with their fire, while the others loaded their muskets and passed them forward.

This is pretty thin data upon which to hang one's hat, but it fits the general tenor of the tactics employed by other nations. It should be noted that there is absolutely no mention of the skirmishers operating in any particularly independent fashion and they did not operate in pairs like the rest of Europe's armies. They were supposedly encouraged with marksmanship training and taught to use cover. Otherwise the tactics described are very primitive and restrictive. It is also unfortunate that no details of intervals between the deployed skirmishers are provided, which prevents a comparison of the density of skirmishers used by the Russians to that used by others.

Other fragmentary evidence can be found which very explicitly states that the Russian line infantry regiments in 1812 did have integral skirmishers. Based on slightly later documentation and a comparison to period Austrian tactics, these skirmishers were probably drawn from the third rank of the line companies. This suggests that there was some philosophical change, but without more documentation it is difficult to determine how significant this change truly was.

It has been repeatedly stated in works discussing its tactics that the Russian army did not have a series of all-encompassing regulations by which it manoeuvred, but that each regimental commander chose whatever suited his fancy. Indeed, a review of the Russian 1799 infantry drill Regulation is almost devoid of drill, concentrating on organisation and standing in formation for reviews. No doubt this affected Russian skirmish tactics as well.

The only other point of note is that in 1812 the *opolochenie* or militia was reported in French documents to have been used in a skirmish role during the Second Battle of Polotsk. It is probable that they were employed in the older, linear system described by Zweguintzov, as that system could easily be employed by less well-trained troops and would be far easier to control by the company officers.

Skirmishing from an American perspective

The only drill regulation uncovered during the research for this work that truly discussed light infantry tactics was Major-General Winfield Scott's American infantry drill regulation. This work was first published shortly after the Napoleonic Wars ended and was reissued several times. Though it was not necessarily identical to the systems used in Europe, it bears some startling similarities to them. Also, General Scott was a student of the French Regulation of 1791, having used it during the War of 1812. Though his work is not, technically, a Napoleonic regulation, it is obviously a compilation of the lessons learned from the period, and is thus worthy of review and consideration. It is also worth noting that the American military system was an interesting mix of the British and French. The Regulation of 1791, for instance, was used by Scott to train his troops in 1811–12. In addition, in 1861 company structure was based on the French model while the number of companies in a battalion was based on British organisation. I am, however, inclined to suspect that the French system of skirmishing had more influence on American tactics than the British.

General Scott's work makes the following statements about light infantry, its use and manoeuvres:

> Skirmishers will be thrown out to clear the way for, and to cover the movements of, the main corps to which they appertain: accordingly, they may be thrown out to the front, to a flank, to the rear, or in the several directions as may be deemed necessary ... They will render their movements subordinate to those of the main corps, so as constantly to cover it in the direction to which they were thrown.

[The movements of skirmishers are] not expected to be made with the same harmony (ensemble) in all their bearings, as if made by closed ranks and file; because, to attain that accuracy, would diminish what is more important in a body of skirmishers – rapidity of execution.

Every body of skirmishers will always have a reserve, the strength and composition of which will vary according to circumstances. If the body thrown out to skirmish be within sustaining distance of the main corps, it will be sufficient for each company to have, in its rear, a small reserve, generally a third of its strength, destined to reinforce the line of skirmishers, and to serve them as a rallying point. [This concept of a reserve is not noticeably different than that advocated by Davout or Valentini.]

If the main corps be at too great a distance, another reserve will be necessary, composed of an entire company or it may be companies, destined to sustain and reinforce such parts of the line of skirmishers as may be hotly attacked. This reserve ought to be strong enough to relieve at least a half of the companies deployed as skirmishers. [Davout specifically says that the reserve is to reinforce the line when attacked.]

Reserves ought to be placed behind the centre of the lines of skirmishers – company reserves at about 140 and the principal reserve, at about 370 paces. This rule however, will not be invariable: the commander, always holding his reserve within sustaining distance, will next take care to profit by any accident the ground may present (such as trees, houses, fences, hollows,) to put it under cover from the fire of the enemy. [This is both more formally presented and a greater distance than that of Davout and Valentini, both of whom used a 100 to 200 pace interval.]

The movements of skirmishers will generally be made in quick time; but in circumstances which demand greater rapidity, *double quick* time, and even the run will be employed. In this instruction, the *double quick march* will be at the rate of 140 steps in the minute: the rate of the run cannot be equally determined. This extreme swiftness will be reserved for cases of absolute necessity, in order not to uselessly fatigue the men and preserve their strength for circumstances in which success may principally depend on rapidity of movement. [Davout allowed the use of the *pas de course* – which was, in essence, running – if the situation required it. This is in surprising contrast to Rottemberg's regulation, which allowed for nothing faster than quick time.]

In all movements, skirmishers (that is, men in open files) will carry their muskets or rifles in the manner which may be most convenient to each skirmisher, taking care to avoid accidents. [Though neither Davout nor Valentini speak of this it seems a reasonable precaution when running about with a loaded flintlock.]

The movements of skirmishers will be executed, as far as possible, by the voice of the commander; but when the line shall be too extended for his voice, he will substitute the sounds of the bugle or beats of the drum. [The use of drums and bugles was widespread in every European army for the control of its troops.]

Officers, and, in case of need, sergeants, will cause each command to be executed as soon as it shall be heard or seen; but when announced by means of the bugle or drum, to avoid mistake, they will wait till the signal is ended, and then commence the movement.

When speaking of a skirmish formation formed by a company deployed as skirmishers, General Scott indicates that they are to be deployed on the frontage of a battalion in line at a distance of 100 paces from the battalion. Note that the distance of 100 paces is identical to Davout and Valentini. He goes on to say, in his discussion of company skirmish tactics:

The deployment *forward* will be adopted when the company is behind the line on which it is to be established as skirmishers; it will deploy *by the flank*, when it finds itself already on that line. In both cases, if the company be in three ranks, the front and centre ranks will form the line of skirmishers, and the rear rank the company reserve. If the company be in two ranks only, it will be divided into three platoons; the right and left, denominated, respectively, *first* and *second* platoons, will form the line of skirmishers; the *centre* platoon the reserve.

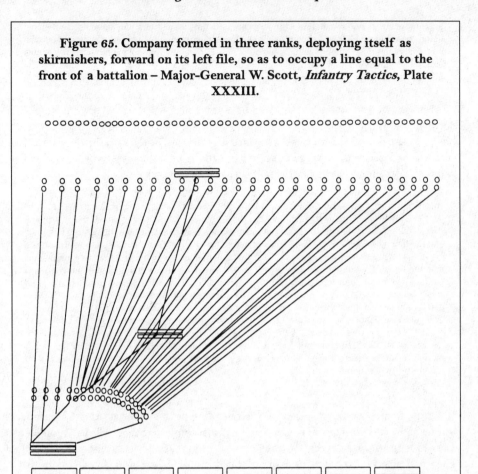

Figure 65. Company formed in three ranks, deploying itself as skirmishers, forward on its left file, so as to occupy a line equal to the front of a battalion – Major-General W. Scott, *Infantry Tactics*, Plate XXXIII.

Davout's instructions deploy two-thirds of the unit as skirmishers with the remaining third, also chancing to be the third rank, as a reserve. This is identical to the deployment Scott uses for a three-rank company. It is, however, different to the system used by the Russians and Austrians for integral skirmishers in their line battalions. In their armies, the third rank was told off and deployed as skirmishers while the first two ranks remained as a reserve. Figure 65 illustrates this formation.

> A company may be deployed, as skirmishers, on its left, on its right, or on its centre file: in this manner the skirmishers may be thrown out upon the line that they are to occupy with the greatest promptitude.
>
> A line of skirmishers ought, as far as possible, to be aligned. To obtain this regularity, advantages which the ground may present for covering the men, ought not to be neglected.
>
> The intervals between files of skirmishers depend on the extent of ground to be covered; but the fire will be too much scattered if the intervals exceed 10, or, at most 15 paces. The front to be occupied to cover a battalion, comprehends the front of the battalion, and half of each interval on the right and left of the battalion. [Davout explicitly uses a 15 pace interval.]

General Scott devotes considerable attention to skirmishers' firing practices. He states:

Skirmishers will fire at a halt, and in marching; in both cases they will observe the method about to be indicated. The fire will be given alternately by the two men of the same file, who will so arrange it between them, that the one or other shall always have his piece loaded; to this end, the front rank man, will fire and reload; the centre or rear rank man, will withhold his fire until the first shall have rammed; the second, in his turn will wait in like manner for the first, and so on in continuation.

This system is identical to that used by every European army where any details of skirmish musketry are discussed – French, Prussian, Bavarian, and British. Scott then states: 'If the line of skirmishers be formed of three ranks, the same order of alternation will be observed, with this difference – the rear and centre rank men will fire together.' When marching and firing, Scott's regulation states:

If the line be advancing, the front rank man of every file will halt, fire, and reload, before throwing himself forward; the centre rank man, of the same file, will continue to march eight or 10 paces beyond the first, halt, fire, and reload, in the manner prescribed; the front rank man, having reloaded, will throw himself forward a like distance beyond his centre rank man, and fire again, conforming himself to what has just been prescribed, and so on in continuation.

If the line be marching in retreat, the front rank man of every file will halt, face about, fire, and then reload whilst throwing himself to the rear: the centre man, of the same fill will continue to march, halt at eight or 10 paces beyond the front rank man, face about, fire, and then observe what is just prescribed for his front rank man; the latter will, when at the same distance in rear of his centre rank man, halt again, face about, finish loading, fire, and then do as he had done before, and thus the alternate fire by the men of the same file will be continued.

If the company be in march by the right flank, the front rank man of every file will face to the enemy, step one pace forward, halt, fire, and throw himself behind his centre (or rear) rank man, who had been next behind him, reloading as he marches: as soon as this second man, who has continued to march, shall judge that the first has rammed, he will, in his turn, face to the enemy, step one pace forward, halt, fire, and throw himself behind his front rank man, reloading as he marches, and thus the fire will be continued.

A little further on Scott speaks of the reloading process. He says that 'skirmishers will be habituated to load their pieces whilst marching; but they will be enjoined always to halt an instant when in the act of forming, and of charging the cartridge. They will also be exercised in loading and firing, kneeling, and lying, leaving each man at liberty to execute those *times* (or pauses) in the manner he may find the easiest.' He also says, like Davout, that skirmishers should 'be taught to take advantage of any chance object the ground may present, to cover themselves from the enemy's fire, and also to judge distances with accuracy, in order to fire with effect.'

Rallying was another important process to understand. Scott states: 'The rally will be made in a run; the assembly in quick time.' The rally was to resist cavalry, while the assembly catered for any other circumstance. When the command to rally the skirmishers on the reserve is given,

the captain will throw himself on the reserve; the third lieutenant will begin the formation of the circle, by throwing back a little the two flanks of the reserve. The skirmishers running in, will form themselves as successively they join the reserve, on its right and left, in two ranks, without regard to height, face outwards, and complete the circle. The officers and sergeants will direct the execution of this movement, and then place themselves within the circle. [Figure 66b shows this manoeuvre and final formation.]

These dispositions being made, the captain will profit by any interval of time the cavalry may allow him for putting himself in safety against its attacks, either by rejoining his battalion, or by gaining some advantageous position: to this end he will reduce the circle, and reform the company into column by platoon, and in two platoons; he will march in this order, by the front or rear rank; and if threatened anew by the cavalry, he will halt and again form circle, by throwing back the right and left files of the two platoons: the second platoon, if not already faced by the rear rank, will first be so faced, and the other platoon by the front rank.

Figure 66a. Company deploying itself as skirmishers by the flank on the centre file – Major-General W. Scott, *Infantry Tactics*, Plate XXXIV, Figure 1.

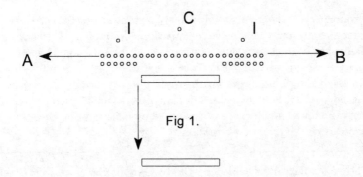

Fig 1.

Figure 66b. Company deployed as skirmishers, rallying on its reserve, and forming the circle to resist cavalry – Major-General W. Scott, *Infantry Tactics*, Plate XXXIV, Figure 2.

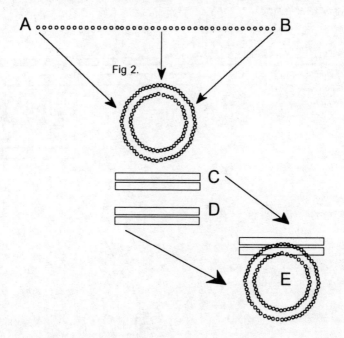

Fig 2.

A–B = Skirmish line.
C   = Reserve beginning to form circle.
D   = Company after having reduced the circle, forms in column to continue its withdrawal.
E   = Company halts retreat and reforms circle to resist cavalry.

If the suddenness of the danger leaves not time to rally the skirmishers on the reserve, the rally will be made by platoon; the first and second lieutenants will each rally his platoon on the ground most advantageous behind the line of skirmishers. Pending this movement, the captain will throw himself on the reserve, and so dispose it as to protect the rallying of the platoons and to resist the cavalry. The platoons being rallied, they will promptly rejoin the reserve.

If the company was deployed as skirmishers and it was necessary to rally it on the battalion the skirmishers would move to unmask the front of the battalion, moving at a run towards the nearest flank and forming behind the battalion. Once the company was reformed it would move to one flank or the other, depending on the choice of the colonel. If assembling on the reserve, the reserve would form in the precise order in which it stood before the deployment. The skirmishers would assemble on it and each skirmisher would resume his place in the previous rank and file. Once the company was reformed it was to rejoin the battalion.

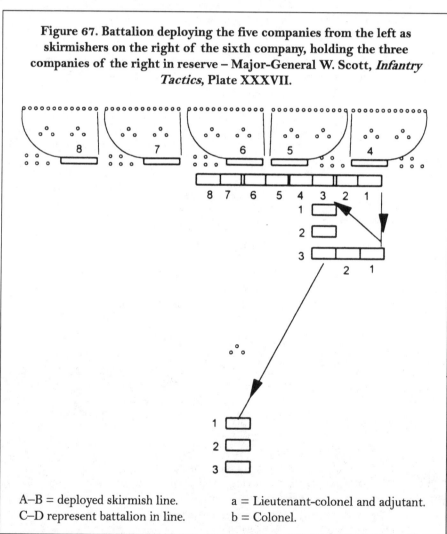

Figure 67. Battalion deploying the five companies from the left as skirmishers on the right of the sixth company, holding the three companies of the right in reserve – Major-General W. Scott, *Infantry Tactics*, Plate XXXVII.

A–B = deployed skirmish line.
C–D represent battalion in line.

a = Lieutenant-colonel and adjutant.
b = Colonel.

Figure 68a. Rallying of a battalion deployed as skirmishers – Major-General W. Scott, *Infantry Tactics*, Plate XXXVIII, Figure 1.

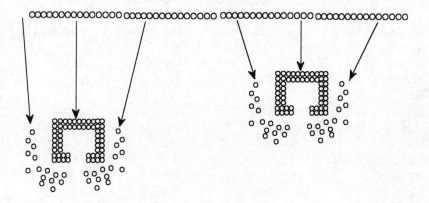

A–B = Skirmish line. Line falls backwards and forms squares on reserves.

Figure 68b. Small squares reforming into columns and directing themselves on battalion reserve – Major-General W. Scott, *Infantry Tactics*, Plate XXXVIII, Figure 2.

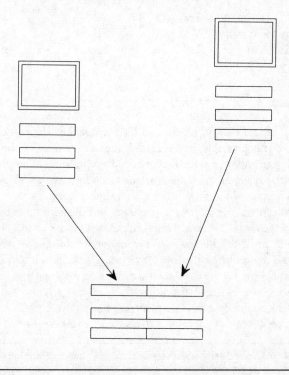

	Table 36. Methods by which skirmishers were organised.		
Nation	Independent light battalions/ regiments	Light companies attached to battalions	Selected men drawn from line battalions
Austria	Yes	No	Yes
Bavaria	Yes	Yes	Yes
Britain	Yes	Yes	No
Brunswick	Yes	Yes	Yes
Cleves-Berg	Yes	Yes	No
Denmark	Yes	Yes	Unknown
France	Yes	Yes	No
Hesse-Darmstadt	Yes	No	No
Hanover	Yes	Yes	No
Mecklenburg	Yes	N/A	Yes
Naples	Yes	Yes	No
Nassau	No	Yes	No
Northern Italy	Yes	Yes	No
Prussians	Yes	No	Yes
Saxony	Yes	No	No
Saxon ducal houses	Yes	Yes	No
Spain	Yes	Yes	No
Sweden	Yes	Yes	No
Russia	Yes	Yes[11]	Yes
Grand Duchy of Warsaw	Yes	Yes	No
Westphalia	Yes	Yes	No
Württemberg	Yes	No	Unknown
Würzburg	No	Yes	No

The question of rallying is mentioned by Davout, but the mechanism is not so clearly discussed. It is probable, however, that the system used by the French and the rest of the European nations would not have been significantly different. Davout speaks of rallying on the reserves, and the Austrians, though not speaking of it directly, imply by the existence of a reserve that it is a rallying point.

When a battalion was completely deployed as skirmishers three of the 10 companies were held in reserve. The regimental lieutenant-colonel and adjutant would assume positions in front of the reserve. The major would dispose the reserve as required. The reserve would be deployed by company in echelon: one company was posted 140 paces behind the right of the skirmish line, a second was united and placed opposite to the interval between the skirmishers of the 4th and 5th companies 110 paces from the line, while the third company was united in the similar gap between the 7th and 8th companies at a distance of 170 paces. The reserves were placed in echelon

[11] The Russians had a *tirailleur peloton* attached to every battalion, but there is no evidence that they operated as an independent unit or as skirmishers in the manner of the French *voltigeur* companies.

so that they could protect each other in the event of a rally, without running the risk of firing on one another. The number of echelons was diminished by uniting contiguous reserves in order to increase their capacity for resisting cavalry.

If attacked by cavalry, the companies would rally on the squares of their respective reserves. Each reserve was to form the front of the square. The skirmishers would, as they rallied on the square, form the lateral fronts and the other files would form the rear of the square. The square was formed in two ranks without regard to height.

Once the rally was effected, the captains commanding the squares were to take advantage of any pause in the cavalry attack to move towards the battalion reserve or to a more desirable position. This movement was to be performed in column, but if threatened the force was to convert itself into square. As the companies arrived near the battalion reserve they reformed and rejoined the battalion without regard to company number or seniority.

As can be seen in Scott's illustrations, these 'hasty squares' are a relatively simple manoeuvre, but more subtle than anticipated by the verbal description. The circular formation, however, fits the description found in many detailed discussions of the formation adopted by the French and Austrians when their skirmishers were obliged to form *Klumpen* in an effort to escape enemy cavalry. The only major difference might be that the French and Austrian 'hasty squares' might not be hollow.

With so many common points readily apparent between Scott's regulation and the few scraps of truly Napoleonic tactical discussion of skirmish operations, it is hard to believe that Scott did not borrow heavily, if not entirely, from the tactics that would have been worked out only a few years before during the largest war the Western world had seen prior to 1900. There had been no weapon changes or improvements in the interim, and Napoleonic tactics were destined to be used throughout the world until the beginning of the American Civil War, when technological improvements in weaponry forced a general reconsideration.

National light infantry formations

Every nation in Europe had skirmishers, but they organised them differently. There were two fundamental systems. The principal one consisted of independent, homogeneous light infantry formations. The other was where light infantry were drawn out of the line infantry battalion, operated as skirmishers, and returned to their parent battalion when required to do so.

There were two variations on this second system. One was to attach a light infantry company, with skirmish duties, to every line infantry battalion. The other was to draw previously selected individuals out of the line infantry company and have them perform the function of skirmishers. Table 36 lists the methods by which every nation in Europe was known to organise its skirmishers.

Another aspect of skirmishing units was that, though the light infantry was usually the only formation specifically trained and exercised in skirmishing, line units and even militia units are known to have operated as skirmishers. It is reasonable to presume that the effectiveness of any line unit, operating in skirmish formation would not be as good as if it were a light unit specifically trained in the tactic. It doesn't need to be said that a militia unit operating in skirmish order would probably be quite ineffective and unable to perform the offensive task satisfactorily.

There are numerous historical examples of the French taking entire line regiments and even divisions of line infantry and deploying them as skirmishers. Fabry, a historian for the French General Staff before the First World War, reports that the Russian General Wittgenstein deployed *opolochenie* (militia) as skirmishers against Oudinot's III Corps late in 1812. Other documents report the Prussians using Silesian *Landwehr* (also militia) in skirmish formations.

It is very probable that at one time or another every nation deployed line or militia units as skirmishers. Unfortunately, no professional evaluation of their effectiveness is available. As a result, it is safe to say that such occasions were exceptions to the general rule and not standard practice. Only the French can lay claim to the universal employment of their line infantry as skirmishers. However, this practice began to decline after the Revolutionary Wars and became less frequent as time went on.

It would also be reasonable to presume that the line infantry of the Grand Duchy of Warsaw was used as skirmishers. There are two reasons for this. Firstly, there were no light infantry in the Polish army until four battalions were raised in Lithuania late in 1812. The use of light infantry was so standard in the French system of warfare that their client states, including the Poles, absolutely had to have someone, aside from the battalions' light companies, capable of performing in a skirmisher role.

The second reason is that the Poles had serious national goals at stake in the outcome of the Napoleonic Wars. Poland had been destroyed by the Russians, Prussians and Austrians in 1795, and they were fighting to restore their nation and to maintain its very existence. Therefore, they could logically be expected to have the morale and discipline necessary to act as skirmishers. This is further reinforced by the fact that the cadre and many of the troops in the army of the Grand Duchy were veterans of the Revolutionary French army in Italy. They would have had whatever experience and training was provided to French line infantry with regard to skirmishing.

Chapter 5

Manoeuvring a Brigade

Operations at brigade level

After reviewing the manoeuvres of the company and battalion, the next manoeuvre element to be reviewed is the brigade. The operation of a brigade is best described as the manoeuvring of several battalions. The manoeuvres of the company and battalion are the building blocks of tactics, but the manoeuvres of the brigade are the domain of generals and the building blocks of a battle. Brigade manoeuvres are occasionally referred to as grand tactics, though there is some greyness in the application of this definition. However, they are certainly where battlefield manoeuvres end and strategic/army manoeuvres begin.

Despite the numbers of armchair generals and the significance of brigade manoeuvres, they are the most poorly understood and the least documented of all army operations. Only two documents exist which contain any significant discussion of Napoleonic brigade tactics. These are Marshal Ney's *Memoirs*, which have an appendix with lengthy discussion of brigade tactics; and Baron Meunier's *Evolutions par Brigades*, which is devoted solely to the tactical operations of the brigade.

The brigade

Meunier's work is a very detailed study. He begins by defining the brigade as a force of four battalions which are manoeuvred in either an extended order or in a *masse*. In extended order the battalions of each brigade are deployed by *pelotons* at full interval or at half-interval. In the *masse* formation the battalions are formed in *masses* by divisions on the wings.

In brigades operating in *masse* the frontage allocated to a battalion was one and a half times the length of a division (two *pelotons*). This interval was known as the 'evolution distance between the battalions', and was established to facilitate the manoeuvres of the artillery. The distance of one *masse* to another was one and a half times the depth of the *masse*, or approximately 66 paces. If one deletes the 19 paces for the depth of the preceding *masse* the result is the true interval, 47 paces. This is only three paces more than the length of the front. With this interval the battalions of the brigade are able to execute in an orderly and successive manner the changes of direction, changes of formation to the right and left, forming into line to the right or left, and, finally, all the manoeuvres necessary for the operation of a battalion in *masse*.

It was possible for the battalions to double-up the *pelotons* by sections and reduce the front of the column to the width of a section. With this movement executed, the interval between successive battalions would increase by six paces. Each battalion could, with equal facility, form a square if attacked by cavalry.

The interval allocated for manoeuvres between successive brigades of the same division was 90 to 100 paces, including the first rank of the last *masse* of the preceding brigade. This means the actual interval was 80 paces.

Meunier on brigade level tactics

Meunier's attention focusses on the evolution of brigades from marching columns into attack formations and back into column. His first linear formation is the deployment from line into column in *masse* by divisions, with evolution distances between the brigades and battalions.

In the example he provides, a line of two brigades in deployed order desires to form into column, right in the lead, by battalions in *masse* by divisions, on the first battalion of the second brigade, with evolution distances between the brigades and battalions. The first battalion of the second brigade would be the centre of the evolution and formed itself in *masse* by division behind the division of the right wing, and remained in place. The three remaining battalions in the brigade formed themselves into *masses* on their right division. They then moved separately by the right flank and by a diagonal to the rear, so as to place themselves in sequential order behind the first battalion

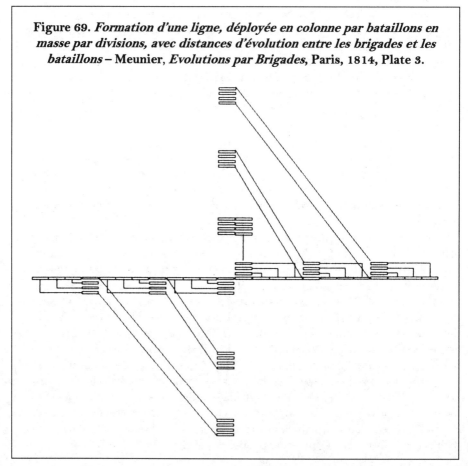

Figure 69. *Formation d'une ligne, déployée en colonne par bataillons en masse par divisions, avec distances d'évolution entre les brigades et les bataillons* – Meunier, *Evolutions par Brigades*, **Paris, 1814, Plate 3.**

at a distance of one and half times the length of the front of their *masse* (the leading division). This distance was measured from the first rank of the preceding *masse* to the first rank of the following *masse* and was known as the 'evolution distance'. The third battalion placed itself behind the second at the same distance, as did the fourth battalion and any others that might have been in the brigade. The first brigade then marched towards its left flank, its four battalions in *masses* forward on their left division.

The fourth battalion, which found itself at the *distance de bataille* from the first battalion of the second brigade, marched forward 90 to 100 paces, the interval established for the evolutions between brigades. Once at this distance, it moved by the left flank and placed itself squarely in the direction of the column, ahead of the leading battalion of the second brigade. The third battalion moved by the flank to the left, diagonally, and placed itself forward of the fourth battalion at the 'evolution interval'.

By a similar manoeuvre, the second battalion placed itself before the third battalion and the first battalion moved in front of the second. After these manoeuvres, the brigades found themselves formed into column, the right in the lead by battalions in *masse* by divisions, with the evolution intervals between the brigades and battalions.

The interval between battalions necessary to allow the comfortable manoeuvring of artillery is 22 to 24 paces. If using this interval, when the brigades and battalions

Figure 70. *Formation à droite ou à gauche, en bataille d'une colonne de plusieurs briagdes, par bataillons en masse à distances d'évolution* – Meunier, *Evolutions par Brigades*, Paris, 1814, Plate 4.

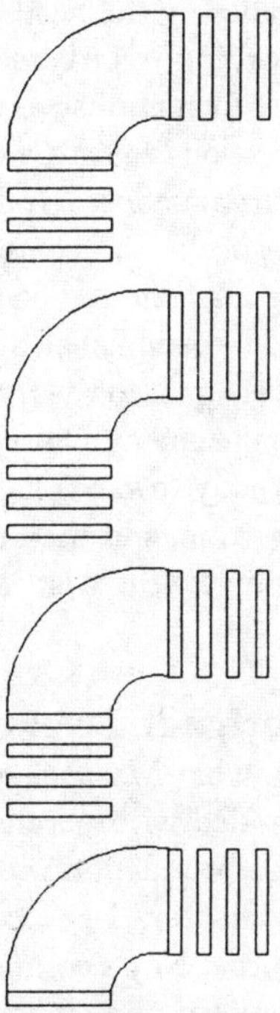

wish to resume their march in column by a conversion they will find themselves at their basic interval.

The regularity of these distances in the formations, and the facility of the execution of the various manoeuvres, are due to the basis which the French had established for the changes of direction for each battalion when in *masse*. During deployments the commander was to maintain only the battalion interval between battalions. If the battalions in *masse* are deployed successively as they arrive, or if they are not deployed until after the *masse* formation is established, there shall be no more than 22 to 24 paces between the battalions.

The *Réglement de 1791* provided two methods for deploying a column of battalions into line. The first, where the column was formed of battalions composed of *pelotons* at full interval, was performed by directing each battalion singly and diagonally towards the new position it was to assume in line. The second method was for columns in *masse*. They were to close up until the battalions were at an interval of six paces from one another. Once at that interval, each battalion was to deploy by the flank, much as a battalion deployed into line, and manoeuvre to assume the proper position.

These two methods were well understood. In the case of a column of several brigades, each brigade could detach itself and manoeuvre diagonally into the centre of the position it was to occupy, and then deploy its battalions accordingly. This method greatly facilitated and speeded up the deployment of a division or larger formation. The order of the formation also gained by this manoeuvre. Each brigade was moved to its new position as a whole unit under its own commander, who directed its movements according to the terrain.

The diagonal movement by brigades by the heads of the column offered a greater facility in deploying them and, according to circumstances, allowed the ready use of the *ordre mixte* or *ordre profond*. These formations were then moved to the points where they were required by the most propitious route. Once there they formed into line, or in echeloned *masses*, depending on circumstances. Indeed, the remainder of Meunier's study is simply one variation after another of columns of battalions (brigades) manoeuvring much as companies were manoeuvred according to the *Réglement de 1791*. An interval between brigades would be established as the brigades marched off to the flanks, diagonally or directly, that was equal to the frontage that the brigade wished to occupy when it was deployed to face the enemy. Once the proper interval was achieved, the brigade turned and marched directly towards its final destination, halted on position, deployed its battalions into position, and then the battalions either remained in column or deployed into line according to the wishes of the brigade commander.

Ney on brigade level tactics

The following is a transcription of what Marshal Ney has to say on grand tactical manoeuvres. His discussion is expanded with parallel comments extracted from the *Réglement de 1791*, which illustrate the foundation and basis of his remarks. In order to tie these directions into the earlier chapters I have inserted notes in brackets where appropriate. It should also be noted that Ney's comments were written with the two-battalion regiment and eight-company battalion in mind. These manoeuvres should be modified accordingly to reflect the later six-company organisation if the reader is more familiar with that.

The March in Column to Out-Flank one of the Wings of the Enemy's Line

I

The attack with four regiments being directed against the right wing of the enemy, the general in command shall form his lines by the left; the battalions shall be formed into columns by platoons [*pelotons*], the left in front, at whole or half-distance [interval between *pelotons* in column]. The columns thus prepared shall, in marching forward, take a diagonal to the left, and by heads of the column formed by each battalion. As soon as the three first platoons shall have taken the given direction, the remainder shall insensibly resume the perpendicular by moving obliquely to the right. The heads of the columns marching on the diagonal to the left, having now sufficiently approached the point fixed for outflanking the enemy's line, and by a rapid movement resumed the perpendicular, shall reform the line of battle by a general conversion to the right.

It will be advisable, if circumstances admit of it, to keep the columns at the distance from each other of only a half-battalion or division [two to four *peloton* intervals], in order to shorten the movement; and also to close the platoons to half-distances [intervals within the column] whenever the columns change their direction. By such means too great undulation would be avoided.

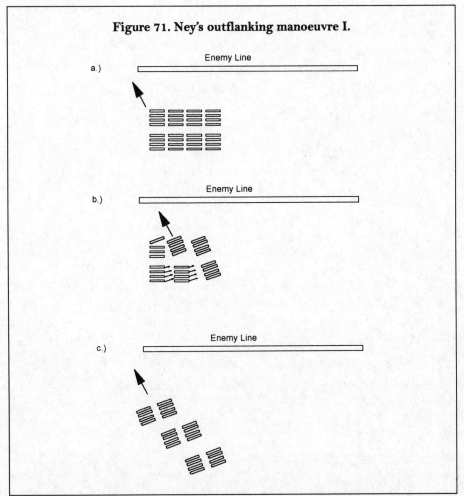

Figure 71. Ney's outflanking manoeuvre I.

II

If, however, the diagonal to the left, taken by each column, should not prove sufficient to outflank the enemy's right wing, the commander-in-chief must form his new line by successive battalions, beginning with the right of his two lines and giving the following word of command: – 'By the right of the two lines, and by successive battalions form line of battle to the right.' The first battalion having executed its movements by platoons to the right in line of battle, shall advance 25 paces, in column by platoon, in order to establish itself upon the oblique line indicated for this movement. The other battalions shall successively continue to march until the right of each is parallel with the left of the last formed battalion. They shall then execute a conversion by platoons to the right, and successively take up their proper position in line.

If the attack be directed against the left wing of the enemy, the lines shall march by the right, the columns having the right in front. This measure is applicable to manoeuvres I and II. It is necessary, during the march of the columns on the diagonal, to designate the last battalions of the two lines as the directing battalions, when the left is in front, and the first battalions, when the right is in front. Care must also be taken to make the columns of the second line march so that their heads be directed between the interval of those of the first line, without, however, losing the distance in line prescribed to them. But the moment the columns march directly forward, those of the second line shall resume the perpendicular.

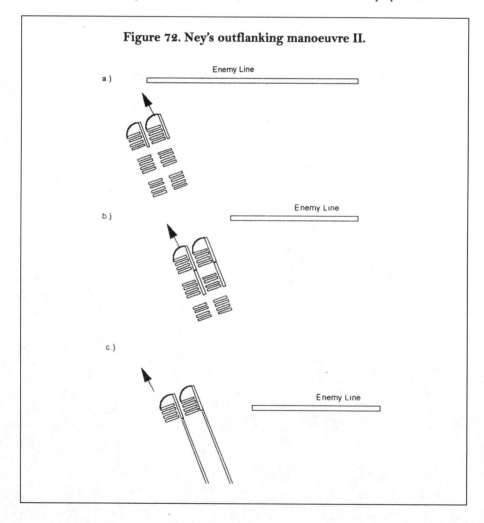

Figure 72. Ney's outflanking manoeuvre II.

III

The enemy being drawn up parallel to the front of your regiments, and it being the intention of the commander-in-chief to deceive them with regard to the true point of attack – if it is meant to be on the enemy's right, the battalions of both lines shall form by platoons to the left, and march on, appearing thus to retreat. So soon as the heads of the two lines have extended the space of one or two battalions beyond the enemy's front, a new oblique line shall be formed in the following manner: On the command, 'Form the oblique line, left wing in front,' the fourth platoon of the third battalion of the first line, and the eighth platoon of the third battalion of the second line or such other platoons as may be directed, shall march by the right flank, and by file to the right; as shall likewise all the platoons preceding those which serve as the axis of movement, upon the new line taken. The platoons in the rear shall move by the left flank, and form a perpendicular to the head. A general wheel to the right shall replace the line in the order of battle prescribed.

IV

If, on the contrary, the commander-in-chief determines to attack the left of the enemy, the battalions of the two lines shall march to the right, and, as soon as the heads of the two columns of the two lines shall have extended beyond the enemy's front, he shall form an

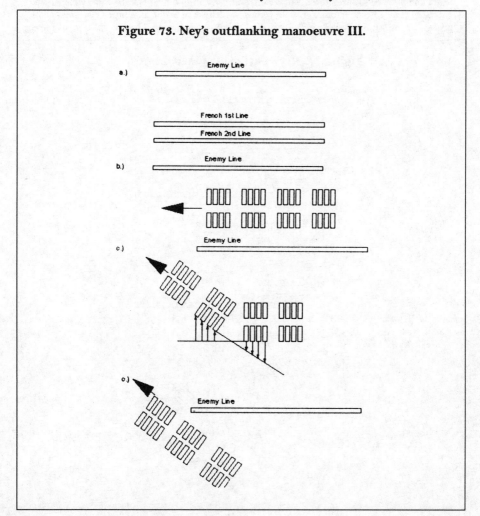

Figure 73. Ney's outflanking manoeuvre III.

oblique line, right wing in front, upon the eighth platoon of the first battalion of the second line. All the divisions preceding those designated for the formation of the oblique line shall operate successively on the flank, and successively establish themselves on the new line; those in the rear shall operate by the right flank, in order to resume the distance and perpendicular of the head. A general conversion to the left will replace the line in the order of battle prescribed.

V

But if the two heads of columns of the lines, the right being forward, should come to the diagonal on the left towards the centre of the enemy's front, and you intend to attack the left of the enemy's line; – in that case the platoons preceding those which are to serve as the axis, shall operate by the right flank, and those in the rear by the left flank; [forming line from column on the centre, lead platoons to the right, rear to the left] and, the perpendicular being taken, the line shall be resumed by a general wheel to the left. Nevertheless, if during the movement the enemy should make a demonstration of attack, it would be prudent to form the platoons in the prescribed line of battle, as they successively came up, for the purpose either of making head against the enemy, or of protecting the manoeuvre.

If, on the contrary, your heads of columns arrive, the left in front, upon the diagonal on the right, and proceed towards the enemy's centre, and you intend to attack the right wing of the enemy's line – all the platoons preceding those which serve as the axis in the two lines shall operate by the left flank, those in the rear by the right flank [forming line on the centre of the

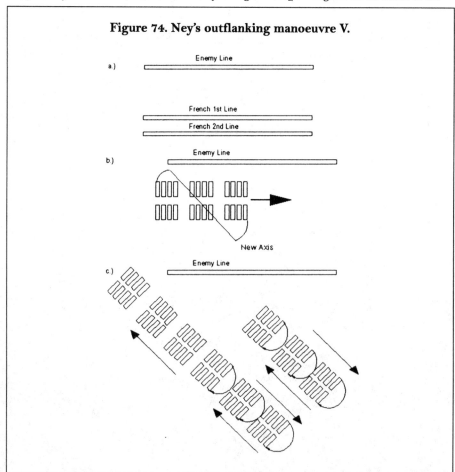

Figure 74. Ney's outflanking manoeuvre V.

column, front *pelotons* moving to the left, rear moving to the right]; and the oblique line of battle shall be reformed by means of a general conversion of platoons to the right.

VI

The four regiments marching in column of platoons, the right in front, on a line parallel to the enemy's front, as if they intended to attack the enemy's left wing, when, on the contrary, their right wing was the objective of the attack; in such a case, the oblique line might be formed, the left wing advanced on the first platoon of the third battalion of the second line, or such other platoons as might be selected; the platoons preceding these to operate by the right flank, and to proceed along the new perpendicular; the platoons in the rear to operate by the left flank and by file to the right. A general wheel by platoons to the left would place the line in the order of battle required.

It is to be observed that this movement must either be rapidly executed, or take place at some distance from the enemy, because the column for a time stands with its rear to the latter [the enemy].

VII

The same manoeuvres may also be performed if the lines march in columns of platoons towards the right of the enemy's line, though the commander-in-chief intends to form his oblique line upon the enemy's left. In this case, the platoons in the rear of those fixed upon the axis of movement shall operate by the right flank and by files to the left; those in front of the axis shall operate by the left flank. The perpendicular being assumed, the line of battle shall be reformed by a general conversion to the right by the two lines. Whenever the commander wishes to change the perpendicular of the columns, he will take care to establish, as in a change of front, the platoon designated for the rest of the troops to form upon.

Some Manoeuvres by Means of the Column

I

Four regiments in columns with intervals, marching, right in front, by platoons or divisions, at whole or half-distance: – If the commander requires to make them march by front of regiments in columns on the reverse flank of the guides in natural order [1st–8th *pelotons* in sequence, right to left] he shall give the following command after halting: – 'By platoons (or divisions) on the uneven or alternate battalions of each regiment, to the right form line of battle.'

This movement being executed, he may resume his line of battle by a change of front on the centre of each regiment, the right wing forward: that is to say, on the first division of the even battalions of each regiment. But if he wanted to form into line of battle by an inversion of regiments to the other flank, the change of front must be effected with the left wing forward: that is to say, on the fourth division of the uneven battalions of each regiment. If he wished to march in column of regiments by the proper pivot flank, he must execute a conversion of the divisions or platoons by inversion to the left.

II

By this distribution of columns of regiments, the commander might easily form his four regiments into a hollow square. If such were his intention, the first regiment would stand fast; the uneven battalions of the second and third, must execute a conversion to the right by battalions or by platoons, half-wheel to the right, and the even battalions must effect a conversion to the left. The fourth regiment, after having closed its ranks, would form the rear face.

III

The commander having reduced the square in order to form into line the same order of columns, the first regiment shall operate by platoons to the right after having cleared the second regiment; the latter shall then advance the space of one division, in order to form the basis for the general line. The first regiment shall halt and form in battle; the third and fourth shall operate to the left by platoons and place themselves successively in the alignment.

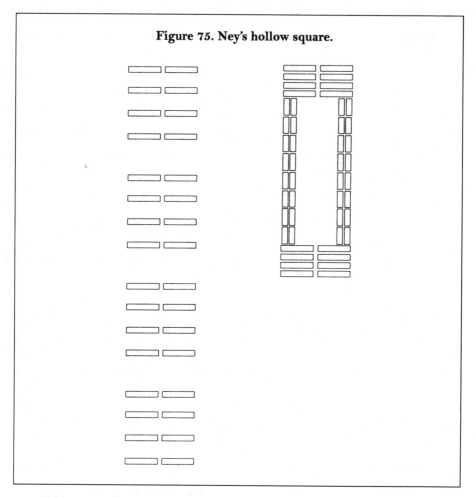

Figure 75. Ney's hollow square.

If this is to be effected in front on the second regiment, the column shall close to division distance, after which, forward and wheel

But if the commander intended to form two lines, the uneven regiments would stand fast, whilst the even numbers would execute the movement above indicated for the third and fourth regiments.

IV

Should the commander, however, find that the movements prescribed for the manoeuvre, No. IV, are too slow of execution, he may form a single column of regiments. He will command to form close column, the right in front, on the colour division of each battalion; and, having closed in mass, he may form into line by battalions in mass, or deploy on any named battalion. [This last manoeuvre was adopted into the Regulation of 4 March 1831.]

V

The four regiments having deployed, and the commander being desirous instantly to form two lines, and to place the uneven battalions in the first, and the even battalions in the second, he shall form a close column of regiments, the right in front on the fourth division of the uneven battalions, then close the masses, at the distance of a battalion [as if formed in line] from each other, upon the second regiment, and afterwards form into line upon the colour division of each battalion.

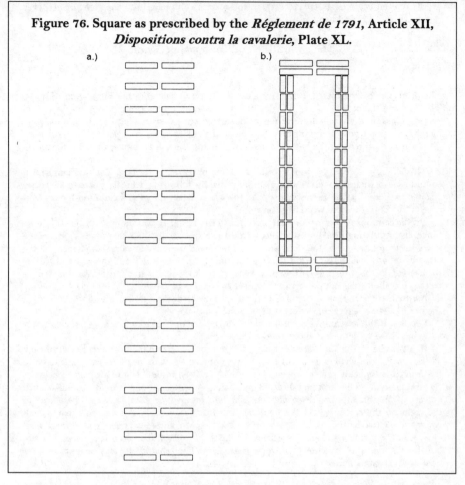

Figure 76. Square as prescribed by the *Réglement de 1791*, Article XII, *Dispositions contra la cavalerie*, Plate XL.

VI

If the commander wants to march in columns with the left in front, by entire regiments in their proper order: (let us suppose that the odd battalions are in the first, and the even battalions in the second line;) he will command a change of front to be effected on the colour platoon of each battalion, right wing to the front. If, on the contrary, he wished to march with the right in front, the change of front must be effected upon the colour platoon of each battalion, the left wing in front. The battalions would thus be in line of battle by inversion.

If the even battalions were in the first, and the uneven battalions in the second line, the column might be formed by fronts of regiments in columns of march, the right in front, by effecting a central change of front in each battalion, left wing forward; and, on the contrary, a change of front right wing forward, if the troops were to march with the left in front. In this case the battalions would likewise be in line of battle in inverted order.

VII

The line of four regiments or eight battalions being fully deployed, as in manoeuvre No. V, if the intention of the commander be to make the eight battalions march in two columns close to each other, in order to conceal his force and give greater precision to his movement, – the regiments shall form, in the rear, into columns by division, viz: the first regiment with the left, and the second with the right in front. The same movement shall be adopted for the second and third regiments. This movement may be executed by the following command – 'To the left of the uneven regiments, left in front, to the rear in column; and to the right of the even regiments, right in front to the rear in column.'

March in Line and Increase of Front

I

The principles of the march in line are clearly enough indicated in the Regulation of 1791. The men and the battalions are placed square to the front, on the ground they occupy, and in perfect alignment; the colours are generally carried six paces in front, when the line is to march, for the purpose of giving the cadence of the step, serving as a point of intermediate direction, and preventing the battalion from outflanking the one appointed to direct the movement.

This alignment, though good in itself, is seldom observed in warfare. The regiments shall continue, nevertheless, to follow this mode, and also the following, which appears to me better adapted to rendering the direction visible to the whole of the line, and facilitating the correctness of the line when the word is given to halt.

On the cautionary command: 'Battalions (or lines) forward,' the colours will remain in the ranks; the regulating battalion shall advance three paces, so that its rear rank is exactly on a line with the battalions to the right and left. The General guides or camp colourmen, of the other battalions shall advance to the same alignment. At the word 'Halt!' the whole shall line themselves on the directing battalion. Whenever the first line is to charge bayonets, the directing battalion shall not move from its place in the line of battle.

As, on many occasions in war, great advantage may be derived from increasing the front of the line, the commander may affect it in the following manner: –

Let us still suppose four regiments or eight battalions upon one or two lines whose front is to be increased by some battalions on the wings.

If it is to be of the four battalions placed at the two wings on the first line, the third rank of those battalions shall make a half-turn to the right, retire 30 paces to the rear, face about to the front, then quickly reforming into two ranks, proceed in double-quick time[12] to support the first platoon of the first battalion. There shall be a lieutenant and two non-commissioned officers to the third rank of each platoon. The non-commissioned officers shall be placed to the right of the sections, and the lieutenant shall act as captain. An adjutant-major shall command the two battalions of each regiment thus formed, and to which four drummers shall be added. The formation shall be the same for the third rank of the two battalions on the left, but the platoons shall execute the inverse movement. These battalions may be employed according to circumstances.

Passage of Lines

The passage of lines may be effected by column in different ways, besides those specified in the regulations: –

I

Two lines of four or eight battalions having to execute the passage of lines to the front by column: the first line stands fast; the battalions of the second, having broken into platoons to the right, shall march forward, change the direction to the left by heads of columns of battalions, pass outside the right of the battalion on the first line, and replace themselves in order of battle, either upon the first platoon or division, or upon one of the divisions or subdivisions of the centre. But if the commander wishes positively to place the first line on a parallel with the second, the heads of columns, after they have passed right of the battalions of the first line, shall oblique to the left in a sufficient degree to regain the platoon front which they have lost by the direct march. This manoeuvre is applicable either to the first or to the second line. [The method of passage of lines in the *Réglement de 1791* is quite defective. Here Ney substitutes a mode of doing it in proper columns, which is more rational. The manoeuvre in the *Réglement de 4 Mars 1831* is very like this method.]

---

[12] The copy of this work consulted was in English. As a result, it is not clear if this 'double-quick time' is the *pas de charge* or the *pas de course*. However, it is probable that it was the latter.

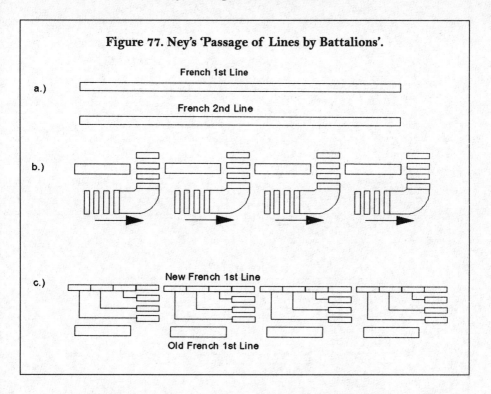

Figure 77. Ney's 'Passage of Lines by Battalions'.

The battalions of the second line may likewise gain ground to the front by proceeding round the left of the battalions in the first line. In this latter case they will break by platoons to the left, and will change their direction to the right on reaching the level of the left of the first battalions which have preceded them.

The movement to the rear is executed in the same manner; the battalions of the first line, after a half-turn to the right, and by platoons to the right, march forward, change their direction to the left and pass round the left of the battalions of the second line, and so on from both sides.

II

The passage of lines to the front may likewise be effected by columns of whole regiments for both lines. In this case the second line must form a close column of regiments, the right in front, either upon the first division of the even battalions, or upon the fourth division of the uneven ones. Each column shall march forward and pass through the interval between the two battalions of each regiment of the first line which precedes them. After having gained sufficient ground, each column shall form into line upon one of the divisions prescribed for its formation. [The column must, therefore, have cleared its last platoon past the front the stationary line.] The passage of line of regiments of the second line may likewise be effected by the latter executing the movement of the passing the defile forward by the centre. This mode is perhaps preferable, because the manoeuvre takes up less time, and the heads of the columns may immediately execute the platoon firing.

The passage of line retrograde, by columns of regiments, would be evidently too dangerous very near the enemy. Those prescribed by the regulation, and those indicated in No. I for columns of battalions, must, therefore, alone be put into practice.

In the supposition of a general attack in front, the heads of columns of each regiment of the second line shall march up to the intervals between the battalions of the regiments which precede them on the first line, and thus uniting the *ordre profound* to the *ordre mixte*, necessarily give more vigour to the ensemble of the charge. The movement being concluded, the regiments shall extend to the front.

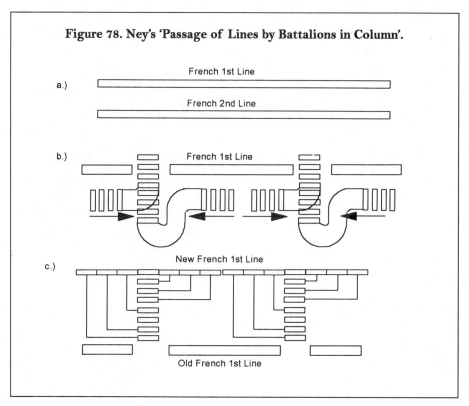

Figure 78. Ney's 'Passage of Lines by Battalions in Column'.

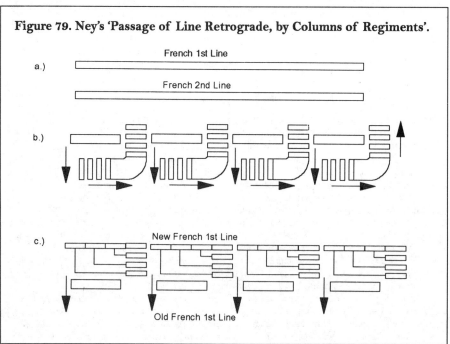

Figure 79. Ney's 'Passage of Line Retrograde, by Columns of Regiments'.

March or Attack by Echelons

This manoeuvre is extremely advantageous in war; but it requires a great perfection in the marching of the troops, in order that the attack upon the enemy may be supported with rapidity and intelligence, and that the battalions which refuse to attack may be in a fit state to execute attentively every movement which circumstances may require.

I

Eight battalions upon two lines having to attack the right wing of the enemy placed parallel to their front:

The movement shall begin by the left at full distances, either by regiments or battalions, whichever may be preferable. So soon as the last battalion of the first line has marched forward, it shall be followed by that of the second line, and so on by the remaining battalions. In the supposition that the enemy refuses its right, and makes a demonstration of attack with its left upon the right flank of the echelons in march; in this case, all the battalions shall effect together a change of direction to the right by battalions; or for the sake of more compactness and greater celerity, a change of front upon the colour platoon of each battalion in the two lines, left wing forward. This manoeuvre being performed, the battalions may continue the attack by echelons, or march forward and place themselves in line of battle upon the first battalions of the right of the two lines, which serve as pivots or *points-d'appui*. By this operation the two wings act alternately on the offensive.

If the attack were to be made on the left wing of the enemy's line, the movement must begin by the right of the two attacking lines. This change of direction by the battalions must be executed to the left; or the change of front made right wing forward.

II

If the commander wishes to attack with only the first line in echelons of battalions, either by the right or by the left, the battalions shall march at full distances, after the echelons are established; and if they are threatened with an attack by cavalry, each battalion should form into column of division at platoon distance, the right in front, upon the colour division of each battalion, if the movement were effected by the right of the line; or the left in front, if the movement were effected by the left in line. This being done, the first division of each head of column would stand fast. The uneven platoons of the second and third division should then wheel to the right, and the even platoons wheel to the left. The fourth division should close up and then face about so as to form squares by battalions placed in echelons.

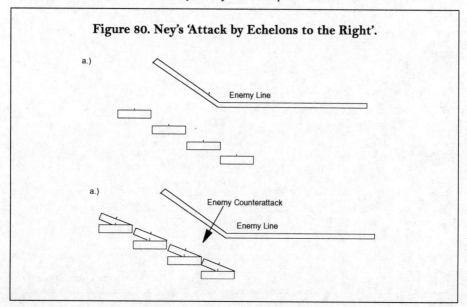

Figure 80. Ney's 'Attack by Echelons to the Right'.

a.)

Enemy Line

a.)

Enemy Counterattack

Enemy Line

**Figure 81. Attack by echelons to the right – *Réglement de 1791*,
Evolutions of the Line, Article 496, Plate XXXVII.**

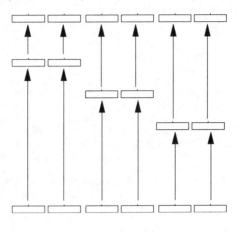

**Figure 82. Ney's 'Attacking with the First Line and Defending Against
Cavalry Attack'.**

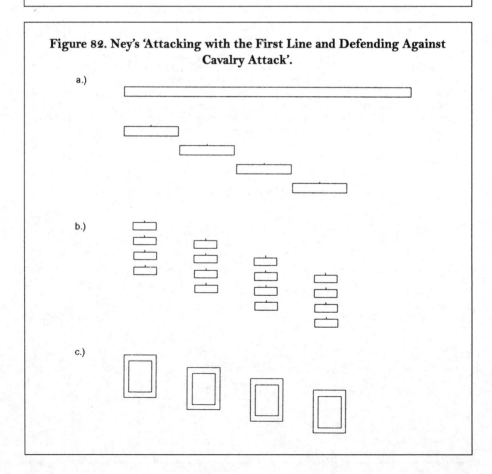

III

The attack in echelons by the centre is in general too dangerous a manoeuvre to be frequently used in war, unless the commander is certain that the enemy has imprudently weakened his centre to strengthen his wings; and that when he has reached the central position he can maintain it, cut off the enemy's wings, and force him to give battle separately. This attack upon the centre requires great resolution and extreme celerity in the march of the assailants.

Let us suppose a first assailant line of eight battalions: in this case battalions Nos. 4 and 5 shall begin to march at half-distance; the other battalions shall in like manner follow at half-distance, so that the movement may be better concentrated. It would be prudent not to make the second line march otherwise than in line of battle, in order that it may serve as a support to the two wings of the echelons of the first line, and be able to receive the first line thus firmed, and protect it in case of necessity.

Retreat *en Echiquier* or Alternate Retreat

The retreat *en echiquier* upon two lines may be effected according to the principals laid down in the regulations, by falling back by battalions a hundred or a hundred and fifty paces. But in order to change alternately the defensive into the offensive, the even battalions of the second line, instead of falling back at the same time as the even battalions of the first line, may form columns by divisions, at either close, half or whole distance behind the first division, the right in front, and then advance outside the right of the even battalions of the line then in retreat, and form into line a few *toises* [a *toise* = approximately six feet) in the rear of the left of the

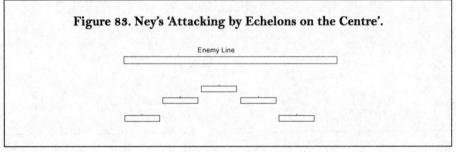

Figure 83. Ney's 'Attacking by Echelons on the Centre'.

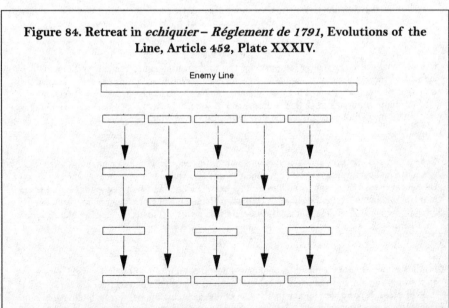

Figure 84. Retreat in *echiquier* – *Réglement de 1791*, Evolutions of the Line, Article 452, Plate XXXIV.

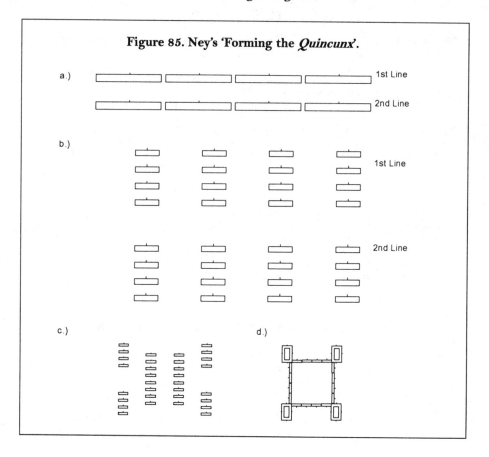

Figure 85. Ney's 'Forming the *Quincunx*'.

uneven battalions of the first line. This movement may be alternate in to two lines, and by
even and uneven battalions, during the whole time that the retrograde movement lasts.

Squares

Squares are formed three deep [in and prior to 1805], in conformity to the Emperor's instructions; and sometimes also by doubling the interior sections, according to the principal laid
down in the Regulations of 1791. Regiments may also be practiced to fire from the four sides
by the simple column; and as this is often seen in war [!!!], the troops generally marching in
that order, it would be advantageous to accustom the men to it.

I

Four regiments crossing a plain in columns with intervals, by platoons or by divisions. If they
were attacked by cavalry, and had not time to form into the prescribed squares, the regiments
should close up in mass, the three files on the proper pivot flank (we suppose that the columns
have their right in front) should form to the left flank; and those on the reverse flank should
form to the right flank; the last division would face about.' [This is exactly like the Austrian
Batallionsmasse.]

II

But if the four regiments marched upon two lines in columns: the first and second regiments
of the first line, the right in front, in column upon the eighth platoon of the even battalions, if
it be by platoons, or upon the fourth division of the same battalions, if it be by divisions; and
the first and second regiments of the second line, with also the right in front, but to the rear

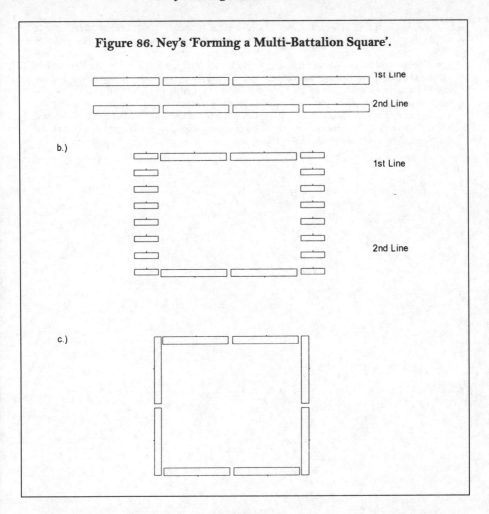

Figure 86. Ney's 'Forming a Multi-Battalion Square'.

in columns upon the first platoons of the uneven battalions, or the first divisions of the same battalions, if it be by divisions. This arrangement would enable the commander to form squares, either by making the uneven platoons wheel to the right, and the even platoons to the left, the column being by divisions at half-distance; or, after having closed up in mass, by making the three files on the right and left flanks of the column face as above to the left and right. Should circumstances permit, the *quincunx* may be formed, in order that the fire may cross without inconvenience to the troops.

III

The four regiments may also be formed in to columns in the following manner: – The first regiment of the first line in front forward into column, the right in front, upon the fourth division of the even battalion; the second regiment in the rear into column, the right in front, upon the first division of the uneven battalion. The first regiment of the second line forward into column, the left in front, upon the first division of the uneven battalion, and the second regiment in rear into column, the left in front, upon the fourth division of the even battalion.

IV

Four regiments upon two lines may easily form the hollow square, and place within it the baggage and implements of war, which they might have to cover or protect on a march. In this case, the two lines should leave no interval between the battalions and the regiments. The first battalion of the first line should break to the rear into column, by platoons, the left in front, at whole distance [full *peloton* interval], upon the eighth platoon; the fourth battalion of the same line into column by platoons, the right in front, behind the first platoon; the first battalion of the second line forward into column, the right in front, upon its eighth platoon, and the fourth battalion forward into column, the left in front upon its first platoon; a wheel by platoons to the right, by the right flank, would close this part of the square, and a wheel to the left, by the left flank would close the other part. The second and third battalions of the second line must make a half-turn to the right. The grenadiers might be so disposed as to cover the exterior and interior salient angles of the square.

Chapter 6

Revolutionary French Tactics: The Attack Column and Other Formations in Combat

It is widely understood and accepted that the French Revolutionary armies practiced a wide variety of tactics in an effort to find a successful compromise between their written regulations and the capabilities of their armies and soldiers.

In 1803 a most unusual dissertation on tactics by *Chef de brigade d'artillerie* Dedon Sr was published. Much of it appears to coincide with regulations, while some differs. In addition, some aspects provide a most interesting insight into battalion-level tactics. The differences from the regulations displayed in Dedon's work are probably formations and manoeuvres that were actually used in the field. I say this because the *Réglement de 1791* was never changed, even to accommodate the changes introduced by the Decree of 18 February 1808, which revised battalion strength from eight to six companies. The changes that the Decree forced on the battalion commander's manoeuvres have already been discussed in detail in Chapter 3. In addition, if Dedon, a senior officer, is displaying and advocating the use of these formations he would have had the opportunity to exercise a battalion to study the feasibility of the manoeuvres he describes or would have been in a position witness their use in battle.

Dedon's illustration of a deployed battalion is interesting in that it shows a slightly different placement of the officers and NCOs. It also puts the officers of the left half of the battalion on the left of their companies.

Figure 87. Battalion deployed in line as presented by *Chef de brigade* Dedon – *Dissertation sur l'Ordonnance d'Infanterie*, p.4, Figure 1. (Note: The file-closers' rank is compressed and the intervals eliminated between them in this illustration.)

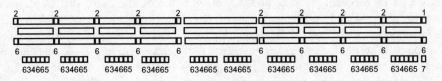

1 = Captain of grenadiers   2 = Captain of fusiliers   3 = Lieutenant

4 = *Sous-lieutenant*   5 = Sergeant-major   6 = Sergeants

7 = Corporal *fourrier* of grenadiers

In the right *demi-bataillon* the two sections on the extreme right were known as the first and second sections and formed the first *demi-peloton*. The sections were paired to the left to form the subsequent *pelotons*. The division formed the first and second *demi-pelotons*, 'which does not exist in our regulations, is indispensable for the formation of attack columns, as well as for diminishing the frontage and for augmenting the depth' of the battalion. This is a very clear indication that Dedon is speaking from experience in the use of this formation to accommodate some shortcomings of the *Réglement de 1791*. In the left *demi-bataillon*, the *demi-pelotons*, sections, and files were numbered from the left to the right. The officers and non-commissioned officers occupied positions that were the mirror image of those occupied by their counterparts in the right *demi-bataillon*.

All of the column manoeuvres were executed in *masses*, and on the centre as much as possible. The disposition that Dedon illustrates facilitates this and, he contends, is preferable to those provided by the *Réglement de 1791*.

For the *demi-bataillon* on the right, Dedon proposes that the captain be on the right of the *peloton*, in the first rank, having behind him the senior sergeant in the third rank. This is as it is presented in the *Réglement de 1791*. The placement of the remainder of the officers and NCOs is at variance with the *Réglement*, as can be seen. The lieutenant is in the file closers' rank two paces behind the second file of the second *demi-peloton*, having at his side, in the centre of the third section, the second senior sergeant. The *sous-lieutenant* is behind the second to last file of the second section. The sergeant-major is behind the same file of the fourth section. The senior sergeant is behind the captain in the third rank. The second senior sergeant is behind the centre of the third section, the third senior sergeant is behind the next to last file on the right of the second section, and the fourth sergeant is behind the second file on the right of the fourth section. The corporal *fourrier* of the grenadier company is behind the second file of the right of the first section. The four other corporal *fourriers* of the *demi-bataillon* form the colour guard. The eight corporals of each *peloton* are on the right and left of each section, in the first rank.

Dedon proposes that the left *demi-bataillon* be formed such that the captain is on the left of the *peloton* in the first rank with the first sergeant in the third rank behind him. The lieutenant is in the file closers' rank, two paces behind the second file on the left of the second *demi-peloton*, having beside him, in the centre of the third section, the second senior sergeant. The *sous-lieutenant* was to stand behind the next to last file of the second section. The sergeant-major stood behind the next to last file of the fourth section. Again, the first sergeant stood in the third rank, behind the captain. The second senior sergeant stood behind the centre of the third section, the third senior sergeant stood behind the second file of the left of the second section, and the fourth senior sergeant stood behind the second file on the left of the fourth section. Again, the company corporal *fourriers* were detached to the colour guard and the corporals of each company were posted on the right and left of each section in the first rank.

The drummers were in two ranks, placed 30 paces behind the file closers opposite the fifth *peloton*. The drum-major stood at the head of the drummers of the first battalion. The corporal drummer stood at the head of the drummers of the other battalions. The musicians stood behind the drummers of the first battalion.

When in battle the adjutant-majors placed themselves a dozen paces behind the file closers aligned with the fourth *pelotons*. The adjutant non-commissioned officers stood on the same line opposite the sixth *pelotons*. The adjutants were positioned so that they were able to repeat the verbal orders being issued by the battalion and demi-brigade commanders.

Dedon felt that this organisation and disposition of the cadre optimised the unit's ability to form into an attack column, which appears to have been his preferred formation, as we will see later.

He states that the attack column, formed on the centre, offered the greatest speed and precision for ploying and deploying the battalion. This has been clearly demonstrated in Chapter 3. He felt that it allowed the battalion to be divided laterally by *demi-bataillon*, in case 'the enemy was to be driven in.' He felt that this allowed the battalion to attack the enemy's wings. He says that, be it to provide shock, or to provide support, an attack should be made in column and that this did not exclude columns of divisions formed on the wings.

'The attack column,' says Dedon, 'could be formed in two manners; by full *pelotons* or by *demi-pelotons* of the right or left, according to the circumstances which gave the greatest depth … One forms an attack column according to need, in its formation, be it at the interval provided for in the *Réglement de 1791*, or be it at the interval of a section, and one must habitually manoeuvre in the *masse*.'

He states that the attack column could, according to circumstances, be formed with two battalions, as well as with four battalions formed laterally and perpendicularly, separated solely by the distance of a section, which can be filled at the head or the tail by the four sections of grenadiers. The senior officers marched on the flanks at the

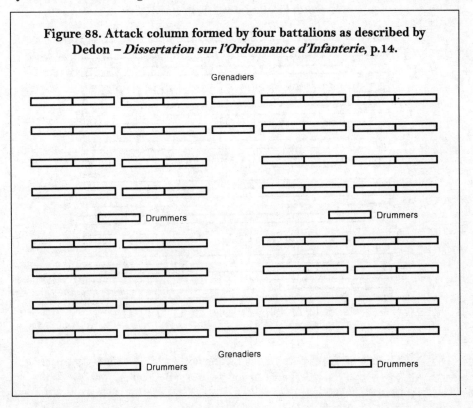

Figure 88. Attack column formed by four battalions as described by Dedon – *Dissertation sur l'Ordonnance d'Infanterie*, p.14.

Grenadiers

Drummers   Drummers

Grenadiers

Drummers   Drummers

level of their battalion or regiment. The drummers marched behind the column of their battalion or regiment.

Dedon states that when the attack column, by *pelotons*, was formed in closed ranks, there remained a one pace interval between each *peloton* for their commanders, their replacements, and for the officers and non-commissioned officers of the companies whose battle stations were found there, *ie* the file closers. Dedon goes into a lengthy discussion of the precise placement of these individuals, which will not be repeated here. He does state that those from the file closers' ranks were placed within the battalion in an effort to prevent confusion and to expedite the replacement of casualties with fresh men from the interior of the battalion.

What Dedon is proposing is a very heavy column, quite similar to the Macedonian phalanx advocated by Mesnil-Durand. It is generally acknowledged that though Gibert's system was what entered the French army as the *Réglement de 1791*, Mesnil-Durand's heavy columns were employed on occasion. One can even argue that Macdonald's at Wagram was such a column and d'Erlon's divisional attack at Waterloo may have been too.

Dedon also states that if a greater depth was desired the attack column could be formed by *demi-pelotons* from both line or an attack column of *pelotons*. In the latter case the conversion would be executed by the normal process of doubling.

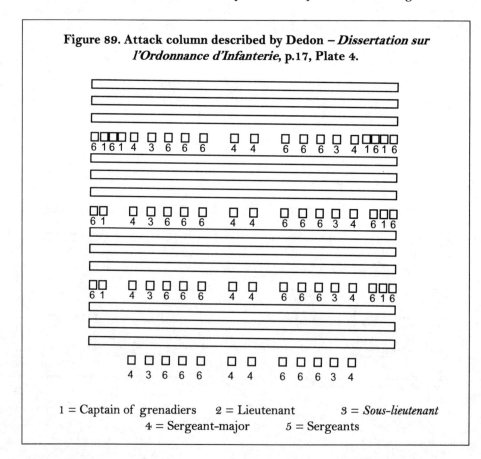

Figure 89. Attack column described by Dedon – *Dissertation sur l'Ordonnance d'Infanterie*, p.17, Plate 4.

1 = Captain of grenadiers   2 = Lieutenant   3 = *Sous-lieutenant*
4 = Sergeant-major   5 = Sergeants

The column would normally be formed in *masse* and it would close to *masse pleine* when advancing on the enemy. In a most unusual passage, Dedon says that 'if the enemy line is broken in its centre by the head of an attack column, and its wings, remaining on the flanks of the column, continue to offer resistance, one may charge them by the right and the left, by dividing the [attack] column in the centre and causing each half-column to act laterally.' The *demi-pelotons* in the half-columns would perform a facing move to the right or left and march with the heads of the files rather than wheeling the *demi-pelotons* and forming into a line perpendicular to the enemy line. This latter manoeuvre is possible, but the attack column would have to expand to a full two-section (*demi-peloton*) interval before it could wheel outward and form into two separate lines. Figure 90 shows the manoeuvre of which Dedon speaks.

However, this manoeuvre is not as unusual as one might initially assume, as it is identical to a tactic described by Folard, and was later adopted officially. It was also, apparently, used during the Seven Years War. It is, therefore, highly likely that this manoeuvre, proffered by Dedon, was in fact a tactic actively employed during the Revolutionary Wars.

When speaking of changes of direction while manoeuvring in *masse*, Dedon provides a clarification of how the mobile pivot worked. He states that the man on the inside of the pivot began taking paces of 162 mm length (6.4 ins) and marched in a

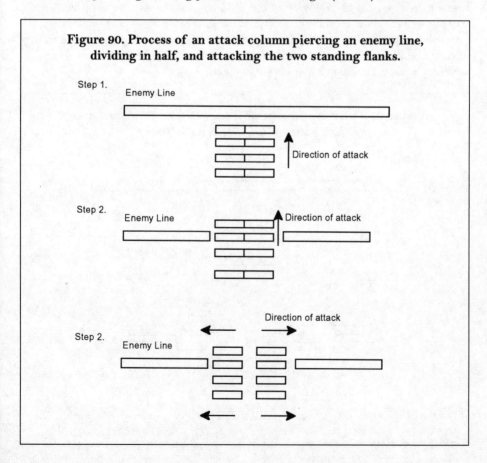

Figure 90. Process of an attack column piercing an enemy line, dividing in half, and attacking the two standing flanks.

circular path while continuing to march forward. The man on the outside flank of the wheel began to take paces of 650 mm (25.6 ins). Men in between maintained the alignment between these two and the man – a corporal who served as the guide for the manoeuvre – on the outermost flank. Dedon also indicates that the manoeuvre was executed at the *pas ordinaire* (76 paces per minute). As soon as the unit completed the pivot it resumed the normal pace length and the appropriate cadence. Dedon's notes indicate that this is the manoeuvre as it is described in the *Réglement de 1788*.

Dedon then turns his attention to the passage of lines. He states that it is one of the most important manoeuvres of warfare. 'It is essential that it be executed in a sure and simple manner, be it employed in a defensive mode, or if it is employed in the attack mode for shock.' In the case of a defence, he states that the method described in the *Réglement de 1791* is unnecessarily complex. Ney, in his tactical notes, agrees with this. Dedon felt that as the forward line fell back it could become entangled in the second line and expose both to destruction. He advocated returning to the method described in the *Réglement de 1776*.

In a retreat, Dedon's essay directs that the first line should make a half-turn to the right to move behind the second line. The commander of the second line was to form by battalion, in attack column on the centre by *demi-pelotons*. The first line could then easily pass through the intervals and the second line would be quite ready to act in any manner desired, be it to deploy, or to attack in column. As soon as the first line had withdrawn behind the second, the second could quickly redeploy in to line, closing the intervals and presenting a strong face to the presumably advancing enemy. The former first line could then reorganise itself and recover in the shelter of the new front line, while at the same time serving as a reserve for it.

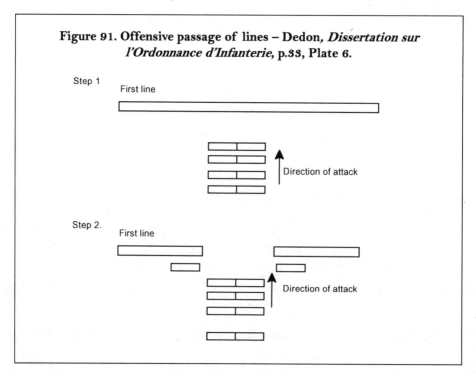

Figure 91. Offensive passage of lines – Dedon, *Dissertation sur l'Ordonnance d'Infanterie*, p.33, Plate 6.

On the offensive, specifically in a bayonet attack, Dedon directs that the second line should form in attack columns by *demi-pelotons* on the centre. They should then be directed to advance and, just prior to their arrival at the first line, the first line would open and provide passages for these battalions. This 'opening' would be effected by the battalion commanders of the front line doubling the two *demi-pelotons* in the centre of their battalions behind their line. Once the attacking battalions had advanced through the line the doubled *demi-pelotons* would advance by the flank back into their original positions and close the first line.

Once the attack columns had passed 200 paces beyond the original front line, the old front line would reorganise itself into attack columns by battalion and prepare to advance, serving as a reserve or to reinforce such attacks as the general may desire.

Dedon also addresses situations where a battalion is attacked by cavalry. Since his dissertation is entirely based on the use of the attack column, it is on this that his discussions regarding moving into square are based. The formation he discusses is

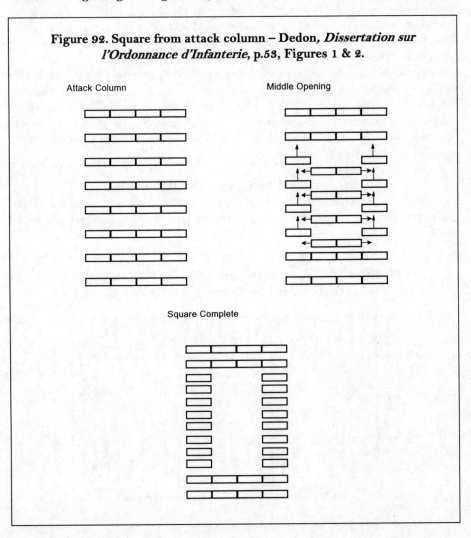

Figure 92. Square from attack column – Dedon, *Dissertation sur l'Ordonnance d'Infanterie*, p.53, Figures 1 & 2.

Attack Column

Middle Opening

Square Complete

precisely like the Russian hollow square formed from a column by doubling the centre companies by sections to the flanks. The method of manoeuvre and the placing of the file closers into the intervals is identical.

The intervals between the sections forming the flanks of the square in Figure 92 are, in fact, the file closers plugging the gaps. Dedon also provides an illustration of a two-battalion square formed following the same procedure. This is presented in Figure 93.

The interesting thing about Dedon's dissertation is that it is a period work by a Revolutionary officer which describes how he feels things should have been done, and may well describe tactics and organisations actually used on the battlefield. The type of square he advocates is identical to one used by the Russians at a later period, so it is highly likely that this style of square was used by the French in this period.

Dedon's discussion of the preferable way to execute a passage of lines is drawn from the *Réglement de 1776*, which indicates that it was a known procedure and highly likely to have been used. Indeed, Ney's comments about the process of a passage of lines support Dedon's position. He disliked what was proposed in the *Réglement de 1791*. However, while Dedon looked backwards to an older system, Ney innovated a new tactical manoeuvre, which was adopted in future regulations.

The only unsupported proposition of Dedon is his breaking of an attack column in half along the axis of advance and marching the two halves to the flank. Did this happen? It's difficult to say. The researches made in the preparation of this study have not located a document that indicates, in a detailed passage, that such a manoeuvre occurred. However, the absence of such a find does not preclude the possibility of its use.

Documented tactics of the Revolution

Few works of the Revolutionary period provide many details on the tactical formations employed by the French Revolutionary armies. There are, however, a few that provide some insight.

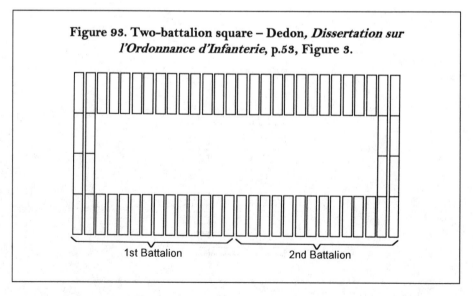

Figure 93. Two-battalion square – Dedon, *Dissertation sur l'Ordonnance d'Infanterie*, p.53, Figure 3.

1st Battalion   2nd Battalion

Prior to the outbreak of war in 1791, the officers of the Royal army were well versed in the philosophical argument between Guibert, advocate of a mixture of line and columnar movements, and Mesnil-Durand, who advocated the use of columns as the sole tactical formation necessary for 'modern' combat. Figure 90 – Dedon's 'Process of an attack column piercing an enemy line, dividing in half, and attacking the two standing flanks' – is an excellent example of Mesnil-Durand's school of thought. The French officer corps had, as a result, divided itself into three camps: those who supported Guibert, those who supported Mesnil-Durand, and those who accepted parts of the arguments of both. Indications are that the vast majority accepted the use of the line for musketry and the column for assaults on villages, posts and entrenchments.

Both Jonquière, in his work *La bataille de Jemappes*, and Colin provide detailed discussions of the engagement at Jemappes. In his account Colin cites Dumouriez's orders for the battle as follows: 'At exactly noon all the infantry formed into columns by battalions.' Jonquière identifies these columns as being dense (*serré*). The French then moved in this formation against the Austrian-held village and the trenches.

This order was not to be retained long. Dumouriez ordered General Ferrand to no longer amuse the enemy's cannons with a preparatory cannonade, but to advance 'boldly'[13] with bayonets. Dumouriez ordered Ferrand to use columns by battalion and to retain this formation when his troops got into the village. He recommended Ferrand make this attack in columns by battalions, to retain this formation in the village of Quaregnon, and not to deploy until his right joined the left of the centre division. This deployment was executed.

Ferrand had his troops fire by files three times. On the right Dampierre had formed his troops in attack columns, not *masses*. The Austrian artillery fired on these troops in an effort to delay or break up their formation. General Dumouriez ordered him to deploy his columns even though Ferrand judged that the fire of 40 guns was too heavy to allow him to do this. Nevertheless, the manoeuvre was performed without flaws. Once the ten battalions had deployed they marched forward at the charge. This force consisted of two *légère* battalions, four line battalions, and four battalions of Parisian volunteers. Dumouriez states that these particular battalions performed this most complex manoeuvre as if they were on a peacetime parade ground, clearly indicating that they were well versed in the linear tactics of the period, and not raw drafts. This is an excellent example of manoeuvring in column, closing to within striking range, deploying into line, and then attacking with the bayonet.

At Limbach, Saint-Imbert, the defense of Ketterich and the retreat on Bitche, the Army of the Moselle continued to fight in linear formations. During the disaster at Pirmasens, indications are that Moreau may have wished to use linear tactics. He advanced his troops in deep columns, but did not have the space necessary to deploy and the Austrian fire on the heads of his columns quickly disordered them.

During the battle at Kaiserslautern, General Ambert speaks of his attack on the rear of the Prussian positions as follows: 'I moved our advanced guard, formed in line, before Oterbach. I then ordered the battalions forming my column to form in *masses*, by division, so that they could move up to the rear of the advanced guard. The light troops moved into the Otterberg gorge and began a skirmish fire on the Prussians.'

---

[13] The term *tête bassée* was used, which means lowered head, literally 'like a bull' in this context.

The basic formation was skirmishers in front, a line of infantry formed to provide the fire power necessary to hold the enemy, and a mass of infantry formed in column sheltered behind the line to manoeuvre for any opening that might develop. This is also one of the rare examples of a complete description of the formations used by the French infantry in battle.

In the diary of Commandant Girardon, commanding officer of the *Bataillon de Réquisition de Chaumont*, a passage describes the tactical deployment of this battalion as it approached the enemy. It advanced during the morning in a column of divisions at full interval until such time as it met the enemy, when it deployed into line. Again, both linear tactics and a tactical process that comes from Guibert's school. In the days following, Girardon states that their army commander had them march in divisions, by brigades, with their right forward, in columns closed into *masses*, so as to facilitate their passage through villages and to be ready on an instant to deploy. As soon as the enemy was observed the columns each deployed on the first *peloton* of their first battalion. When, near Neustadt, the Austrians withdrew, the French continued their advance formed in line. In the details of the battles by Nothweiler, Giradon's diary clearly indicates that all the combat occurred in skirmish formation or in small columns because of the broken terrain.

In 1793, as at all other times, the battalions detached skirmishers. Giradon describes this process as the detaching of about 100 skirmishers from each battalion. In an engagement near Mietesheim, seven battalions were sent forward to take the edge of a small wood near Mietesheim. Each battalion detached 100 skirmishers and sent them forward to clear the woods of Austrians. Unfortunately, the Austrian skirmishers maintained such a lively fire that the French battalions were unable to support their own skirmishers and the army was obliged to withdraw.

The French appear to have never engaged in an action without detaching from 30 to 100 skirmishers per battalion. As there were no *voltigeur* companies in the French infantry at this time, and the grenadier companies were generally stripped from the battalions and converged, these were men drawn from the fusilier companies. These detached skirmishers generally appear to have then been united into a single formation that operated across the front of the French army.

The frequency with which these various tactics were utilised is difficult to establish, but Dr John Lynn has, in *The Bayonets of the Republic*, prepared a list of the instances of various formations being used in combat between 1792 and 1794. This listing is summarised in Table 37.

In addition, French skirmishers were not always particularly effective. Duhesme states clearly that, in his experience, the French light infantry was heavily outnumbered, and that the Austrians made effective use of their light infantry by passing them down the flanks of the French battalions, which they then attacked while hiding behind such terrain features as might be found. Indeed, Brossier commented in 1800 that the Austrian attacks in 1792 were always accompanied by a cloud of skirmishers. This would indicate that it was the Austrians who taught the French how to skirmish.

There are some discrepancies, however, in the suggestion that the French were always outnumbered. Duhesme goes on to say that the less exercised and more poorly-trained national guard battalions of the French army were often used as light troops because they were unable to successfully handle the linear movements of the remnants of the Royal army. He goes on to say that 'in truth, by the end of 1793, it can be said

Table 37. Formations used in combat 1792–4.

Formation	Use	Frequency
Line	Defence	13
Line	Defence in retreat	7
Line	Defence, passage of defiles	2
Line	Preliminary formation	17
Line	In support of skirmishers	6
Line	On the march	3
Line	In the attack	3
Column	Attack, deploying into line	1
Column	Attack, 'column' specified	14
Column	Charge, 'in order/*masse*'	9
Column	Bayonet attack	7
Column	Attack against cavalry	4
Column	Preliminary formation	3
Column	Retreat, manoeuvre formation	3
Column	Column by *pelotons*	5
Square	Square	6

that the French armies had nothing but light infantry.' The reference speaks of the decline in strength of the old Royal regiments and the explosion of 'volunteer' units. In *The Bayonets of the Republic*, Dr Lynn provides a listing of documented uses of skirmishers 1792–4, as shown in Table 38.

It is apparent that the casualties suffered during the 1792 campaign amongst the French line troops had greatly reduced those capable of performing the linear manoeuvres of the Frederickian style of warfare. The new troops being raised and sent to the front were not well versed in such manoeuvres. Despite that, linear tactics continued to be used, with the more poorly-trained units being employed as skirmishers until such time as they could be properly drilled in linear techniques. Lynn's accounting clearly indicates a significantly larger number of column attacks – 14, compared to three attacks in line. Though this suggests a predisposition to columnar attacks, it must be remembered that the figures are based only on published material, and do not

Table 38. Use of skirmishers 1792–4.

Type of troops	Frequency
Unknown	34
Not trained as skirmishers	3
Total battalion dispersed	5
Trained light infantry	4
Trained light infantry company	5
Trained light infantry battalion	22

cover every action. Authors notoriously omit such details from their works, so though a trend may be assumed, it cannot be proven with any certainty.

There were still large numbers of veteran soldiers in the French army. The new recruits did not total more than a third of the army's strength and these men, even after formal training, were generally placed in the second rank of the companies so that they were surrounded by veteran soldiers. Furthermore, there were incentives provided by the Revolutionary government that enticed soldiers from the regular regiments into the National Guard battalions, giving them a very high proportion of veterans. In fact, the only serious shortcomings of these troops was their lack of solidity, and their inability to withstand the shock of prolonged combat and heavy losses.

On many occasions French units would see their new recruits bolt at the first volley. It is not a unit's military instruction or knowledge of the theory of manoeuvres that enables it to face enemy fire, but its cohesion or collective courage. During the assault on Berg-op-Zoom in 1814 even two veteran British battalions, the 55th and 69th Regiments of Foot, broke and fled simply because they were advancing in the dark to assault a fortress. Not a shot was fired at them, nor was a single Frenchman seen.

The year 1793 was one of training for the new French armies, and by 1794 they were capable of engaging in sustained fire-fights. All that they lacked during this period was the ability to consistently manoeuvre successfully in extended or linear formations, and to manoeuvre under fire. By contrast, new recruits drawn into the French army in 1813 were capable not only of manoeuvring in linear formations and manoeuvring under fire, but they had learned their trade while marching from the recruit depots to the front! This is probably not because of the capabilities of the troops themselves, but because of the skill and knowledge of their cadres, the commissioned and non-commissioned officers who directed such complex manoeuvres. It needs to be recalled that in 1792–4 the French army was undergoing a complete purge of all officers of royal ancestry. In their place were men who had been elected to their positions of authority. Very often these were veteran soldiers, because the other soldiers recognised that they needed to be told what to do by someone who knew the manoeuvres. Occasionally, however, incompetents were elected on the grounds of popularity, political correctness, or seniority, and overall the quality of the cadres was greatly diminished. It took time to train the officers and NCOs who performed such tasks, and in the early days of the Revolution they were seriously lacking in numbers and skills.

By 1796 the French cadres had begun to master the art of war. One begins to see all units operating in both column and line. The line continued to be the preferred method of attack, but use of the attack column was now common. The latter had evolved into a tool that was recognised and was being used with greater frequency by all French generals; but it was not the mindless sledgehammer, thrown against enemy lines to bludgeon them into submission, that it is sometimes made out to have been.

Mixed order

It was in 1796 that Napoleon appears to have introduced the *ordre mixte*, employing it with great success at Tagliamento. Whether the situation here obliged his adoption of this order because the terrain did not permit the formations to fully deploy, or if it was a stroke of genius, is not known, but the compromise between column and line resulted and a new phase of tactical manoeuvre began.

It was, in fact, Guibert who developed the *ordre mixte*. He stated that it was appropriate to mix columns and lines, be it to march on the same front or to support the lines. He strongly advocated the use of both lines and columns in the attack so that, by acting in concert, the advantages and strengths of both could be fully exploited. However, it should be remembered that it is one thing to sit in one's study and philosophise on manoeuvres and quite another to execute them on the battlefield. It is Roguet, son of the general, who states that the first combat use of this tactic occurred on 16 March 1797 at Napoleon's passage over the Tagliamento. In his own report of his dispositions to the directory, Napoleon stated: 'Each of these divisions [Guieu and Bernadotte] formed their grenadier battalions, deployed for battle [in line], each having a light infantry demi-brigade before them, supported by two battalions of grenadiers and flanked by cavalry. The light infantry was deployed in skirmish formation ... I ordered each demi-brigade to form their 1st and 3rd Battalions in closed [*serré*] column on the wings of their 2nd Battalion.'

Napoleon used this formation again a few days later during his passage over the Isonzo. The history of the 12th Demi-brigade specifically cites his personal intervention in the selection of this formation:

> The division was formed in line on the banks of the Isonzo. The enemy fired his artillery on it from the left bank. The commanding general [Napoleon] arrived and directed the formation of the troops in the following order: The 12th [Demi-brigade] formed in a *bataillon carré* without depth, that is the 2nd battalion in line and the 1st and 3rd Battalions in closed [*serré*] columns by divisions on the flanks of the 2nd Battalion. The 64th Demi-brigade formed in closed [*serré*] columns by divisions, the right forward. The grenadiers of these two demi-brigades stood on the left of the line in closed [*serré*] columns. A battalion of the 21st *Légère* Demi-brigade stood on the head of each of these columns.

The report of the 64th Demi-brigade states that 'one of its battalions was formed in line and the other stood closed in columns behind in *masse* and *en potence*.' It is worth noting that the *ordre mixte*, as employed, often consisted of a single battalion in line and a single battalion in column.

In 1800 Generals Watrin and Rivaud fought at the Battle of Montebello. Watrin, who advanced across the plain, formed his troops in line. The Austrians had a significant force and cannonaded the French with a brisk fire. Watrin formed two battalions of the 6th *Légère* Demi-brigade into line to the right of the road, giving them an order to turn the enemy artillery. At the same time a battalion of the 40th Demi-brigade was ordered to take the Casteggio heights in order to turn the other flank. The movement of the 40th took too long and Watrin saw that the Austrians were on the heights in force. He detached a battalion of the 22nd Demi-brigade to engage them while the rest of the demi-brigade remained in line in their original position.

Rivaud, who attacked the heights, was unable to act against it except with skirmishers and narrow columns. The 1/43rd Demi-brigade[14] advanced on the left and the 2/43rd advanced on the right in skirmish formation. The 3/43rd advanced in the centre in column. The 3/43rd advanced without firing a shot, but under the covering fire of the skirmishers advancing on either flank. The 1/96th and 2/96th Demi-brigades moved

---

[14] This should be read as the 1st Battalion, 43rd Demi-brigade.

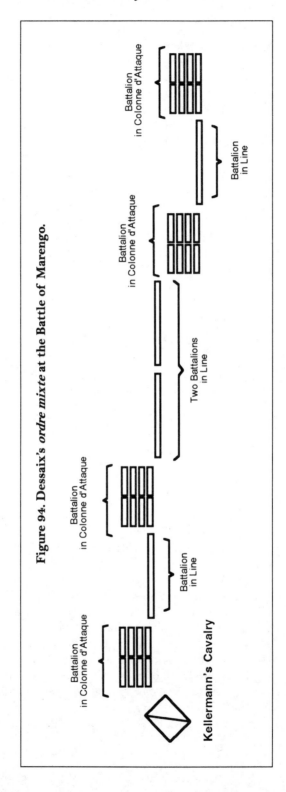

Figure 94. Dessaix's *ordre mixte* at the Battle of Marengo.

past the village of Casteggio in a closed (*serré*) column of *pelotons*. After their advance past the village they deployed into skirmish formation.

This same tactic was used at Marengo with no less success. When Dessaix arrived on the battlefield he deployed Boudet's division into mixed order. The 1st Brigade formed on the left of the main road, with one part deployed and the other in closed column. The 2nd Brigade assumed the same disposition on the right of the road. The 1st Brigade, which contained the 9th *Légère* Demi-brigade, was ordered to advance. The Austrian musketry, however, was sufficiently heavy to oblige Boudet to deploy skirmishers in front of the 9th *Légère*. The 2nd Brigade, also formed with closed columns, was then ordered forward.

After training his army at Boulogne in 1805, Napoleon did not hesitate long in putting it to the test. In December he was to employ his mixed order at Austerlitz with the same effect as at Tagliamento and Isonzo. His orders directly stated: 'Each brigade shall have its first regiment in line. The second regiment in closed column by division, the first battalion to the right and to the rear of the first battalion of the first regiment and the second battalion (of the second regiment) to the rear and to the left of the second battalion (of the first regiment).' This is exactly the same formation as was employed at Tagliamento, except that the frontage of the force in line is doubled.

Soult relates that Napoleon strongly recommended to his generals that they remain constantly in two lines of battle and a third line of light infantry. They were to retain the battalions in column by division formed at half (*peloton*) intervals, so that they would in all circumstances be able to quickly form square as well as be able to manoeuvre rapidly. They were to maintain this formation throughout the engagement and, if some battalions were deployed into line, it would not expose too great a frontage to the enemy.

However, despite Napoleon's recommendations, his generals appear to have had their own opinions regarding how to manoeuvre their forces and what manoeuvres and formations were preferable. Austerlitz is one of the very few instances where Napoleon violated his own general rule of allowing his subordinates to choose their own unit-level tactical deployment. Vandamme used this disposition in his orders to General Ferey when faced by allied infantry and cavalry. Ferey's brigade formed its first line of two battalions in line, while his second line was two battalions formed in square.

During the Battle of Jena, Suchet wrote that in order to take the village of Closwitz he formed Claparède's brigade in line, followed by two guns. Reille's brigade, on his right, was formed in two lines with artillery in the intervals. The 40th Demi-brigade was in column with orders to deploy as soon as the terrain permitted, and behind them, 200 yds to the rear, stood Vedel's brigade, formed in *masse*. When they arrived at the head of the wood, the division, mostly formed in closed (*serré*) *masses*, with some brigades deployed, found a large force of cavalry on the plain before it. The 17th *Légère* lacked sufficient ammunition and found itself at a particular disadvantage. The 34th Demi-brigade was ordered to replace it using a passage of lines. The 2/34th and 3/34th Demi-brigades, which had advanced in good order, were then ordered to charge three enemy battalions with an advancing fire (which indicates they were probably intended to be in line, not column), and by a change of front with the right wing forward, to overthrow the Prussian grenadiers and capture their supporting artillery. The Prussians covered their withdrawal with fire. A battalion of the 88th Demi-bri-

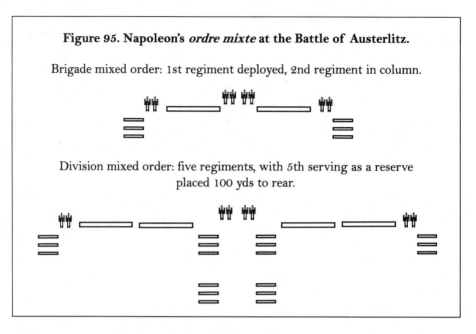

Figure 95. Napoleon's *ordre mixte* at the Battle of Austerlitz.

Brigade mixed order: 1st regiment deployed, 2nd regiment in column.

Division mixed order: five regiments, with 5th serving as a reserve placed 100 yds to rear.

gade launched an aggressive pursuit, supported by a battalion of the 21st *Légère* formed in *masse*. However, Lannes, in lieu of using multiple columns, fought the battle in line. Yet he still formed his divisions in two lines.

Further examples of this can be found in the twin battles of Jena–Auerstädt. At Jena, Lannes disposed his corps in a mixed formation of line and columns. His artillery was deployed in the intervals between the battalions. He prepared, by a change of direction to the right, to strike the village of Closewitz. Later, in response to a withdrawal of the Prussians, he ordered a charge by the 100th and 103rd Demi-brigades formed in *masse*.

Lannes used two formations at Austerlitz and at Jena. However, he generally used an *ordre mince* (linear formation). Soult, by contrast, manoeuvred most of his battalions in column in two lines, with cavalry on the right.

The 1st Division of Augereau's Corps was formed in two lines as well. The 1st brigade made an oblique change of front, placing its right forward. The second line copied this movement and extended further to the left with its two left-most battalions. The 1st Brigade subsequently broke by *pelotons* to the left and marched forward

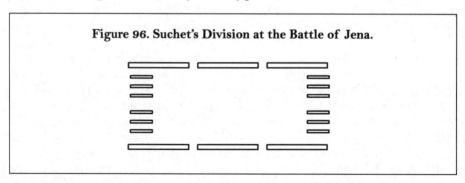

Figure 96. Suchet's Division at the Battle of Jena.

in this formation to drive the Prussians from the woods. As soon as the 7th *Légère* Demi-brigade began to clear the woods, and seeing many wounded French leaving the woods to the left (which indicated that it contained a force of Prussians), it was ordered to form a line facing to the left to counter this potential threat.

The 16th *Légère* Demi-brigade reported that it had moved to the left towards the woods. The 3/16th *Légère* deployed into skirmish formation and pushed into the woods, while the 1/16th and 2/16th *Légère* advanced to the right of the woods in column. Once past, they deployed into line within musketry range of a Prussian battery. Their line formed, they began a brisk musket fire against the Prussians and advanced to within pistol range. From there they advanced in skirmish formation and in a sharp fight captured 11 guns from the Prussians.

The 14th Line Demi-brigade reported that once the 16th *Légère* had pushed back the Prussians on the right, it formed line in the position that the Prussians had just abandoned. When the French VI Corps arrived, it moved to the left. While doing so, it was obliged to perform many manoeuvres under the fire of the Prussians, which it did without significant discomfort. Shortly afterwards the regiment, supported by the 44th Demi-brigade, was ordered to seize a ridge. The 2/14th Demi-brigade was had deployed in line and the 1/14th had remained in column since they had cleared the woods. However, the regiment then reformed into closed (*serré*) columns, because of the threat of cavalry.

The 44th Demi-brigade reported forming on the right of the 2nd Brigade of the 1st Division of VII Corps. It was formed in line to the right rear of a burning village. At 10:30 am, it was ordered by Napoleon to break by *pelotons* to the right. It then detached a company of *voltigeurs* to observe the enemy movements before it. After this was complete it prepared to advance out onto the plain. As it moved out the 1/44th Demi-brigade formed in line while the 2/44th, formed in closed column, stood behind the 8th *peloton* (left flank) of the 1/44th.

The 105th Demi-brigade found itself formed in column by the left. It arrived on the plain and promptly deployed into line, marching forward to the edge of the woods. The Prussians withdrew in disorder before it, taking their artillery with them. With the threat of the artillery gone, the 105th formed column and crossed the plain at the *pas de charge* in order to seize the heights that dominated the road. Once on the ridge it deployed into line and began a fire of two ranks, which would last for two hours.

Though the Prussian infantry was driven back, their cavalry moved against the left of the regiment. The 105th then withdrew *en échiquier* by battalions at an interval of 50 paces, reformed line, and ordered the 2/105th to change its facing to an oblique behind the grenadiers and began a two-rank fire which drove off the Prussian cavalry. The left flank of the infantry was uncovered, and, still fearing the cavalry which had once again rallied, the colonel of the 105th ordered the 2/105th to form column, while the 1/105th remained in line.

Upon arriving at Friedland with the I Corps in 1807, General Victor was ordered to form his forces before the village of Posthenen in a fold in the ground and act as the reserve for the whole army. Each division was formed by brigade, with part of it deployed into line. The other part of the brigade remained in column on the flanks, *ie* an *ordre mixte*.

The Battle of Friedland began with a major skirmish. Oudinot had deployed two full battalions as skirmishers into the Sortlack woods, while five or six others ad-

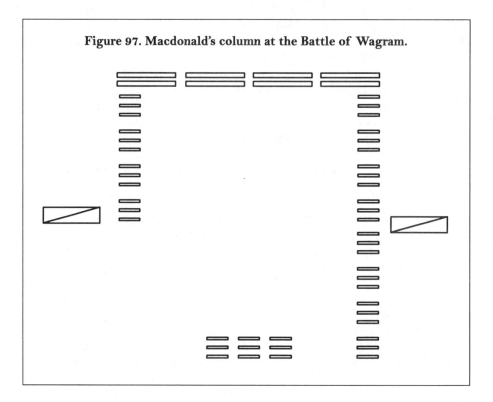

Figure 97. Macdonald's column at the Battle of Wagram.

vanced behind them. Lannes acted in a similar manner. Behind a screen of skirmishers favoured by the broken terrain, he repeatedly sent forward a battalion of skirmishers to drive back the Russian skirmishers. He formed two columns, each consisting of a full brigade. He employed them alternately, striking at different points as the battle progressed.

When Napoleon arrived, Ney's two divisions were engaged. The five regiments of Marchand's division had formed into a single closed (*serré*) column in order to be able to move as quickly as possible and strike the Russian flank. Bisson's division formed in echelons on the left. The Russian artillery fire and an attack by its cavalry inflicted heavy losses on Marchand's division, driving it back in disorder. Seeing Marchand's fate, Bisson deployed to the left. Marchand rejoined him and his nine regiments deployed, for the most part, in an *ordre mince* (line) in order to maximise the utilisation of their available fire power and to minimise the effect of the enemy's fire. Their line extended along a front of 6000 to 7200 ft (1.14 to 1.36 miles). Across their front a 'cloud' of French skirmishers were locked in combat with their Russian counterparts.

After a terrible fusillade, this long line was driven back by a cavalry charge. At that point Napoleon intervened and directed Dupont to form his division into a mixed order. One brigade was deployed, and the second, with six battalions, stood in a line of *masses*. The three regiments of Ney's corps remained firm on the extremities of the line and were formed in square. As Dupont encountered the Russians, he found himself separated from them by a stream. He deployed in line. Ney advanced his forces and deployed a battalion into skirmish order, sending them into the ravine. Finally, as he closed on Friedland he sent the 59th Demi-brigade forward in a closed column.

At the Battle of Wagram one finds Macdonald's attack described as a massive column. However, it can be argued that Macdonald's famous column here was, in fact, a massive mixed order formation. Its front consisted of two lines, each with four deployed battalions. On each wing there was a column of four or five battalions in *masse*. It was a heavy column, incapable of rapid deployments and various manoeuvres, and if charged by cavalry it could only form one immense square.

Little remains of the tactical details of the Battle of Borodino except that the assault made on the great redoubt was made in a mixed order. Morand formed the 1st Division into the classic formation.

With the 1813 campaign there came major changes in the tactics practiced by the French army. Though there is not any evidence that the mixed order was no longer employed, there is little documentary evidence of its use. What the evidence does show is a major philosophical change. The lack of French cavalry in 1813 obliged Napoleon and his marshals to make use of massive formations. Before Lützen, Napoleon directed that his generals 'should in case of action, manoeuvre in such a manner as to hold their left on the Saal River, forming as many lines in *masse* and by brigade as they have divisions in their army corps. Each regiment is to be in one column formed of divisions at a half [*peloton*'s] interval. There shall be a 200 metres interval between regiments, so that one could form six or eight squares in two lines in each division.' Each regiment, in this formation, was to form a distinct and individual column, and according to regulation would form a single square.

The attacks made on Gross-Görschen and Kaya were made with closed columns. When the 8th Division was repulsed, it moved behind the 10th Division by means of a well executed passage of lines. At Bautzen both lines and columns were employed, but there were some variations. The 8th Division and the advanced guard of III Corps moved against the heights before them. They were supported by the 9th Division, formed in closed columns by division, and by the 10th Division, deployed in two lines and forming the corps reserve. This formation was retained until Preititz was taken. At that time the 9th Division moved forward still in columns, while the 10th and 11th Divisions deployed.

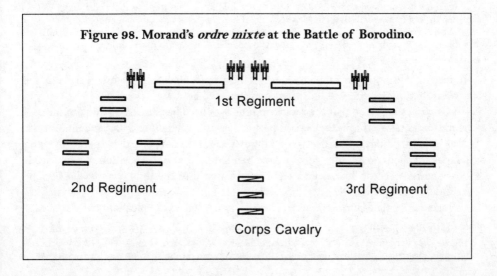

Figure 98. Morand's *ordre mixte* at the Battle of Borodino.

1st Regiment

2nd Regiment

3rd Regiment

Corps Cavalry

It would appear that beginning in 1809 there was a transition in French tactical methods. Macdonald's column appears to be the first example of a trend away from battalion and regimental tactics towards divisional and corps tactics. It is also noteworthy that the two divisions that took Preititz did so while in line and that the divisions formed behind them in column never took part in the battle. Again, this is a mixed order, but on a macro scale.

Attack column

Under the Empire, General Meunier appears to have totally abandoned the attack column, because in his book *Evolutions par Brigades* he employs only *colonnes par division*. General Pelet, in his later works, still shows the attack column, to which he ascribed several desirable features. He wrote that it was, by its nature, essentially isolated. One could not form a large column without infinitely complicating all its movements, as well as risking mixing the various *pelotons*. The advantage of the attack column was that it consisted of a single battalion, operating by itself under the fire of the central division. The first advantage was considerable, because it allowed rapid and efficient manoeuvres. The column was the quickest formation for conversions to square or line, as well as for many other manoeuvres, as was shown earlier. The second advantage was less important in a line of several battalions.

General Chambray stated that:

> the attack column is not employed as often as one might believe and here is the reason. When the infantry marches on roads and when it is some distance from the enemy, it marches by the flank. When it is time to approach the enemy it is then time to form up. The infantry then leaves the roads and forms by *pelotons*. First the divisions form up and they close to an interval of a section. Finally they shoulder arms and march out at the *pas acéléré*, if it is necessary. One sees that, in order to form an attack column, it was previously necessary to deploy [into line].

General Morand, one of Davout's famous divisional generals, appears to have been an advocate of the *colonne par divisions*. He felt that it was

> the most convenient in various terrains and circumstances and that it gave the facility to change to other formations in the least time and with the greatest possible order. A battalion in *colonne par divisions* at a *peloton*'s interval seems to me the best in these conditions. In effect, it cannot be surprised on the rear or flanks by an infantry or cavalry shock. The battalion can deploy in a few seconds, with order and without danger. A column can change its front without deforming, by pivoting on itself. It is the sole formation to assume in a broken or hilly plain, and it is useful in all terrain. It seems to me that it is basic with regard to the basic and fundamental order of the battle.

He also said that, in an attack, each battalion must maintain an interval from the adjacent battalions that was sufficient to allow it to deploy.

It is often suggested that the attack column was used because one could put inexperienced infantry in it and they could perform satisfactorily. That was, in fact, not the case. General Duhesme said: 'It is a singular error to suppose that the ardour and inexperience led the infantry to adopt the formation of the attack column. The battalions who received no instruction were assimilated into the light troops and became rare, and were in the minority.'

Speaking in generalities, Gouvion Saint-Cyr described a typical attack:

> I shall suppose that a division, formed with four line demi-brigades and one *légère* demi-brigade, are charged with attacking the front of an enemy line. Here is the attack order which I would prescribe. The three *légère* infantry battalions would advance, formed in two ranks,

their files separate from one another at a range of two to three paces, in such a manner that the three battalions cover the front of the 12 other battalions of the division and mask its movements. At the moment of the attack, the 12 battalions shall close into column by battalions, each column being formed of four divisions [two *pelotons – colonne par division*] at an interval of 3 paces [*serré*].

When the signal to attack is given the light infantry, standing at a distance of 150 paces in front of the columns, shall march forward in a lively manner and begin a supporting [skirmish] fire. The 12 columns shall follow at the *pas de manoeuvre* [120 paces per minute – same as the *pas de charge*] and when the light infantry is 50 paces from the enemy it shall stop. If the enemy holds fast, the skirmishers shall redouble their fire. The *colonnes serrés* in *masse* by divisions, the first [division] with lowered bayonets, the remaining three [divisions] with shouldered arms, shall double their pace, while conserving their deep formation, passing through the skirmishers and place themselves by *pelotons* in the intervals, and charge with bayonets against the enemy.

If charged by cavalry the columns simply close ranks until they touch one another [the *masse*].

One more note needs to be added to provide a full explication. Apparently, with the quality of the gunpowder being what it was, the skirmishers could actually mask the manoeuvres of the columns behind them with the smoke from their fire.

When III Corps fought at Auerstädt it appears to have almost uniformly adopted and executed its manoeuvres by battalions in column of divisions at a half-interval (*peloton* distance) or closed interval (*serré*). This was probably because it found itself attacked by large numbers of Prussian cavalry and was heavily engaged in fighting in villages. However, despite the reasons for the formation's use in the first line of battle, almost all of the manoeuvres behind the lines also appear to have been in the same formation, column of divisions. The 111th Demi-brigade, upon its arrival before the Prussians, was ordered to form square. It marched forward in this formation, but soon changed into an attack column and continued its march until it joined the 3rd Division. Then, because of heavy casualties caused by canister, it was obliged to change formation into line.

Morand's Division, III Corps, moved up to the battle in column of divisions at half-*peloton* interval. The 13th *Légère*, with two 4-pdrs, led the Division. It was ordered to march with one of its battalions in a closed column and the other deployed. When the Prussians lined up 8000 cavalry and executed their attack, Morand responded by forming his division, with the exception of the 13th *Légère*, into an echelon of battalion squares with artillery at the corners. When the cavalry attack was defeated, Morand reformed his infantry into a single line of battalions, in columns of divisions, and resumed his advance.

In the 1809 campaign the process continued. On 19 April, at the Battle of Teugen, Davout sent the skirmishers of the 3rd Line Regiment forward in a rush, as there was no time to form up. This movement permitted the 57th Line Regiment to form into attack column, which then moved up a ridge and deployed on the summit under enemy fire. This attack, in turn, permitted the 3rd Regiment to rally and to form into line on the right of the 57th. At this time the 57th, most of which remained in line, had folded its left back into square, because of a threat from some Austrian cavalry.

The Spanish experience

In Spain things were different. French generals fighting there appear to have been seized with a passion for the attack column. Despite that, examples of the mixed order can still be found. At Albuera, Girard formed his division into a mixed order with two battalions in line. In the centre of the formation were eight battalions in attack column, and on the outer flanks of the two deployed battalions there were two battalions in attack column at full intervals. At Fuentes de Oñoro a mixed order was formed with two battalions in line and three in column. At Almonacid another mixed order was formed, but the lines were too long and the columns were too deep. This had four battalions deployed in line with three closed columns, each formed of three battalions.

Though it was not always done it was general practice to cover attacking columns with a line of skirmishers. For example, on 23 July 1813, not far from Pampluna, Soult attacked the British with closed columns which he covered with skirmishers because of the heavy fire they faced, the objective being to screen the advancing columns and prevent the British from manoeuvring to meet the French attack. However, as the Napoleonic Wars had progressed it had proven unnecessary to provide such cover, since the simple forward rush and élan of the French columns would often prove sufficient to break Prussian, Russian and Austrian lines. In some instances this tactic succeeded without a single shot having to be fired.

However, the British were always covered by a chain of skirmishers, while the French were often not. This put the French at an initial disadvantage. As in Spain they generally advanced in columns of *pelotons*, and only rarely columns of divisions, when they pushed through the British skirmishers their frontage would be from 40 to 80 men, with a depth of from nine to 18 formed in three-rank companies. The rear ranks served only to support the morale impetus of the column and added nothing to its firepower. When faced by a British battalion in line, where every musket could be brought to bear and the column provided an unmissable target, the only hope the French had was that the élan of their attack would have the same effect on the British as it did on the Spanish, Austrians, Prussians and Russians. Somehow, however, the French never seemed to learn that the British simply refused to allow themselves to be shaken.

In cases where the French did precede their attacks with heavy skirmish lines, *eg* at Talavera and Busaco, they still did not succeed. And then there is Albuera, where

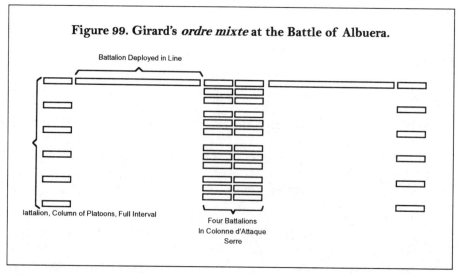

Figure 99. Girard's *ordre mixte* at the Battle of Albuera.

Battalion Deployed in Line

lattalion, Column of Platoons, Full Interval

Four Battalions
In Colonne d'Attaque
Serre

three British brigades pushed a French army twice their strength from the dominant position which Soult had chosen for it. This was done, not with bayonets or élan, but with the sheer force and accuracy of their musketry.

Squares

The tactical history of the Revolutionary and Napoleonic Wars is filled with multitudes of references to infantry forming squares. Their use is very straightforward, but there remain a few minor questions that need to be answered, starting with the manoeuvrability and speed at which a square could be marched.

In his description of an attack at Geisberg, Girardon states that the Chaumont Battalion moved onto an open plain in column by *pelotons*, until it was just below Geisberg. At that point it formed itself into square, because the terrain was open and the threat of cavalry significant. It was joined by the 2/33rd Line Regiment, which also formed in square on its left. Together the two battalions 'charged' the enemy with bayonets, deploying (into line) and moving across the plateau at the *pas de charge* and striking two Austrian battalions. The French continued the pursuit, probably in line as no reference is made to any formation change, until they arrived before the Geisberg Château, where they reformed their line. This means that the charge was probably made in square, not column or line. If such a manoeuvre could be made by a Revolutionary battalion, there is no reason why it could not have been done by any regular, line infantry formation during the entire period. The likelihood of it being done very frequently, however, is open to debate.

The Battle of Lützen in 1813 provides a good example of several uses of the square. It should be remembered that the French were, in the spring of 1813, desperately short of cavalry of their own and were under constant threat by that of the Allies. As Marmont advanced onto the battlefield towards Pergau he acted in accordance with Napoleon's instructions. He advanced his forces in nine columns on several lines, ready to form square instantly and advancing in echelon. The 20th Division crossed Starsiedel at the *pas accéléré*[15] with Bonnet's 21st Division *en echelon* to the left and Friederich's 22nd Division in the rear.

Marmont's corps was attacked by Prussian cavalry, which surprised his forces. The 37th *Légère* Regiment formed square, but broke and fled in terror. The 1st Marine Artillery Regiment, outfitted as an infantry regiment, formed in squares to the east of Starsiedel when it was charged by the Brandenburg Cuirassier Regiment. Though the Brandenburgers had caused the 37th *Légère* Regiment to break, the 1st Marines repelled them easily. No doubt the surprise of the attack had worn off and the 1st Marines had the time to set their square.

Marmont withdrew Compan's 20th Division to the edge of Starsiedel and formed his forces into several squares, so that any new attack would not throw them into the same disorder that had struck the 37th *Légère* Regiment. These squares were placed so close to each other that they could not fire unless the enemy cavalry actually passed between them.

Also at Lützen we have an instance of how difficult terrain was handled by units marching in square. Around 3:00 pm, IV Corps was advancing slowly towards Pobles and the crossing of the Grünabach. Facing it was Winzingerode, who occupied the

---

[15] The *pas accéléré* was a march rate of 250 paces per minute and was, in essence, a cadenced run.

east bank of the Grünabach stream. Though faced with enemy artillery the French were advancing in square because of the cavalry threat. Under the cover of French guns, Morand's 12th Division broke into columns, crossed the stream, and reformed itself into squares to resume its advance.

There is an instance of a Confederation of the Rhine formation using squares within IV Corps which is also enlightening and should be considered when reviewing the use of squares. This involved two Hessian regiments moving against Klein-Görschen, of which the Hessian *Leib-Garde* Regiment formed into square. The Regiment *du Corps* moved in the second line to the left and the Fusiliers moved on the extreme left, formed in column and covering the whole advance. The force was covered by a screen of Hessian skirmishers and had redoubled artillery fire in support. The attack advanced at the *Sturmschritt* (storming pace) to seize the bridge to Klein-Görschen. Here we have infantry both attacking and advancing at the *Sturmschritt*, which was the Hessian equivalent of the *pas de charge*. Therefore the square was obviously not slower than any other formation, despite modern thoughts on that point.

In another discussion Colin presents column tactics which Schauenbourg trained his division to use. At least twice, in major exercises, Schauenbourg had his division convert from a line of battalions into a massive square, these formations bearing very strong similarities to Macdonald's Wagram column. However, the intended use of these squares is not clear. Schauenbourg's notes do not indicate if the formation was adopted as a defence against cavalry or for other, unnamed purposes.

In one example of a massive square formed by battalions in lieu of companies, the line folded back into a square with each battalion marching backwards to the required depth, performing a perpendicular turn towards the centre and marching to its final position. The front of the square was formed by battalions that retained their initial position. The rear was formed by the flank battalions marching directly to the rear, halting at the prescribed distance, turning inwards, and marching in a line to their final position. This is very much like the ploying of a line into an attack column.

In a second manoeuvre Schauenbourg used a system of folding the line on the centre much like the Prussians used to form square from line under the directions of the 1788 Regulation. The line folded on the centre battalions, much as in the previous example. However, the French battalions marched independently of one another, in

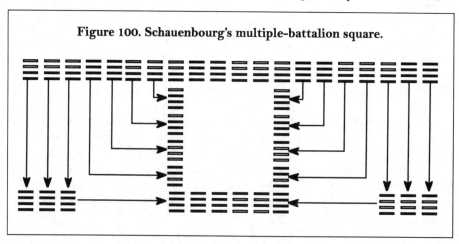

Figure 100. Schauenbourg's multiple-battalion square.

great sweeping movements towards their final position. This type of manoeuvre may seem very theoretical until one realises that it is essentially the formation that Macdonald employed at the Battle of Wagram. There are also other examples of this type of formation being used, though Macdonald's is the most famous.

Chapter 7

Cavalry Tactics and Quality During the Revolutionary and Napoleonic Wars

In order to understand the tactical operations of cavalry during the period between 1792 and 1815 it is necessary to begin with their organisation, on the grounds that though tactics may determine organisation, more often organisation determines tactics.

There are a number of characteristics that need to be examined, starting with the ratio of men to officers and non-commissioned officers. This is the 'leadership ratio'.

	Officers	NCOs	Troopers	Leader-ship ratio	No of squadrons
Table 39. Comparison of national leadership ratios.					
Hesse-Kassel (1796–1806)					
Dragoons	5	11	122	7.625	3
Cuirassiers	5	11	122	7.625	3
Hussars	5	13	132	7.333	4
Saxony (1810–15)					
All	11	12	164	7.130	4
Prussia (1787–1808)					
Cuirassiers	7	15	144	6.545	4
Dragoons	7	15	144	6.545	4
Hussars	5	15	144	6.545	4
Prussia (1812–15)					
Cuirassiers	6	12	101	5.600	4
Dragoons	6	12	101	5.600	4
Hussars	6	12	101	5.600	4
France (1799–1803)					
Heavys	8	16	114	4.750	3
Dragoons	8	28	192	5.333	4
Hussars	8	28	192	5.333	4
Chasseurs	8	28	192	5.333	4
France (1803–15)					
Cuirassiers (1803–6)	8	16	150	6.250	4
Cuirassiers (1806–12)	8	16	166	4.611	4

continued

Table 39 continued

Cuirassiers (1812–15)	8	16	204	5.777	4
Dragoons (1803–11)	8	28	184	5.111	4
Dragoons (1811–15)	8	28	242	6.722	4
Lancers	8	28	220	6.111	4
Hussars	8	28	174	4.833	4
Chasseurs	8	28	174	4.833	4
Grand Duchy of Warsaw (1807–13)					
All	8	28	162	4.500	4
Britain					
Dragoon Guards	8	20	172	6.143	4
Light Dragoons	8	20	172	6.143	4
Russia (1802–12)					
Cuirassiers	3	14	132	7.765	5
Dragoons	3	14	150	8.824	5
Hussars	3	12	132	8.800	10
Russia (1812–15)					
Cuirassiers	3	14	132	7.765	5
Dragoons	4	14	140	7.778	5
Hussars	7	13	132	6.600	10
Uhlans	7	12	132	6.974	10
Bavaria (1803–15)					
All	4	9	134	10.31	4
Baden (1812)					
Hussars	8	26	164	4.824	6
Hesse-Darmstadt (1812)					
All	3	11	77	5.500	4
Kingdom of Northern Italy (1812)					
All	8	16	150	6.250	4
Naples (1812)					
All	6	28	154	4.529	4
Westphalia (1807–14)					
Cuirassiers	8	16	136	5.667	4
Chevaulégers	8	28	122	3.389	4
Hussars	8	28	122	3.389	4
Württemberg					
Kreis-Dragoons (1793)	6	10	124	7.750	4
Jäger zu Pferd (1805)	4	8	90	7.500	3
Chevauxlegers (1806)	3	9	113	9.410	4
Chevauxlegers (1807)	4	13	124	7.290	4
Chevauxlegers (1809)	4	11	111	7.920	4
Chevauxlegers (1813)	5	14	100	5.260	4
Austria (1807–15)					
Cuirassiers	6	12	140	7.778	6
Dragoons	6	12	140	7.778	6
Hussars	6	12	150	8.333	8
Uhlans	6	12	150	8.333	8

Table 40. Leadership ratios by nation.

Leadership ratio

Westphalian (1807–14)	Chevaulégers	3.389
Westphalian (1807–14)	Hussars	3.389
Grand Duchy of Warsaw	All	4.500
Naples (1812)	All	4.529
France (1806–12)	Cuirassiers	4.611
France (1799–1803)	Heavy	4.750
France (1803–15)	Hussars	4.833
France (1803–15)	Chasseurs	4.833
Baden (1812)	Hussars	4.824
Hesse-Darmstadt (1812)	All	5.500
France (1803–11)	Dragoons	5.111
Württemberg (1813)	Chevauxlegers	5.260
France (1799–1803)	Dragoons	5.333
France (1799–1803)	Hussar	5.333
France (1799–1803)	Chasseurs	5.333
Prussia (1812–15)	Cuirassiers	5.600
Prussia (1812–15)	Dragoons	5.600
Prussia (1812–15)	Hussars	5.600
Westphalia (1807–14)	Cuirassiers	5.667
France (1812–15)	Cuirassiers	5.777
France (1811–15)	Lancers	6.111
Britain	Dragoon Guards	6.143
Britain	Light Dragoons	6.143
Northern Italy (1812)	All	6.250
France (1803–6)	Cuirassiers	6.250
Prussia (1787–1808)	Hussars	6.545
Prussia (1787–1808)	Cuirassiers	6.545
Prussia (1787–1808)	Dragoons	6.545
Russia (1812–15)	Hussars	6.600
France (1811–15)	Dragoons	6.722
Russia (1812–15)	Uhlans	6.974
Saxony (1810–15)	All	7.130
Württemberg (1807)	Chevauxlegers	7.290
Hesse-Kassel	Hussars	7.333
Württemberg (1805)	Jäger zu Pferd	7.500
Hesse-Kassel	Dragoons	7.625
Hesse-Kassel	Cuirassiers	7.625
Württemberg (1793)	Kreis-Dragoons	7.750
Russia (1812–15)	Cuirassiers	7.765
Russia (1802–12)	Cuirassiers	7.765
Russia (1812–15)	Dragoons	7.778
Austria (1808–15)	Cuirassiers	7.778

continued

Table 40 continued		
Austria (1808–15)	Dragoons	7.778
Württemberg (1809)	Chevauxlegers	7.920
Württemberg (1812)	Chevauxlegers	8.070
Russia (1802–12)	Dragoons	8.824
Russia (1802–12)	Hussars	8.800
Austria (1808–15)	Hussars	8.333
Austria (1808–15)	Uhlans	8.333
Württemberg (1806)	Chevauxlegers	9.410
Bavaria (1803–15)	All	10.31

Note that the dates denote the period in which the organisation shown was effective. By contrast, the nationalities shown with the date of – for example – '(1812)' indicate solely that the cavalry of the country involved had the organisation as given during that particular year.

One can make a number of reasonably accurate assumptions about the quality of any given cavalry unit by an examination of the leadership ratios shown in Table 39. It is reasonable to assume that if there are more officers and non-commissioned officers per trooper they should be able to provide superior control over the unit. However, it should not be assumed that the leadership ratio alone is sufficient to indicate which regiment is the best. It is purely an indicator of what should be the case. Some nations were noted for their horsemanship while others were noted for their indiscipline. Either national characteristic could offset any leadership ratio indications.

Another variable that should be recognised is that this analysis looks solely at theoretical strengths. In the field men would be lost and these numbers would change. However, historical evidence shows that officers and non-commissioned officers remain with the colours longer and tend to have a higher survival rate than troopers. This suggests that campaign casualties would improve the leadership ratio rather than reduce it.

Taking Table 39 and reorganising it according to the leadership ratios we arrive at the information in Table 40.

Using this analysis the Westphalian light cavalry should have been the best in Napoleonic Europe. However, as mentioned earlier, national characteristics can intervene. The one historical fact that would support a high rating is that Westphalia was one of the horse-breeding areas of Germany, and would consequently have had a tradition of horsemanship. Unfortunately, its military activities are not well enough recorded for this high rating to be supported.

The second best rating belongs to the Poles. This is not surprising. The Poles lived on the edge of the steppes and had a tradition of horsemanship. Their army had 16 cavalry regiments and 12 infantry regiments, which shows a decided pre-disposition towards cavalry.

One would then logically presume that the Russians, living in the steppes, would have had a similar tradition and have a higher leadership ratio. This, as we know, was not true. The average Russian peasant did not ride a horse until he was drafted into a cavalry regiment. This could well explain their low ranking on the list.

The position of the Saxons is quite interesting inasmuch as they had a tremendous reputation as horsemen. This is attributed to the quality and spirit of their horses, as well as the skill of their horsemen. Despite their reputation, their placement in this listing is unusual and does not match their reputation.

The worst leadership ratio belongs to Bavaria. This is unsurprising when one remembers that Bavaria is mountainous, and therefore not a place where one would expect to find good horsemen. However, the same excuse cannot be offered for Württemberg, which brings up the rear with Bavaria, since, by contrast, it is not particularly mountainous.

The other interesting placements are those of France. They would appear to be quite near the head of the list and certainly ahead of their principal rivals. More interesting is the relationship the listing demonstrates between the French and the British. The latter were known as horsemen and famed for the quality of their horses. They were well trained and highly professional, which initially makes this relationship unusual. However, historical evidence of French and British cavalry engagements shows that it is correct.

There is a famous quotation by Wellington which supports this relationship: 'I considered one of our squadrons a match for two French, yet I did not care to see four British opposed to four French, and still more so as the numbers increased'. Wellington went on to say: 'They [the British] could gallop, but could not preserve their order.' Their inability to preserve order was no doubt directly related to their command and control structure.

The Prussians are in the middle of the leadership ratio chart. It is interesting to note that they improved after the Jena-Auerstädt fiasco. However, despite this improvement there are no indications that they were anything unusual when it came to being horsemen.

It is surprising to see where the Austrians stand in this list, principally because their Hungarian hussars had a reputation of being excellent horsemen. This, however, may well be based on individual horsemanship rather than on their skill as organised cavalry. There is significant documentation confirming that the French regularly defeated them, but a standing at the bottom of the list would not, initially, appear to be justified.

One country which stands high in this list, but should not be there, is Naples. Its structure might justify such a rating, but historically the Neapolitans did not enjoy a reputation for martial quality. Their army was rife with secret societies which undermined the authority of their officers, and they had a history of desertion. Indeed, when the Neapolitan forces in Spain deserted they had a nasty habit of turning to brigandage. Their historical reputation is so bad that they should really be placed on the bottom of the list.

Table 40 needs to be refined and simplified to permit easier understanding of what it shows. Table 41 condenses it using an averaging technique.

As can be seen, Westphalia and the Grand Duchy of Warsaw are still on top of the list and Württemberg and Bavaria are still on the bottom.

If one looks at the actual formation of the squadrons further support for this ranking can be found. Figures 101–103 provide examples of the actual placement of the officers, non-commissioned officers and troopers. Figure 101 shows the French systems used between 1799 and 1815. The principal features of this, and the other squad-

Table 41. Simplification of Table 40 using averaging technique.	
Country	*Average leadership ratio*
Westphalia	4.148
Poland	4.500
Naples	4.529
Baden	4.824
France	5.416
Darmstadt	5.500
Britain	6.143
Northern Italy	6.250
Prussia	6.473
Saxony	7.130
Hesse-Kassel	7.528
Russia	7.787
Austria	8.050
Württemberg	8.070
Bavaria	10.310

rons shown in Figures 102 and 103, are: 1) the forward leadership; 2) the body of the squadron; and 3) the file closers' rank.

In the French system the command element in front is fully developed – each of the four manoeuvring elements has an officer leading it and controlling its front. The presence of officers in front of the manoeuvring elements ensured that it will go in the precise direction desired. It also ensured that the troopers could not advance too far forward and thereby lose their alignment. In the body of the squadron each of the four manoeuvring elements has a non-commissioned officer on both of its flanks. This provided lateral control, preventing the files from becoming too 'loose', as well as providing guides for the manoeuvring elements to align themselves on laterally. The file closers' rank closed the rear of the squadron. Its functions were to push the men forward and ensure that they 'closed up' their ranks, and to prevent men from stopping or deserting to the rear when faced by the enemy.

The French system provided a large degree of control on every flank and face of the squadron, thereby ensuring that it should behave as desired in battle and that, once it had completed a charge, it should rally more quickly.

Figure 102 shows the cavalry formations of various French client states, whish either raised them in accordance with the French model or were greatly influenced by it. An examination shows that their structures are fundamentally identical to those of the French.

Figure 103 shows the formations of five other nations, each of which had a different system. They all have the same three elements: 1) forward leadership; 2) the body of the squadron; and 3) the file closers' rank, to a greater or lesser degree.

The Hesse-Kassel system is related to the older structures used during the Seven Years War. It has a forward leadership equivalent to that of the French. It also has non-commissioned officers on the flanks of the principal manoeuvring elements, the

Figure 101. French cavalry squadron formations.

a) Dragoon, chasseur and hussar regiment, 1799.

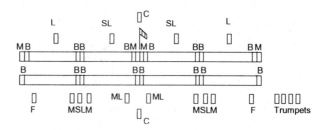

b) Heavy cavalry squadron, 1799.

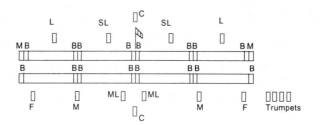

c) Cavalry squadron, 1812.

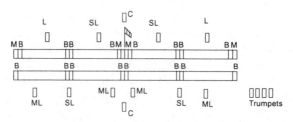

C = Captain	M = *Maréchal des logis*	L = Lieutenant
F = *Brigadier Fourier*	SL = *Sous-lieutenant*	B = *Brigadier*
	ML = *Maréchal des logis chef*	

Figure 102. French allied cavalry squadron formations.

a) Westphalian light cavalry squadron.

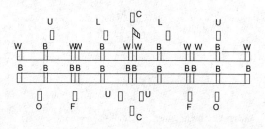

b) Westphalian cuirassier squadron.

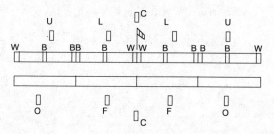

C = Captain	W = *Wachtmeister*	L = *Leutnant*
B = *Brigadier*	U = *Unterleutnant*	F = *Fourier*
	O = *Oberwachtmeister*	

c) Grand Duchy of Warsaw cavalry squadron.

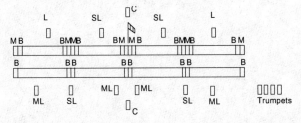

C = Captain	M = *Maréchal des logis*	L = Lieutenant
F = *Brigadier fourier*	SL = *Sous-lieutenant*	B = *Brigadier*
	ML = *Maréchal des logis chef*	

continued

Figure 102 continued

d) Saxon cavalry squadron.

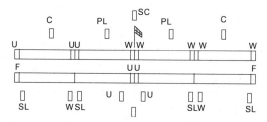

SC = Squadron commander   W = *Wachmeister*   C = Captain
U = *Unteroffizier*   PL - *Premierleutnant*   F = *Fourier*
         SL = *Sekondeleutnant*

Figure 103. Allied cavalry squadrons.

a) Hesse-Kassel cavalry squadron, 1796.

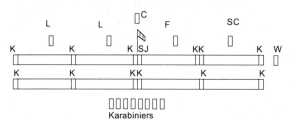

Karabiniers

C = Captain   F = *Fahnrich*   SJ = *Standartjunker*
SC = *Stabcapitan*   W = *Wachtmeister*   K = *Korporal*
       L = *Leutnant*

b) Prussian cavalry squadron, 1812.

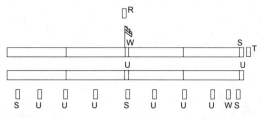

R = *Rittmeister*   W = *Wachtmeister*   P = *Premierleutnant*
U = *Unteroffizier*   S = *Sekondleutnant*   T = Trumpeter

continued

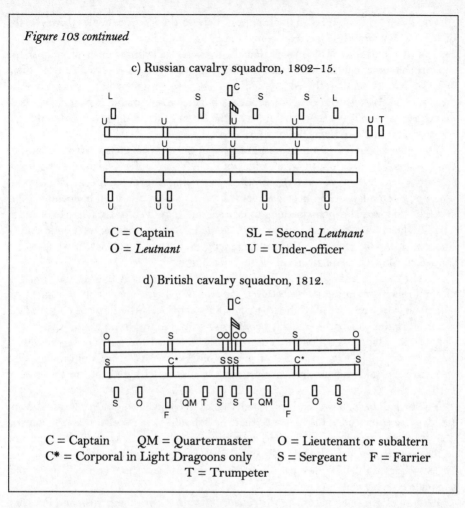

Figure 103 *continued*

c) Russian cavalry squadron, 1802–15.

C = Captain   SL = Second *Leutnant*
O = *Leutnant*   U = Under-officer

d) British cavalry squadron, 1812.

C = Captain   QM = Quartermaster   O = Lieutenant or subaltern
C* = Corporal in Light Dragoons only   S = Sergeant   F = Farrier
T = Trumpeter

Züge. However, it does not have a developed file closers' rank – there are *Karabiniers* there, but the Hessian 1796 Regulation does not specify their precise positioning, nor does it indicate that they served as file closers. Indeed, the designation of *Karabinier* indicates that they were skirmishers equipped with a carbine and subject to being detached from the squadron for independent duty. The result of this would most likely be that a Hessian squadron would be well controlled in every direction except to the rear.

The Russian system is very similar to the French. The forward leadership should, therefore, provide an equal degree of forward control. The distribution of non-commissioned officers in the body of the squadron is also similar in general arrangement to that of the French, but there are not as many. The few that are there are on the ends of the manoeuvring elements, but there are several ranks these whose flanks do not have one. It is therefore reasonable to assume that the Russians could not control the 'lateral' alignment of their squadrons as well as the French could. The file closers' rank has solely non-commissioned officers, and not as many as in the French system. The rear control cannot, therefore, have been as good.

The Prussian system is yet another variation on the French theme. However, the officers, except for the squadron commander, are integrated directly into the front rank of the squadron. This means that the forward leadership consisted of just the squadron commander. In this situation he has too many thing to do, to do any of them well. He has to evaluate the enemy and move the entire squadron in an appropriate direction; he also has to provide directional guidance to the manoeuvring elements of his squadron as well as ensure that none of the troopers draw ahead of the front rank. He must have had problems performing all of these tasks.

The officers and non-commissioned officers in the body of the squadron are rather thinly spread. In addition, there are none on the left flanks of the manoeuvring units, so that in action there was the risk of these becoming disordered; in the French system a non-commissioned officer was posted there to keep this from happening. This suggests that lateral control is going to be poor and that the files are likely to open up. The file closers' rank is well manned and should be able to perform its function more than satisfactorily. However, this arrangement shows a philosophical predisposition towards pushing the squadron rather than leading it.

The British system is quite similar to the Prussian, but has evolved in the direction of the French, providing a link between the two. The British have only the squadron commander in front. As with the Prussians, this provided little forward control over the front rank and left the squadron commander attempting to do too much by himself. The resultant loss of forward control was a historically frequent occurrence with British cavalry. The French system of placing officers ahead of the front rank allowed them to keep the troopers from losing their heads and charging off in the heat of battle.

The British have, however, integrated 60% of the squadron officers into the front rank of the squadron. This indicates that they should have excellent lateral control. The manoeuvring elements should be rigidly controlled, and wheels, etc, should be well executed. The British system, like the French, boxes the troopers in laterally and keeps the files tight. The file closers' rank is quite dense and should provide more than adequate rear control.

Because of the open nature of the squadron front in both the British and Prussian systems it is highly probable that not only would stopping a charge be difficult for both nations, but rallying a squadron after a charge would also be comparatively more difficult than a country employing the French or modified French system.

The Austrian system went one step further than than the British, eliminating all officers from the front of the squadron. This would have made forward control very difficult, at best. Lateral control, however, is stronger than that of any other nation, placing every 14 troopers between two NCOs whose attention is totally devoted to controlling those troopers. Rear control is fundamentally the same as that used by most other nations.

Table 42 provides a numerical summarisation of several of these countries. The figures shown for forward, rear and lateral control are based on the specific units' formations for the years indicated. The forward control ratio is generated by taking the number of officers, etc, in front of the squadron and dividing it into the number of troopers in the squadron. The rear control ratio is generated in the same way, and the lateral control ratio is simply the number of officers, etc, positioned within or on the flanks of the body of the squadron, divided into the number of men in the squadron.

Table 42. Numerical summarisation of cavalry quality.

Country	Year	Unit type	Leader-ship Ratio	Forward Control Ratio	Rear Control Ratio	Lateral Control Ratio
Westphalia	1807–14	Chevaulégers	3.389	24.40	17.43	12.20
Westphalia	1807–14	Hussars	3.389	24.40	17.43	12.20
Poland	1807–13	All	4.500	32.40	23.14	6.75
France	1806–12	Cuirassiers	4.611	33.20	23.71	16.60
France	1799–1803	Heavy	4.750	22.80	16.29	11.40
France	1803–15	Hussars	4.833	34.80	24.86	7.25
France	1803–15	Chasseurs	4.833	34.80	24.86	7.25
France	1803–11	Dragoons	5.111	36.80	26.29	7.67
France	1799–1803	Dragoons	5.333	38.40	17.45	8.00
France	1799–1803	Hussars	5.333	38.40	17.45	8.00
France	1799–1803	Chasseurs	5.333	38.40	17.45	8.00
Prussia	1812–15	Cuirassiers	5.600	101.00	9.18	20.20
Prussia	1812–15	Dragoons	5.600	101.00	9.18	20.20
Prussia	1812–15	Hussars	5.600	101.00	9.18	20.20
Prussia	1812–15	Uhlans	5.600	101.00	9.18	20.20
Westphalia	1807–14	Cuirassiers	5.667	27.20	27.2	11.33
France	1812–15	Cuirassiers	5.777	40.80	29.14	20.40
France	1811–15	Lancers	6.111	44.00	31.43	9.17
Britain	1800–15	Dragoon Guards	6.143	172.00	15.64	12.29
Britain	1800–15	Light Dragoons	6.143	172.00	15.64	12.29
France	1803–6	Cuirassiers	6.250	30.00	21.43	15.00
Prussia	1887–8	Hussars	6.545	144.00	28.80	14.40
Prussia	1887–8	Cuirassiers	6.545	144.00	28.80	12.00
Prussia	1887–8	Dragoons	6.545	144.00	28.80	12.00
Russia	1812–15	Hussars	6.600	18.86	16.65	26.40
France	1811–15	Dragoons	6.722	48.4	34.57	10.08
Saxony	1810–15	All	7.130	27.33	27.33	12.62
Hesse-Kassel	1796–1808	Hussars	7.333	26.4	–	10.15
Hesse-Kassel	1796–1808	Cuirassiers	7.625	24.4	–	11.09
Hesse-Kassel	1796–1808	Dragoons	7.625	24.4	–	11.09
Russia	1812–15	Cuirassiers	7.765	44.00	16.50	22.00
Russia	1802–12	Cuirassiers	7.765	44.00	16.50	22.00
Russia	1812–15	Dragoons	7.778	35.00	17.50	23.33
Austria	1808–15	Cuirassiers	7.778	–	22.40	7.00
Austria	1808–15	Dragoons	7.778	–	22.40	7.00
Russia	1802–12	Dragoons	8.824	50.00	18.75	25.00
Russia	1802–12	Hussars	8.800	44.00	16.50	33.00
Austria	1808–15	Hussars	8.333	–	25.60	8.00
Austria	1808–15	Uhlans	8.333	–	2.560	8.00

Though seemingly chaotic, this chart provides a high degree of correlation with the data found in the initial leadership ratio study. Table 43 compares the rankings in Table 42 with those found in Table 41. As can been seen, there is a distinct similarity between the findings regarding overall leadership and the figures developed in the forward, rear and lateral control analysis. Only the British and Prussians have changed places. All of the other nations remain in the same sequence.

Based on this numerical analysis it is reasonable to assume that the relationships shown in Table 42 equate closely to the comparative combat value of each nation's cavalry. However, this is an analysis based on squadron and regimental capabilities, not on the capabilities of the individual trooper.

It should also be recognised that this analysis is purely theoretical. It is generally accepted that, of the major armies, the French cavalry was the best in Europe. It was destroyed by the Russian campaign and winter, not action with the enemy. It was also destroyed by the actions of some generals, notably Murat, who tended to charge it around, chasing after everything that came into his field of vision, and did not give it time to recover from the privations of the 1812 campaign. By December 1812 most of the French cavalry had ceased to exist and the lack of a strong cavalry arm caused the French to lose the 1813 and 1814 campaigns. What cavalry the French did field in 1813 consisted of a small quantity of veteran cavalry drawn from Spain, a small number of remounted survivors of the 1812 campaign, and many new recruits.

In the historical sense, prior to 1813 the French cavalry was victorious over everyone it encountered on a tactical level above the regiment. There are individual instances of the French being beaten by other cavalry, but in most of the major cavalry engagements, French organisation and control seems to have given their cavalry victory. The French cavalry triumphed over the Russian cavalry at Friedland, Eylau and Borodino. The Battle of Borodino was notable for its massive cavalry engagement on the French left. The Austrian cavalry was regularly defeated by the French in 1805 and 1809. In 1806 the Prussian cavalry was not engaged by the French on a large scale or in many pure cavalry clashes. It was, however, totally incapable of holding back the French pursuit after Jena-Auerstädt.

Only the British seem to have been able to beat the French cavalry in individual regimental engagements, but they regularly threw away their victories by charging

Table 43. Summations of Tables 41 and 42.

Summation Table 42	*Summation Table 41*
Westphalia	Westphalia
Poland	Poland
France	France
Prussia	Britain
Britain	Prussia
Saxony	Saxony
Hesse-Kassel	Hesse-Kassel
Russia	Russia
Austria	Austria

off like a band of fox-hunters. Once they broke into pursuit the more organised French regularly used their reserves to slaughter them. This occurred most notably at Waterloo, when the French cavalry destroyed the blown Union Brigade.

The cavalry of Hesse-Kassel had all but vanished before 1800, while that of Westphalia was so small in number as to be hard to evaluate. There was a division of Westphalian, Polish and Saxon cuirassiers at Borodino. It was this formation which eventually overran the Great Redoubt. They were, no doubt, magnificently competent horsemen. Unfortunately the engagements around the Great Redoubt were so confused that the only statement that can be made regarding the quality of this division is that it defeated the Russian cavalry it encountered there.

There are other accounts of the Russians engaging Poles, at Mir and other smaller skirmishes. These battles generally resulted in a stand-off. Numbers were seldom equal and the elements of surprise and ambush featured heavily in them. However, at the Battle of Ostrovno a regiment of Polish lancers overthrew the opposing Russian cavalry in a stand-up engagement. The Poles were probably superior horsemen to the Russians, but documentation is scarce. Their potential superiority to the British cannot be confirmed or denied, since there appear to have been no engagements between British and Polish cavalry.

During the 1809 campaign the Poles fought with the Austrians, but their army was newly formed and it would be unreasonable to compare the exploits of green troops with those of the veteran Austrian cavalry. In addition, the Hungarian cavalry found in the Austrian army had a long history of outstanding horsemanship. After 1813 the surviving Polish cavalry would have been mostly veterans and could not have rebuilt its forces very far with new recruits, as most of the Grand Duchy of Warsaw was overrun by the advancing Russians. Its performance in the 1813 campaign was excellent, engaging and defeating Austrian cuirassiers in one instance during the Battle of Leipzig.

The Saxons had a history and reputation of being excellent horsemen. They fought well during the 1806 campaign, but were stripped of their horses by the victorious French army to mount several dismounted French cavalry regiments. After the war these horses were returned. There are two possible reasons given. The first is the political implications of restoring property to a nation which was then a new French ally. The second reason often given is that the horses were too spirited for the French to control. Either way the return of its horses allowed the excellence of the Saxon cavalry to continue. Only in 1813 did its quality decline.

The Westphalians never engaged the British and were totally wiped out in 1812, after which the old regiments were fleshed out with new recruits. In late 1813 all of them, save one, deserted to the Allied side. With the exception of the Guard Chevaulegers, the Westphalian cavalry were not very high quality troops. Much the same can be said of the cavalry of Bavaria; unlike the Westphalians, they changed sides at the command of their sovereigns. On the other hand, the cavalry of Hesse-Darmstadt, Württemberg, and Baden performed as well as any other cavalry in the field.

A summation of the probable relative rating of cavalries of Europe during this period is shown in Table 44. Each tier of cavalry is essentially of equal quality.

Though the Swedish, Portuguese, and Spanish cavalry have not been discussed before now it is appropriate to mention them briefly. Swedish horses were not well founded, nor were they suitable for cavalry. The Swedes had no notable history of cavalry after

Table 44. Relative cavalry ratings.			
First tier cavalry	*Second tier cavalry*	*Third tier cavalry*	*Fourth tier cavalry*
Poland	Britain	Austria	Sweden
Saxony	Prussia	Westphalia	Spain
Baden	Russia	Württemberg	Portugal
France	Northern Italy	Bavaria	Naples
Hesse-Darmstadt		Hesse-Kassel	

the time of Gustavus Adolphus and were, according to British sources of the Napoleonic period, very poor horsemen. The Spanish and Portuguese have a mixed military reputation, the Spanish being the worst. Both nations suffered from few and poor horses. Neither nation's cavalry performed in any significant manner during the period and the general military history of these countries was so poor that it was generally acknowledged that only Naples had a worse army.

Theoretical tactical employment

There were three principal types of cavalry during this period – heavy, dragoons, and light. These were distinct forces with decidedly different functions. Napoleon wrote to the Minister of War on 30 *Frimaire*, Year XII: 'I want you to consider the cuirassiers, the dragoons, and the hussars as forming three different arms and that you never propose to me that the officers of one corps be transferred to the other.'

The function of the heavy cavalry, sometimes more appropriately called 'battle cavalry', was to smash enemy formations with a concentrated charge. It was the reserve force, to be used at the decisive moment. After dispersing the enemy cavalry, the heavy cavalry was to turn and attack the flank of the enemy infantry. Its formation, organisation and tactics were developed with these goals in mind.

The light cavalry too was quite often employed as 'battle cavalry' and it could stand in line of battle, but its principal task was reconnaissance and pursuit of a beaten enemy. It was to serve in the army's advance guard, its rear guard, and on the wings to protect it from ambush. It was intended to be broken into smaller units for use as pickets and vedettes in conjunction with its reconnaissance role. This accounts for the higher number of sergeants and corporals in the French light cavalry than are found in their heavy counterpart. In other nations this numerical variance may not always be apparent, but the function of the light cavalry was the same.

Current parlance has often distorted where the dragoons fit into this scheme. One often hears the term 'medium' cavalry used with regard to dragoons, but no period literature reviewed by the author to date ever used that term. It is interesting to note that the French did transfer the dragoons to the light cavalry category during the Revolutionary Wars to make up for a shortage of this arm. This designation appears to have faded and the dragoons assumed a somewhat 'dual-purpose' role, as well as taking on a flavour entirely their own. However, they were not 'medium' cavalry. Their function was viewed by Napoleon as being something between that of the heavy and the light cavalry. It could and did act to supplement the operations of these more specialised types, providing, for instance, heavy support for the light cavalry which screened the main army.

Since the origin of dragoons was as mounted infantry they could also be used in that capacity. That this mounted infantry tradition had begun to fade prior to the French Revolution, however, is testified by the uniforms dragoons wore during this period. These were very ill suited to infantry operations. However, their equipment did not significantly change. The dragoons of most countries appear to have continued to carry a bayonet throughout the period 1792–1815. There were, of course, exceptions. In 1812 the Russians stripped all their cavalry of muskets and bayonets for re-issue to their infantry. However, it was a shortage of infantry weapons, not a change of tactical philosophy, that led to this. The only real organisational change was the disappearance of drummers, who are to be found in the organisational listings of some dragoon units until as late as 1806. The French continued to maintain a few dragoons per regiment who were designated as sappers until long after 1815.

The French often used their dragoons in the historical foot role. They were extensively trained in foot tactics, and during the 1805/6 campaigns regiments of foot dragoons were formed. (Regiments of foot hussars had also appeared during the Revolution, but these resulted from a lack of horses, and as soon as horses were found the foot hussars disappeared). During the Spanish campaign French dragoons frequently served on foot, be it in fighting guerrillas or the British. The most notable example was during the British evacuation of Corunna. The town and surrounding terrain was unsuitable for cavalry tactics, so the dragoons dismounted and went in on foot. The regulations of all nations during this period devoted some time, if not a great deal, to foot manoeuvres.

The structure of the French dragoon regiments continued to reflect aspects of both the light cavalry and the cuirassiers. Review Table 45, and compare the numbers of officers and non-commissioned officers for the dragoons in every period shown to those of the light cavalry. The number of dragoon officers is identical to that of the cuirassiers, but the number of non-commissioned officers falls between that of the two other types of cavalry.

No doubt the dragoons retained a higher number of non-commissioned officers for the purposes of patrols, pickets and vedettes. This betrays, to a degree, their intended usage. However, when the dragoons were employed at brigade and division levels they were more often found operating with the cuirassiers as heavy cavalry. Indeed, after 1804 pure dragoon divisions were always referred to as 'heavy cavalry divisions'. They were employed as battle cavalry during most engagements.

Table 45. French squadron strengths 1805.

	Light cavalry	*Dragoons*	*Cuirassiers*
Officers	8	6	6
NCOs	28	22	16
Troopers	192	144	148
Trumpeters	4	2	2
Total	232	176	172

After 1800, whenever the French cavalry was brigaded the cuirassiers and dragoons were invariably put into homogeneous brigades. Occasionally a light regiment might be added to one brigade of a 'heavy' cavalry division, to provide it with some reconnaissance capability, but this was an administrative assignment more than one for battlefield operations. Prior to 1800 the French cavalry had not always been organised into homogeneous brigades, but were put together in formations which had a little bit of everything. The cavalry was not always concentrated by type. It would appear that around 1800 someone had realised the value of a concentrated heavy cavalry formation and it was thereafter adopted by the French.

The French light cavalry appears to have been mixed almost with impunity. Hussars, lancers and chasseurs seem to have been considered functionally identical.

After 1807 the Russians appear to have adopted the same system as the French and formed homogeneous heavy cavalry brigades, divisions and corps. Before that they had been organised in mixed brigades of all cavalry types. By 1813 the Russians had also organised their light cavalry into hussar, chasseur, and uhlan divisions. The Austrians too followed the French lead, and changed from mixed to pure heavy and light brigades sometime before 1805.

The Prussian army after 1808 was too small to form the massive cavalry corps of the French, Russians, and Austrians. They did form their four cuirassier regiments into two brigades which were assigned to the Allied Guard Corps in 1813/14, but prior to Jena-Auerstädt their practice was to form integrated brigades and divisions with a heterogeneous mixture of cavalry types.

The British did not organise major forces of cavalry in which brigading became an issue until late in the Spanish campaign. At that time they appear to have always organised light dragoons into light dragoon brigades and their heavier counterparts into heavy brigades.

Attack formations

Once the target was selected, the regimental or squadron commander would decide what formation was appropriate. He would study the terrain to be crossed, and evaluate any other threatening enemy units that might be in the area. The unit commanding officer had a series of possible attack formations, which are presented in Figure 104.

The line of battle

The principal battle formation used by cavalry was the line. This allowed the regiment to extend to its full length and make the most efficient use of every lance or sabre. It also gave the regiment the potential to outflank a smaller enemy regiment by the sheer width of its frontage.

Its principal characteristic was that in a charge the entire regiment impacted at, to all intents and purposes, the same time. The shock of this massive impact would, theoretically, shatter the enemy formation. A cavalry line is illustrated in Figure 104a. It was universally used by every nation.

The British and others used a system of two lines. The first was the main battle line, and the second line was a reserve. It is best described by a passage from the British 1799 Regulation:

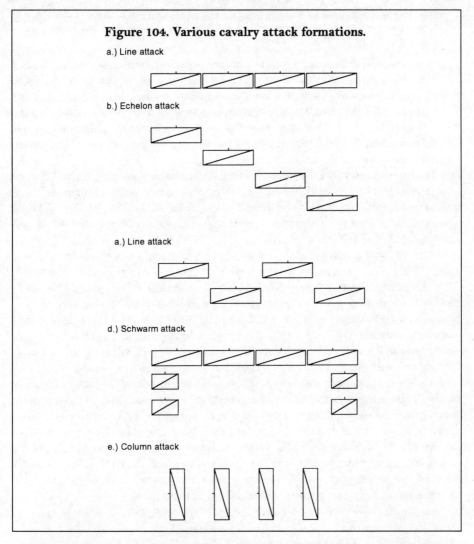

Figure 104. Various cavalry attack formations.

a.) Line attack

b.) Echelon attack

a.) Line attack

d.) Schwarm attack

e.) Column attack

There may be situations where a small body of cavalry, such as two or three squadrons, is to attack another nearly similar body, and can depend on its superiority of movement and agility. – For this purpose it may divide into small bodies of 14 or 16 files each, with intervals equal to their front, and the second line, or reserves, must cover those intervals at 150 paces to the rear. – This enables it to turn the enemy's flank rapidly, by having a more extended front, and several light and movable bodies. – If there are three squadrons, the first line may be formed of six small troops, and the second of three, each of which latter will be subdivided into two; five of these cover the intervals, and the sixth outflanks to right or left as may be ordered. – If there are only two squadrons, the first line is of four small troops, the second of two, which are again subdivided, three of them covering the intervals and one outflanking.

The second line is not only used as a support, but it may also be sometimes brought up in part, on the flank of the first line, while advancing to the attack, in order suddenly to turn the enemy's flank. – If there are six troops in a first line covered by six smaller ones, two of these latter may be taken from one flank to turn that of the enemy: this leaves one interval uncovered, because, if these two small troops are taken from the flank on which the second line does not outflank, then this second line covers to that hand one interval more, which changes the troop that before outflanked into a covering troop. – Sometimes the advantage to be gained by outflanking an enemy appears so great, that half the second line will be taken away for that purpose, being enabled to leave some intervals uncovered, in consequence of the disorder the enemy is thrown into by this manoeuvre.

Before 1806 the Prussians used a linear attack known as the *Attacke mit drei Gliedern,* or 'attack with three ranks'. This was established by the Regulation of 1796. Tactically it was a two-rank line with a third rank formed behind them which acted as a flanking corps. This rear rank was formed by drawing the four files from the left wing of each *Zug.* The third rank was then divided into two groups which were posted behind each wing of the regimental line. It would then swing out and attack the enemy flank and rears as opportunity permitted.

The Prussian 1812 Regulation laid down strict instructions that a small reserve was to be formed behind either flank to protect the squadron from a flank attack as well as to swing out in an attack on the enemy's exposed flanks. The 1st *Zug* of the 1st squadron formed the reserve on the right and the 3rd and 4th *Züge* of the 4th squadron formed that of the left.

Before 1806 the Prussians also used a form of attack known as *en murial,* or a 'wall attack'. This was a massive linear attack which began at a range of up to 1500 paces from the enemy. The last 700 to 1000 paces were executed at the gallop. This attack had both advantages and disadvantages. The massive line had a tendency to form clumps and to break up as it advanced over the 1500 pace distance. It also totally exhausted the horses by the time the charge was complete, so that any enemy cavalry reserve could damage it tremendously at that stage. However, whatever units it came into contact with during the charge were often swept away by its impetus.

On a larger scale, light and heavy cavalry would often operate together. The light cavalry then acted either as a screening force or as a second line. When the light cavalry led the heavy cavalry it screened it against hostile fire and concealed its advance from the intended target. If the light cavalry advanced behind a line of heavy cavalry, it formed behind its flanks. When the heavy cavalry had locked the enemy in melee, the light cavalry would swing out and strike him in the flank. This invariably resulted in the enemy breaking and retiring in disorder. Instances of this can be found in battle accounts of many nations, most notably the Russians.

Echelon attack and echiquier attack

The echelon attack (Figure 104b) and the *echiquier* attack (Figure 104c) are variations on the linear theme. In both the leading element(s) of the attacking formation struck the enemy before the other elements. This initial impact would begin the process of breaking up the linear integrity of the defending unit. As the enemy line began to destabilise a second, fresh force would strike it, accelerating its disintegration. In the case of an echelon attack there would be several successive shocks that, theoretically, would ensure its destruction.

Though the British 1799 Regulation speaks of echelon attacks formed with several regiments, the theory also applied to single regiments. The Regulation states:

> The echellon movements of a great corps, place it in an advantageous situation; to disconcert an enemy; to make a partial attack, or a gradual retreat. Different [preliminary] manoeuvres ought always to have diverted the attention of an enemy, and prevented him from being certain where the attack is to be made. It may be formed from the centre, or from either of the wings reinforced: If successful the divisions move up into line to improve the advantage: If

repulsed, they are in a good situation to protect the retreat. In advancing the several bodies move independent, act freely, and remain ready to assist. In retiring, they fall gradually back on each other, and thereby give mutual aid and support.

The echellons of a line are, according to its strength, of three, four or five squadrons each. Though their flanks seem multiplied, they are not exposed, as they cover each other.

Echellons seen at a distance appear as if a full line: being short and independent lines, they can easier march obliquely to outwing an enemy, or to preserve the points of appui to a wing; and such movement may not be perceptible to an enemy

The Hesse-Kassel 1796 Regulation contains both the echelon and *echiquier* attack. It states that one of the principal advantages of these two forms of attack was that the units were independent and could take advantage of flanks when they were encountered. It also states that the echelons that were not in the front line drew less fire and were more likely to be fresh when they contacted the enemy.

The Prussians before 1806 made extensive use of echelon attacks. The process was delineated in the Regulation of 1796. The echelons were placed 30 paces apart. They found the echelon attack naturally easier to handle and manoeuvre than the long, undivided linear attack. Surprisingly, the Prussian 1812 Regulation does not speak of the echelon attack.

The Saxons, as the Prussians, British and Hessians, used echelons in advancing and retiring. The French *Ordonnance* of 1805 speaks of echelon formations, but not the *echiquier*. No discussion of the utilisation or philosophy of the echelon formation is provided. However, in *Die westphälische Armee* one finds that the echelon attack was used for attacks against infantry in line or square. As the Westphalians were a French client state whose army was closely modelled on the French, it is reasonable to assume that this philosophy was drawn from French tactical doctrine.

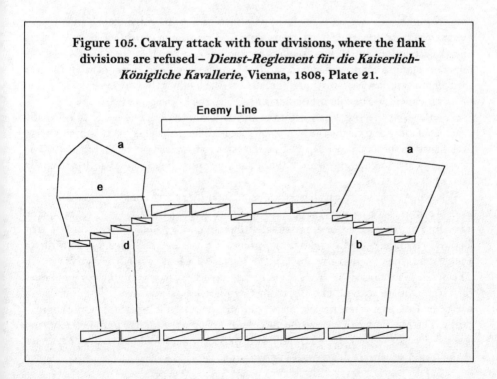

Figure 105. Cavalry attack with four divisions, where the flank divisions are refused – *Dienst-Reglement für die Kaiserlich-Königliche Kavallerie*, Vienna, 1808, Plate 21.

Enemy Line

The Austrian 1808 Regulation provides an illustration of an echelon-style attack though, unfortunately, it provides no discussion of it beyond the notes on the illustration that explain how the echelons swung backwards and forwards.

Schwarm attack

The Prussian *Schwarm* attack is illustrated in Figure 104d. It existed in the 1796 hussar Regulation, and may have existed before. It was formed in two ways. Upon the signal to form the *Schwarm* attack every fourth *Zug* drew forward and formed a skirmish screen which covered the advance. These skirmishers would, with their fire, draw the enemy fire onto themselves and screen the main body behind them. It was principally used as a system for attacking infantry in square. The Prussians formed it by combining light and heavy cavalry. A heavy cavalry regiment would advance on the infantry and tease it into firing. Light cavalry, concealed behind the heavies, would then swing out and strike the infantry before the latter had a chance to reload. The intent was to cross the dangerous fire zone while the infantry could not fire, come into contact with them, and engage them in melee without suffering the effects of their musketry.

The Saxons also used this attack. It was designated solely as being for use against infantry. A line of flankers preceded the main cavalry line by 50 to 60 paces. The flankers would advance far enough to fire their weapons on the enemy infantry. Then the cavalry line would advance and attack the infantry.

Column attack

The column attack was an older form of attack used principally against infantry. In *Die westphälische Armee* one finds the quotation: 'The column attack, which in the wars of the French Revolution was frequently used by the French cavalry, after 1804 was used only against infantry in column and was employed against heavy cavalry. In 1813 the column attack was re-instituted because of the badly trained troopers, who could be better controlled in column than in line. This attack was executed at the trot.'

The Prussians before 1806 employed the column attack. They used it principally against infantry and formed it in a *Zug* column. The principals for this attack were established in the *Instruction for the General-majors of Cavalry* of 16 March 1759. The Prussian 1812 Regulation formed this attack by squadrons. It was still principally used against squares.

When one examines a cavalry attack on an infantry square some of the reasons for using a column become quickly apparent. A typical Russian battalion, formed in square, had a frontage of 50 men, or approximately 86 ft. A cavalry squadron of 100 troopers, formed in two ranks, had a frontage of 50 men. If three feet is allowed for the width of a horse and rider, we find that the cavalry squadron would have a frontage of 150 ft. The overlap is tremendous. If the cavalry regiment were formed in line it would miss the target square with all but approximately half of one squadron. The squadron's narrower frontage when in column would still overlap the square, but not significantly. The remaining squadrons in the column, even more so than in the echelon and *echequer* attacks, were sheltered from hostile musketry and would, it was hoped, arrive at the target square fresh and still in good order.

Attack à la débandade

The Saxons had an unusual attack known as *à la débandade*. This was executed in the widest open interval and was principally used by light cavalry. The Regulation does state that the cuirassiers could, on rare occasions, use this form of attack. It was to be used against unformed infantry or uhlans. When used against uhlans it allowed the Saxon cavalry to get behind them, as well as lessening the effectiveness of their lances – the effectiveness of the lance, it was felt, would be reduced because the target was not concentrated and the uhlan would have to constantly aim his lance at a specific, moving target, rather than just point it forward to hit a massed target.

Lava attack

Researches have revealed one other sort of attack. This was the famous cossack *lava* attack, which was surprisingly similar to the Saxon *à la débandade*. In his work on tactics, Oberst Balck says:

> The *lava* may be classed as a charge in extended order in a restricted sense only, as it serves as much for manoeuvring [reconnaissance and screening] as for an actual attack. The *lava* is the combat formation of the Cossacks and was originally transmitted to them by Asiatic nomad tribes of horsemen. Yelling and firing, the Cossacks swarm in a dispersed formation all around the enemy, in order to induce him to disperse likewise, thus enabling them in hand-to-hand combat, to bring into play their superiority in riding and handling their weapons.

The *lava* was formed either from line or from column. When forming a *lava* attack the first *sotnia* (squadron) formed a line of half-platoons 50 paces apart to the front, on the centre platoon, and then deployed that line so that there were four paces between each cossack along the front. Thus deployed, the average *sotnia* will cover about 400 paces of frontage. Another platoon or squadron followed the deployed *sotnia* in close order at a distance of up to 350 yds. If it deployed, one non-commissioned officer and six cossacks remained with the guidon to act as a rallying point known as the *majak* (lighthouse).

The extreme length of the *lava* allowed the cossacks to simultaneously envelope one or both flanks of the enemy and subject him to attacks on the front and rear. Any breaks in the enemy formation could, subsequently, be taken advantage of. The *lava* was not intended to come into contact with a formed body of cavalry, but rather to wear it down by continual harassment. The *lava* was also used for the pursuit of a beaten enemy and the screening of movements by other bodies.

Pre-attack reconnaissance

In his treatise on marches, Jarry provides some insight into pre-attack cavalry reconnaissances. He states that a cavalry commander should never order a charge or movement to the front without having previously sent out skirmishers to ascertain whether there was some obstacle which had not been observed, *eg* the sunken road at Waterloo. This rule was frequently ignored. It was, therefore, the duty of the staff officers to reconnoitre the ground to circumvent blunders that might be made as a result of the over-aggressive nature of some generals and regimental officers.

Jarry felt that a reconnaissance could be confidently made within pistol shot of a line of enemy cavalry. The enemy cavalry would not move just to charge an individual. The most that could be expected was that an officer might ride forward and discharge a pistol, 'which is not very dangerous.' If this reconnaissance was made by a number of hussars or dragoons, they should be selected for their known bravery and the quality of their mounts. Of course, a well-mounted staff officer could make such a reconnaissance in person.

Passage of lines

The purpose of this manoeuvre was to allow a fresh regiment to pass through a fatigued or shattered unit and assume its position in the front line. It was performed by either unit, advancing or retiring through the intervals between the squadrons of the other. In the French army the manoeuvring unit formed its squadrons individually into columns by *pelotons*, and these four separate columns passed through the gaps in the stationary regiment. Once they had passed through they wheeled, marched perpendicular to the stationary unit and deployed back into line parallel to it.

Cavalry versus the square

It was very difficult for cavalry to break a formed infantry unit, unless the morale of the infantry was weakened. Only under circumstances where the infantry had suffered excessively either during or prior to the battle, so that its morale had decayed, did the cavalry have a very good chance or breaking it. In those cases, the cavalry often had only to present itself before the infantry and march towards it with a firm step to obtain the required result. In those instances where the infantry's morale remained intact a charge in a single line rarely succeeded. It was desirable, therefore, to always precede a cavalry charge with a liberal application of canister or musketry. Even then, an attack on infantry advantageously emplaced should always be avoided.

However, when a square or other formed body of infantry was successfully attacked it would invariably be totally destroyed. On 25 March 1814, at La Fère-Champenoise, several French squares were crushed and entirely dispersed. At the Battle of Dennewitz on 6 September 1813, the Prussian cavalry crushed two French squares. On 1 May 1809 Austrian dragoons under Colonel Heimroth crushed a square at Riedau. At the Battle of Cateau on 26 April 1794, Colonel Prinz Schwarzenburg, at the head of six Austrian and 12 British squadrons, attacked a column of French infantry. A total of 2000 men were killed and 277 were captured, along with 22 guns and 29 caissons. Of course, numerous similar examples can be given of French cavalry crushing Allied squares, *eg* at Eylau, Wagram, and Borodino.

On the other hand, history is equally filled with instances where cavalry attacks failed miserably. Waterloo is probably the best example. Here Ney despatched the French cuirassiers against Wellington's line, and they broke upon the British squares, having about the same impact as a wave breaking on a rocky shore.

Success or failure against a square seems to have been dependent on the steadiness of the troops on either side. However, since a horse could not be forced to impale itself on a bayonet, the key was the steadiness of the infantry: if it was green and not confident in its ability to defend itself in square, it would have a problem. If it was being pounded by infantry fire or cannon fire while under attack by cavalry, its chances of withstanding the cavalry attack appear to have been diminished. In addition, the cumulative level of casualties suffered by the infantry prior to a cavalry attack would also have affected its ability to withstand it.

Brigade level attacks

On the multi-regimental level, the cavalry of the Napoleonic Wars was organised in a series of successive lines. Generally each line consisted of a single regiment or brigade. The lines were deployed, with the regiments or brigades placed one behind the other, forming a dense column with barely any distance between each rank.

The first line was nearly always formed of light cavalry, followed by dragoons and finally cuirassiers. It was in this formation that the cavalry moved to the attack, not as a single block, but as a wave of successive lines. During the attack the intervals between the ranks would expand significantly. As the leading line struck the enemy and broke, it would swing around to the flanks of the 'column' of advancing lines and rally on the flanks or would perform a 'passage of lines'. Once at the rear of the formation they would reform into line and advance into the attack as often as necessary.

This tactic was employed at Hoff, when Murat advanced his light cavalry division supported closely by a dragoon division. When they were thrown back a second dragoon division, under Grouchy, advanced. It was insufficient and slowly d'Hautpoul's cuirassiers were fed into the battle. At Eylau Murat formed 80 squadrons into an immense column by brigades and charged in 10 successive lines of cavalry, as we saw earlier. At both Essling and Wagram we find eight to nine charges by successive lines. At Waterloo the cuirassiers of Milhaud and Kellermann and the lancers of Lefebvre-Desnouëttes charged 11 times.

The process of the attack

Whichever formation the regimental officers adopted in a charge, there was a definite sequence of steps through which they put their troops. When the cavalry began to advance, it would move first at a walk, then a trot, then a gallop, and finally it would come to the charge and impact on the enemy. After impact the victor would chase the defeated unit, if possible, and both would attempt to rally. Though this general charge sequence was followed by every nation there were variations in each, as follows:

In the British 1812 Regulation we find the following discussion of the charge: 'In a charge of either infantry; or cavalry, though a momentary disorder may take place; yet the instance the enemy gives way, the line must be again formed, and the pursuit continued by light troops, or by detached troops or companies only. – These follow the enemy with the utmost vigour, and as soon as the line is in order, it advances again and completes defeat.'

Table 46. Charge sequences and ranges.

| | Range in paces from target at which the cavalry begins to | | | |
	Walk	Trot	Gallop	Charge
French	Not specified	Not specified	230	80
Prussian (pre-1806)	1000	950–750	650–450	300–200
Prussian (1812)	8–600	Not specified	220	100–80
Hessian	8–600	6–400	200	80–70
British	Not specified	Not specified	250 yds	80 yds

The Prussians and other nations also had specific smaller forces identified to be detached in pursuit of the defeated enemy formation. The Regulation continues:

> When cavalry attack cavalry, the squadrons must be firm and compact; but when they attack infantry the files may be opened, and the men may bend down on their horses necks [so as to be able to strike the soldiers below them]. It may be expected that under a severe fire both the cavalry and infantry lose to a degree their regular order before they arrive on the enemy, but cavalry acting against cavalry can profit by its manoeuvre and order till the very last moment; for till the horses' heads come up against each other, there is nothing that ought to prevent a cavalry soldier from being as steady in the ranks, as if he was at a common exercise.

In another chapter the Regulation goes on to say:

> Whatever distance the squadron has to go over, it may move at a brisk trot till within 250 yards of the enemy, and then gallop. – The word CHARGE! is given when within 80 yards, and the gallop increased as much as the body can bear in good order. – Any attempt to close the files at the instant of the charge, would only increase the intervals in a line, and tend to impede the free movement of each horse, who at no time requires to be more independent than when galloping at his utmost exertion, and every rub to right or left diminishes that effort in a degree.
>
> At the instant of the shock, the [trooper's] body must be well back; the horse not restrained by the bitt, but determined forward by the spur; rising in the stirrups, and pointing the sword, will always occasion a shake in the squadron; it will naturally be done when necessary.
>
> It is in the uniform velocity of the squadron, that its effect consists; the spur as much as the sword tends to overset an opposite enemy; when the one has nearly accomplished this end, the other may complete it.
>
> In every part of the charge and in quick movement, the standard must be very exact in following the leader; and the men particularly attentive in keeping up to, and dressing to their standard. They will have their horses in hand, and perfectly square to the front, their heads well up, which will keep them under command. – Men must remain firm in their saddles, an unsteady man will always make a horse so; one such will interfere with the movement and effect of a whole squadron.
>
> When the shock of the squadron has broken the order of the opposite enemy, part may be ordered to pursue and keep up the advantage; but its great object is instantly to rally and to renew its efforts in a body, either to the front, or by wheeling to take other squadrons in the flank.
>
> If the squadron fails in its attack, and is itself put in disorder or confusion, it must retire as well as it can, to make way for those that support it, and must rally as soon as possible under the protection of others. [Failure to withdraw made a unit terribly vulnerable to counter-attack and defeat in detail.]
>
> A squadron should never be so much hurried as to bring up the horses blown to the charge, and this will much depend on circumstances and the order they are in.
>
> When after the charge, part of the squadron disperses to pursue, they should open out and cover the front and intervals. When they return and form, each man should observe his point, come around by his proper flank, and by the rear of his respective rank and on no account cross near the front of the squadron.
>
> Every soldier who is attacked, and whose order is broken, looks upon himself as beaten, and is not easily brought to rally, if the first advantage is pursued; and the operation is in itself difficult, after he has once turned to the rear. – But the body that attacks, though put in confusion, will easily unite while its motion is progressive and forward, and acts with a confidence and exertion which will never be found in those that stand still.

In addition, the British Regulation speaks of other points which are of extreme interest. One such comment is that 'though circumstances of situation may prevent a line [of cavalry] from advancing much, it should never absolutely stand still to receive the shock, otherwise its defeat is inevitable.' The French regulations also speak of this, but there are several recorded instances where French cavalry nevertheless chose to receive a charge standing and firing a defensive volley before the charge struck them. In every historical incident read in the preparation of this study, the standing cavalry was unable to stop the attack with its defensive volley, and was broken by the charge. However, since this was done so often by the French over so many years, it begs the question why, if it apparently always failed, did the French continue to attempt this?

Rallies after charges appear to have been controlled by bugle-calls and the position of the standard. The appropriate bugle-call would be made and, hopefully, the troopers would return to their squadron or regimental colours.

Cavalry skirmishing

In addition to melee weapons, cavalry often had carbines or musketoons. Their use was often left to specific individuals, as in the case of Hesse-Kassel, where a number of men in the regiment were designated as *Karabiniers*. The Hessian *Karabiniers* positioned themselves 30 paces in front of the main body of their squadron and adopted an open interval. Here they screened the main body and executed controlled volley fire.

The French did not designate specific individuals as skirmishers, but would detach *pelotons* into skirmish order. They were known as *flanqueurs*. Like their infantry counterparts, cavalry skirmishers seems to have operated in pairs. The line formed 60 paces from the main body with one skirmisher forward and the second on his left rear. That heavy cavalry also assumed this skirmish role, using their pistols and carbines, is supported by Chevalier Mercer in his account of Waterloo, where he reports single cuirassiers riding up to his battery to fire on his gunners, then calmly riding away to reload.

The musketry from a French cavalry skirmish line does not appear to have been controlled in volleys, but was a voluntary fire. However, the second rank of the skirmish line did not fire. Instead it held its fire to defend the front rank of skirmishers if attacked. As in the case of infantry, the pairs of soldiers would alternate loading and firing so that there was always one with a loaded weapon. The execution and cessation of musketry were controlled by bugle-calls.

The *flanqueurs* executed all manoeuvres at the gallop. They were never to take their firearms in hand until they were forward of the main body and dispersed. This was to prevent accidents. If necessary, the French regulations allow for a formed *peloton* to be sent forward to act as a support for the skirmishers.

The British system of skirmishers is slightly different. They sent theirs 200 yds in front of the squadron, the remainder of which always stood with swords drawn ready to support them. The British felt that 'all firings [were] best performed on the move, and it is unnecessary to halt for that purpose only.' This would tend to eliminate any possibility of accurate aimed skirmish fire by British cavalry.

The British skirmishers worked in two ranks. The first rank would fire, then the second would advance to take up the forward position and the line that had fired would reload. Like the French, they too did not want the skirmish line to be caught with unloaded muskets, and the forward line is very carefully enjoined from firing until it is sure that the second line has reloaded. The British sent out small skirmishing detachments on occasion. These were distinct from a skirmish line, and were posted 250 yards from the squadron. However, they appear to have operated much as the other skirmish formation.

The Austrian skirmishing system was not dissimilar. Figure 106, drawn from the Austrian 1808 Regulation, is the only formal diagram to be found which illustrates how this was done.

Figure 106. Austrian cavalry skirmishers – *Dienst-Reglement für die Kaiserlich-Königliche Kavallerie*, Vienna, 1808, Plate 22, Figures 1 & 2.

'Figure 1': Advancing a skirmish screen with the 1st *Zug* of a division.

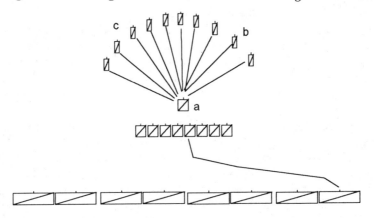

a) Position of the *Zug* before the middle of the division.
b) First rank under the direction of the 2nd corporal, deployed as skirmishers.
c) Grouping of the skirmishers in small formations at intervals of 50 paces.

'Figure 2': Advanced guard with two *Züge* of a division.

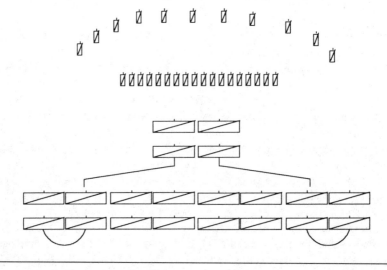

Chapter 8

Cavalry Tactics:
Theory in Practice

One is always asked if the theory espoused in the regulations was indeed put into practice in the field. In order to ascertain this we are limited to reviewing the historical accounts of various engagements. Unfortunately, these are generally too vague, detailed accounts being extremely scarce.

Let us begin with an examination of cavalry actions in the 1812 campaign. These quotations are excerpted and condensed so as to cover only the various points of interest. They do not provide a complete picture of any battle, nor are they complete quotations.[16]

There were a number of cavalry engagements before and during the Battle of Ostrovno. Two of these are of interest to our study:

> As the battle continued [and] the 16th Chasseurs prepared themselves and reorganised after traversing the broken terrain they were attacked by the cossacks opposite them. They stood fast and unsuccessfully attempted to break the Russians' charge with carbine fire. They held their fire until the Russians were 30 paces from them and fired a volley. Despite the effect of the French fire, the Russians closed with them and drove them back in disorder.
>
> In their haste to escape, the 16th Chasseurs became trapped in the ravine. The remains of the 16th Chasseurs rallied behind the 53rd Line Regiment, part of General Broussier's division, which had hastily formed squares in echelon. The fire of the 53rd drove the Russian cossacks back, saving the French artillery that was about to fall into the Russians' hands. The Russian cavalry charged the squares repeatedly, but were eventually driven back.
>
> The charge of the Russian cossacks carried them to the foot of Napoleon's observation post on the hill. Some of the Chasseurs à Cheval de la Garde, posted to protect Napoleon, drove off a few aggressive cossacks with a few well-aimed shots. The Russian cossacks withdrew and passed directly over the voltigeurs of the 18th *Légère* Regiment.

This passage provides an historical example of one of the points already discussed earlier – *ie*, that cavalry could never stand and hope to overthrow charging cavalry by its defensive fire. In his work *On the Napoleonic Wars*, Dr Chandler provides an account of another such attempt by French cavalry to engage charging cavalry with musketry, at the Battle of Sahagun in 1808. What is troubling about this is that there are repeated accounts of such incidents. Obviously the French believed they could stop a charge with cavalry musketry. I strongly suspect that there is a hole in the literature, and that this tactic falls into that hole. If it failed so regularly, why did the French rely on it so often? It is highly probable that it had some benefit and *could* be successful. If it never succeeded, it would have quickly been abandoned.

It also indicates fairly clearly that the cossacks could not have been tightly organised if, though their charge was turned back by the fire of the infantry, others still

---

[16] All 1812 passages are drawn from G.F. Nafziger, *Napoleon's Invasion of Russia*, 1988, Novato, CA, Presidio Press.

came into contact with Napoleon's personal escort. This was probably the famous *lava* attack.

After the French drove the Russians out of Smolensk they set out in pursuit. They caught up with them a short distance from Smolensk, and the Battle of Valoutina-Loubino was fought. During this the Westphalians under Junot executed a grand tactical flanking manoeuvre and appeared behind the Russians. There was a series of infantry and cavalry engagements. 'Hammerstein, the commander of the Westphalian cavalry, formed his cavalry into echelons and struck the superior force of Russian cavalry. His attack was not very successful. The Guard Chevauléger Regiment lost one dead and seven wounded officers, 36 dead and 93 wounded, and five prisoners.'

This is one of the few instances where a cavalry formation is actually described. It shows that the echelon attack was used against cavalry as well as infantry. Unfortunately, it shows little that might confirm or refute the supposition that Westphalians were amongst the better European cavalry. This is the only detailed battle account encountered during the preparation of this study that describes Westphalian cavalry in action.

The next series of engagements is from the Battle of Borodino. This battle is one of the richest in cavalry engagements and, as a result, is very useful for our purposes.

> Prince Eugene of Württemberg was leading the 17th Division of the 2nd Infantry Corps south towards the battle around the *flèches* and halted it behind the redoubt at 10.00 am, when the French attacked him. He was resting his troops when he found himself attacked by the French III Reserve Cavalry Corps. The three cuirassier and four dragoon regiments moved forward with their light cavalry brigade screening their advance. This mass of cavalry swarmed around the Russian infantry, forcing it to form square quickly.

This sequence is interesting in that it clearly shows that light cavalry was used to screen heavy cavalry.

> The French attack on the centre of the Russian position around Semenovskaya was led by Friant's 2nd Division. He was flanked by the heavy cavalry of the I and IV Reserve Cavalry Corps. This force advanced directly on the rubble that had been Semenovskaya. The assault was heralded by a tremendous artillery barrage that furthered the destruction of the already ravaged village.

This excerpt illustrates the tactical use of cavalry on the flanks of advancing infantry in a combined-arms attack. This was a very common use of cavalry.

> The Russian artillery replied and directed much of its fire on the French cavalry. About 10.00 am the French assault began and the cavalry quickly began their advance. Latour-Maubourg's forces advancing in half squadrons, his forces divided into two columns. As he crossed the Semenovskaya stream his right hand column was the 7th Cuirassier Division, commanded by Lorge.
>
> The right column contained the Saxon cuirassier regiments – Garde du Corps and Zastrow (8 squadrons); the Polish 14th Cuirassier Regiment (2 squadrons); and 1st and 2nd Westphalian Cuirassier Regiments (8 squadrons).
>
> The left column was formed by the 4th Light Cavalry Division: 3rd, 11th, and 16th Polish Uhlan Regiments (12 squadrons).
>
> As the leading two and a half squadrons of the Saxon Garde du Corps crossed the stream, they encountered a Russian battery supported by the Russian 2nd Grenadier Division formed in square. General Thieleman formed the remaining squadrons in echelon to the left and charged the Russians. One square was broken and the others forced back.

The columns described here are columns of regiments formed in line, as described earlier. Imagine Figure 104e being four regiments formed in a column rather than four squadrons. Each regiment is then formed into a column of eight half-squadrons. We see both the use of an echelon formation against an infantry square and a prepared, standing square being broken by a cavalry charge.

> In their pursuit of the withdrawing Russian infantry they encountered the dragoons of General Siever's 4th Cavalry Corps. The dragoons were supported by the fire of the 2nd Guard Light Artillery Battery. This was insufficient to halt the Saxons and they pressed beyond the village and found themselves facing the Ismailov and Lithuanian Guard Infantry Regiments formed in six battalion squares.
>
> The French cavalry assault was furious, but the Ismailov Guard withstood them. In one of three historically recorded instances the Ismailov Guard actually executed a bayonet charge against the attacking cavalry. They did so with the support of the 1st Guard Light Battery and the two Guard Position Batteries.

Though not specifically relevant to cavalry melee, this excerpt does refer to one of the most unusual historical events in the history of the Napoleonic Wars. This passage is in error in stating that there were only three such instances of bayonet charges against cavalry. In fact, during the last few years several such instances have come to light. See the discussion on the bayonet in Chapter 1.

> At the same time General Borosdin II, with his 1st Cuirassier Division (Emperor, Empress and Astrakhan Cuirassier Regiments) struck the Saxons frontally and the Akhtyrka Hussar Regiment struck them in the flank. The Saxons suffered heavy casualties from the ensuing cavalry battle because they had left their cuirasses in Saxony. They were driven back behind a crest to the right of Semenovskaya.

Here we see heavy cavalry co-operating with light cavalry. The heavies struck the Saxons frontally and the Russian hussars struck them in the flank. The following series of paragraphs jump to the northern flank of the Battle of Borodino. The Russians committed their cavalry reserve in a major grand tactical flanking effort.

> The Russians sent a major cavalry force on a flank manoeuvre in an effort to turn the French left. They crossed the Kolocha near Maloe about 11.00 am.
>
> The first French forces they encountered were the 84th Line Infantry Regiment and the Bavarian and Italian light cavalry of General Ornano.
>
> The Russians formed the Elisabethgrad Hussar Regiment and the Guard cossacks into their first rank. Behind them formed the Guard Dragoon, Uhlan and Hussar Regiments, the Niejine Dragoon Regiment and the 2nd Guard Horse Battery. The Guard Hussar Regiment attacked the 84th Line Regiment, which was in square. They attacked three times without artillery preparation or success.

Here we find a typical example of cavalry hitting a prepared square and losing the engagement. As the excerpt goes on we find that the solution to the cavalry's ineffectiveness was to bring up horse artillery so that it could break up the square:

> Eventually, the Russian artillery unlimbered and forced the 84th Line Regiment to withdraw behind the river and abandon its two regimental guns. The remainder of the Russian cavalry drove back the Bavarian and Italian cavalry.
>
> Pavlov had crossed the Kolocha with nine cossack *pulks* in an attempt to manoeuvre on the French rear, but the regular cavalry operating with them was stopped by Delzon's division and the reformed Italian and Bavarian cavalry. The French moved cavalry north to support that flank. General Grouchy's III Reserve Cavalry Corps was the first to move north. The 11th Light Brigade, formed by the 6th Hussar and 8th Chasseur à Cheval Regiments, engaged the Russians with deadly effect.

Here we find a large force of cossacks being stopped by a smaller force of regular cavalry. It contrasts with the earlier account around Ostrovno, where the cossacks defeated a single unit.

The next series of paragraphs covers the biggest cavalry engagement during the Battle of Borodino. At one instance as many as four cavalry corps were engaged in combat during this engagement. In the first passage we find two or more lines of cavalry operating against an enemy cavalry formation. We also see the second and most famous instance of a cavalry charge overrunning an earthwork.[17]

> The Garde du Corps drew out to the left and advanced directly on the redoubt's breastwork, unmasking the Zastrow Cuirassier Regiment. The Garde du Corps and the nearest squadrons of the Zastrow Cuirassier Regiment poured up and over the breastwork, while the other squadrons forced their way through the rear and embrasures of the breastwork.
>
> Once the redoubt was secured, Eugene began to mass all available cavalry behind it, including the II and IV Reserve Cavalry Corps. Grouchy's III Reserve Cavalry Corps was released when the Russian threat to the northern flank had passed. At that time Grouchy's cavalry joined the others behind the redoubt. Once these three cavalry corps had completely reorganised, they advanced beyond the redoubt to face the Russians again.
>
> Barclay took personal command of the forces in the Gorki ravine and directed the 24th Division to retake the redoubt. However, before the counter-attack could begin, the 14th Polish Cuirassiers descended into the ravine in a column of threes, stopped the counter-attack, and drove the Russians back.

The column of threes is a transit formation, not a battle formation. Once at the bottom of the ravine the Poles must have reorganised into at least a column of demi-*pelotons*. The column of threes would have been totally inappropriate for this situation and would have resulted in their rapid destruction.

> The Chevalier Guard was formed by squadrons, in two lines with gaps between the two squadrons in the first line sufficient to permit the squadrons of the second line to pass through. The Horse Guard was posted in line to their left. Facing them were the Saxon Garde du Corps, followed by the Zastrow Cuirassier Regiment and the Polish 14th Cuirassier Regiment. The Horse Guard moved against the flank of the advancing Saxons and were countered by the 14th Cuirassiers. The Poles, having already been heavily engaged and suffered many losses, were insufficient to hold them back. The Saxons and Poles were forced back.

In this account we find the Russians using a combined echelon and flank attack against the Poles and Saxons, who were advancing in an *echiquier* attack. The Poles were able to manoeuvre in reaction to the Russian flank threat and engaged in melee with it. It is also worth noting that the Saxons and Poles had been defeated in an earlier melee and were able to reorganise themselves and engage in further combats (this one and the seizure of the Great Redoubt).

'At the same time the 2nd Cavalry Corps arrived and the Isoum Hussar Regiment and the Polish Uhlan Regiment attacked Wathier's and Defrance's forces. The Russians were not able to halt the French advance and were themselves thrown back by the 1st Cuirassier Regiment and a half squadron of chevauléger-lanciers.' Here is an account of French light cavalry operating in conjunction with heavy cavalry. Though not stated, this was probably a frontal attack by the heavies and a flank attack by the light cavalry. This would then be similar to earlier accounts of similar tactics used by the Russians.

> The Russian 3rd Cavalry Corps arrived on the field and dispatched five of its six regiments into what quickly developed into a two-hour melee. The cavalry of both armies intermingled, dust rose obscuring all vision. Small groups of cavalry pulled into and out of the battle to

---

[17] The first instance of this known to the author occurred during the Battle of Jemappes in 1792 and was executed by the Chamborant Hussar Regiment.

rally, reorganise and charge back into the fray. All control of the battle passed from the hands of the generals and into the tiny knots of soldiers.

This is a very unusual passage. Initially it would seem to indicate a two-hour cavalry melee, but this is not the case. Instead, it was a series of melees by the cavalry units that formed four complete cavalry corps. This account does provide some interesting insights into the process of a large cavalry melee. The statement that small groups of cavalry pulled out of the melee, reorganised, and charged back in suggests that cavalry could charge, reform, and charge again rather quickly if not pursued.

Discussion of cavalry versus cavalry actions in the Peninsula is relatively easy, in that we can simply provide quotations from Oman that refer quite directly to the issues at hand:

> There were cases, no doubt, where English regiments threw away their chances by their blind fury in charging, and either got cut up pursuing an original advantage to a reckless length, or at any rate missed an opportunity by over-great dispersion or riding off the field. The earliest was seen at Vimeiro just after Wellington's first landing in the Peninsula, when two squadrons of the 20th Light Dragoons, after successfully cutting up a beaten column of infantry, pushed on for half a mile in great disorder, to charge Junot's cavalry reserves, and were horribly maltreated – losing about one man in four.

This excerpt clearly indicates that the British had a propensity for charging off rather wildly and losing control once the charge was on. This supports the suggestion that the organisation of the British squadrons was such that the officers had poor forward control and could not influence their units once they began a charge.

> An equally irrational exploit took place at Talavera, where the 23rd Light Dragoons, beaten off in a charge against a square which they had been ordered to attack, rushed on beyond it, against successive lines of French cavalry, pierced the first, were stopped by the second and had to cut their way back with a loss of 105 prisoners and 102 killed and wounded – nearly half their strength.'

In this instance the cavalry struck and bounced off a square. It then reorganised itself sufficiently to attack and defeat some French cavalry. However, once again it charged wildly off over hill and dale, totally out of control, to be savaged in its turn by the more controlled French. It also sounds as if the defeated French cavalry was able to quickly rally behind the British charge and close in behind them.

> An equally headlong business was the charge of the 13th Light Dragoons at Campo Mayor on March 25, 1811, when that regiment, having beaten in a fair fight the French 26th Dragoons, and captured 18 siege guns which were retreating on the road, galloped for more than six miles, sabering the scattered fugitives, till they were actually brought up by the fire of the fortress of Badajoz, on whose very glacis they had made their way. The captured guns, meanwhile, were picked up by the French infantry who had been retreating behind their routed cavalry, and brought off in safety – the 13th not having left a single man to secure them. Here, at any rate, not much loss was suffered, though a great capture was missed, but similar galloping tactics on June 11, 1812, at the combat of Manguilla, lead to complete disaster.

This action is an even more incredible account of no control being exercised over charging cavalry. Not only did they defeat a French dragoon regiment and capture a siege train, but they galloped six miles down the road, lost all formation and control, and totally forgot to guard what they had captured. One can only suspect that even the officers got swept away with the excitement of the charge. Tally ho!

Slade's heavy brigade (1st Royals and 3rd Dragoon Guards) fell in with L'Allemand's French brigade, the 17th and 27th Dragoons. Each drew up, but L'Allemand had placed one squadron in reserve far beyond the sky line, and out of sight. Slade charged, beat the five squadrons immediately opposite him and then (without reforming or setting aside any supports) galloped after the broken French brigade in complete disorder for a mile, till he came parallel to the unperceived reserve squadron, which charged him in the flank and rear: the rest of the French halted and turned; Slade could not stand, and was routed, having 40 casualties and 118 prisoners. Wellington wrote about this to Hill: 'I have never been more annoyed than by Slade's affair. Our officers of cavalry have acquired a trick of galloping at everything. They never consider the situation, never think of manoeuvring before an enemy, and never keep back or provide for a reserve. All cavalry should charge in two lines, and at least one-third should be ordered beforehand to pull up and reform, as soon as the charge has been delivered, and the enemy been broken.

This is another exceptional example of the total lack of control the British had over their cavalry. This excerpt rather clearly covers the perception of British cavalry held by senior commanders when it notes that 'our officers of cavalry have acquired a trick of galloping at everything.' This and one of the previous excerpt clearly use the term 'disorder' with the adjectives 'great' and 'complete.'

Three accounts are recorded in Balck's tactical study of the use of the *lava* attack and its effectiveness:

At Luckenwalde, August 19th, 1813, a French Cuirassier regiment advancing at the trot in column of squadrons, was attacked by Cossacks, the flankers that it had thrown out being forced back. The French advanced against the centre of the Russians. The latter's thin line at once dispersed, all the Cossacks throwing themselves against the flanks and rear of the French. The French column halted when it no longer had an enemy in its front. Meantime, the Cossacks thrust or fired into the flank files and rear of the French Cuirassiers. After a while, the French column was in such confusion that orderly movement was out of the question. The Cossacks, though numerically inferior and unable to disperse the French column by charging it in close order, were elated because they felt that they were better horsemen than the French, and continued with great glee to fire their rifles and thrust their lances into the French ranks. The flank files and rear line of the French finally turned to the flank and grasped their carbines. The Cuirassiers were not relieved from their unhappy predicament until fresh cavalry arrived.

At Boragk, September 19, 1813, 1,200 Cossacks attacked 2,000 French Dragoons. The latter remained passive, received the attack with carbine fire and sought to form line in place to avoid being enveloped. The action terminated with the rout of the French cavalry. In a quarter of an hour the Cossacks made 19 officers and 400 men prisoners.

During the engagement of Rudnia, August 8, 1812, Count Bismark had his troopers form square without dismounting, and repulsed the attack of the cossacks at a halt. But his situation was not relieved until reinforcements arrived, otherwise he would, doubtlessly, have succumbed.

As can be seen from these passages, if regular cavalry was not supported with either infantry or other cavalry and faced equal numbers of cossacks, the tactics of the day were unable to deal with the latter. The first of these passages is also interesting in that it indicates that French cuirassier regiments did deploy portions of their forces as skirmishers. Another point of interest is Count von Bismark's tactic of forming his cavalry in square. This is unusual in that the square is an infantry manoeuvre, and is not generally used as a defensive formation by cavalry.

In these various quotations we have seen numerous historical examples of the attack techniques covered in the earlier discussion of tactics as described in the drill regulations. The discussion of leadership qualities and control is strongly supported, in its estimation of the relationship between British and French cavalry, by the Duke of Wellington himself. The rest of its projections are not supported by specific examples here, but, with the exception of the position of Neapolitan cavalry, are probably reasonable projections of their relative worth.

The following are translations from General Bonie's *Cavalerie au Combat*, written to address the subject of French cavalry tactics after the Franco-Prussian War of 1870. Because of its later date it would be unwise to include his discussion of tactics, but he gives a large number of detailed accounts of Napoleonic cavalry actions that do merit inclusion. The particular value of these is that they deal with the French use of cavalry on a brigade and divisional level.

The first is from the Battle of Marengo. It is noteworthy because it describes the process by which successive waves of cavalry struck an enemy formation, cleared the field of combat, and struck it again in order to complete the destruction of that enemy.

> At the Battle of Marengo General Kellermann was leading a force consisting of the 2nd, 6th, and 20th Cavalry Regiments, 8th Dragoon Regiment and a squadron of the 12th Chasseur à Cheval Regiment. Around noon he found the Austrian cavalry under Pilati, crossing the Fontanowe and turned to face this threat.
>
> Kellermann attacked with his regiments formed in two lines. He ordered the 8th Dragoons to deploy into line and to charge and supported this movement with the other squadrons in line.
>
> The 8th Dragoons struck the head of the enemy column, driving it back, but losing order. Kellermann ordered it to demask the Austrians and rally behind the rest of his troops.
>
> He then led the rest of his brigade, deployed in line, against the enemy. He marched his force calmly to within 50 paces of the Austrians, then ordered them to charge a force significantly their superior in numbers. The Austrians broke and fled.

In Bonie's discussion of the Battle of Austerlitz we find the following accounts of cavalry actions:

> Kellermann's division formed the head of the left wing of the French army. It was formed in two columns by squadron (that is, by brigades *en masse* at the interval of deployment) and at 7.00 am advanced onto the heights that overlooked the battlefield.
>
> The divisions of Beaumont, Nansouty, Walther, and d'Hautpoul were formed behind Kellermann by regiments *en masse* and in two lines. The six regiments of the first two divisions and one brigade of each of the latter two formed the first line. The remaining two brigades of the latter two divisions formed the second line. The brigades of Treilhard and Milhaud formed themselves in a single line on the left of the army.
>
> When Kellermann's forces arrived at the crest of the heights they encountered 2,500 enemy cavalry and were forced to withdraw on the main body, formed in two lines.
>
> As he withdrew the Russians struck the 4th Hussars. During the shock, Kellermann executed a 'change of front to the right on the first *peloton* of the second brigade at the gallop'. He then led his three other regiments into the flank of the Russian cavalry. Russian General Essen, seeing this manoeuvre led forward an uhlan regiment which threw Kellermann back on Cafarelli's infantry. Kellermann's cavalry fell in disorder through the gaps in the infantry.
>
> Under the cover of the infantry fire, which stopped the Russian attack, Kellermann reformed his division in two lines and led it forward 'by regiment on the right in advance by echelons'. They struck the Russian uhlans and drove them back on their own infantry.
>
> Prince Johann von Lichtenstein threw forward Uvarov's regiments and the first echelon of Kellermann's force was enveloped. The three other echelons riposted and struck the Russian cavalry in the flank. This attack was supported by General Sébastiani, who then fell upon the allied cavalry striking the French right. Uvarov's cavalry was driven back. Kellermann quickly reformed his forces 'in echelon on the most advanced squadron' and advanced in a single line to sweep up the fugitives.
>
> The allies brought forward their reserves. Kellermann drew his cavalry behind Sébastiani's cavalry and the combined force reorganised itself into two lines. Walther's division formed

behind this force to support it and defend its flanks. Kellermann and Sébastiani's combined cavalry attacked the advancing allied reserves. A tremendous melee resulted and, when Kellermann was wounded, the French withdrew behind Walther's division to reform. Walther attacked with his three brigades in two lines to cover Kellermann's withdrawal.

Kellermann's division reformed in two lines and advanced again, supported by Sébastiani's brigade and the two other brigades of Walther's division. Bagration's cavalry reserve was driven forward for the second time into combat and for the second time it was thrown back.

Again, Lichtenstein drew together three cavalry brigades. He organised them in two lines. There were two brigades in the first line and a third brigade in the second line at the distance of a brigade.

The French struck and drove back the first line. Nansouty's 2nd and 3rd Cuirassiers pursued the fugitives, chasing them behind their infantry, while the rest of the French cavalry reformed.

At 11.00 am, four hours after Kellermann began his attacks, the allies organised a force of 82 squadrons. The French organised the bulk of their cavalry behind Cafarelli as the allies struck towards Cafarelli's right.

The cuirassiers of d'Hautpoul and Nansouty moved to the right of Cafarelli. They moved through his ranks at the trot in 'columns by pelotons' and in two parallel columns. Once clear they formed line to the right, attacked and threw back the allied cavalry.

The cavalry of d'Hautpoul moved forward organising itself with Walther's division, formed in two lines. Sébastiani's brigade formed the first line and Roget's was in the second, acting as a reserve.

It was supported on the left by Treilhard's brigade and on the right by Kellermann's division. Behind the centre stood d'Hautpoul's division. When the allies advanced the French redeployed their lines so that d'Hautpoul's cuirassiers formed the first line, supported on the right by Treilhard and on the left by Kellermann. Both Treilhard and Kellermann were deployed in two lines.

This passage is interesting for three reasons. The first is the repeated use of cavalry in two lines in every attack at some interval – once stated to be a 'brigade interval'. The function of these two lines was a wave attack. The first line broke the enemy's formation and disordered them. That line quickly cleared out of the way and the second, fresh line struck the disordered enemy and chased them off the field.

The second reason is the number of charges. Kellermann's division participated in no less than five charges and five melees in four hours. It then acted in support of one more charge. This adds a rather interesting light on the idea of fatigue in combat. Five charges and melees in four hours is an incredible amount of galloping and combat. It suggests that only after the fifth assault were Kellermann's forces so fatigued that they had to resign themselves to a secondary role.

The third point worth noting is that the cavalry worked in conjunction with the infantry, passing through it, sheltering behind it, and supporting it when attacked by enemy cavalry.

Any discussion of cavalry tactics requires that the massive cavalry attack at Eylau be discussed. Bonie provides us with the following details:

The centre of the Russian army stood menacingly before the French. Napoleon directed Murat to form 80 squadrons of his chasseurs, dragoons and cuirassiers and prepare to strike.

The squadrons were formed in several strong lines, each consisting of a brigade formed in line. Grouchy's dragoons led the column, then came the cuirassiers. The order was give that each echelon was to form itself to the left of the column when the signal was given to charge and to quickly demask the following echelons. The Guard cavalry was sent forward to join in the assault.

The enemy infantry, supported by its cavalry, arrived before the cemetery where Murat had formed his forces. Murat advanced at the gallop through the defile between the cemetery and Rothenen. As Grouchy's dragoons cleared the defile they formed into line of battle and struck the Russians.

Though dehorsed, Grouchy remounted and took command of his second brigade, leading it forward in support of his first. The second shock broke the Russian cavalry's formation and paved the way for the advance of the remaining columns.

The 24 squadrons of d'Hautpoul's cuirassiers moved up behind the dragoons. Despite the vigour of their attack, the first brigades had not completely broken the Russians and they returned to the rear of the column to reform themselves.

The fourth brigade striking the Russian cavalry pushed a hole through to the Russian infantry where it cut a hole opening access for the following French cavalry. The Russian second line of cavalry found itself overwhelmed and fell back, under the cover of its artillery.

The Russian second line renewed the attack and the Grenadiers à Cheval of the Imperial Guard advanced to support the dragoons and cuirassiers under the command of General Lepic.

The single most significant point is that Grouchy led his division through a defile and formed line at the gallop. This has some very interesting ramifications vis-a-vis the speed of manoeuvre on the battlefield. Earlier we did see comments about Kellermann's cavalry at Austerlitz wheeling to the flank at a gallop so as to strike, but that is a very simple manoeuvre when compared to the passage of a line through a defile. Aside from that we have the continual use of lines and the somewhat unusual comment about the leading elements of the multi-wave column swinging back to the rear of the column, in a caracole-like manoeuvre, to reform, reorganise, and renew the charge.

Chapter 9

Manoeuvring a Cavalry Regiment

It is not possible to present time and motion studies for the cavalry on the same scale that they were presented for the infantry. There are two reasons for this. The first is that the horse does not regulate its step to a specific distance and it does not march in cadence; and the second is that the speed at which it moves is, consequently, relatively uncontrollable. As a result, the speeds of manoeuvre that will be used in this analysis are subjective, but based on period documentation. Indeed, the figures generated are intended solely for the purpose of comparing the manoeuvring systems, and they probably bear only a vague similarity to what might have actually occurred on the battlefield.

For the purposes of this study, the French *Ordonnance provisoire sur l'exercice et les manoeuvres de la cavalerie* has proven to be a fountain of useful information. It provides standard intervals and speeds for horses at every rate of movement, which have been used throughout the following time and motion studies. It also provides the standard dimensions used by French cavalry officers to calculate the manoeuvres of their squadrons and regiments. These will be applied as needed for each nation, on the premiss that a Prussian horse was not significantly different from a French horse. The *Ordonnance* provides speeds of manoeuvre in Title III, Article II, paragraph 347, as shown in Table 47.

Title III, Article VII, paragraph 404 states that two ranks of cavalry were six metres deep. Title I, Article XII states that the ranks had an interval of 0.666 metres, measured from the tail of the front horse to the nose of the rear rank. Finally, Title I, Article XIV states that for sizing a squadron, a horse should be considered to have a width equal to one third its length. The *Ordonnance* assigns them a width of one metre. It goes on to say that a *peloton* of 12 files would in fact occupy a frontage of nine to 10 metres, while a squadron of heavy cavalry would occupy a distance of 37–8 metres, a squadron of dragoons 36–7 metres, and a squadron of chasseurs or hussars 35–6 metres. However, these figures are for a squadron with a strength of approximately 100 men and horses, which is not accurate in light of the actual organisational and field strengths and will be modified accordingly.

No doubt this slight difference in the width of the different types of squadron was due to the sizes of the horses that were generally selected for each type of cavalry. Table 48, extracted from Margueron, provides the size of horses provided by the French to the different cavalry regiments. As can be seen, the smallest horses were in the chasseur, hussar, and chevauléger regiments. As the chevauxleger were raised long after the initial issuance of the *Ordonnance*, and as it was not updated until after 1815, they are not addressed in the 1805 *Ordonnance*.

Table 47. Speed of horses.

Pace	Metres per minute
Walk	97–107
Trot	194–214
Gallop	300

Table 48. Size of horses by regiment.

Type of regiment	Size of horse (metres)
Carabiniers/Cuirassiers	1.556–1.597
Dragoons	1.529–1.556
Hussars/Chasseurs	1.488–1.529
Chevauxléger	1.461–1.502

Table 49. Rates and distances used for analysis.

Width of 12 files	10 ft
Depth of two ranks	20 ft
Interval between ranks	2 ft
Walk	330 ft per minute
Trot	660 ft per minute
Gallop	990 ft per minute

For the purposes of this analysis all of these measurements were distilled down to feet and are summarised in Table 49. Where specific figures were not available for a particular nation the figures in this table were used.

Manoeuvring by 'threes' and 'fours'

In another source we find a discussion of an aspect of the manoeuvring process that is not generally considered when one's experience lies solely with the close-order drill of infantry. This relates to the manoeuvring of cavalry by 'threes' and 'fours' in some countries. In this process a horse was calculated as being one pace wide and three paces long. When positioning the second rank it was generally placed about two feet further behind the tail of the first horse, allocating to each horse an area of one pace by approximately four paces. Because of this calculation evolutions were conducted by 'fours', because this block of horses was a perfectly square manoeuvring element. The idea of conversions by 'threes' was the invention of the Prussian General Kalkreuth, and was adopted by the Prussians and, eventually, most of Europe. However, it was not adopted by Russia during the period of the Napoleonic Wars.

Movement by both 'threes' and 'fours' presented equal difficulties when forming a dense column (*colonne serrée*) and during flank marches. It was commonly used in the *demi-tour* or half-turn. Here the flank horse would remain stationary and the two or three horses to its side would wheel to the right or left in a pin-wheel fashion, until they had marched 180 degrees and were facing to the rear. This placed the file closers and second rank in front, the first rank in the middle, and the regimental and squadron officers behind the regiment. Hence the *demi-tour* was not a practical evolution in the presence of the enemy, because the *peloton* commanders were behind the front of their troops and because the colonel of the regiment was dependent on the good will of the second rank. Usually such manoeuvres were executed by *pelotons*.

Only in one instance does such a conversion seem to have been done, and done successfully. This was in the Battle of Dennewitz (6 September 1813) when a chevauléger regiment executed a demi-turn to the right under canister fire and in the presence of a numerous enemy cavalry. It was able to perform this manoeuvre solely because it was a veteran unit commanded by veterans. It was able to make its withdrawal without the slightest disorder.

French cavalry

The initial problem in dealing with French cavalry is that its strength varied considerably and was invariably below the authorised strength. Just prior to the 1812 campaign every squadron was theoretically brought up to a strength of 250 men and horses. Needless to say, not only was this not achieved, but whatever increase in strength was achieved was quickly lost in the snows of Russia. In 1813 it was terribly understrength and matters did not improve in 1814. There is also the problem of foot dragoons in the 1805–6 campaign, and foot hussars even earlier.

In the infantry it was felt to be safe to use the standard theoretical organisation because it was not uncommon for a unit to actually achieve that strength. However, for the reasons mentioned earlier, for the purpose of this analysis a French cavalry squadron will be considered to have 166 troopers. This figure is based on a quick analysis of average squadron strengths for the 1805, 1806, and 1809 campaigns. It was noted in this averaging process that the cuirassier squadrons tended to be smaller and that the chasseur/hussar squadrons tended to be larger The theoretical strength of a squadron in this period was as shown in Table 50.

This sets the width of an average French squadron at 83 files. Using the dragoon horses as an average horse width, and 48 files of dragoons being 36–7 metres an average width of a French squadron would have been about 63 metres or 208 ft. This should offset the strength differences to a degree.

For the purpose of this study only two formations, the column and the line, will be examined. The column has been calculated at the full and closed interval. Only the

Table 50. Theoretical squadron strengths 1805–9.

Cuirassiers	172 men
Dragoons	280 men
Chasseurs/Hussars	232 men

Figure 107. Fifth Manoeuvre, *Formation en avant en bataille –
Ordonnance provisoire sur l'exercice et les manoeuvres de la cavalerie,*
Paris, 1800, Title IV, Article II, Paragraphs 551–9 & Plate 107.

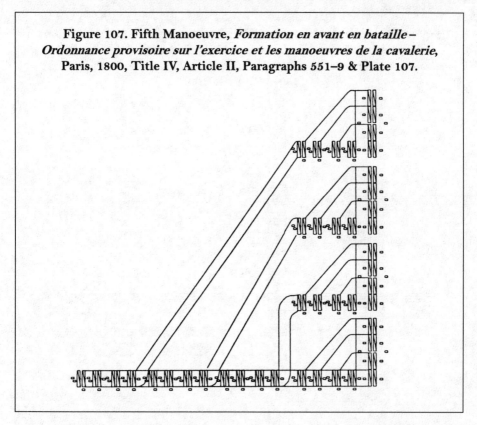

forms of column commonly used by each army will be reviewed. There has been no
attempt to force the various national cavalry units into using common formations because there appear to have been insufficient common manoeuvres to allow a comparison of manoeuvring systems.

Deploying from column to line

The first French manoeuvre to be examined is the changing of a column of *pelotons* to
line of battle. Figure 107 illustrates this manoeuvre. As can be seen, it closely resem-
bles the infantry manoeuvre of deploying on the head of a column to one flank.

One last interval must be defined before the analysis can be done. Note that the
regiment is formed with gaps between the squadrons and that the column also has
gaps between the squadrons. Title I, Article 14, which defines the intervals of a regiment, states that the interval between squadrons in a regiment should be 10 metres.
This interval was maintained, no matter what the formation, and was maintained between the *pelotons* in column as well. Also, since the formation was at full interval, the
interval between the leading *peloton* of one squadron and the rear *peloton* of the next
squadron would also include one *peloton*'s interval. This means that the length of a
regiment was 932 ft when the regiment was formed in line.

In the Fifth Manoeuvre, therefore, the last *peloton* would advance three intervals
(156 ft), perform a quarter-wheel using a moving pivot (40 ft), advance laterally a
distance determined by the frontage of the regiment less two *peloton* intervals (828 ft),

Figure 108. Seventh Manoeuvre, *Former en avant en Bataille sur le 1er Peloton du 3e Escadron – Ordonnance provisoire sur l'exercice Et les manoeuvres de la cavalerie*, Paris, 1800, Title IV, Article II, Paragraphs 560–67 & Plate 109.

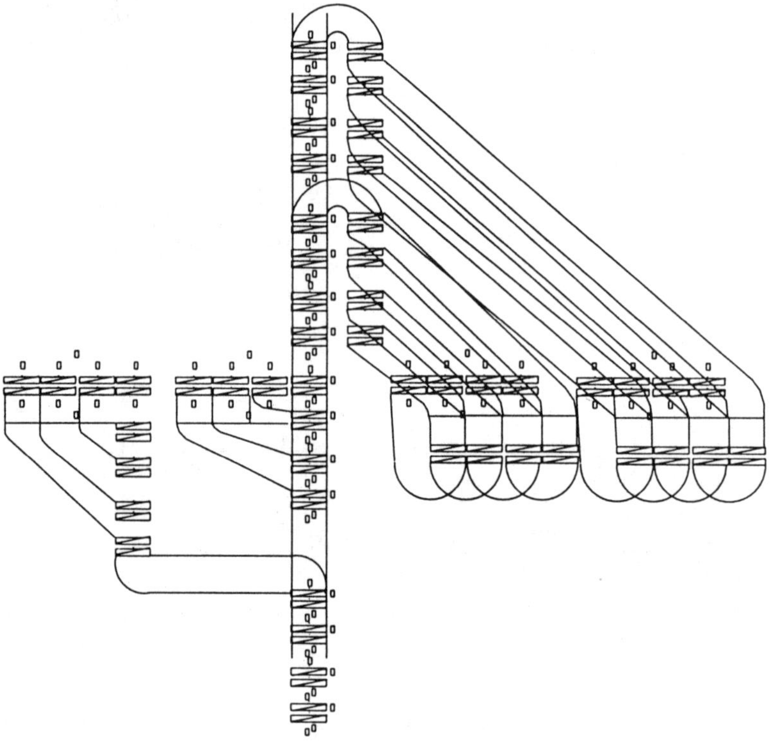

and the entire length of the column (724 ft). Using Pythagorean theorem this comes to 1190 ft. Finally the *peloton* performed a quarter-pivot into line (40 ft). The total manoeuvre takes the last *peloton* 1387 ft. As these manoeuvres were performed at the trot, they required 2.1 minutes to complete. If the regiment was deployed from column of *pelotons* to line on the centre, the Seventh Manoeuvre was used (Figure 108). Here the regiment formed on a *peloton* of one of the middle squadrons.

This time the lead *peloton* of the column had the greatest distance to cover. It would pivot 180 degrees (150 ft), advance three *peloton* intervals (156 ft), pivot 45 degrees (40 ft), advance 540 feet along the hypotenuse of a triangle with sides of eight *peloton* intervals plus two squadron intervals (482 ft) and four *peloton* intervals and two squadron intervals (241 ft), pivot 45 degrees (40 ft), advance a *peloton* interval (52 ft), pivot 180 degrees (150 ft), and advance an interval into position (52 ft). The total distance moved was 1138 ft, which, moving at a trot, required 1.7 minutes.

The next method of forming line from column is done by forming on the column's head to both the left and the right. Figure 109 shows how this was done.

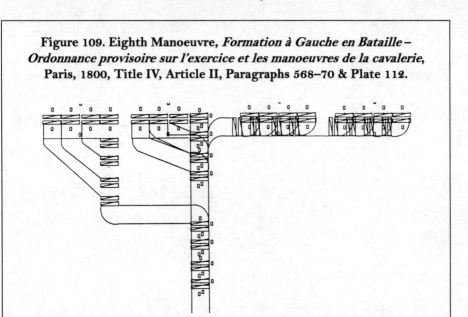

Figure 109. Eighth Manoeuvre, *Formation à Gauche en Bataille – Ordonnance provisoire sur l'exercice et les manoeuvres de la cavalerie*, Paris, 1800, Title IV, Article II, Paragraphs 568–70 & Plate 112.

The longest march was made by the rearmost *peloton*. It advanced three full squadron lengths, plus two 10 metre squadron spacing intervals, did a quarter-wheel, transitted the lateral distance to the end of the line, and did a quarter-wheel to fall into position. The total distance moved was 1263 ft, which at a trot would take 1.9 minutes. If the regiment wished to perform the same manoeuvre and face to the rear,

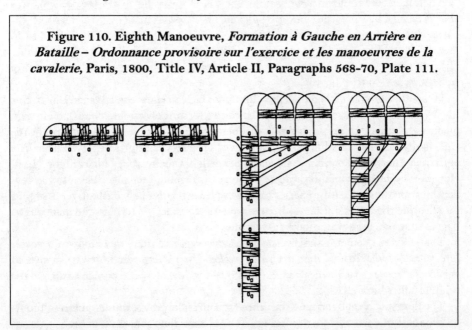

Figure 110. Eighth Manoeuvre, *Formation à Gauche en Arrière en Bataille – Ordonnance provisoire sur l'exercice et les manoeuvres de la cavalerie*, Paris, 1800, Title IV, Article II, Paragraphs 568-70, Plate 111.

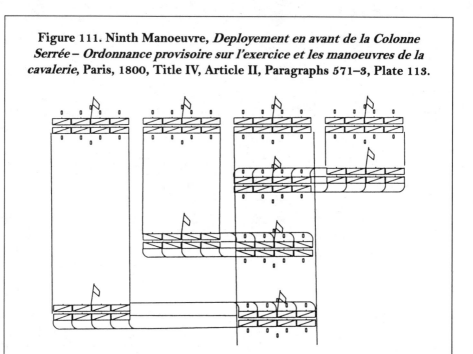

Figure 111. Ninth Manoeuvre, *Deployement en avant de la Colonne Serrée – Ordonnance provisoire sur l'exercice et les manoeuvres de la cavalerie*, Paris, 1800, Title IV, Article II, Paragraphs 571–3, Plate 113.

it did everything as previously described and then advanced one *peloton* interval, did a 180 degree wheel, and advancd one *peloton* interval and fell into position. The last *peloton* had travelled 1519 ft, which at a trot would have taken two minutes.

The other column formation used by the French was the *colonne serrée*. This was always formed by squadrons, never by *pelotons* or any other manoeuvre element. It was a heavy, dense formation where the interval between the squadrons was reduced to 10 metres (33 ft). The sole reported purpose of this formation was to conceal the number of troops present. The Ninth Manoeuvre addressed the conversion of a column of squadrons *serré* into a line of battle.

When the column wished to deploy into line the lead squadron advanced 20 metres (66 ft), and each of the rear squadrons faced to the right or left and did a flank march, much as the infantry performed this manoeuvre. Once they had advanced outwards sufficiently far, they faced forward and moved up into position. The fourth squadron again had the longest march. It advanced to the left, then marched forward for 742 ft. However, as with the infantry, the accordion effect would take place because the cavalry wheels by twos. This expands the line by two-thirds the length of a horse plus two feet for the normal interval between ranks. This adds 510 ft to the manoeuvre. The total manoeuvre would take 1.9 minutes.

The next manoeuvre from the *colonne serrée* is *par la queue de la colonne à gauche (droite) en bataille*. In this manoeuvre the *colonne serrée* expanded forward and each squadron, from the rear, wheeled left (or right) into line of battle perpendicular to the original line of march.

The first squadron must move out three squadron intervals, plus 30 metres (100 ft) to maintain the proper interval between squadrons, then wheel 90 degrees and advance six metres into line. As the rear squadron wheeled immediately, the first squadron actually advanced something less than three full squadron intervals. The basic formation was 54 metres (180 ft) thick. This means the first squadron advanced three squadron intervals (624 ft) less 260 ft, or 364 ft. The wheel required the outermost file to move 294 ft. Then the formation advanced six metres (20 ft) into line. The total manoeuvre required the squadron to move 678 ft and took one minute at a trot.

Ploying from line into column

The French appear to have had one principal method of converting a line into a column. This can be found only by examining the *Ecole de l'escadron à cheval* and is not addressed in the regimental manoeuvres section. Not surprisingly, this comprised a direct march into column by a 45 degree wheel towards where the column is to be formed, an oblique march to position, and a 45 degree wheel to fall into position. The flank *peloton* marched forward and each successive *peloton*, using the oblique march, fell into position behind it.

The result of this was that the last *peloton* in the regiment completed its movement just as the head *peloton* caused the column to advance sufficiently for the forming column to have cleared its position. This meant that the leading *peloton* had to advance 16 *peloton* intervals before it occupied the desired position of the last *peloton*, and another 16 *peloton* intervals before that position was cleared by the 15th *peloton*. This was a total of 32 *peloton* intervals and six squadron spacing intervals, or a total of 1862 ft, requiring 2.8 minutes to complete.

Of course, the quickest method of forming line or column was to do so by wheeling 90 degrees by *pelotons* (or squadrons) and form perpendicular to the original line of march. This manoeuvre required a minimum amount of time. To do so by *pelotons* required just a few seconds, probably no more than 10 or 15. I hesitate to be precise because it is in the first few seconds of manoeuvring that the orders are passed, horses are required to accelerate, and everyone figures out what is going on. The same ma-

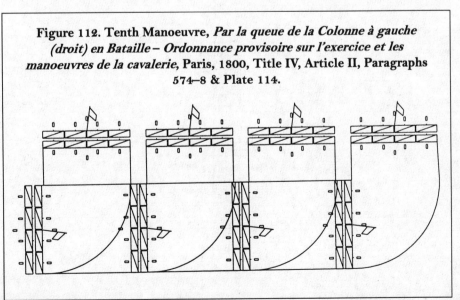

Figure 112. Tenth Manoeuvre, *Par la queue de la Colonne à gauche (droit) en Bataille – Ordonnance provisoire sur l'exercice et les manoeuvres de la cavalerie*, Paris, 1800, Title IV, Article II, Paragraphs 574–8 & Plate 114.

Figure 113. Ploying from line into column – *Ordonnance provisoire sur l'exercice et les manoeuvres de la cavalerie,* **Paris, 1800, Title III, Article VIII, Paragraph 465,** *L'escadron marchant de front, le romper en avant par pelotons,* **& Plate 92.**

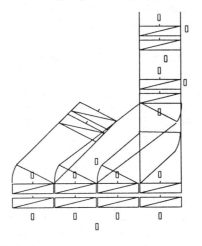

Figure 114. Wheeling a column into line on the flank. Title IV, Article II, Third manoeuvre, *Former à Gauche en Bataille –* *Ordonnance provisoire sur l'exercice et les manoeuvres de la cavalerie,* **Paris, 1800, Paragraphs 545–8 & Plate 105.**

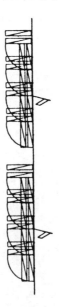

noeuvre by squadrons certainly took longer, but probably still took no more than 30 seconds to complete. Again, mathematical calculations for such a quick movement are not valid.

British cavalry

The strength of British cavalry regiments varied considerably because of the method by which Parliament funded its army and politics. This makes any study based on theoretical organisations almost impossible. Their authorised strengths from 1804 to 1815, as drawn from Parlimentary records, are shown in Table 51. As can be seen, their strengths varied from 415 to 1152 men.

Table 51. British cavalry regiments.

Total Authorised Strength

Regiment	1804	1805	1806	1807	1808	1809	1810	1811	1812	1813	1814	1815
1st Life Guards	415	417	416	416	416	416	416	416	417	583	673	473
2nd Life Guards	415	415	415	415	415	415	415	415	416	582	672	472
Royal Horse Guards	482	654	654	654	654	654	654	654	655	816	816	599
1st Dragoon Guards	1083	1083	1082	1082	1082	1083	1084	1084	1085	1085	1085	726
2nd Dragoon Guards	905	905	904	904	904	905	906	906	907	907	907	584
3rd Dragoon Guard	905	905	904	904	904	905	916	916	917	917	917	585
4th Dragoon Guards	905	905	904	904	904	905	906	906	917	917	907	584
5th Dragoon Guards	905	905	904	904	904	905	906	906	917	917	917	584
6th Dragoon Guards	905	905	904	904	904	905	906	906	907	907	907	584
7th Dragoon Guards	905	905	904	904	904	905	906	906	907	907	907	584
1st Dragoons	905	1125	904	904	904	905	916	916	917	917	917	584
2nd Dragoons	905	905	904	904	904	905	904	906	907	907	907	584
3rd Dragoons	905	906	905	905	905	905	907	907	918	918	918	585
4th Dragoons	905	905	904	904	904	905	916	916	917	917	917	584
5th Dragoons	905	Disbanded										
6th Dragoons	905	905	904	904	904	905	904	906	907	906	906	584
7th Dragoons	905	1125	904	904	904	905	905	906	696	917	917	1097
8th Light Dragoons	720	720	720	720	720	928	928	929	942	942	941	1051
9th Light Dragoons	905	905	904	904	904	905	696	696	727	727	727	584
10th Light Dragoons	905	905	904	904	904	905	906	906	907	907	1097	584
11th Light Dragoons	905	1125	904	904	904	905	904	906	917	917	907	584
12th Light Dragoons	905	905	904	904	904	905	906	906	917	917	917	584
13th Light Dragoons	905	1125	904	904	904	905	916	916	917	917	917	584
14th Light Dragoons	905	1125	904	904	904	905	916	916	917	917	917	917
15th Light Dragoons	905	1125	904	904	904	905	906	906	907	907	1097	584
16th Light Dragoons	905	905	904	904	904	905	916	916	917	917	917	584
17th Light Dragoons	905	905	904	904	890	940	940	1151	1152	1257	1251	1151
18th Light Dragoons	905	1125	904	904	904	905	916	906	907	907	1097	584
19th Light Dragoons	720	720	720	720	904	695	485	696	697	697	697	697
20th Light Dragoons	905	905	904	904	904	905	916	916	917	917	941	721
21st Light Dragoons	905	905	904	904	904	905	941	941	942	1152	1151	1151
22nd Light Dragoons	720	720	720	720	878	928	928	929	942	1152	1151	1151
23rd Light Dragoons	905	1125	904	904	904	905	706	696	697	907	907	584
24th Light Dragoons	720	720	720	720	720	928	928	929	1152	1152	1151	1151
25th Light Dragoons	?	720	711	720	890	940	1150	1151	1152	1152	1151	1151
26th Light Dragoons	Disbanded											
27th Light Dragoons	720	Disbanded										
28th Light Dragoons	Disbanded											
29th Light Dragoons	720	727	Disbanded									

The theoretical strengths did vary, but generally there were 100 files per squadron. Since they tended to keep their strength better than the French this figure will be used for the analysis. This gives a British squadron a theoretical width of 300 feet. The regulation does specify that a file was a yard wide, which is not significantly different from the French measurements. The figure of one yard has been used in the following analysis.

The interval between British squadrons was one third of their actual front, but there was no additional or different interval between regiments or brigades. This meant that a British regiment of four squadrons had a total frontage of 1500 ft. It is interesting to note that a French four-squadron regiment had an average frontage of 862 ft and at full strength (250 men per squadron maximum) had a frontage of 1247 ft.

The British provide no estimates of the speed of the walk, trot, or gallop, so the French rates will be used. It is worth nothing that the British regulation states that in a flank march the cavalry occupied three times the interval it occupied when facing to the front. It is also worth noting that the British used a movable pivot, like the French.

Deploying from column into line

The British used two columns, the open column and the closed column. The British open column was the equivalent of the French column of fours, only it was done with

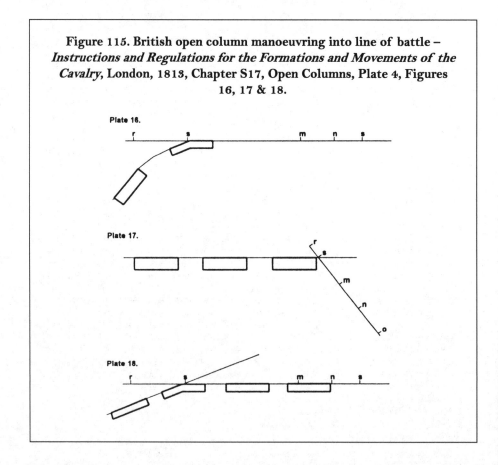

Figure 115. British open column manoeuvring into line of battle – *Instructions and Regulations for the Formations and Movements of the* ***Cavalry,*** **London, 1813, Chapter S17, Open Columns, Plate 4, Figures 16, 17 & 18.**

Plate 16.

Plate 17.

Plate 18.

a frontage of at least six files and at most 12 files. Apparently they formed line from this formation by streaming in a long queue, following the leader, and, once they were marching along the position where they wished to form line, wheeled by threes to the right (or left). Figure 115, extracted from the Regulation, demonstrates this.

Assuming that the cavalry regiment chose to perform this manoeuvre with a frontage of 12, the regulated maximum, each squadron would theoretically break into eight segments. The squadron still occupied an interval of 300 ft plus 'one third their actual length', or a total of 400 ft. The accordion effect does not come into play because of the extended frontage of each element. For the regiment to move into the position where it wishes to form line, it needs only to march its entire length (1500 ft) and wheel, by twelves, into position. The wheel would take 51 ft, so the manoeuvre covered 1551 ft, which would take 2.35 minutes.

The British also used a variation of the French manoeuvre of marching diagonally directly to their final position. However, instead of wheeling forward, their units wheeled backwards. Once pointed in the correct direction they marched off to the intended line and wheeled into final position.

The reverse wheel was in fact a series of individual circling movements where each trooper turned his horse about, walked to the rear, and turned it about again. In a tight formation this must have been a difficult manoeuvre that more closely resembled a series of dominoes falling, each horse moving in its turn from the outermost (furthest moving) flank of the wheeling troop inwards. In addition, it has to have been done at a walk. If we assume a column of troops to be performing this manoeuvre the length of time for the troop to wheel to the rear may have been as great as 30 seconds. This is,

Figure 116. British direct march – *Instructions and Regulations for the Formations and Movements of the Cavalry*, London, 1813, Chapter S20, Changes of position of a Regiment, Plate 2, Figures 7 & 8.

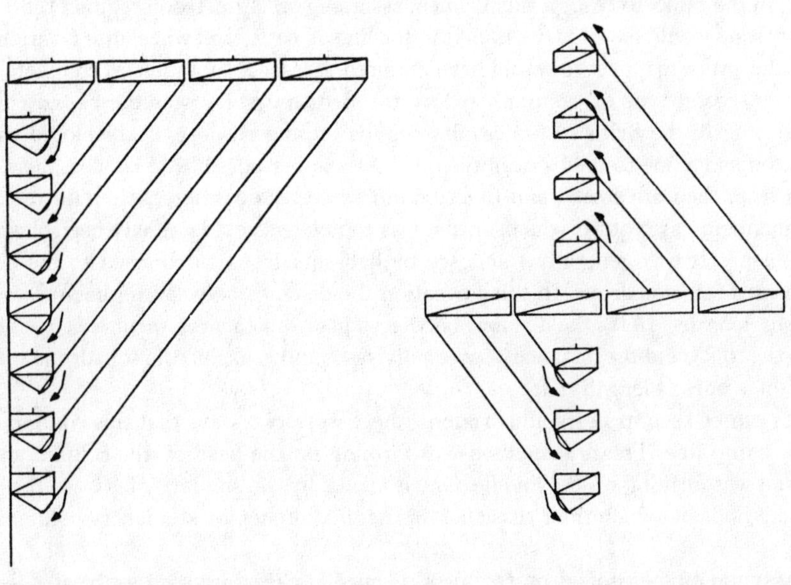

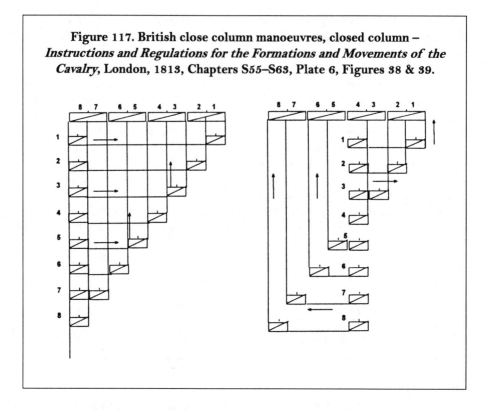

Figure 117. British close column manoeuvres, closed column –
Instructions and Regulations for the Formations and Movements of the
Cavalry, London, 1813, Chapters S55–S63, Plate 6, Figures 38 & 39.

however, an estimate, based on the 120 ft the outermost horseman had to cover and the assumption that once they had all walked back to position there would be some jostling in the ranks to realign them. Then, assuming an eight-troop regiment, the rearmost troop would have to trot 1909 ft to the line of battle and wheel into position (115 ft). The entire manoeuvre would have required at least 3.1 minutes to complete.

The second type of column used by the British cavalry was the closed column. According to the British 1799 cavalry regulation, the purpose of the closed column was to form a line to the front in the quickest manner possible, to conceal their numbers from their adversary, and to extend in whatever direction the circumstances of the moment may require, which, until it was completed, could not have been obvious to the enemy. It was generally composed of half-squadrons, in contrast to the French who used full squadrons. In this formation the distance between regiments was two horses' lengths (18 ft), the distance between squadrons in a regiment was one horse's length (10 ft), and the distance between divisions and ranks of the squadrons was one half of a horse's length (5 ft).

As can be seen from the illustrations, there were two ways that this column could deploy into line. The first method was forming on the head of the column and the second was forming on the middle. One is struck by the similarity between these and the methods by which the Prussian 1788 Regulation deployed infantry columns into line.

Assuming a four-squadron regiment, formed at closed interval we have a distance of 205 ft from the nose of the rearmost troop to the head of the column. If the system

Figure 118. Line of battle to column of troops – *Instructions and Regulations for the Formations and Movements of the Cavalry,* **London, 1813, Chapter S56, When the Regiment From Line Forms Close Column, Plate 6, Figure 34.**

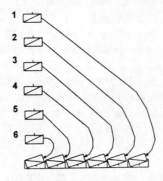

in Figure 117 was used, the rearmost half-squadron filed to the left by twos. It advanced seven troop intervals (1050 ft), plus three squadron spacing intervals (150 ft) and suffered the accordion effect (450 ft), moving a total of 1650 ft to the flank. Assuming that the wheel to the front took no time it only remained for the rearmost half-squadron to advance forward into line 205 ft. The manoeuvre would take 2.8 minutes. If the system shown in Figure 118 was used, the half-squadron at the head of the column set the pace. It moved to the flank by twos, as described earlier, and travelled a total of 1650 ft. This manoeuvre took 2.5 minutes. If the system shown in Figure 119 was used the rearmost half-squadron moved four half-squadron intervals to the left, two squadron separation intervals, and accordions. This is a total of 900 ft. It then advanced the 245 ft to the front. This manoeuvre covered 1145 ft and took 1.75 minutes.

Figure 119. Line of battle to column of troops on the centre – *Instructions and Regulations for the Formations and Movements of the Cavalry,* **London, 1813, Chapter S56, When the Regiment From Line Forms Close Column, Plate 6, Figure 33.**

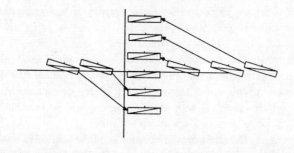

Ploying from line into column

When the British ployed a line into a closed column they used a direct marching system. The troops did a counter-march by threes from the opposite flank, passed behind the line, and marched directly to their final position.

As this was done by threes there was no accordion effect problem. The rearmost troop, again, moved the furthest. It was obliged to move 1514 ft at a trot, which it would do in approximately 2.3 minutes.

The British could also go to a column by forming on the central troop. It did this by a direct march, without a counter-march, and was significantly faster, requiring the regiment to move 421 ft and taking 0.65 minutes.

And, as with the French, the British could always take a column of squadrons or troops and wheel them 90 degrees into a line perpendicular to the line of march (see Figure 114). For a column of troops this manoeuvre required 0.4 minutes. For a column of squadrons it required 0.7 minutes.

Prussian cavalry

The Prussian 1796 Hussar and Bosniaken Regulation is an interesting document. Unfortunately the theory regarding the proper use of light cavalry in the Prussian army at this time was not that it should stand in the battle line, but that it would act more or less as mounted skirmishers. Yes, the Regulation speaks of line and regimental attacks, but it devotes considerably more time to attacks that support the operations of battle cavalry, to flank and rear attacks, and to the *Schwarm* attack. Also it only provides descriptions of squadron manoeuvres, not of regimental manoeuvres, with the exception of some by hussars as they swing around the flanks of their own cavalry to strike the flank and rear of an enemy cavalry line.

As a result, this analysis is based solely on the 1812 *Exerzir Reglement für die Kavallerie der Königlich Preussischen Armee* and is, unfortunately, only entirely valid for the period 1812 to 1815. Prussian regulations have a nasty habit of assuming that the reader is already familiar with many minor details and these are regularly left out of this Regulation, but, fortunately, it was possible to find most of the required figures. That the Prussians formed their cavalry with a two *Fuss* (approximately two feet) interval between the ranks is based on a pencilled note in the regulation citing the Cabinet Order of 17 February 1795. The intervals between squadrons were four paces (which is treated as 12 ft). The intervals between regiments were 12 paces.

Prussian sources provide no dimensions for their horses, nor do they provide speeds, so the French figures will be used for those calculations. Consequently the 1812 Prussian cavalry squadron, which had 58 files, had a width of approximately 145 ft.

Deploying from column to line

The Prussians had two basic columns, column of half-squadrons and column of squadrons. They had two intervals, open (*geöffneten*) and closed (*geschlossenen* or *masse*). The open column had intervals equal to the size of a *Zug* or squadron. It also had an additional four feet (the interval appears to change when in closed column) between each squadron, be the column in *Züge* or squadrons.

When deploying on the head of the column the first *Zug* advanced six paces and stopped. Each successive *Zug* wheeled to the right (or left) and marched directly on the

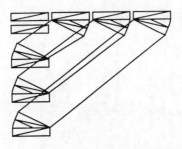

Figure 120. Deploying an open column through swinging – *Exerzir-Reglement für die Kavallerie der Königlich Preussischen Armee,* **8th Chapter,** *Entwicklung der Colonnen, 2. Aufmarsch einer geöffneten Colonne durch das Einschwenken.*

diagonal to its final position and wheeled left (or right) when its flank touched the opposite flank of the *Zug* that preceded it in the column. The rearmost *Zug* moved the greatest distance, doing two 45 degree wheels and advancing along the diagonal. The manoeuvre required it to advance 421 ft and would have taken 0.64 minutes.

The Prussian closed column could be formed either by squadron or by half-squadron. Though not mentioned specifically, the manoeuvres it performed necessitated that it was formed at a *Zug* interval. When formed by squadron and deploying into line the 2nd, 3rd, and 4th squadrons wheeled by *Züge* to the right (or left), advanced parallel to the intended line of battle until they were opposite their final position, when they would wheel to the left (or right) and advance into it. Any of the *Züge* in the last squadron advanced the same distance. They performed two 90 degree wheels, advanced 12 *Zug* intervals and three squadron spacing intervals to the flank. The squadron then advanced three *Zug* intervals. This manoeuvre took slightly over one minute (1.05 minutes).

Figure 121. Deploying a regiment to the right, swing squadrons by *Züge* **to the right, Prussian General Staff –** *Urkundliche Beiträge und Forschungen zur Geschichte des Preussischen Heeres, Abbild* 17, *Regiment – rechts deployiert!, Eskadron mit Züge rechts schwenkt – Marsch! Trab!*

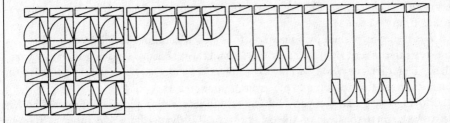

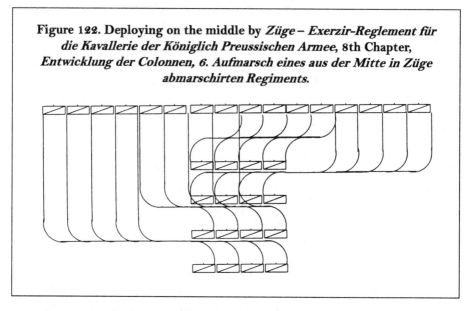

Figure 122. Deploying on the middle by *Züge – Exerzir-Reglement für die Kavallerie der Königlich Preussischen Armee,* **8th Chapter,** *Entwicklung der Colonnen, 6. Aufmarsch eines aus der Mitte in Züge abmarschirten Regiments.*

If the closed column deployed on the middle the 1st and 2nd squadrons wheeled by *Züge* to the right while the 3rd and 4th squadrons wheeled by *Züge* to the left. By this means the column expanded in both directions simultaneously and the junction of the second and third squadrons formed where the centre of the original column had lain. The 4th squadron's *Züge* made the longest move. They performed two 90 degree wheels, then advancd five *Zug* intervals and one squadron spacing interval to the left, and finally advanced three *Zug* intervals. This manoeuvre took 0.63 minutes.

Ploying from line to column

The Prussians used two basic systems to ploy from line to column. In the first, when forming a column of squadrons or *Züge,* the manoeuvre elements filed by twos to the flank where the column was to be formed and, thence, directly to the rear. Continuing in Indian file until the squadron or *Zug* had withdrawn to the depth of its position in the intended column, it would turn 90 degrees towards the final column's location and march to its final position. The principal problem with this manoeuvre's timing was the accordion effect. By filing by twos, what was formerly two metres wide (two horses side by side) now became three metres long (the length of a horse). In addition, the normal interval between horses in the same file is inserted between each brace of horsemen. This takes a *Zug* and expands it from 36 to 173 ft, while a squadron expands from 145 to 694 ft.

When ploying a line by squadrons to a closed column the file moved three *Zug* intervals to the rear, then 12 *Zug* intervals and three squadron spacing intervals to the flank. That distance is 471 ft. The accordion effect added 694 less 145, or 549 ft, to the manoeuvre so that the time to ploy was 1.5 minutes.

Ploying to the half-company column (at full interval) is slightly different. The *Zug* that was to form the head of the column actually advanced one *Zug* interval, thereby reducing the distance moved by the last *Zug*. The last *Zug* wheeled 90 degrees (51 ft),

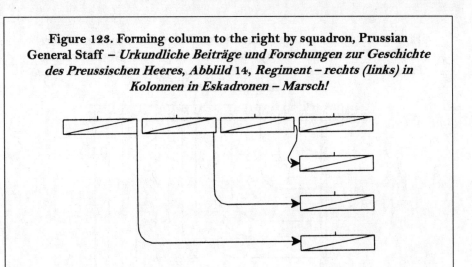

Figure 123. Forming column to the right by squadron, Prussian General Staff – *Urkundliche Beiträge und Forschungen zur Geschichte des Preussischen Heeres, Abblild 14, Regiment – rechts (links) in Kolonnen in Eskadronen – Marsch!*

marched diagonally to its final position (300 ft), then marched one further *Zug* interval (36.25 ft). Adding in the accordion effect (173 – 35 = 138 ft) the total manoeuvre covered 526 ft and took 0.8 minutes. This is significantly longer than the previous manoeuvre because the column was formed at full interval, not the compressed interval of a closed column.

One last manoeuvre was the ploying from line into *Zug* column. This was quite similar to the previous manoeuvre and took 1.7 minutes.

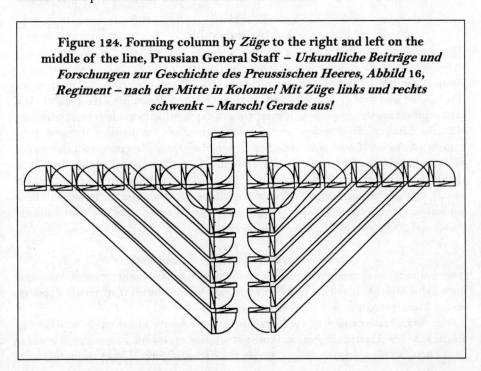

Figure 124. Forming column by *Züge* to the right and left on the middle of the line, Prussian General Staff – *Urkundliche Beiträge und Forschungen zur Geschichte des Preussischen Heeres, Abbild 16, Regiment – nach der Mitte in Kolonne! Mit Züge links und rechts schwenkt – Marsch! Gerade aus!*

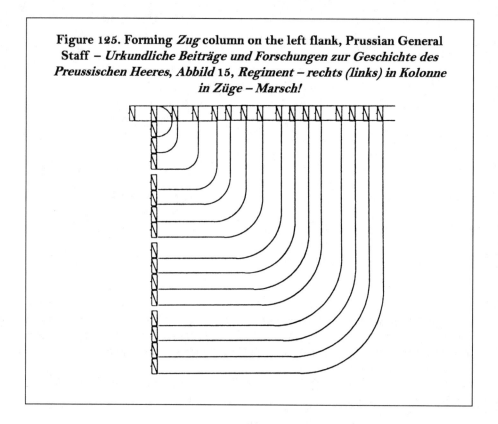

Figure 125. Forming *Zug* column on the left flank, Prussian General Staff – *Urkundliche Beiträge und Forschungen zur Geschichte des Preussischen Heeres, Abbild 15, Regiment – rechts (links) in Kolonne in Züge – Marsch!*

Austrian cavalry

The organisation of the Austrian cavalry was different to that of the other nations examined so far. Each Austrian cuirassier and dragoon regiment had six squadrons. A *chevauxleger* or *uhlan* regiment had eight squadrons. The hussar regiment had up to 10. There were also four slightly different field squadron organisations. In addition each regiment had a reserve squadron that served as a depot, which was only slightly smaller than the field squadron and in wartime was disbanded and distributed to the field squadrons. As the *Dienst-Reglement für die kaiserlich-königliche Cavallerie* (1808) provides no indication of a 'wartime' organisation, it can only be assumed that the distribution of the reserve squadron into the field squadrons was intended to bring them up to full strength. As a result, all calculations will be based on a 'full complement' field squadron. There were really only two different squadron organisations, heavy squadrons having 134 men and light squadrons 150.

Squadron organisation, dimensions, and speeds

The Austrian squadrons were formed in two ranks. The Regulation provides no guidance to the interval allowed for each trooper, nor does it address manoeuvring speeds, so the French statistics will be used for these.

For the cuirassier and dragoon (heavy) squadron we have 112 troopers, or 64 in the front rank. The Austrian Regulation does not provide any estimate regarding the width of a horse, so we are again obliged to use the French figures. Using the dimensions provided for a French cuirassier horse, this gives a squadron frontage of 160 ft. For the *chevauxleger*, hussar and uhlan (light) squadrons we have 128 troopers, or 72 in the front rank. Using the dimensions provided for a French chasseur/hussar horse, this gives a squadron frontage of 170 ft.

These heavy and light squadrons were then organised so that two squadrons formed a division. Each squadron consisted of two half-squadrons (80 and 85 ft respectively) or four *Züge* (40 and 42.5 ft respectively). To simplify matters, the heavy regiments will all be considered to have six squadrons and the light regiments will be considered to have eight squadrons. The figures for hussar regiments, which had 10 squadrons, will be placed in parentheses after the light cavalry manoeuvring times.

It is also interesting to note that the 1808 Regulation provides no illustrations of regimental manoeuvres, but limits itself to those of divisions and squadrons. This is a not-so-subtle clue that Austrian focus was not on the regiment, but on the squadron. If this is the case, it partly explains why the French cavalry was so regularly successful against Austrian cavalry. If the Austrians operated theirs as more or less independent squadrons these would have found themselves facing the crushing superior regimental organisation of the French and would most certainly have been at a terrible disadvantage.

The Austrian 1808 Regulation is a miserable document which devotes more time to church services, payrolls and musters than it does to military manoeuvres. The only truly 'military' material it contains is found in the plates at the back. Needless to say, it does not provide any estimations of the speed of a horse, so we are again obliged to use the French figures. This means that at a trot a heavy squadron would have covered its length in approximately 0.245 minutes and a light squadron in 0.26 minutes. A 90 degree wheel required 1.257 minutes for a heavy squadron and 1.335 minutes for a light squadron.

Deploying into line

The Austrian manoeuvres strongly resemble those of the other nations. Figure 126 shows what was probably the quickest method of forming line of battle from a column. In this the entire manoeuvre is controlled by the time taken to pivot. Table 52 summarises the type of column and the time required to execute the manoeuvre.

Figure 127 shows a manoeuvre nearly as simple as that shown in Figure 126. As each half-squadron reached its turning point it wheeled to the flank and stopped. The last half-squadron determined the time required for the manoeuvre. In a heavy squadron it advanced 12 half-squadron lengths, wheeled, and advanced another half-squadron interval. The 13 half-squadron intervals (1040 ft) plus the half-squadron wheel

Table 52. Austrian cavalry manoeuvring speeds.		
	Time to manoeuvre (minutes)	
Column	*Heavy regiment*	*Light regiment*
Column of squadrons	1.257	1.335
Column of half-squadrons	0.628	0.668
Column of *Züge*	0.314	0.334

Figure 126. Deploying from column into line by swinging to the flank – *Dienst-Reglement für die kaiserlich-königliche Cavallerie*, Vienna, 1808, *Stellung einer Division Cavallerie zu Pferd nebst der Schwenkung mit Züge und halb escadrons*, Plate 1.

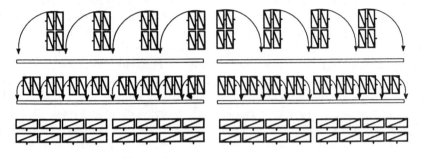

Figure 127. Deploying into line behind the front – *Dienst-Reglement für die kaiserlich-königliche Cavallerie*, Vienna, 1808, *Aufmarsch mit Abthielangen hinter der Front*, Plate 10.

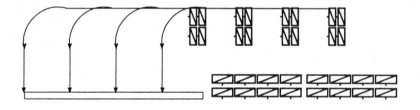

Figure 128. Deploying a column of *Züge* on the column head – *Dienst-Reglement für die kaiserlich-königliche Cavallerie*, Vienna, 1808, *Deploirung Einer Colonne von Züge in das Alignement der Tete*, Plate 11.

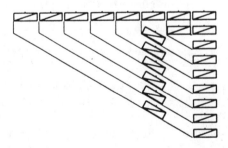

(126 ft) covered a distance of 1166 ft and would have taken 5.83 minutes at a trot, or 7.43 (9.03) minutes for a light regiment.

Figure 128 shows a manoeuvre identical to that performed by French infantry when they deployed from column into line. This is the only example of a cavalry unit performing a filing type of march that was uncovered during the research for this book. Here the accordion effect could have had a tremendous effect, as the horse is three times as long as it is wide. Unfortunately, the 1808 Regulation doesn't tell us whether this manoeuvre was done by twos or threes. As it was a relatively common practice, we are obliged to assume that it was done by threes.

The first *Zug* remained stationary and the other *Züge* moved to assume position in line in relation to it. As usual, the rearmost *Zug* determined the time required to complete the manoeuvre. In the case of a heavy regiment, it must advance along the hypotenuse of a triangle determined by the length of the column, 23 *Zug* intervals, and the length of the line, 23 more *Zug* intervals, plus one *Zug* interval to advance into line. A heavy regiment required 6.707 minutes to execute this, and a light regiment 9.477 (11.961) minutes.

Ploying into column

A study of the Regulation shows that there were more methods of forming column from line than there were for forming line from column. However, these variations

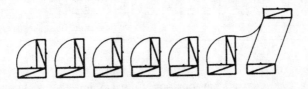

Figure 129a. Forming a column on the right flank *Zug – Dienst-Reglement für die kaiserlich-königliche Cavallerie*, **Vienna, 1808,** *Formirung einer Column vor dem rechten Flugel Zug*, **Plate 13, Figure 1.**

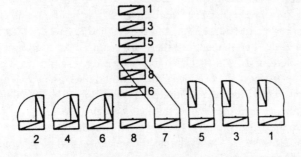

Figure 129b. Forming a column on the 8th *Zug – Dienst-Reglement für die kaiserlich-königliche Cavallerie*, **Vienna, 1808,** *Formirung einer Column vor dem achten Zug der Division*, **Plate 13, Figure 2.**

Figure 130a. Forming column on the division middle by half-divisions – *Dienst-Reglement für die kaiserlich-königliche Cavallerie*, Vienna, 1808, *Abmarsch mit halben Escadron aus der Mitte ein Division*, Plate 17, Figure l.

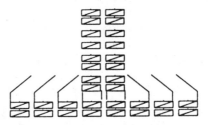

Figure 130b. Forming column with half-squadrons on the middle of two divisions – *Dienst-Reglement für die kaiserlich-königliche Cavallerie*, Vienna, 1808, *Abmarsch mit halben Escadron aus der Mitte zweyer Divisions*, Plate 17, Figure 2.

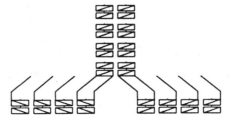

result more from the desire of the commanding officer to position one squadron, one division, or one *Zug* in a particular position in the column, than from anything else.

Figure 129a shows the procedure for forming a column on the right flank *Zug*. This simple manoeuvre was close enough to being the reverse of that shown in Figure 126 to permit comparison. The flank *Zug* merely marched obliquely to provide sufficient room for the following *Zug* to wheel properly, then it marched straight forward with the other *Züge* in tow. As usual the last *Zug* set the time for the manoeuvre. A heavy regiment had 24 *Züge*, so the last *Zug* had to cover 23 *Zug* intervals and two 90 degree wheels. The light regiment had 32 *Züge*, and the last had to cover 31 *Zug* intervals and two 90 degree wheels. The manoeuvre therefore required 5.228 minutes for a heavy regiment to complete, and 7.271 (8.975) minutes for a light regiment. It could be done on a regimental level, but it is more likely that it would have been done on a divisional basis; the divisions would then queue into position, acting as independent sub-formations of the regiment, until the final formation was developed.

In Figure 129b the same column is formed on the middle *Zug*, the two flanks wheeling to the middle. However, if one examines the sequence of the *Züge* one will see that the odd-numbered ones come first and the even-numbered ones follow in reverse or-

Figure 131a. Changing facing on a flank – *Dienst-Reglement für die kaiserlich-königliche Cavallerie*, Vienna, 1808, *Formirung der Front auf der Stelle in die rechts Flanque*, Plate 7, Figure 1.

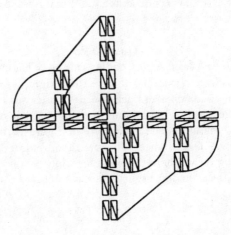

Figure 131b. Changing facing on the centre – *Dienst-Reglement für die kaiserlich-königliche Cavallerie*, Vienna, 1808, *Gebrochene Schwenkung auf der Mitte einer Division*, Plate 7, Figure 2.

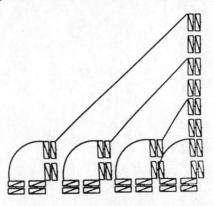

der. This is to allow the division to fold. The manoeuvring time of the last *Zug* in the column is the same as in Figure 129a, because it had to wait for the previous seven *Züge* to take their positions. However, it is worth nothing that this manoeuvre could probably not be executed by a regiment. If it was attempted, too many problems would have occurred with the mixing of *Züge* from other squadrons.

The two illustrations in Figure 130 are most definitely not manoeuvres that would be executed by a regiment. In fact, since they are illustrated in the Regulation on a divisional and a squadron level, there is strong reason to suspect that they were never intended to be executed on a regimental level. Unfortunately, as the Regulation provides absolutely no descriptive text on this or any other manoeuvre, we are obliged to make some assumptions regarding how it was carried out. It is most probable that the *Züge* made quarter-wheels, marched laterally until above their final position, quarter-wheeled again, and marched forward one interval into place. To expand this into a regimental manoeuvre would require assumptions that are not justified and, therefore, no calculations for this are provided.

Pivoting a line

These manoeuvres were performed by half-squadrons. That in Figure 131a required the furthest half-squadron to wheel 90 degrees to the right, then 45 degrees to the left, advance along a line of march 4.243 half-squadron intervals long, and wheel 45 degrees to the right. For a heavy division this manoeuvre would require 4.2 minutes, for a light division 4.475 minutes. The manoeuvre in Figure 131b required a 90 degree wheel to the right, a 45 degree wheel to the left, a movement of 1.414 half-squadron intervals, and a 45 degree wheel to the right, for which a heavy squadron would have required 3.078 minutes and a light squadron 3.273 minutes.

Chapter 10

Artillery During the Napoleonic Wars

In order to understand Napoleonic artillery it is easiest to begin with an examination of the history of its evolution and the philosophies which guided it.

The artillery used by the French Royal Artillery establishment had undergone a considerable change in the years immediately preceding the Revolution, having been transformed into a single, systematically organised force as a result of the efforts of Vallière and Gribeauval. The Gribeauval System, established on 3 October 1772, remained in use until 1803, when it was replaced by the System of the Year XI. It was restored during the Second Restoration in 1815, and finally abandoned in 1827 in favour of the System *de Valée*.

Vallière's reforms of fortifications and siege artillery were not altered by Gribeauval, whose attention was focussed on establishing a new field artillery system based on three standardised weapons. This move towards reform resulted from disastrous experiences in the Seven Years War, in which France lost the use of much of its artillery as a result of its lack of mobility. Louis XV recalled Gribeauval from foreign service, drawing together the latest technology and best military expertise he could obtain. Louis' goal was to get the best that could be gleaned from the Prussian and Austrian systems, and in Gribeauval he found the architect for his new system.

Gribeauval had directed the Austrian artillery establishment nearly single-handedly and was later second in command of the Prussian artillery under Frederick the Great. He felt that the keys to solving France's artillery problems were absolute uniformity of equipment, and the construction of all its guns to conform to the manner in which they were intended to be used. He also sought to separate field from siege artillery.

Gribeauval's first modification to French artillery equipment was to decrease the calibre of the guns by shortening them to 18 calibres. Thus he reduced the weight of the field-pieces, and later the weight of their carriages, so as to permit easier movement on the battlefield. He also had field-pieces cast in bronze, because it was significantly lighter than iron. The next step was to eliminate all of the heavy, siege artillery from the field train. The largest field-piece was to be a 12-pdr. Gribeauval felt that larger guns were only a hindrance: they lacked mobility and did not fire fast enough, nor with sufficient destructive force, for use against formed troops. The expense and difficulty involved in dragging them around the battlefield was therefore unjustified.

Types of artillery

There were three fundamental types of artillery: field, coastal and siege. The last two differed only in usage, both consisting of heavy guns – 16-pdrs and larger – mortars, and heavy howitzers. Siege guns were designed to inflict damage on fortifications and tended to be very unmanoeuvrable. Their goal was to punch holes in earthworks or masonry fortifications to create a breach for the besieging infantry. They rarely appeared on the battlefield after the Seven Years War. When they did, it was either because they were being transported and had the misfortune to be on the field when the battle began, or because they were caught up in a sally from a besieged fortress. Field artillery consisted of lighter guns – 12-pdrs or smaller – that were mounted on field-carriages and were used in conjunction with infantry and cavalry on the battle-field. It was sub-divided into foot and horse artillery. In a foot artillery battery the gunners marched alongside their guns and rarely rode the limbers. In a horse battery the gunners were mounted. Depending on the nation and the period, they either rode the limbers, gun-carriages and team horses, or were mounted independently.

The advantage of horse artillery over foot artillery was that it was far more mobile and more adapted to following the movements of the infantry and cavalry. It was able to respond quickly to sudden attacks by the enemy, and to reinforce weak points. On the other hand, it was far more expensive than foot artillery; it was rarely equipped with guns larger than a 6-pdr and therefore had less firepower; required a large number of horses; and the gunners themselves required more training than in a foot battery.

The philosophy of horse artillery was probably most clearly stated by Major E.S. May in 1896, when he wrote:

> In the old days of round shot and case a good horse artillery range was 400 yards: 200 yards was even better. The horse artillery guns were comparatively useless unless they galloped right into a fight, and their whole energies were concentrated on getting to close quarters as soon as possible. Even on the battlefield itself they might gallop up to within a few hundred yards of a mass of infantry, unlimber and come into action without excessive loss, and then a pitiless storm of case was often more than a match for the musketry fire which clumsy flint-locks could bring to bear.

D'Urtubie states that because of its lightness, this type of artillery could be attached to cavalry and support their manoeuvres by its fire. He advocated the massing or fragmenting of horse batteries to deceive the enemy, and the equipping of French horse artillery of the Revolution with 8-pdr cannons and 6-inch howitzers. He states that the 12-pdr was acceptable in a horse battery and at times during the Revolution it was indeed equipped with 12-pdr guns, though not often. However, the 12-pdr had the problem of being very heavy, making rapid manoeuvres difficult. D'Urtubie favoured the 8-pdr because, at a maximum range of 3600 ft, its shot could penetrate completely through masses of troops; and the 6-inch howitzer because its exploding shell – containing 61 balls, which made it especially murderous – would cause chaos in ranks of horses when fired at them.

Some other interesting aspects of horse artillery come to light in reading Seruzier's *Mémoires*. Seruzier states very clearly that in the battles of Heilsburg (against Russian and Prussian cavalry), Wagram (where they seized an Austrian battery), and Borodino (against cossacks) he ordered his horse gunners to mount up and attack an enemy formation as if they were cavalry. The account of the British horse battery in Spain cutting its way through a regiment of French chasseurs is, therefore, neither an historical aberration, nor in any way unusual.

I cannot speak for British training, but the French horse artillerists, when formed between 1794–8, were organised with a few trained artillery specialists and large num-

Table 53. Foot artillery division crews.

	French artillery company 1805	British artillery company 1803	Westphalian artillery company 1808
Officers	4	5	4
NCOs	9	16	5
Gunners	86	116–24	90
Musicians	2	3	4
Others	4	2	1
Total	100	142–50	107

	French train company 1805	British train company 1803	Westphalian train company 1808
Officers	1	1	3
NCOs	10	7	10
Drivers	84	100	86
Others	2	10	6
Total	99	118	105

	Russian artillery company 1803	Bavarian artillery company 1811	Saxon artillery company 1810
Officers	7	3	7
Cadets	12	–	–
NCOs	1	9	10
Gunners	85	138	96
Musicians	2	1	2
Others	15	1	14
Train	31	–	40
Total	153	151	167

	Austrian artillery company 1805	Polish artillery company 1812	Prussian artillery company 1809
Officers	4	5	5
NCOs	14	18	14
Gunners	159	140	116
Musicians	2	2	2
Others	3	8	1
Train	–	–	15
Total	184	172	152

Table 54. Horse artillery division crews.

	French artillery company 1805	*British artillery company 1803*	*Westphalian artillery company 1808*
Officers	4	5	4
NCOs	10	16	8
Gunners	86	116–24	75
Musicians	2	3	–
Others	4	2	3
Total	100	142–50	90

	French train company 1805	*British train company 1803*	*Westphalian train company 1808*
Officers	1	1	3
NCOs	10	7	10
Drivers	84	100	86
Others	2	10	6
Total	99	118	105

	Russian artillery company 1803	*Bavarian artillery company 1811*	*Saxon artillery company 1810*
Officers	6	3	4
Cadets	12	–	–
NCOs	1	9	12
Gunners	82	138	100
Musicians	2	1	2
Others	9	1	2
Train	23	–	40?
Total	135	151	121

	Austrian artillery company 1805	*Polish artillery company 1812*	*Prussian artillery company 1809*
Officers	4	5	5
NCOs	14	10	7
Gunners	159	136	132
Musicians	2	1	2
Others	3	9	9
Train	–	–	15
Total	184	161	172

bers of trained cavalrymen. This was done in an effort to compromise between the time necessary to train gunners and the time necessary to train horsemen. To train a good gunner takes longer than to train a horseman, but it was felt that under the guidance of a single expert several inexperienced cavalry troopers could successfully lay and fire a gun. Since trained cavalry troops were more common and more easily replaced than gunners, they were used in large numbers to flesh out the horse batteries.

With a cavalry background it is hardly surprising that they might be able to perform as cavalry, and attack the enemy. However, it is also possible that this is an effort on Seruzier's part to make himself out to be a hero. On the other hand, I know of no rebuttal ever being written to refute his memoirs, as Gorgaud refuted Segur. If his pronouncements were beyond the realms of possibility I have no doubt some published comment would have been made. Though this lack of known refutation is not in itself conclusive, it is reasonable to assume that there is some truth in what he says. It would also seem reasonable to assume that this capability would be limited to the horse artillerists of those nations whose gunners rode individual horses, and not *Wurst* batteries (for details see pages 260–1). This would preclude Bavarian, Austrian and pre-1800 French horse artillery from performing such manoeuvres.

Tactical organisation

Though this varied between nations, there were three basic systems. The first simply used an overabundance of gunners to man the guns and the train; the second divided the artillerists from the train and assigned them to separate organisations; and the third, used by the French and their allies, consisted of an artillery company and a

---

Table 55. French artillery division equipment, Gribeauval System.

Material	*Division of eight guns* 12–pdrs	8–pdrs	4–pdrs	Howitzers
Guns	8	8	8	8
Replacement carriages	1	1	1	1
Artillery caissons	24	16	8	12
Infantry caissons	*	*	*	*
Divisional wagons	1	1	1	1
Forges	1	1	1	1

Material	*Division of six guns* 12–pdrs	8–pdrs	4–pdrs	Howitzers
Guns	6	6	6	6
Replacement carriages	1	1	1	1
Artillery caissons	18	12	6	18
Infantry caissons	*	*	*	*
Divisional wagons	1	1	1	1
Forges	1	1	1	1

Table 56. Gun crews, Gribeauval System.

| | Number of men serving each gun | | | | Number of horses | |
| | Foot battery | | Horse battery | | Foot | Horse |
	NCOs	Men	NCOs	Men	battery	battery
12-pdr gun	1	10	–	–	6	–
6-pdr gun	1	8	1	10[18]	4	6
Howitzer	1	10	1	10[18]	4	6

Table 57. Gun crews, Austrian system, 1792.

| | Number of men serving each gun | | | Number of |
	Corporals	Gunners	Handlagers[20]	horses per gun
Regimental 3-pdr	1 per 2 guns	5	6	2
Line 6-pdr	1 per 2 guns	5	8	4
Reserve 12-pdr	1 per gun	5	10	6
6-pdr *Wurst*	1 per 2 guns	6	–	6
7-pdr howitzer	1 per 2 guns	6[19]	7	3
7-pdr *Wurst* howitzer	1 per 2 guns	5[19]	–	4
10-pdr howitzer	1 per gun	2[19]	4	3

train company. The artillery company consisted solely of guns and gunners. It was, by itself, immobile. When a train company, with the drivers and limbers, was merged with an artillery company it became mobile and was known as a *division d'artillerie*.

The strength of the artillery division varied, depending on the number of guns and the type of battery involved. Larger guns required more men to serve them, more horses to draw them, and more men to drive the additional horses. Horse batteries were designed for rapid manoeuvring, so they had more horses and more men per gun, to handle them as rapidly as possible. Table 53 provides a few examples of the organisation of artillery divisions of several nations so that comparisons can be made. It is interesting to note that the British seemed to have a significantly larger crews manning their artillery.

The number of infantry caissons indicated by an asterisk in Table 55 varied, but there was generally one with the battery and four with the infantry. When the regimental artillery was disbanded these caissons were returned to the artillery parks. Only the 12-pdr guns were drawn by six horses, the others being drawn by four, as were other wagons. Each 12-pdr and howitzer had three caissons, while the 6-pdrs had only two. Under the System of the Year XI the weapons were served as illustrated in Table 56.

---

[18] Includes horse holders or guards.
[19] Includes one bombardier.
[20] A *handlager* was a non-specialist artilleryman whose function was to push the gun around and handle the heavy manual labour. He was not a trained gunner.

Artillery equipment

Gribeauval's reforms standardised the French artillery into three calibres of field-cannon and one field-howitzer, the characteristics of which are noted in Table 58. In addition, there were a number of standardised siege and coastal guns. They were as illustrated in Table 59.

The Gribeauval System introduced a new type of gun-carriage that had two positions for mounting the gun. There was a forward position for use when firing the gun, and a rear position which was used when transporting it. This latter position was located to allow better balance when manoeuvring. When the gun was brought into action it was shifted forward to the firing position with little effort. However, inexperienced gunners were occasionally known to accidentally dismount the gun – that is, drop the barrel off the limber – when trying to shift it from travelling to firing position.

On 2 May 1803 the Gribeauval System was replaced by the System of the Year XI. It is reported that the latter evolved because after the Battle of Marengo the Army of Italy was so deficient in artillery that General Allix had been ordered to form a train of 250 guns in Turin. Being pressed for time he was unable to cast new guns, so he made use of a number of 6-pdr guns and 24-pdr howitzers he found in Turin, which

Table 58. Gribeauval System equipment statistics.

Gun	Muzzle diameter (mm)	Length of barrel (mm)	Weight of barrel (kg)	Projectile (kg)
12-pdr	121.3	299	880	6
8-pdr	106.1	200	580	4
4-pdr	84.0	157	290	2
4-pdr	84.0	235	560	2
6.4-inch howitzer	165.7	76	330	12

	Muzzle velocity (m/sec)	March weight (kg)	Caisson weight (kg)	Crew size
12-pdr	415	2100	1800	15
8-pdr	419	1650	1700	13
4-pdr	416	1050	1500	8
6.4-inch howitzer	170	1450	1600	7

	Caissons	Number of draft horses	Total no. of shot in caissons	Total no of canister in caissons Large	Small
12-pdr	3	6	153	36	24
8-pdr	2	4	137	20	40
4-pdr	1	4	118	26	24
6.4-inch howitzer	3	4	147	13	–

Table 59. Gribeauval System siege artillery statistics.

Gun	Calibre (mm)	Tube length (mm)	Gun weight (kg)
24-pdr	152.7	353	2740
16-pdr	133.7	336	2000
12-pdr	121.3	317	1550
8-pdr	106.1	285	1060
4-pdr (long)	84.0	235	560
8-pdr howitzer	223.3	94	540

Mortars with cylindrical chambers

12-pdr	324.9	81	1540
10-pdr (long range)	274.0	81	980
10-pdr (short range)	274.0	74	780
8-pdr	223.3	58	270
Perrier	406.1	–	735

Mortars with truncated chambers

12-pdr	324.9	91	1320
10-pdr	274.0	88	1200

Coastal artillery

	Calibre (mm)	Tube length (mm)	Gun weight (kg)
36-pdr	174.6	–	3520
24-pdr	152.7	353	2500
16-pdr	133.7	336	1900
12-pdr	121.3	317	1510

were introduced into service by the order of 2 March 1803 (Year XI). This would indicate that initially the 6-pdr guns of the System of the Year XI were captured rather than French weapons; indeed, it is quite certain that there were hundreds of captured 6-pdrs available after the various battles with the Austrians and Prussians. Eventually, however, all the 6-pdr guns were of French manufacture.

The new system replaced the 8-pdr with a 6-pdr gun and theoretically abandoned the 4-pdr. However, the 4-pdr continued in use until the end of the Empire and the System of the Year XI never fully replaced the Gribeauval System in the field or in fortresses. Table 60 provides the statistical data that is available on the System of the Year XI, for comparison with the older Gribeauval System.

The new guns were reputedly stronger and more powerful than the old ones. In addition, the adoption of the 6-pdr resulted in the temporary elimination of regimental artillery. The 4-pdr was said to be too heavy to readily follow the infantry and it was not felt to have sufficient missile weight to justify its existence. This is surprising, because in 1809 regimental artillery began to reappear in the French army.

The 6-pdr was heavier than the 4-pdr and could only further embarrass the movements of the infantry if it was assigned to the role of regimental artillery. The other

	Gun weight	Shot diameter	Powder charge	Muzzle velocity
Gun	(kg)	(mm)	(kg)	(m/sec)
12-pdr	880	117.7	1.958	419
8-pdr	587	102.1	1.223	413
6-pdr	400	93.1	0.979	416
4-pdr	293	81.0	0.634	420

Table 60. Statistics for the System of the Year XI.

problem with the 6-pdr – loss of firepower resulting from the replacement of the 8-pdr – was felt to be more than offset by the gains resulting from the manoeuvrability of the lighter 6-pdr. The System of the Year XI consisted of the following weapons: short 24-pdr gun, long 12-pdr gun, short 12-pdr gun, long 6-pdr gun, short 6-pdr gun, 3-pdr mountain gun, 24-pdr howitzer, and 24-pdr mortar.

Later, a 6-pdr mortar and a 6-pdr howitzer, known as *à la Prussienne*, were adopted into the system. For that matter, even though the System of the Year XI was the standard, in practice the Gribeauval system continued to be used in Spain, and a variety of field-howitzers continued to be used by the *Grande Armée*.

There were and continued to be 3-pdr guns of Piedmontese origin in service in the French army. These were found on light, medium, and heavy carriages. They were generally designated as mountain guns, but were occasionally assigned as regimental artillery. Firing one of these guns on a quarter-charge would cause a round to carry 472 yds, and the gun would recoil 12 ft. If a one-third charge was used the round would carry 512 yds and the gun would recoil 15 ft. With a full charge the gun could be fired rapidly and continuously until, after somewhere between 600 and 700 rounds, the barrel would burst.

The System of the Year XI also discarded the copper pontoons used by the pontooneer companies and replaced them with wooden pontoons.

The artillery equipment of the various other nations was not dissimilar from that of the French. As the manufacture of artillery was an expensive proposition, many of the smaller nations bought their artillery rather than made their own, but the major powers – France, Prussia, Austria, Britain, and Russia – all manufactured their own. Table 61 provides a comparison of the available information on the artillery equipment of some of the major powers.

French ammunition

The projectiles employed by the guns varied. There were three basic types: shot, canister and shell. Shot was a solid ball fired from the field-pieces; canister was a container of small shot that produced a shotgun-like effect; and shells were explosive charges, fired solely by the howitzers. In addition, there were shrapnel shells, which were a howitzer-like shell fired from cannons; only the British had these.

In the French army most shot took the form of a shot and a sabot joined to a powder bag. This pre-prepared cartridge permitted a significantly higher rate of fire. Only the 16-pdr and larger guns used loose powder and separate shot, because the size of their shot made cartridges impractical.

Table 61. Comparison of artillery statistics for various nations.

	Weight of tube (lb)	Carriage weight (lb)	Charge weight (lb)	Muzzle diameter (ins)	Barrel length (ins)	Horses for gun and limber
France						
4-pdr[21]	645	860	1.61	3.23	57.5	8
8-pdr[21]	1270	1255	2.64	4.18	72.5	10
6-pdr[22]	880	1130	3.19	3.78	65.5	8
12-pdr[21]	1936	–	4.29	4.78	117.7	12
12-pdr[22]	1950	1490	4.29	4.78	84.0	12
6.54-inch howitzer	700	1365	2.69	6.54	30.0	10
Britain						
6-pdr (HA)	672	1065	1.5	3.67	60.0	4
6-pdr (FA)	1372	1065	1.5	3.67	84.0	4
9-pdr	1510	1760	3.0	4.2	72.0	6
5.5-inch howitzer (HA)	532	1125	2.0	5.5	26.8	4
5.5-inch howitzer (FA)	1120	1125	2.0	5.5	33.0	4
Saxony						
Old 12-pdr	2410	1627	5.0	?	?	?
New 12-pdr	1700	1408	4.0	?	?	?
Old 8-pdr	1600	1173	3.25	?	?	?
New 8-pdr	1120	1019	3.0	?	?	?
Prussia						
6-pdr	962	1210	2.31	3.71	64.0	6
12-pdr	2100	1675	4.12	4.66	80.5	8
5.8-inch howitzer	792	1340	1.28	5.8	37.0	6
6.7-inch howitzer	1415	1675	1.82	6.7	42.5	8
Austria						
3-pdr	530	?	?	?	45.0	2
6-pdr	911	?	?	?	58.3	4
6-pdr *Wurst*	880	?	?	?	58.3	6
12-pdr	1786	?	?	?	75.0	6
7-pdr howitzer	502	?	?	?	?	3
7-pdr *Wurst* howitzer	616	?	?	?	?	4
10-pdr howitzer	1676	?	?	?	?	3
Russia						
12-pdr	806	2160	4	4.579	77.5	?
6-pdr	352	1280	2	3.634	63.8	?
18-pdr licorne[23]	682	2160	?	5.927	64.3	?
9-pdr licorne	357	1280	?	4.668	53.0	?

[21] Gribeauval System.

[22] System of the Year XI.

[23] A licorne was essentially a howitzer, except that it had a longer range and was more accurate. Physically, it tended to be longer barrelled than a howitzer.

	12-pdr	*8-pdr*	*4-pdr*	*3-pdr*	*Howitzer*
Table 62. Gribeauval System canister specifications.					
Length of cartridge (cm)					
Large	27	19	15	13	19
Small	20	18	17	–	–
Canister weight (kg)					
Large	10.3	6.9	3.4	2.5	1.4
Small	9.3	6.3	4.2	–	–
Number of balls in canister					
Large	41[23]	41[23]	41[23]	–	–
Small	112[24]	112[24]	63[25]	–	–

French canister came in two sizes, large and small, consisting of either large or small balls encased in a metal canister that ruptured on firing. Details of the canister types are shown in Table 62.

The French prepared canister cartridges for the 4-pdr cannon, but not the larger calibres. This is because the cartridges for those guns would have been too long and fragile to be successfully employed in the field.

Mortar bombs and howitzer shells contained various numbers of shot and were properly called 'grenades.' They were intended to be lobbed over fortifications or other obstructions and rolled into locations where troops were concealed. In the field the howitzers bounced their shells like field-pieces, but when the fuse burned through the shell exploded with the same effect.

Other nations' ammunition

The use of several sizes of canister shot appears to have been universal. According to B.P. Hughes the British used only two: light canister balls weighing 1.5 oz, and heavy canister balls weighing 5 oz. A 9-pdr light canister round contained 126 1.5 oz balls, and the heavy round contained 41 5 oz balls. The 6-pdr light canister contained 85 1.5 oz balls and the heavy canister had 41 5 oz balls. However, in Scharnhorst's *Handbook* we find the data shown in Table 63.

Russian canister balls came in nine sizes, ranging from No 1 canister, which was 13 oz, to No 9, which was 2 oz. See Table 64. The Russians also prepared fixed cartridges like the French. For field ammunition shot and howitzer shell were fixed to their powder charges with a wooden sabot and formed into a cartridge.

---

[23] Formed solely of No 1 shot.
[24] Formed of 80 No 2 shot and 32 No 3 shot.
[25] Formed of 24 No 1 shot and 39 No 2 shot.

Table 63. British canister specifications.

	Number of case balls	Weight	Cartridge weight
12-pdr medium	15	18 oz	18 lb 8 oz
	42	6.5 oz	17 lb 11 oz
12-pdr light	12	14 oz	14 lb 14 oz
	34	6.5 oz	14 lb 11 oz
6-pdr medium	15	8.5 oz	9 lb
	42	3.5 oz	8 lb 14 oz
6-pdr light	13	8.5 oz	7 lb 3 oz
	34	3.5 oz	7 lb 7 oz
3-pdr medium	15	4.5 oz	4 lb 10 oz
	42	1.5 oz	4 lb 6 oz
3-pdr light	12	4.5 oz	3 lb 10 oz
	34	1.5 oz	3 lb 11 oz

Table 64. Russian canister specifications.

12-pdr canister	41 No 8 shot and 151 No 3
6-pdr canister	41 No 8 or 72 No 2 and 27 No 1
18-pdr licorne canister	48 No 7 or 94 No 5
9-pdr licorne canister	55 No 5 and 5 No 4 or 141 No 3

There is a mixture of data available on the Austrians. They reportedly used two sizes of canister, light and heavy. The 3-pdr gun's heavy canister contained 30 balls. The 6-pdr light canister had 60 1.5 oz balls and the heavy canister had 28 3 oz balls. According to another source the 12-pdr light canister contained 120 balls. Yet another states that it had 28 6 oz balls, and that the 12-pdr heavy canister contained 12 16 oz balls. Some of these figures are in agreement with the data in Scharnhorst's *Handbook*, which I am inclined to believe is the most reliable source document. It is, however, possible, that the other documents reflect changes that occurred later in the Napoleonic Wars, and as Scharnhorst was published in 1806, such changes could not have been reflected in his work.

Table 65. Austrian canister composition (Scharnhorst's *Handbook*).

	Number of shot	Weight of each ball
4-pdr	41	2.4 oz
6-pdr	28	3 oz
12-pdr	28	6 oz
7-pdr howitzer	67	3 oz

Table 66. Danish canister specifications.

	Number of shot	*Weight of each ball*
12-pdr	100	4 *loth* (approx 64 gm)
6-pdr	100	2 *loth* (approx 32 gm)
3-pdr	100	1 *loth* (approx 16 gm)

The Saxon old 12-pdr canister contained 40 4 oz shot, while the new 12-pdr contained 48. The old 8-pdr canister contained 28 4 oz shot and the old 4-pdr contained 27 2 oz shot. The new 6-pdr gun's canister round, adopted in 1811, contained 41 3 oz shot.

The Danish appear to have been very uniform in their canister. Indeed, its effect must have been very much like birdshot because of the number and smallness of the shot.

Spherical case or shrapnel

In 1784 Lieutenant H. Shrapnel, RA, designed the spherical case shot in an effort to improve the performance of field-artillery. It consisted of a hollow iron sphere containing 60 bullets, a bursting charge, and a fuse. These shells were not issued for service use until 1803–4. They were an immediate success and widely used thereafter, dramatically increasing the firepower of British light artillery. A single shell was known to kill every horse in the team of an enemy limber, even at long range. The French hated it because they could not reply to it. Tables from the 1820s show it having a range of up to 2000 yds, and trials showed that it could score hits on the order of magnitude of 48% at ranges of 1000 yds.

Range and accuracy

The range of the shot depended, naturally, on the weight of the powder charge placed behind it and the elevation of the muzzle. The charge was generally one-third of the weight of the shot. Ranges for the French Gribeauval System are shown in Table 67. These are theoretical ranges based on experiment and not obtained under actual bat-

Table 67. Gribeauval System ranges.

Elevation	*Gun*	*Range (metres)*
45 degrees	24-pdr	4200
	16-pdr	4000
6 degrees	12-pdr siege	1900
	8-pdr siege	1800
	12-pdr field	1800
	8-pdr field	1250
	4-pdr long	1600
	4-pdr short	1500

Table 68. Range for Gribeauval System guns firing canister.

	Gun	Range (metres)	Shot
Extreme practical range	4–pdr	500	Petit
	12–pdr	800	Grand
Best range	4–pdr	400	Petit
	12–pdr	600	Grand
Maximum range	12–pdr	880	Grand
	12–pdr	600	Petit
	8–pdr	700	Grand
	8–pdr	600	Petit
	4–pdr	600	Grand
	4–pdr	400	Petit

tlefield conditions. The generally accepted maximum range was 3000 ft. D'Urtubie confirms this when he also states, in his *Manual d'Artillerie*, that the greatest distance that an 8-pdr or 12-pdr gun should be fired on the battlefield is 500 *toises*, or 3000 ft. Point-blank range in the Gribeauval System was 470 metres for a 12-pdr, 460 for an 8-pdr, and 440 for a 4-pdr.

The effective range of canister also varied from calibre to calibre and according to Colonel d'Urtubie the 12-pdr should use canister at no more than 400 *toises* (2400 ft), the 8-pdr at no more than 350 *toises* (2100 ft), and the 4-pdr at no more than 300 *toises* (1800 ft). D'Urtubie provides practical, effective ranges as shown in Table 68.

The range of howitzers and the effectiveness of their fire varied also. The shell produced from 25 to 50 fragments, that could carry from 165 to 220 yds, but they were only dangerous within 22 yds of the explosion.

The French 12-pdr of the System of the Year XI would carry a maximum of 2200 yds, though its practical range was only 1900 yds. The maximum range of the 6-pdr

Table 69. Comparative range table.

France	Ball, maximum	Ball, effective	Canister, effective
12-pdr[27]	2200 yds	1900 yds	800 yds
6-pdr[27]	1900 yds	–	600 yds
3-pdr	1600 yds	–	500 yds
4-pdr[28]	–	1600 yds	550 yds
8-pdr[28]	–	1250 yds	600 yds
12-pdr[28]	–	1800 yds	875 yds
Prussia	Ball, maximum	Ball, effective	Canister, effective
12-pdr	–	1800 yds	550 yds
6-pdr	–	1600 yds	550 yds
Howitzer	–	2000 yds	400 yds

continued

Table 69 continued

Saxony	Ball, maximum effective	Canister, maximum
12-pdr heavy	2000 paces	700 paces
12-pdr light	2000 paces	700 paces
8-pdr heavy	2000 paces	700 paces
8-pdr light	2000 paces	700 paces
4-pdr regimental	2000 paces	500 paces
8-pdr howitzer	2000 paces	500 paces

Russia	Ball, maximum	Ball, effective	Canister, effective
3-pdr	1200 yds	–	–
6-pdr	1920 yds	1000 yds	450 yds
12-pdr (short)	2800 yds	1200 yds	500 yds
12-pdr (medium)	3000 yds	1200 yds	500 yds
9-pdr licorne	2272 yds	1000 yds	600 yds
18-pdr licorne	2345 yds	1000 yds	700 yds

Britain	Ball, maximum	Ball, effective	Canister, effective	Shrapnel effective[29]
12-pdr (medium)	–	–	–	2340 yds
9-pdr	–	1400 yds	500 yds	2215 yds
6-pdr	–	1200 yds	450 yds	–
12-pdr howitzer	1400 yds	1100 yds	400 yds	–
24-pdr howitzer	1700 yds	1025 yds	400 yds	–

Austria 1792	Ball or shell, maximum	Ball or shell, effective	Canister, effective
3-pdr	–	1500 paces	400 paces
6-pdr	–	2100 paces	600 paces
12-pdr	–	2400 paces	1000 paces
6-pdr *Wurst*	–	2100 paces	600 paces
7-pdr howitzer	–	1100 paces	500 paces
7-pdr *Wurst* howitzer	–	1100 paces	500 paces

Denmark		First strike	Ball at rest
10-pdr howitzer[30]	Minimum range	338 paces	2000 paces
	Maximum range	2304 paces	2363 paces
10-pdr howitzer	Minimum range	280 paces	1605 paces
	Maximum range	3500 paces	3500 paces
5-pdr howitzer	Minimum range	216 paces	1575 paces
	Maximum range	1949 paces	1980 paces

[27] System of the Year XI.
[28] Gribeauval System.
[29] Range dates from the 1820s.
[30] 18-pdr barrel bored out only to 10-pdr calibre.

was 1900 yds and that of the 3-pdr 1600 yds. Despite these maximum ranges, actual combat ranges were generally shorter. Canister ranges were much as those listed for the Gribeauval System, but tactical doctrine called for the use of canister from 300 to 1200 yds.

The rate of fire of a smoothbore cannon was two balls or three canisters per minute. This difference existed because there was a greater need to lay or aim a gun firing ball than there was when firing canister. Though not a necessary consideration for determining the accuracy of a weapon, it is a major consideration when evaluating the number of casualties a battery could cause in a given span of time.

There is a surprising wealth of data on accuracy to be found in Muller's *Die Entwicklung der Feld-Artillerie*. He addresses the accuracy of both ball and canister fire, providing the results of several artillerists' experiments as well as the percentages of hits considered probable by the various military experts of the day. Table 70 lists the results of several experiments and the accepted accuracy of ball fire. It should be noted that all the targets were approximately the frontage of an average infantry company. The data in Table 70 shows what one would expect – a diminishing accuracy as range increased. It also shows that the 12-pdr was more accurate at long range than the 6-pdr, which is not too surprising.

Chart 4 uses these percentages to project overall probable effectiveness at all ranges. This is a regression analysis based on the limited number of points provided. Despite this, it should be a reasonable projection. In preparing this and the following charts, in order to generate the proper shape of curve a point was selected where it was assumed the gun would hit the target 100% of the time. For round shot, it was presumed that a trained crew firing a smoothbore gun could not miss a 31 × 1.90 metre target at a range of 50 yds.

Table 70. Accuracy of high angle fire with round shot.

Source	Target (metres)	Gun	Hits on target at (metres)			
			600	750	900	1200
Decker	31 × 1.9	12-pdr	50%	40%	29%	–
		6-pdr	42%	33%	27%	–
Scharnhorst	31 × 1.9	12-pdr	–	–	35%	25%
		6-pdr	36%	–	33%	–
Oelze	31 × 1.9	12-pdr	55%	–	36%	25%
		6-pdr	50%	–	32%	16%
Artillery Officers' Handbook	31 × 1.9	12-pdr	60%	48.3%	40%	25%
		6-pdr	53.2%	43.5%	32.2%	15.5%
Official Treatise on Artillery	31 × 1.9	12-pdr	55%	47%	36%	25%
		6-pdr	50%	42%	32%	16%
Average		12-pdr	55%	45.1%	35.2%	25%
Average		6-pdr	46.2%	39.5%	31.2%	15.8%

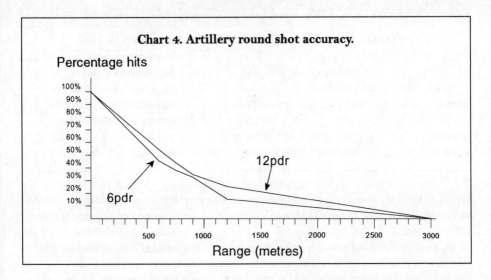

Chart 4. Artillery round shot accuracy.

Percentage hits

Range (metres)

The data in Table 70 also enables us to project the accuracy of a smoothbore cannon. However, in order to do so it is necessary to make a number of assumptions. The assumptions used in the following analysis were:

1) The fall of shot would be random and normal in its distribution.
2) The point of aim would be the centre of the target.
3) The ground is an even surface which would deflect any short shot at the same angle it struck the ground and along the same line of fire.
4) Shot that fell short of the target would 'skip', or bounce, and have the same chance of striking the target as a ball that did not strike the ground.
5) The area of shot distribution, over which it was normally distributed, would be semi-circular (skip shots bounding up, not penetrating into the ground under the target).
6) The semi-circular area of shot fall would contain all shot and the radius of that semi-circle would be equal to the maximum deflection of the ball from the line of aim.

As the ball is a sphere passing through a cylindrical chamber, it must be reasonably expected to have an equal chance of exiting the muzzle at any angle, be it horizontal or vertical. As a result the pattern of distribution must be basically circular and since there is an equal chance of the ball varying from the central line of aim the distribution of shot must be normal. Knowing that the guns were inaccurate, it would be the natural tendency for gunners to aim at the middle of their target.

Rounds would usually skip when they struck the ground, so those rounds falling short would have bounced up and continued in the general direction of the target. The assumption that the ground would be a perfectly flat surface is unrealistic. However, in the context of this analysis the unevenness of the ground would contribute to the inaccuracies of the fall of shot and has, in essence, been considered by the assumption of a normal distribution of shot fall. The problem comes when different pieces of ground, varying from battlefield to battlefield, are examined. These experiments were

	Radius of shot fall (feet)		Deflection in degrees	
Range	*12-pdr*	*6-pdr*	*12-pdr*	*6-pdr*
600	6.7	7.17	0.0002	0.0002
750	7.25	7.55	0.0002	0.0002
900	7.75	7.93	0.0001	0.0002
1200	8.23	8.63	0.0001	0.0001

Table 71. Accuracy of round shot from smoothbore cannon.

probably run on generally level and smooth artillery ranges. Battlefields are invariably worse than any test range. This would cause this analysis to be an 'optimum' case study.

Because the ground is hard, and because it is highly unlikely that these tests were run on wet ground that would absorb any short shots, it is reasonable to assume that the shots would bounce and continue towards the target, as the pattern of shot, without consideration of the ground, must be circular. If we assume the ground would deflect upwards, the shot that would otherwise strike the bottom of the circular pattern must then fall into a semi-circular pattern. Therefore the pattern of shot fall is a semi-circle and, as the distribution is normal, the shots with the greatest inaccuracy must be on its outer rim. The radius of the semi-circle must, therefore, be their deflection from the line of aim. That is to say, the radius is the linear measurement of their inaccuracy, which can be reduced mathematically to a deflection angle.

As Muller has provided the percentage of hits that fall within the target and the relevant ranges, the determination of the radius of the semi-circle can be calculated. The results provide the data shown in Table 71. As can be seen, the angular error of round shot from a period smoothbore cannon was not very significant. This clearly shows that the round shot from cannon that was fired directly at a target, not skipped in its direction, was highly accurate.

Table 72 provides the accuracy of fire using the skipping technique that was uniformly employed to increase the effectiveness of artillery by keeping it closer to the ground. It should be understood that this type of fire was aimed at several targets at once and passed through them all. It was achieved by firing the gun at a very small angle of elevation. The projectile then fell on the ground at an angle less than 10 degrees and rebounded. It could even be skipped across the surface of water, at elevation angles of less than five degrees.

It was used in counter-battery fire, as well as to harrass an enemy when formed or in the act of forming behind rising ground or an obstacle or taking a position in woods, or when firing on an enemy's flank. It was able to reach objects that, because of the intervening terrain, could not be reached by direct fire.

The data in Table 72 consists of the percentage of hits scored on a single target at specified ranges. As this is skip shooting, the shot could well have struck several other targets before it arrived at the final target, so its effectiveness against massed formations is higher than these percentages might otherwise suggest.

It is interesting to note that the accuracy for this type of fire does not seem to vary with range. It appears that any skip shot had approximately a 25% chance of striking

Table 72. Accuracy of skip or roll shooting.

Source	Target (metres)	Gun	Hits on target at (metres)			
			980	1130	1200	1350
Decker	25 × 1.9	6-pdr	24%	23%	23%	–
		12-pdr	26%	235	20%	22%
Oelze	25 × 1.9	6-pdr	24%	–	20%	–
		12-pdr	24%	–	22%	–
Artillery	25 × 1.9	6-pdr	24.5%	24%	–	24%
Officers'		12-pdr	25%	26.5%	–	24.6%
Handbook		7-pdr howitzer	40.7%	33.9%	–	21%
	Average	12-pdr	25%	24.8%	21%	23.3%
	Average	6-pdr	24%	22.5%	21.5%	24%

its final target. Then there is the incidental damage to all of the intervening formations to be considered.

Chart 5 was generated in the same manner as Chart 4. It was assumed that at 0 metres' range every shot would hit and an exponential curve fitted to the data points. This shows a dramatic decrease in accuracy up to about 250 metres range and a subsequent stabilisation to a slightly declining line.

Table 73 provides Muller's figures for the accuracy of canister fire. This is juxtaposed against Table 74, which shows the results of the famous Strasbourg experiments run by Gribeauval. This is summarised in Charts 6 and 7 using the same regression programme used in Chart 4. Chart 7 indicates that the French Gribeauval gun system was both more accurate and had a longer range than the guns used in the various tests (mostly Prussian and Austrian) listed by Muller. It also has a closer curve fit. It would not, however, be reasonable to assume, based on these two graphs,

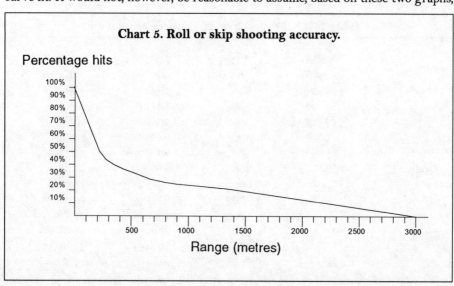

Chart 5. Roll or skip shooting accuracy.

Percentage hits

Range (metres)

that French canister was superior to that of the Prussians and Austrians. It would be more reasonable to assume that there are insufficient data points for a proper comparison. Nonetheless, these curves do provide an interesting insight into the accuracy of canister over a given range.

Table 73. Accuracy of canister fire.

			Hits on target at (metres)					
Source	*Target*	*Gun*	*300*	*375*	*450*	*525*	*600*	*675*
Scharnhorst	50 × 2.5	6-pdr	16%	–	13%	–	7%	–
		12-pdr	–	–	–	–	12.7%	13%
Decker	30 × 1.9	6-pdr	–	13%	10%	8%	6%	–
		12-pdr	–	–	13%	11%	9%	–
		7-pdr	30%	14%	12%	–	6.5%	–
Gravenitz	31.4 × 1.9	6-pdr	–	8%	–	4%	–	–
		12-pdr	–	–	–	7%	–	3%
Austrian	Unknown	6-pdr	7%	5%	–	–	–	–
Military		12-pdr	5%	3%	2%	–	–	–
Newspaper		7-pdr	10%	6%	6%	–	–	–
Oelze	30 × 1.9	6-pdr	13%	–	10%	8%	–	–
Handbook		12-pdr	15%	–	11%	9%	–	–
	6-pdr		16%	–	10%	5%	–	–
Artillery	30 × 1.9	6-pdr	13%	12%	10%	7.5%	–	–
Officers'		12-pdr	14.5%	14%	12%	10.5%	–	–
Handbook		7-pdr	16%	13%	10%	7.5%	–	–
	Average	12-pdr	11.5%	8.3%	9.5%	10.1%	10.9%	8%
	Average	6-pdr	12.3%	9.5%	10.8%	6.9%	6.5%	
	Average	7-pdr	18%	11%	9.5%	6.3%	6.5%	

Table 74. Gribeauval System canister accuracy.

	Number of balls	*Range of fire (metres)*	*Balls striking the target*	*Percentage*
12-pdr	41 (large)	800	7–8	18%
		700	10–11	25%
	112 (small)	600	20–25	20%
		500	35	31%
		400	40	35.7%
8-pdr	41	700	8–9	20.7%
		600	10–11	25.6%
	112	600	25	22.3%
		500	40	35.7%
4-pdr	41	600	8–9	20.0%
		500	16–18	41.5%
		400	21	51.2%

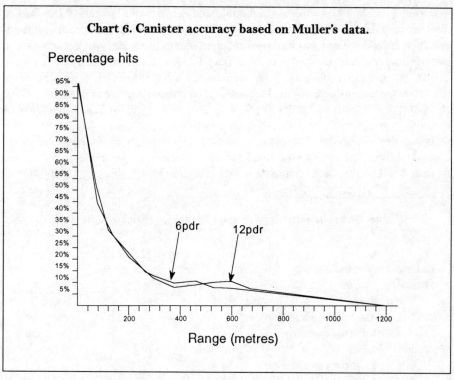

Chart 6. Canister accuracy based on Muller's data.

Percentage hits

6pdr   12pdr

Range (metres)

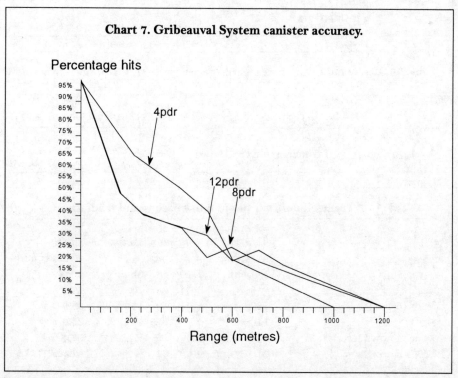

Chart 7. Gribeauval System canister accuracy.

Percentage hits

4pdr

12pdr 8pdr

Range (metres)

Caissons

The French Gribeauval System had two basic types of caissons, the 12-pdr and the 4-pdr. The 12-pdr caisson was designed to carry ammunition for the 12-pdr, 8-pdr, 6-pdr (after adoption of the System of the Year XI), howitzers, and muskets. The 4-pdr caisson was designed solely for 4-pdr ammunition and musket cartridges. The interiors of these caissons were divided into large, watertight containers designed to keep the munitions as fresh and as dry as possible. They were adjusted to accommodate the material stored in them, be it 12-pdr shot, 8-pdr shot, etc.

In addition to those two types of caissons there was the *Wurst* caisson used by the horse artillery. This *Wurst* was a copy of the Austrian horse artillery system and consisted of a leather saddle which was on top of the caisson, allowing the artillerists

Table 75. French artillery caisson loading, Gribeauval System.						

	Calibre		*Number of shots, canister*			
Caisson	*of munition*	*Shot*	*Grand*	*Petit*	*Total*	*Total*
12-pdr	12-pdr	48	12	8	20	68
	8-pdr	62	10	20	30	92
	6.4-inch howitzer	49	–	–	3	52
	Infantry cartridges					14,000
4-pdr	4-pdr	100	26	24	50	150
	Infantry cartridges					12,000
Wurst	8-pdr	51	–	–	6	57
	6.4-inch howitzer	27	–	–	3	30

Table 76. Ready munition in gun-carriage ready chest, Gribeauval System.

12-pdr	9 ball
8-pdr	15 ball
4-pdr	18 ball
6.4-inch howitzer	4 canister

Table 77. French munitions per gun in caissons and ready chest.

		Total no. of shot in caissons	*Total no. of canister in caissons*		*Total ammunition per gun*
	Caissons		*Large*	*Small*	
12-pdr	3	153	36	24	222
8-pdr (6-pdr)	2	137	20	40	212
4-pdr	1	118	26	24	186
6.4-inch howitzer	3	147	13	–	164
5.5-inch howitzer	3	210	20	–	234

to ride the caisson into battle. This provided them with greater mobility, and eliminated the need for individual mounts. This cut down costs, as well as preventing the gunners from deserting individually should the battle become too hot for them. The *Wurst* caissons were designed for 8-pdr ammunition and were only superficially different from the 12-pdr caisson.

Despite the extensive redesign and modification of the French caissons, they continued to receive much criticism for having their axles too low and for being too heavy for four horses to draw. The caisson was not suspended on a spring carriage, and the constant shaking caused the ammunition they carried to deteriorate rapidly. There was also insufficient protection against humidity.

The conversion to the 24-pdr (5.5-inch) howitzer that occurred with the adoption of the System of the Year XI led to some problems. It was too light for some of the

	Round shot	Canister	Shell	Incendiary shells	Fire balls	Total
Table 78. Prussian ammunition storage, 1809–15.[51]						
Foot artillery						
6-pdr limber	45	25	–	–	–	
6-pdr caisson	143	45	–	–	–	
Total rounds per gun	120	47	–	–	–	167
7-pdr howitzer limber	–	6	14	–	–	
7-pdr howitzer caisson	–	20	60	3	2	
Total rounds per gun	–	26	74	3	2	105
12-pdr limber	12	9	–	–	–	
12-pdr caisson	70	25	–	–	–	
Total rounds per gun	82	–	–	–	34	114
10-pdr howitzer limber	–	1	4	–	–	
10-pdr howitzer caisson	–	8	36	2	2	
Total rounds per gun	–	9	40	2	2	53
Horse artillery						
6-pdr limber	45	15	–	–	–	
6-pdr caisson	90	25	–	–	–	
Total rounds per gun	105	31	–	–	–	136
7-pdr howitzer limber	–	6	14	–	–	
7-pdr howitzer caisson	–	16	49	3	2	
Total rounds per gun	–	22	53	3	2	80

[51] A Prussian 6-pdr foot battery had two 6-pdr caissons and two howitzer shell wagons. The horse battery had four 6-pdr caissons and two shell wagons. The 12-pdr battery had six 12-pdr caissons and four shell caissons.

duties which its 6.4-inch predecessor had handled. However, the caisson could now carry 75 rounds, as compared to 50 6.4-inch rounds. In addition, the 24-pdr howitzer required only two powder charges to the three required by the 6.4-inch. The 24-pdr field howitzer's charge was also interchangeable with that of the 24-pdr siege howitzer, which saved space and reduced inventories and powder consumption.

Ammunition provisions

The generally accepted rate of fire for a field-piece was about two rounds per minute. This would put the average rate of fire for a period gun at about 100–120 rounds per hour of steady firing. Because this is a reasonably high rate of fire the ammunition stock provided to support a gun, battery or army should provide a good indication of the utilisation of artillery. If one considers that battles often lasted from sunrise to sunset, and a few went on for two days or more, ammunition consumption could be prodigious.

The ammunition available to a battery consisted of what it carried with it in limbers, in the gun-carriage ready chests, and in the caissons. Tables 75–77 provide a quick listing of the ammunition carried in the French Gribeauval System, with some data from the System of the Year XI.

When the System of the Year XI was instituted the 5.5-inch howitzer replaced the 6.4-inch howitzer. This change allowed 75 shells to be carried per caisson, plus four more in the gun-limber ready chest, a total of 234 rounds per gun. The 12-pdr was unchanged and there was no change in ammunition availability. A figure for 6-pdr ammunition was not found, but it cannot have been less than that allocated for the 8-pdr. It is best to assume that it was the same, or slightly more, in that the 6-pdr now served as the replacement for both the 4-pdr and the 8-pdr. For the purposes of this analysis its ammunition storage has been treated as being the same as for the 8-pdr.

The ammunition provided for Russian guns was not dissimilar to that provided by the Prussians. The 12-pdr caissons carried 54 rounds each and there were three caissons per gun. In addition there were 12 in the limber. The 18-pdr licorne caisson carried 40 rounds and had no limber storage. The two 6-pdr caissons per gun carried 77 rounds each. There were 20 more rounds in the 6-pdr limber. The 9-pdr licorne

Table 79. British allocation of ammunition per gun.					
	Ball	*Case*	*Shrapnel*	*Shell*	*Carcass*
6-pdr (horse artillery)	132	28	20	–	–
6-pdr (foot artillery)	149	19	26	–	–
9-pdr	88	16	12	–	–
12-pdr howitzer	–	8	68	56	4
24-pdr howitzer	–	8	42	32	2
Hanoverian 1792					
6-pdr	228	60	–	–	–
7-pdr howitzer	110	290	16[32]	–	–

[32] Incendiary shells.

Table 80. Austrian allocation of ammunition per gun, 1792.

	Ball	Case	Shell	Incendiary
3-pdr	132	44	–	–
6-pdr	160	34	–	–
12-pdr	70	20	–	–
6-pdr *Wurst*	160	34	–	–
	108[33]	24[33]		
7-pdr howitzer	–	10	80	3
7-pdr *Wurst* howitzer	–	10	80	3

Table 81. Austrian allocation of ammunition for a campaign.

		18-pdr	*12-pdr*	*3-pdr*	*7-pdr howitzer*
With the gun	Shot	56	70	132	80
	Canister	8	32	36	10
In reserve or park	Shot	192	155	120	108
	Canister	32	40	16	16
In depot	Shot	248	255	252	188
	Canister	40	72	52	26

caisson carried 54 rounds plus 12 in the limber. The 3-pdr had 90 rounds in the caisson and a further 30 in the limber. Each cannon appears to have been provided with at least 120 rounds, averaging 80 round shot, 20 large canister, and 10 small canister. The 18-pdr and 9-pdr licornes had 20 large canister, 80 shell, and 10 incendiary shell.

An interesting and obscure comparison is the provision of ammunition in the Danish artillery. During the Napoleonic period this was as shown in Table 82. It is interesting to note that the Danish considered the 6-pdr the work horse of the battlefield, allocating to it a tremendous quantity of round shot. The 12-pdr, however, appears to be a defensive weapon, overloaded with canister to break up assaults.

The Saxon allocation of ammunition per gun was as indicated in Table 83.

Table 82. Danish allocation of ammunition.

	Round shot in caisson	*Canister in caisson*	*Rounds in ready chest*
12-pdr	28	44	12
6-pdr	166	53	24
3-pdr	176	58	24
Regimental 3-pdr	80	20	None

[33] These different figures for ammunition are found in Scharnhorst.

Table 83. Saxon allocation of ammunition per gun.

	With gun			In reserve caissons		
	Ball	*Case*	*Grape*	*Ball*	*Case*	*Grape*
Heavy 12-pdr	140	40	20	200	60	40
Light 12-pdr	140	40	20	200	60	40
Heavy 8-pdr	140	40	20	100	30	20
Light 8-pdr	140	40	20	100	30	20
Regimental 4-pdr	90	60	–	100	30	20

	With gun		In reserve caissons	
	Shell	*Case*	*Shell*	*Case*
4-pdr grenade thrower	99	49	99	49
8-pdr howitzer	96	40	134	66

A comparison of the data provided for the various nations (see Table 84) shows some startling differences in their attitudes towards the use of artillery. The French felt that the 12-pdr was the principal battlefield piece and were lavish in their provision of shot for it. The Prussians seem to have had a similar appreciation for the 12-pdr, but were rather niggardly in their allocation of ammunition for all of their artillery. The Russians' attitude towards the quantity of fire was somewhere between those of France and Prussia.

Table 84. Comparison of total ammunition allocated per gun in various armies.

	France	*Prussia*	*Russia*	*Britain*	*Austria*
12-pdr	222	114	172	–	150–210
9-pdr	–	–	–	106	–
8-pdr	212	–	–	–	–
6-pdr	212	167	154	194	210–30
6-pdr (horse artillery)	–	136	154	180	130
4-pdr	186	–	–	–	–
3-pdr	–	–	120	–	220
6.4-inch howitzer	164	–	–	–	–
5.5-inch howitzer	234	–	–	–	–
7-pdr howitzer	–	105	–	–	140–60
7-pdr howitzer (horse artillery)	–	80	–	–	–
10-pdr howitzer	–	53	–	–	–
12-pdr howitzer	–	–	–	136	–
24-pdr howitzer	–	–	–	84	–
9-pdr licorne	–	–	130	–	–
18-pdr licorne	–	–	120	–	–

Battery tactics

Very little has been found to be in print on this subject. The regulations tend to limit themselves to the duties of each individual in the battery. A French work, *Manoeuvres des batteries de campagne pour l'artillerie de la garde impériale*, provides as much insight as any into the operations of the battery. This states that the six caissons (one per gun) followed the battery and manoeuvred with it. The rest of the ammunition provision is formed as a reserve, under the direction of the *garde d'artillerie* or non-commissioned officer designated to fulfill those duties. The train was commanded by the officer commanding the train company and he directed its movements.

The battery was divided into three sections, each section having two guns and two caissons. It could also be divided into two demi-batteries, each of three guns and three caissons. Three officers, or in their absence the three most senior non-commissioned officers, commanded the three sections. The first section was commanded by the most senior, the third by the second most senior, and the second by the junior. A non-commissioned officer commanded each gun, and an artificier was assigned to each caisson.

When the battery moved, the foot gunners marched in two files on each side of their gun. In the horse artillery the gunners rode in two ranks behind the gun. When a French battery fired it did so from right to left, facing the enemy.

The speed of movement is an interesting topic on which there is little data readily available. Escalle, in his work *Des marches dans les Armées de Napoléon*, provides some actual rates of movement for horse artillery, stating that a French horse battery moved at the rates shown in Table 85.

It is interesting to note that he says a distance of 13,328 metres (8.33 statute miles) could be covered in one hour if the line of movement was not obstructed, and he quotes Gassendi as stating that on the road, a convoy of artillery could cover 1500 *toises* (about 3000 metres or 0.94 miles) in about an hour. Longer distances, of course, varied with the loading of the horse. A horse carrying 180 *livres* (75.6 kg or 166 lb) and pulling 750 *livres* (315 kg or 690 lb) could travel between 31 and 32 km (about 20 miles) per day, or it could pull a load of 1500 *livres* (630 kg or 1380 lb) the same distance on even, horizontal terrain. If the terrain was rougher, it could pull only about a quarter as much. Escalle then provides the loading for the Gribeauval System and the horses assigned to it, as shown in Table 86.

The *prolongue* – a series of lines run out in front of the gun, used to pull it forward – was used only in front of the enemy and was constantly deployed, except when no fire was seen. These lines were drawn by six horses and were 18 metres (27 ft) long. If, for some reason, there were no horses, they could be drawn by hand by the gunners. Caissons were posted behind their guns at a distance of 36 metres (54 paces or 117 ft).

Table 85. Rates of movement of French horse artillery.

Speed of movement	Rate of movement (metres per minute)	(feet per minute)
Walk	86.4	280
Trot	189.0	614
Gallop	370.0	1202

Table 86. Loading per horse, Gribeauval System.		
Weapon	*Per horse (kg)*	*Per horse (lb)*
12-pdr cannon	700	1540
8-pdr cannon	825	1815
4-pdr cannon	525	1155
6.4-inch howitzer	725	1595
12-pdr caisson	900	1980
8-pdr caisson	850	1870
4-pdr caisson	750	1650
6.4-inch caisson	800	1760

The gunners' horses and limber-horses were on the gun side of the caissons, while the caisson horses were on the near side, towards the guns. The distance was this great so that when the guns fired and recoiled, the caissons and horses would be far enough away that the guns would not hit either of them.

The battery captain generally placed himself in the middle of the battery, eight paces between the gun horses and the caisson horses. The caissons were 18 metres or 20 yds (27 paces) from the guns. This regulation states that when deployed for combat the distance between each battery, was to be 36 metres (54 paces or 117 ft). When a battery moved in column each gun preceded its caisson. The column of eight guns with its attendant caissons was 105 to 110 metres long (113 to 120 yds).

Philosophy of artillery usage

Though there are a number of period drill regulations for artillery, there is very little readily available on the philosophy of artillery usage. The most thorough discussion comes, surprisingly, from a Spanish source, T. de Moria's *Tratado de Artillerie* of 1816, which provides a number of maxims that are most enlightening. Though most of these are listed below, some have been deleted because they are relevant to specific situations rather than general usage.

De Moria's first maxim is: 'When in the sight of the enemy and when the artillery manoeuvres, manoeuvre it with the prolong or by hand.' This ties in closely with the second maxim, which is: 'Artillery should be manoeuvred by prolong when within range of enemy artillery and when the distance to be traversed is short, but not over broken or rough terrain, or when the movement is large.' It was felt that the prolong was the quickest way to move short distances and that it kept the gunners close to their firing positions. It was also felt that unless the move was significant, it was inappropriate to risk exposing the limbered battery to enemy fire.

The third maxim is: 'When the movement of the artillery is short, the guns should be moved forward by hand.' The prolong was not as quick over short distances.

The fourth maxim is: 'When manoeuvring artillery, never manoeuvre munitions and reserves with the brigade guns, because they complicate manoeuvres.'

The fifth maxim is: 'The artillery should manoeuvre according to the movements of the infantry.' Failure to operate in close conjunction with the infantry columns might result in there being insufficient space between them for the artillery to deploy. A single gun was considered to occupy the space occupied by the smallest manoeuvring element of an infantry battalion. Therefore if the infantry formed without consideration for the artillery it would be crowded out.

The eighth maxim is: 'Batteries should endeavour to take up positions which enfilade the enemy, or at least fire on him obliquely.' This increases the killing power of each shot by maximising the depth of the enemy formation that it penetrates. There are recorded instances of a single ball from an enfilade shot passing through a company and killing 10 men or more. The impact of a shot into the flank of a dense formation was devastating.

The ninth maxim is: 'Never put your batteries in front of your troops, nor behind them on slightly raised elevations.' Artillery posted in front of the infantry was felt to increase the target for the enemy, as well as impeding the movements and breaking up the order of one's own troops. If the artillery was above the infantry and firing over their heads, it tormented the infantry by its noise and hurt them with the spillage of its cartridges and rounds that fell short.

The tenth maxim is: 'Do not position the batteries until it is time to commence fire.' The intention here was to prevent the enemy from altering his dispositions once he knew the positions of the opposing artillery.

The eleventh maxim is: 'Always conceal a portion of your artillery from the enemy.' This was in order both to maintain a reserve and to mislead the enemy into committing himself to a manoeuvre without knowing that it would be exposed to artillery fire.

The thirteenth maxim is: 'Always position batteries on the flanks so that they can fire on the enemy cavalry when it advances.'

The fourteenth maxim is: 'If artillery is assigned to protect your cavalry the number should be large enough to ensure victory and it should, if possible, be posted in a position that is inaccessible to the enemy cavalry.'

The sixteenth maxim is: 'When the artillery is posted before the main line of battle it is necessary to support it with either grenadier companies or complete battalions.'

The seventeenth maxim is: 'The artillery pieces in a battery should be positioned ten paces apart. If the enemy threatens to enfilade the battery one gun may be advanced in front of the others.' This maxim establishes the Spanish interval between guns. Such intervals varied from country to country, the Prussian 1812 Regulations stating that it should be 20 paces. The movement forward of one gun was intended to minimise the impact of an enfilade by enemy artillery.

The nineteenth to twenty-second maxims are closely related. They are as follows: 19) 'When the position or order of battle is defensive, position the heaviest calibre guns so that they cover the most likely avenues of enemy advance. The smaller calibre guns should be held in reserve so they can be sent where they are needed.' 20) 'The major portion of the heavy artillery should be posted where it protects those portions of your forces which are exposed to the enemy.' 21) 'Always post a heavy battery in a fortified position which covers one wing or the centre of the enemy's line.' 22) 'Light artillery, not heavy artillery, should always accompany an attack or rapid movement.'

These maxims basically state that the heavy artillery is best used defensively. It was too difficult to manoeuvre with ease and would embarrass manoeuvres, or simply could not advance quickly enough to support an attack or counterattack. The idea of positioning the heavy artillery on the most likely avenues of enemy advance was simply the most rational way of using it. If it was difficult to manoeuvre, it made sense to position it where it could be used effectively and with the least requirement for repositioning.

The twenty-third maxim is: 'Since the effect of artillery can be decisive, it is necessary that the batteries be strong, that their fire protects themselves and that their fire be crossed.'

The twenty-fourth maxim is: 'Artillery should never abandon the infantry and, similarly, the infantry should never abandon it.' Neither is able to withstand the enemy without the support of the other. Therefore it is logical that they remain closely tied to one another.

The twenty-fifth and twenty-seventh maxims are closely related. They say: 25) 'The conservation of ammunition should be one of the major objectives of the artillery officer'; and 27) 'The first of all the rules for the service of artillery is to economise artillery for the essential and decisive moments.' In view of the limited stores accompanying a battery, ranging from 100 to slightly over 200 rounds depending on the nation involved, a battery could shoot off its ammunition in as little as 50 minutes or at most 100 minutes of continuous fire. A battery which had shot off all its ammunition was worthless and could not defend itself, let alone the infantry.

Maxims twenty-seven to twenty-nine relate to the range of fire. The twenty-seventh maxim says: 'Do not commence fire at a range of greater than 450 *toesas* [2700 yds] from the enemy.' Long range fire was uncertain and inefficient. Unless an excellent target presented itself, long range fire could be little more than a waste of ammunition.

The twenty-eighth maxim says: 'Between 450 *toesas* [2700 yds] and 250 *toesas* [1500 yds] fire ball slowly. If no enemy columns are available for fire, fire still more slowly.'

The twenty-ninth maxim says: 'Between 250 and 130 *toesas* [1500–780 yds] fire large canister, or if able to fire enfilade or against columns, fire ball at a rapid rate.'

The thirtieth maxim says: 'Under 130 *toesas* [780 yds] fire small canister. Do not fire ball unless you have an exact enfilade of the enemy line or unless friendly troops are very near the line of fire. The rate of fire should be precipitous.'

The thirty-first maxim is: 'If you do not have canister, continue to fire ball until the enemy is 90 *toesas* [540 yds] from the battery and then fire bags of musket balls.'

The thirty-seventh maxim speaks of howitzer fire. It says: 'Howitzers may begin firing at a range of 600 *toesas* [3600 yds] only when the enemy is manoeuvring at that distance, and should not use canister until the enemy is within 150 *toesas* [900 yds].' Of course, these last several maxims on range are closely associated with the effective ranges of the guns involved, and should be viewed with that consideration taken into account.

The most significant maxim is the thirty-second, which speaks of target selection. It says: 'The primary target of the artillery is the enemy's troops and not his artillery.' To dedicate one's batteries solely to counter-battery fire is a 'waste of ammunition' that 'seeks in vain to achieve its objective ... Even if the counter-battery fire was successful, what has it achieved if the enemy's forces have overthrown your own?' Counter-battery fire was strongly discouraged, and was acceptable only if it was necessary to support and defend your own troops. This particular point is found repeatedly in instructions and actions by many of the Napoleonic generals. Wellington expressly forbade his artillery to engage in counter-battery fire and the French generally discouraged it unless there were no other targets.

In his discussion on the use of artillery in battle, de Moria states that 'the principal and unique objective of the artillery in battles is the protection of the troops, supporting their manoeuvres and attacks, and the destruction of the obstacles which oppose them'. The treatise goes on to advocate that artillery be positioned at the heads of infantry columns when they attacked, so that they might, with their fire, soften the enemy and prepare him for the infantry assault.

In the Regulation for horse artillery written by General Kosciusko in 1800 there is also a section on the philosophy of artillery usage. Kosciusko says: 'The use of artillery in battle is not against the artillery of an enemy, for that would be a waste of powder, but against the line of the enemy in a diagonal direction when it is destructive in the extreme.' Though he doesn't provide reasons, Kosciusko clearly states that counter-battery fire is not to be used.

Kosciusko says that the tactics of the period

> have established it a rule that only a part of the artillery shall be ever engaged; but then this part by being constantly supported from the park and that park, again supported from a reserve at a distance, is kept up in full vigour and is as entire in all its parts at the end of the action as it was at the commencement of it; two-thirds of the artillery is therefore always out of danger, and as fast as any piece becomes injured from any cause whatever it is instantly replaced by a perfect one, while the injured piece, if susceptible to repair, is in the way of being refitted in the rear, totally undisturbed by the enemy, so long as the front keep their ground.
>
> By keeping the artillery on the flanks instead of [the older practice of] mixing it in the line [of battle], it never can impede the movements of the latter, which are totally independent of it; on the other hand, when artillery is placed in the centre, the movements of the line, being of a different nature from those of the artillery, can never accord with them; the pieces are therefore always in the way and the movement, whatever it may be, is in some way or another impeded by them, and they by the troops.

Further philosophical considerations for the tactical employment of smoothbore artillery are found in the *Handbook of Artillery* issued for the US Army in 1863. Much of its guidance supports that found in de Moria's treatise. It says that artillery should never be used in numbers less than two guns operating in a mutually supporting section. Like de Moria's thirty-second maxim, it states that counter-battery fire is not productive and should only be undertaken 'when [the enemy's] troops are well covered and his guns exposed, or their fire very destructive. Their fire should be directed principally against columns of attack, and masses, or upon positions which are intended to be carried.'

In concert with de Moria's comments about the conservation of ammunition, the *Handbook* states that 'ammunition should be at all times carefully husbanded, particularly at the commencement of an action, as the want of it at the close may decide the fate of the day; it should also be sparingly used in skirmishes and minor affairs, especially when at a distance from supplies or in anticipation of a general reserve.'

The employment of artillery reserves should be

> when a particular point of the line requires additional support, a favorable position is to be seized, an impression has been made on the line by the enemy, a forward or retrograde movement is in contemplation, or when a determined attack is to be made on him, then the reserve should come up and take part in the action; and it is of the utmost importance that this should be done as expeditiously as circumstances will permit.

Table 87. Artillery ranges and ammunition when under cavalry attack.

Cavalry attack No. of rounds to be fired	Type of round	Range (yds)	Infantry Attack No. of rounds to be fired	Type of round	Range (yds)
7	Shrapnel	1500–650	19	Shrapnel	1500–650
2	Ball	650–350	7	Ball	650–350
2	Canister	350–0	8	Canister	350–100
			2	Canister	100–0

Artillery reserves were to be placed 'in the rear with the second line, out of the range of shot, and as little exposed as circumstances will admit, but always in such a position as to have ready access to the front or rear.'

When supporting infantry formed in square to resist the charge of cavalry, the *Handbook* states that

the guns should be placed outside the angles of the square, the limbers horses, etc., inside. Should the detachments be driven from their guns, they will retire into the square, after discharging their pieces, and taking with them the sponges and other equipments; the moment the enemy has retired, they recommence their fire. Supposing the infantry formed in echelon of regimental squares, and that the time or small extent of the squares, would not admit the limbers, etc., being placed inside, then the wagons and limbers should be brought up with their broadsides to the front, so as to occupy, if possible, the space between the guns, leaving no intervals for the cavalry to cut through: the *prolongue* or drag ropes might also offer an effectual momentary impediment to them, if properly stretched and secured.'

The *Handbook of Artillery*, as well as the *Madras Artillery Manual* of 1848, also provide scenarios for the use of artillery against advancing cavalry and infantry. Surprisingly, the two tables are identical and because of the lack of significant innovation in the world of artillery, they are probably very representative of the Napoleonic period. Table 87 shows the ranges and ammunition for use when the battery was under various forms of attack.

The only statistics available on the actual casualties that were ever inflicted on an attacking unit come from the German historian Müller and are given in Table 88. He served in the King's German Legion and assessed the numbers of casualties inflicted by a 6-pdr during such an attack. In addition, he used a higher rate of fire in his calculations. The average was two round shot per minute or three canister, but Müller seems to believe that the artillerists could reach a rate of eight rounds per minute when being charged. Unfortunately, he does not indicate the type of formation being fired upon, which would make a considerable difference in the number of casualties likely to be inflicted. Inasmuch as cavalry generally operated in line it must be assumed that the figures for cavalry casualties are based on firing on such a formation. With that assumption, one should also assume that he was consistent in his assessments and that the infantry were also formed in line.

In his book *The Face of Battle*, J. Keegan says that a smoothbore cannon could keep its front clear of attacking troops with its fire. B.P. Hughes, in his book *Firepower*, supports this. There is certainly no doubt that if a single gun could maintain the rate of fire indicated above, its front would be kept clear of any attacking troops.

French artillery usage

During the Revolutionary Wars the French used whatever artillery they had wherever they needed it. Batteries were distributed amongst the infantry in a support role and often employed by sections. Indeed, individual batteries might have two different calibre cannons, in addition to their assigned howitzers. However, after 1800 the battery's equipment was standardised and it was the general practice of the French to assign at least one battery per infantry division. This was generally a foot battery, but they often attached horse artillery to the infantry divisions as well. The divisional artillery was always an 8-pdr or 6-pdr battery. Horse artillery was generally assigned to the cavalry formations and, during the Revolution, consisted of 8-pdr guns. The use of 4-pdr regimental artillery continued until 1805. The 12-pdr batteries were assigned on a corps level in the artillery reserve. In addition, depending on the availability of equipment, the corps reserve could contain a number of light foot batteries or horse batteries.

Though banished earlier, in 1809 Napoleon decided that the regimental artillery should be re-established and by 1812 most infantry regiments had it again. In 1812 it became standard practice for the divisional artillery to consist of a foot and a horse battery. Equipment and horse shortages rendered this policy difficult to maintain through 1813 and 1814, but whenever possible the practice was continued.

Napoleon, being an artillery officer, made his single biggest tactical contribution in the use of artillery. He devised the concept of the *grande batterie*, which was the massing of as many as a hundred guns on a single section of the battle line. The object was to shred the enemy line and provide a hole through which he could drive his infantry and cavalry. Table 89 lists a few instances of the use of the Napoleonic *grande batterie*.

Austrian artillery usage

In Italy between 1800 and 1805, the Austrian armies were not particularly large and their artillery was assigned to the various infantry divisions. However, though seem-

---

Table 88. Casualties inflicted on an attacking unit (Müller).

Cavalry

Range (yds)	Killed	Wounded	Total
1600–800	4	2	6
800–400	6	4	10
400–0	9	23	32
Total	19	29	48

Infantry

Range (yds)	Killed	Wounded	Total
1600–800	4	4	8
800–400	8	2	10
400–0	30	90	120
Total	42	96	138

Table 89. French and other grand batteries.

Battle	Number of guns	
Castiglione	19	(French)
Marengo	18	(French)
Austerlitz	24	(French)
Jena	42	(French)
Eylau	60 and 70	(Russian)
Friedland	32	(French)
Deutsch-Wagram	112	(French)
Borodino	102	(French)
Bautzen	76	(French)
Dennewitz	34	(Prussian/Russian)
Leipzig	137	(French)
Leipzig	220	(Russian, Prussian and Swedish)
Hanau	50	(French)
Ligny	60	(French)
Waterloo	84	(French)

ingly organised as a divisional force it was, in fact, employed on a piecemeal basis. Batteries were scattered between the brigades and even broken up further, with gun sections being employed in the line. The Austrian army at Austerlitz was organised so that its artillery was assigned in the same manner. There was not an Austrian tactical army reserve composed of 12-pdr guns. Regimental 4-pdr guns were used during the Revolutionary Wars, but seem to have disappeared around 1800.

During the 1809 campaign the Austrians assigned a 6-pdr brigade battery to every line brigade. The light brigades had either a *Wurst* battery or a 3-pdr brigade battery. They also assigned their heavier 12-pdr batteries on a corps level as an independent reserve, indicating that they had learned from the French practice of maintaining large reserves. In 1813 these corps reserves generally consisted of a 12-pdr position battery and two 6-pdr position batteries, but in 1809 they varied considerably.

Prussian artillery usage

Prior to 1806 the Prussians distributed their artillery on a brigade basis. An examination of the armies under *Feldmarschal* Brunswick-Lüneburg and *Fürst* Hohenlohe indicates that there was little regard for what was assigned to any brigade. Some had horse batteries, others 3-pdr, 6-pdr or 12-pdr foot batteries. Surprisingly, the reserve division had less artillery than the others. The brevity of the 1806 campaign means that there is little that can be determined of their usage during it, but if the actions of the Prussians during the Revolutionary Wars are examined we find the typical infantry support role. There was no indication of any operational independence – indeed, the artillery was quite tied to the infantry in its manoeuvring. During the Revolution the Prussians had used regimental 4-pdr guns, but they do not appear after 1800.

After the 1809 reorganisation no doctrine on the use of artillery was established until the issuance of the 1812 series of regulations, which all repeat a set of directions on the use of combined arms. A Prussian brigade, which was the equivalent of other nations' divisions, was standardised and theoretically equipped with one 6-pdr foot and one horse battery. The foot battery operated in two half-batteries, posted on the flanks of the brigade while the horse battery remained in the rear ready to deploy to whichever flank required the additional firepower. It was to act as a brigade ready reserve force, however in actual practice the horse battery was rarely assigned. The 12-pdr batteries were assigned on a corps level and acted as the corps artillery reserve, much as that of the French. This corps reserve also contained varying numbers of 6-pdr foot and horse batteries, depending on the equipment available.

The Prussians did not mass their divisional artillery, but had the option of forming *grande batteries* from their corps reserve should the necessity arise. However, there are very few examples of the Prussians massing their artillery in this manner. Much of this is probably due to their having distributed their army as corps in various mixed allied armies and not having the opportunity to form a purely Prussian *grande batterie* until Leipzig in 1813.

British artillery usage

The British use of artillery during the Napoleonic Wars is effectively Wellington's use of it. He did not believe in concentrating his artillery and rarely did so, preferring to work with small units placed in well chosen spots, and often concealed until the critical moment. Guns were spread in front of a position rather than massed, and in most cases must have been regarded as an infantry-support weapon rather than an independent force with aims and goals of its own.

Much of this might be attributed to the small quantities of artillery available to Wellington in the Peninsula. He was unable to provide even one British battery for his eight divisions and had to depend on the Portuguese for artillery support.

Russian artillery usage

In early 1810, Barclay de Tolly, the Russian Minister of War, wrote the Czar a report that addressed his philosophy of artillery assignment. He said that the distribution of artillery in the infantry divisions was done on a regular and equal basis. He said that there were

> two considerations on this subject [of artillery assignment]: a) it is necessary that the infantry divisions are not encumbered with an excessive quantity of heavy artillery which opposes the rapidity of movements by its transportation difficulties; b) the heavy artillery should be judiciously distributed between the infantry divisions and the excess assigned to the artillery reserve of each army. These reserves, placed under the immediate authority of the [army] commander-in-chief, can be employed with great advantage at the decisive moment of a battle.
> In accordance with these considerations I have the honour to propose (to your Highness), that each corps be assigned two reserve artillery batteries, composed of heavy and horse artillery.

By the beginning of the 1812 campaign, when these guidelines were implemented, each infantry division was assigned an artillery brigade that consisted of two light (6-

pdr) batteries and a heavy or position (12-pdr gun) battery. At a corps level another brigade was assigned that usually had a position battery, a horse battery and one or two light batteries. This general organisation persisted through 1815.

Prior to 1810 the Russians did not establish corps artillery reserves. Artillery was assigned on a divisional level and could consist of as many as two position (12-pdr) batteries, three light (6-pdr) batteries and a horse battery. They continued the use of regimental artillery through to the Battle of Austerlitz, but it is not found in their orders of battle after that time.

The idea of an army artillery reserve did not exist in the Russian army before Barclay's letter, though there were massive corps reserves. Only in the Battle of Eylau do they seem to have employed it as such. No doubt Barclay noted the destructiveness of the two Russian *grande batteries* at Eylau, as well as the French use of artillery reserves, and chose to follow their example. At Borodino a massive reserve was established, but due to the poor generalship of Kutusov and the untimely death of the artillery reserve commanding officer, very little of it was employed.

The failure of the Russian artillery reserve system at Borodino does not seem to have sunk into the Russian military intellect. Russian commanders grew to like these large reserves, but had a real problem with using them. At both Lützen and, especially, at Bautzen the Russians organised large reserves but failed to employ them. It was not until the Battle of Leipzig that they finally got their artillery reserves into combat. However, in this instance it was because the Russians involved were with the Army of Silesia, under Blücher, and he was sending everything he could into the line.

Chapter 11

Operation of Combined Arms

The operational and tactical structure of an army, the types and distribution of troops and their organisational hierarchy, were developed and functioned on the basis of two considerations. The first was the relationship and interaction between the individual components. The second was national preference and historical precedence.

The relationships were well-known during the period 1792–1815. They had not changed significantly since 1757, though there were some technical innovations – the use of skirmishers, for instance, was an evolving process that reached its zenith in the French Revolutionary armies. Another innovation was the development of horse artillery. Both of these had an impact on the conduct of warfare, but they appeared before 1792. No major technical innovations occurred between 1792 and 1815, and there were few tactical innovations or changes in tactical and grand-tactical systems.

The other consideration in the development of army operational and tactical organisation was national and historical precedence. Because of the influences of their specific neighbours and the type of warfare in which an army consequently found itself engaged, formations and organisations unique to a particular nation often evolved, such as the 'lava attack', causing some armies to have particularly outsized cavalry or infantry organisations (*eg* the Grand Duchy of Warsaw, which had an army with more cavalry regiments than infantry regiments, and Switzerland, which had almost no cavalry at all). As a result each nation, having its own preferences for various branches of the armed forces and various tactics, had to weave them into an operational force where the strengths and weaknesses of its infantry, artillery and cavalry, could be employed to best effect. This process evolved into what is known as combined-arms operations.

Inter-relationships of the three arms

In a manner not dissimilar to the children's game of 'rocks, scissors, paper', each of the three combat arms in the period from the 17th through to the early 19th century was both superior and inferior to the other two arms. None could stand by itself if opposed by an enemy force composed of any two of the other arms. Yet, in any given tactical situation, one arm could defeat one other isolated combat arm.

In a general sense infantry was impervious to cavalry if it had assumed the proper defensive formation. Once in square it would shoot the cavalry down until the latter had enough and decided to leave. However, if it was caught out of square its chances of survival were far less. If the cavalry made a frontal charge on infantry formed in line it would win if one of two things happened: 1) if they survived the fire that they were sure to receive, or 2) the infantry's morale failed and they fled. The latter could happen if the infantry lost its nerve and refused to stand, knowing they were in the wrong formation to receive cavalry, even though trained, veteran troops could receive such frontal attacks successfully (as had been shown in the Seven Years War). It could also happen if the troops involved were simply insufficiently trained and unwilling to take the chance that their officers knew what they were doing. In any other situation where the infantry was either deployed as skirmishers, or struck in the flank or rear, the infantry formation was certain to meet a swift and sure demise.

In a similar sense, artillery could defend its front with a bloody certainty. However, it had terribly exposed flanks that could easily be overrun by either infantry or cavalry. It was also subject to sniping by skirmishers who could pick off the gunners slowly, but surely. In fact, this was a very common method for dealing with artillery, and several accounts exist of skirmishers being deployed specifically to counter artillery.

Cavalry could always ride away from what it could not defeat. Its mobility was its most powerful weapon, and it was certain to crush anything it caught in the flank or rear. However, any frontal attack by cavalry on prepared infantry or artillery was certain to fail.

To resolve these strengths and weaknesses, to weld them into a powerful tool for defeating one's enemies and conquering enemy territory, the generals of the Napoleonic period strove to devise the proper formations and mixes of troop types to best handle each situation. The concept of combined arms arose during the Seven Years War or even earlier, perhaps, but it came of age during the Napoleonic period.

What is a combined-arms operation?

A combined-arms operation is one in which all three arms work in unison so as to defeat the enemy. It works by playing on the strengths and weaknesses of each arm in such a way as to: 1) establish morale ascendancy over the enemy and cause him to collapse; 2) hold him in place and punish him until he collapses; or 3) manoeuvre him into such a position that he has no chance of success and collapses. A combined attack can operate with just two of the three arms. Properly handled, it will push the enemy into one of the aforementioned three situations.

The Prussian series of regulations published in 1812 all provide diagrams and a discussion of a standardised combined arms attack by their 'brigades', which were in fact combined-arms forces on a divisional scale. The general operation is shown in Figures 132a-d, which are drawn unmodified from these regulations.

As you can see, the formation consists of a main body of infantry formed in two lines. The use of two successive lines in the main body is very classical and dates back beyond the War of the Spanish Succession (1700–15). The two lines of regular infantry are preceded by a skirmish screen and have the artillery and cavalry posted in the rear. The skirmish screen was to deal with the enemy's own skirmishers, as well as his formed infantry. The main body of infantry was to lock the enemy infantry in place so that the artillery could position itself advantageously. Once sufficient damage had been done to the engaged enemy force, the cavalry would theoretically swing out and strike the weakened enemy, shatter him, and drive him from the battlefield.

That is the divisional combined-arms attack. On a smaller scale, the combined operation worked like this. The attacking infantry would engage the opposing infantry force. In order to meet an infantry threat the general process was to extend into line so as to bring as many muskets to bear as possible. The appearance of attacking cavalry

Figure 132. Prussian combined-arms attack – *Exercir-Regelment für die Kavallerie der Königlich Preussische Armee,* **Berlin, 1812.**

132a. *Aufstellung einter entwicklten Brigade* (Positions of a formed brigade).

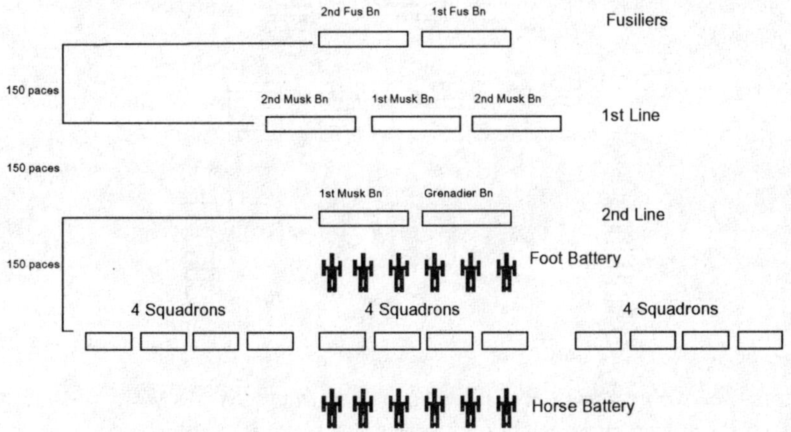

2nd Fus Bn 1st Fus Bn	Fusiliers
150 paces	
2nd Musk Bn 1st Musk Bn 2nd Musk Bn	1st Line
150 paces	
1st Musk Bn Grenadier Bn	2nd Line
150 paces	Foot Battery
4 Squadrons 4 Squadrons 4 Squadrons	
	Horse Battery

132b. *Formirung zur Attaque* (Forming to attack).

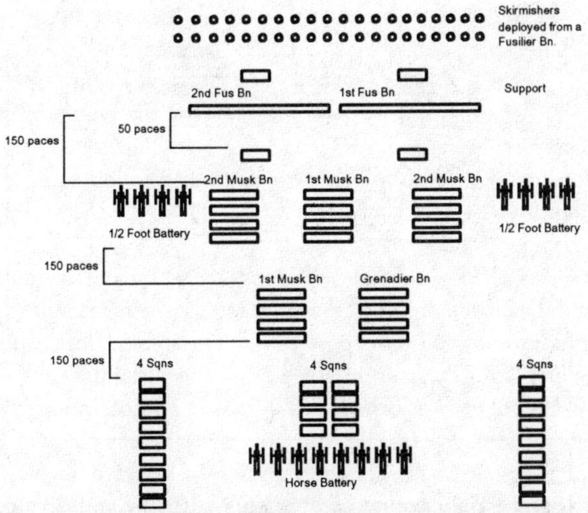

Skirmishers deployed from a Fusilier Bn.

2nd Fus Bn   1st Fus Bn   Support

150 paces   50 paces

2nd Musk Bn   1st Musk Bn   2nd Musk Bn

1/2 Foot Battery   1/2 Foot Battery

150 paces

1st Musk Bn   Grenadier Bn

150 paces   4 Sqns   4 Sqns   4 Sqns

Horse Battery

continued

would oblige the defending infantry to change formation to defend against the greater threat – a strike in the flank or rear by the cavalry – which in turn reduced the number of muskets he could bring to bear on the attacking infantry. The change from line to square also provided a much denser target for artillery, ideal for having the maximum number of casualties inflicted on it, but provided the only protection against cavalry. The presence of the cavalry would oblige the defending infantry to keep in square, thereby allowing the artillery or attacking infantry to fire on the square until it was a

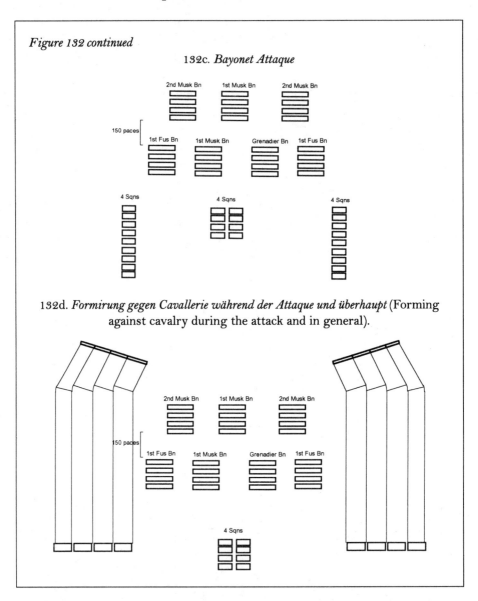

Figure 132 continued

132c. *Bayonet Attaque*

132d. *Formirung gegen Cavallerie während der Attaque und überhaupt* (Forming against cavalry during the attack and in general).

shambles, at which point the cavalry or attacking infantry could bring it into close combat and crush it. The square was *not* a good formation for defending against artillery or infantry attack, but the trick of a combined-arms attack was to force the enemy to choose between two equally bad alternatives. Having obliged him to assume a hopeless situation, the action was won before the first shot was fired.

In situations where just cavalry and artillery operated together the square would be pounded until it broke and the cavalry rode down the survivors. This is not very different to the scenario described above. In the case of infantry and artillery operating together, the process became very prolonged, the lack of cavalry giving the defending infantry no reason to go into square. Instead he would remain in line, which is

Figure 133. Use of cavalry and horse artillery in the attack – *Dienst-Reglement für die Kaiserlich-Königlich Kavallerie*, Vienna, 1808, Plate 29.

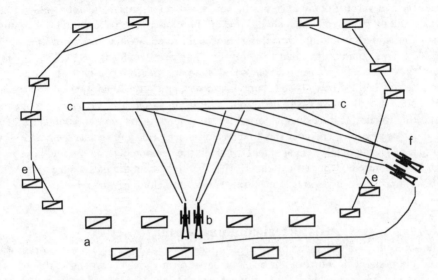

a = Cavalry regiment with horse battery 100 paces in front of it.
b = Horse battery.
c = Enemy line.
d = Movement of the battery to the middle or flank.
e = Detachment of the advanced guard.
f = Detachment from the horse battery, covered by the flank division, which fires on the enemy line.

the best formation for receiving frontal artillery fire. This would result in the battle becoming a fire-fight and no swift solution was likely if both forces were of equal morale. Only if a huge mass of artillery could be brought to bear, or could move up very close to the infantry fire-fight where it could add canister to the exchange of musketry, could it influence the battle. This latter effort would be limited by the amount of defending artillery and its willingness to engage in counter-battery fire.

When cavalry and artillery worked in conjunction against enemy cavalry the process was similar, but the goal of the artillery was to weaken and demoralise the enemy cavalry to such a point that the attacking cavalry was assured of victory. Figures 133 and 134 are drawn from the Austrian 1808 cavalry regulations. They clearly show the desired manoeuvres, including the positioning of the artillery so as to enfilade the enemy line, thereby inflicting the maximum number of casualties. They also show the placing of small detachments of cavalry adjacent to the horse battery, to protect it from attack as well as to act against the flank of the enemy line.

In the situation where infantry and cavalry worked together, one would find much the same situation as when infantry and artillery operated together. The victor in a battle between numerically equal forces would be decided as much by the chance breaking of a unit as a carefully orchestrated manoeuvre and superior tactics.

There is a third basic situation where the two opposing sides have approximately equal forces and each has a combined-arms force involved in the battle. The key to such an engagement was the outcome of the cavalry battle. Once that was decided and one side had cavalry dominance on the battlefield, an unimpeded combined-arms attack could be mounted, which should prevail. Faced with such a situation, the opposing commanders would do everything they could to ensure the victory of their own cavalry. This could be handled in two ways. The first would be to goad the enemy cavalry to strike the infantry squares and dissipate its strength; once the attacking cavalry was winded it would be counter-attacked, and in its disorganised and weakened state it could more easily be beaten. The second approach was to single out the attacking cavalry as the principal target for the defending artillery and bombard them as much as possible. The goal was to damage their morale and reduce their numbers, so that when the cavalry engagement occurred the defender's cavalry could have morale ascendancy and numerical superiority. Though it might not ensure victory, it would improve the odds in favour of the counter-attacking cavalry.

Historical combined-arms forces

The ability to establish a combined-arms attack depended heavily on corps organisation. The general structure of the order of battle of any given army shows the mechanisms and the level on which the combined-arms action was planned to occur. Prior to 1800 all of the European armies distributed cavalry on a divisional level with great frequency. The armies planned for combined-arms attacks on a divisional level, using the mass of divisional infantry as the pivot around which the divisional artillery and cavalry operated. This process continued through 1815 on a smaller scale, represented by the various advanced guards employed by the Austrian and Russian armies. Though the advanced guard was a highly specialised force, it operated in much the same manner as the pre-1800 division when it came to combined-arms attacks.

The typical division-sized advanced guard consisted of light cavalry, light infantry, and light artillery – usually horse batteries or similarly mobile guns. This force was developed to move quickly, scout out the enemy and defend itself long enough to disengage if it was trapped by a superior enemy force. Its speed capabilities indicate a reconnaissance role, but its mix of all three arms show that it was intended to be able to deal with equal-sized or slightly larger line forces, seize vital positions, and defend itself as necessary if it had to hold a bridgehead or city against a significantly larger force. The various arms were extensively trained in advanced posts, skirmish operations, and the normal types of large-scale combat that could be expected of them. The major difference between these and line troops lay principally in the first two areas of specialised training.

In the pre-1800 division-sized combined-arms force, the attack and defence employed the methods of combined-arms attack already described, though the design of the formation was based on a different set of goals than that of the advanced guard. After 1800 there was a move away from the assignment of cavalry on a divisional level. This process was begun by Napoleon, who began establishing cavalry corps. His goal was no longer the divisional combined-arms attack, but the army combined-arms attack. Superficially, in the case of the cavalry corps, the concept of 'combined arms' is a little more difficult to perceive. The reason for this is that the concentrated cavalry

**Figure 134. Use of cavalry and horse artillery in the withdrawal –
Dienst-Reglement für die Kaiserlich-Königlich Kavallerie, Vienna,
1808, Plate 29.**

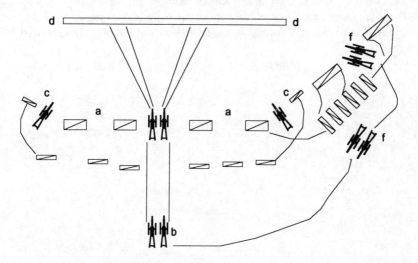

a = Regiment withdrawing in *echequer*.
b = Horse battery in the middle of the withdrawing squadrons.
c = Advanced guard which is on the right and left wings of the
 withdrawing units.
d = Advancing enemy line.
f = Detachment of guns, positioned according to terrain, that engage the
 enemy's flank.

force is not obviously used in combination with the other two arms; but if one examines orders of battle for the French and other major armies one will note that these large cavalry formations almost always had horse artillery assigned on a divisional level. This is one indication that they were intended for combined-arms operations. Another comes from a study of their tactical employment on the battlefield.

The general procedure of combined-arms operations for the cavalry division or corps comes from the use of other divisional or corps-level infantry formations. This infantry force engaged the enemy line with musketry and artillery until such time as the enemy was so weakened that the thundering advance of a huge mass of cavalry was more than their morale could handle. Once casualties and wavering morale began to form a hole in the line of battle the cavalry would pour through and the domino effect would bring about a collapse of the entire enemy line. This technique was used at Jena, Auerstädt and other battles with devastating effect. It was tried at Eylau, but didn't have quite the desired effect because the Russian line had not been sufficiently battered to have its morale broken by the cavalry advance. And the most notable failure to properly employ such a combined-arms attack was at Waterloo, when Ney thought the British were withdrawing and ordered the cavalry to attack without infantry and artillery support. This attack degenerated into the situation described earlier, where the solid infantry squares methodically shot down the attacking cavalry until it ceased to be a viable military force and quit the field.

The combined-arms attack was the ultimate weapon of its day. It combined the best attributes of each arm and blended them so as to synergise the arms' abilities into something far more capable than the sum of their individual parts. It had its weaknesses, and could fail if the timing was mishandled, but if properly exercised it was invariably victorious.

Chapter 12

Grand Tactical and Strategic Operations

Command and control

If any one significant innovation can be attributed to the period 1792–1815, it must be the development of the army staff. When the French Revolutionary Wars erupted, armies had very rudimentary staffs. Generals had small groups of aides to whom they allocated various duties, and there were a few major functions that were assigned to senior officers, *ie* the intendance or provision of materials and food stuffs, provost duties, and the baggage-masters who oversaw the army trains. It was the French, and most probably Napoleon himself, who brought the first truly modern military staff into existence. When the *Grande Armée* invaded Russia it had a Chief of Staff with nine aides; a Baggage-master to the Chief of Staff; a General Staff with five generals (including Baron Jomini, who was assigned the duties of Staff Historian), 11 adjutants, and 50 supporting officers; a Geographical Engineers (cartographers) department with 14 officers and cartographers; three senior officers assigned to the Imperial Gendarmerie; 19 officers defined as 'General Officers, Senior Officers, and others Assigned to the General Staff'; an Imperial Administration with 19 officers, disbursing agents, and war commissioners; an Inspector of Reviews with three inspectors; Administrative Services with 10 surgeons, hospital managers, and commissary personnel; an Artillery Staff with four generals and colonels; a Bridging Train with six senior officers; a Siege Train with six senior officers; and a General Engineering Staff with four senior officers. In addition to these individuals, who would best be described as majors and above and senior civil servants, there was a large contingent of enlisted men supporting their operations. This staff provided the administrative, logistical, and communications support that Napoleon found necessary to make his army operate over long distances and in unknown territories.

Napoleon's staff and those that have followed in the ensuing 180 years have provided their commanders with eyes and ears, minds to process and analyse data, and hands to attend to the thousand chores that are necessary for any army to operate smoothly. The staff has now become so important that where once there were thousands of combatants to a single staff officer or soldier, the administrative tails of armies now outnumber the actual combatants.

Intelligence

The function of the Geographical Engineers was to march before the main army. They would do this either during peacetime on something between covert and overt reconnaissance, or with a military escort during a campaign. They would draw maps of the terrain over which the French armies would advance and fight. These maps would be copied and passed to Napoleon's marshals and corps and divisional commanders, permitting them to have an accurate understanding of the terrain they were about to encounter.

Other reconnaissance forces deployed by armies consisted of light troops, most often only light cavalry, advancing or posted several miles from the main formations. These forces were charged with observing any major formations and with capturing stragglers. Stragglers would be interrogated for information as to their units, directions of march, commanding officers, and plans. It is surprising, but is confirmed by every account read in the preparation of this study, that common soldiers and even officers showed little hesitation in telling their captors anything and everything they knew. The requirement to give only name, rank, serial number and date of birth had yet to be established. All of the European armies used this method of obtaining intelligence.

The question of espionage and non-military methods of acquiring data is a totally different thing. Little data is readily available on this topic, but it is known that Napoleon regularly employed the traditional disguised spy trained in covert operations, as well as businessmen and travellers forwarding observations back to the main army, and the historical activities of consulates and ambassadorial officials. A constant stream of material gathered by these men flowed into Napoleon's headquarters, and he used it in making decisions on how to conduct the real-time grand tactical situation. It was such information that led him to the battlefield at Lützen in May 1813 and only chance, not a lack of proper intelligence, that denied him a decisive victory.

It is not my intention to suggest that at no time did any of the other nations use such intelligence-gathering tools. Documentation exists in Russian correspondence that their military attachés regularly reported details of the force, organisation and equipment of other European allies. A work published in 1912 by the Russian General Staff, *La Guerre nationale de 1812*, is filled with examples of such reports. Margueron's *La Campagne de Russie*, is also filled with more examples of French espionage reports from spies as well as military attachés.

Napoleon also used other, less obvious methods of gathering information. He regularly read or had reviewed every newspaper in Europe. There was no control over what was published, and the French were able to gather an amazing amount of information from these sources. Newspapers regularly reported the presence of this officer or that at a major social event given in honour of the advancing Allied army. They often listed the regiments that were bivouacked in their cities. By innocence or design, 18th and 19th century newspapermen gave away just as many military secrets as today's do. The only major difference was that most military men of the Napoleonic period do not appear to have been sufficiently smart to recognise this, or were neither able nor willing to control the press. In view of the general lack of concern, or even desire for the 'freedom of the press' that is so cherished in the free world today, it is more likely that they didn't realize the impact of what was being reported.

It is interesting to note that Napoleon understood that this tool worked both ways and in a letter to the Duc de Bassano dated 2 March 1813 he expressly states that he wants the Duke to write the *chargés d'affaires* in the various states of the Confederation of the Rhine to direct that they control or censor their newspapers. It appears that the *Gazette de Frankfurt* had published a rather complete account of French movements. Napoleon stated: '*Cela a le plus grand inconvénient*' (this was very inconvenient).

Once the intelligence was gathered it had to be analysed. In the French army this appears to have been done by a small portion of Napoleon's staff, with most of it being done by himself. Though he maintained a force of clerks who accumulated and sorted the data for presentation to him, in contrast to modern practice he appears to have done his own analysis.

The intelligence having been gathered and analysed, decisions were made and transmitted to the various corps commanders. Napoleon would dictate his orders to his clerical staff, and they were then transmitted to the Chief of Staff of the imperial staff, Marshal Berthier, for duplication and retransmission. Supporting Berthier was yet another staff of clerks and scribes, who wrote the orders that were then despatched to the various general officers. It is worth noting that these were frequently encrypted so as to prevent their being of use if captured by the enemy. Orders were carried to their ultimate destinations by a multitude of aides-de-camp, orderly officers, and messengers, who were to be found in all armies of the period.

Once the intelligence was processed and the orders delivered, the next step was strategic manoeuvre.

Strategic manoeuvre

There was one goal for all manoeuvres – to put the enemy in the given situation where battle could be delivered on the terms most favourable to the manoeuvring general. This could be effected by seizing territory, cities, or supplies and forcing the enemy to either give battle to defend those assets, or to commence a precipitate withdrawal to prevent starvation or other calamity befalling him. It could also be effected by getting there 'firstest with the mostest',[34] and thereby outnumbering the enemy so as to be able to destroy him before he can obtain reinforcements.

In the first situation the manoeuvring commander played on two key considerations – national politics and food. The seizure of a national capital was always politically shattering , but it seems to be far more so today than it was before 1860. Napoleon regularly captured Vienna, and he captured Berlin and Moscow, but in each of these instances the governmental bureaucracies were able to re-establish themselves and continue functioning without significantly degrading their effectiveness. In this era only the capture of Paris in 1814 had the effect of destroying a nation's will to continue fighting. However, after 23 years of war it is not surprising that the Parisians were willing to take any opportunity that presented itself to find peace.

The significance of the capture of a capital in the Napoleonic and pre-Napoleonic period was more significant for the loss of the magazines and manufacturing facilities in what was, usually, a country's largest city. Even so, this would have only a long term impact. In the short run it generally did nothing to prevent an army being able to continue fighting.

The strategic manoeuvre aimed at food stuffs had a more significant impact. Armies required a continual flow of food. If it did not arrive, the army would begin to disintegrate and the rate of disintegration would increase geometrically the longer adequate food supplies were unavailable.

The French were better able to withstand this because they had a highly developed ability to forage for food. The armies of other nations, including the various French

---

[34] This phrase reputedly originated with General Forrest, CSA, during the American Civil War.

allies, though able to forage, did not have an organised system whereby foragers brought food back to the main force to feed their fellows. This latter trait is why Massena was able to survive before Torres Vedras for months, even after Wellington had assumed it to have been stripped bare of foodstuffs.

Once faced with being severed from his supply of provisions, the general had two choices: 1) fight his way out; or 2) move as quickly as he could to escape the situation. If he chose to fight, then the enemy general had achieved his probable goal of bringing the other army to battle under conditions of his choosing. Also, by forcing the enemy to attack he could pick the ground to defend and give himself every advantage of terrain.

The second reason for manoeuvre, getting there first with the most, was to locate, isolate, and destroy a smaller enemy force. Probably the most outstanding example of this occurred in early February 1814, when Napoleon, with the shattered remains of his once powerful armies, found Fieldmarshal Blücher had foolishly scattered the corps of the Army of Silesia along the road to Paris, with none of them being within supporting distance of any other. This led to Napoleon's four stunning victories at Champaubert, Montmirail, Château Thierry, and Vauchamps. Vauchamps almost cost Blücher his freedom or possibly even his life. Instead, these four battles cost him about 20,000 casualties.

The ability of any general to do this was dependent on a number of things. The first was his intelligence-gathering machinery. If he was able to identify a sufficiently isolated enemy force he could manoeuvre against it. If it was not sufficiently isolated, the general could manoeuvre his forces so as to be able to isolate it long enough for him to be able to deal with it, and then turn on any advancing relief column. This situation required a constant stream of accurate intelligence, gathered either by reconnaissance forces or by spies.

Having gathered the intelligence, identified the targets, and developed plans, it remained only to move the armies into position to implement them. This required the most basic of the Napoleonic weapons – feet. It was with their feet that all armies moved to execute their master's commands and bring war to their enemy.

Speed and dimensions of marching armies

This is not a very popular or common topic in military literature. Most comments are usually limited to statements of how many miles a division or corps marched in an effort to reach a battlefield and engage in a battle. However, two works devoted to this topic came to light during the preparation of this work, both by French authors. These were Escalle's *Des marches dans les armées de Napoléon* and General Jarry's *Treatise on the Marches and Movements of Armies*. What follows was developed from these. Firstly, however, there are a number of general points that must be taken into consideration when reviewing the movements of armies. These are: 1) the road system and terrain; 2) the organic structure of the armies manoeuvring; 3) the location of magazines and other support; and 4) the general form of the advance (formation).

Europe's road system in the early 19th century was quite different to that of even as long ago as 1900. All of the traffic was wheeled and drawn by horses. Few of the roads were metalled in any way. There were major routes only between the large cities, though in western Europe the countryside was also criss-crossed with a spider's web of secondary and back roads that could be used to march parallel to any major route. This web of secondary roads allowed considerable flexibility in large scale manoeuvres, but the quality of road-maps was often so poor that the analogy of a web fits better than one might otherwise assume. Bad maps and meandering roads could take formations miles from where they were needed. To combat this the reconnaissance forces charted roads, and most armies had cartography staffs attached at army level to update and draw new maps.

There were restrictions on these secondary roads resulting from terrain. Such things as mountains, heavy forests and large rivers provided bottle-necks which funnelled traffic through a few, widely spaced passages. Obviously these terrain features limited manoeuvring and its effectiveness. In addition, the roads, even in western Europe, were such that many tended to become impassable muddy quagmires in heavy rains.

The organic structures limited the manoeuvrability of armies. This is best appreciated when one reviews the 'lightning' manoeuvres of French armies across all 23 years of the Revolutionary and Napoleonic Wars. The French army flew across northern France in 1805 at speeds unimaginable to the rest of Europe's army commanders. Napoleon dropped out of the clouds of Switzerland in 1796, passing through terrain thought impassable for an army, to strike and destroy the Austrian armies in Italy. Davout's corps marched a prodigious 90 miles in the incredibly short period of three days to reach Austerlitz in time to defeat the Austro-Russian army.

There were three reasons for this speed. The principal reason was the organic structure of the French army, the second was its baggage trains, and the third was the youth of its soldiers. To deal with the last point first, and only briefly, the French had flooded their armies with younger men who were more fit and able to endure the rigours of marching. The rest of the European armies – most notably the Prussian pre-1806 army, in which there were many soldiers over 60 – were filled with older men less capable of keeping up the rigorous pace. However, this difference subsequently diminished as France's enemies adopted conscription and expanded their armies beyond their traditional levels.

The effects of youthfulness, however, were only a contributary factor. The major consideration was the organic structure of the marching army; or, to be more specific, what that army chose to drag along with it – its supply train. The French were unique among European armies in not allowing massive numbers of carts and pack animals for the portage of officers tents and property. Nor did regiments have numerous carts, wagons and pack animals to carry its tents and camp equipment.

There are two things to consider about army baggage trains. Firstly, since they couldn't march unescorted they acted as a millstone about the neck of a marching army, slowing it to the reduced rate of the supply wagons, which was slower even than the artillery. Secondly, these huge tails filled the roads with non-combatant traffic that was deemed necessary by the various armies. It clogged the arteries and slowed the entire process of manoeuvre. The French, forced by necessity, paucity and revolutionary egalitarianism, eliminated the trains that had followed French royal armies and marched without. Not being impeded by a mass of wheeled traffic, the French could therefore simply out-march anyone else they encountered.

The fourth factor influencing manoeuvre was the location of magazines and other support. This is tied closely to the existence of the various trains that followed the armies about. Because of the inability of most European armies to live off the land they relied on a system of magazines to provide for their needs. Though a more serious consideration before the Revolutionary Wars, any general would think twice before he went too far from the magazines that fed his troops.

The last, and most significant, consideration is the general form of the advance, which includes the army's formation. Many European armies selected a single main road for their line of advance and stuck to it. As a result all of their traffic moved down a single road in a great line, like beads on a string. There were two reasons for this: poor maps and limited knowledge of the back-roads made using them too risky; and officers liked to bivouac in larger towns if possible. Neither consideration was of much importance to the French. Their cartography staffs were the most developed in Europe at the time, while the residue of revolutionary egalitarianism and the unprivileged background of many of the officers resulted in less concern for physical comforts.

These two factors gave the French greater freedom to manoeuvre on the back-roads. Once using these, Napoleon discovered that he was able to advance against his enemy on a broad front. This meant that a larger percentage of his forces were able to advance onto the battlefield at a much higher rate than the enemy, whose tail was still miles from the battlefield, queued up behind the head and body of the column. The details of train size, however, will be discussed later.

The historical record of strategic marches

In his discussion of the French advance on Ulm, Escalle relates that General Malher's 3rd Division, VI Corps, generally set out between 4.00 am and 6.00 am each day, and stopped between 10.00 am and noon. He also states that though the daily marches might vary from 12 to 40 km, they were generally about 25 to 30. This would indicate an average daily march of six hours covering approximately 27½ km, or a rate of advance of 4.58 kph (2.86 mph). If one takes into account the five-minute break every hour and the half-hour break at the three-quarters mark, the march is reduced to five hours and the velocity rises to 5.5 kph (3.43 mph). During the 1812 campaign Napoleon reckoned on his army advancing an average of 25 km per day. This is close enough to what Malher was doing in 1805 to indicate that the process of marching six hours and resting in bivouac for the rest of the day was quite typical.

In the days before the Battle of Austerlitz, portions of Davout's III Corps performed a march of truly historic proportions. Unfortunately there is considerable disagreement on what the march actually was. In consulting several sources Table 90 has been constructed. The speed of the march has been calculated two different ways. The first column of calculated speeds (minimum speed) was determined by total distance divided by the total hours of the march. The second column (probable maximum speed) was determined assuming that the French troops conformed to the usual marching techniques – five minutes' rest every hour and one hour for lunch – and an assumption of five hours' sleep in every 24 hours. This would allow for 16.5 hours of marching in every 24.

Viger's figures are significantly outside of the range of the others. A review of the standard deviations with (σ No 1) and without (σ No 2) show that Viger is a statistical outlier, and he has therefore been eliminated in calculating the mean. This table shows that Davout's troops were able to average a steady march of 2.5 mph over long periods

Table 90. The march of Davout's III Corps.

Author	Miles	Hours	Minimum speed (mph)	Probable maximum speed (mph)
Chandler	80	50	1.60	2.33
Chandler	70	46	1.52	2.21
Duffy	76	46	1.65	2.40
Elting	70	36	1.94	2.82
Haythornthwaite	70	48	1.46	2.12
Young	80	50	1.60	2.04
Viger	99	36	2.75	4.00
σ No 1	9.60	5.63	0.48	0.63
σ No 2	4.53	4.76	0.15	0.25
Mean	74.3	46.0	1.65	2.50

of time. Remember that Jarry, a period general, said that troops could average 2.27 mph over good roads. Davout's march was, therefore, superior to that, but within a reasonable range of what it was known that marching troops could maintain.

Only limited records of the marches of Allied forces are available, but these were invariably slower than those of the French. However, some insight can be found in McCelland's report to the Secretary of War, where he states that the Russians marched at 2.66 mph. This compares very favourably to the figures of Davout's march, but it should be remembered that some assumptions were made about the length of time that Davout's troops slept, and McCelland does not say how long the Russians could maintain this rate of march.

In the advance of Craufurd's light brigade from Navamoral to Talavera in late July 1809, we find another phenomenal march. The first leg was from Navamoral to Calzada, 14.5 miles, made in five hours (averaging 2.9 mph) under the searing Spanish sun. The British rested briefly then marched to Oropesa, another seven miles, in three hours (2.33 mph). They departed after a five hour rest and marched to the Talavera battle-field in eight hours, covering about 20 more miles (averaging 2.5 mph). Though not as long, this is certainly comparable to Davout's famous march to Austerlitz. In addition, marching in a Spanish July under full pack and Mediterranean sun was probably harder than marching in an Austrian December with or without pack.

There is even one noteworthy case to be found during the Second World War of a similar march. Indeed, one could argue that it exceeds Davout's march. In Sicily, on 20/21 July 1943 the US 3/30th Infantry Regiment, 3rd Infantry Division, marched on foot across the mountains from Aragona to San Stefano. It covered 54 miles in 33 hours, and two hours after its arrival it was committed to the attack on San Stefano. If they had marched non-stop this would work out to 1.6 mph. If the Napoleonic French strategic march system was applied, but they were marched for 15 hours per day, then they travelled at a rate of about 2.5 mph over Italian mountains in the Mediterranean sun.

Obviously the strategic march regulations and documents of the day accurately reflected what a soldier was capable of doing in a long distance, strategic march.

Movements in the presence of the enemy

The work by the Revolutionary French General Jarry is aimed at reviewing the best manner of manoeuvring in the presence of the enemy, *ie* marching onto the field of battle.

His first principal was that it is best to arrive on the battlefield in as many columns as possible. He states that the measures and precautions in all marches were governed by the nature of the country, by the distance from the enemy, and by the circumstances between the two armies. In addition, he states that, for any of a multitude of reasons, an army may have a driving desire to engage in a battle or to avoid battle at any cost.

Jarry felt that the first measure to be attended to in a march was that of the time required for an army to arrive at the desired point. This calculation was based on the number of columns, the number of troops in each column, and the width of the roads and passages through which they must march. An army marched in order of battle, when the battalions and squadrons were broken into divisions or sections, that exactly corresponded with the extent of ground which such battalions and squadrons should cover. A column filed whenever it occupied more ground than the battalions and squadrons which composed it ought to cover when drawn up in order of battle. The time that a column used to arrive by filing was in inverse proportion to its front. That is to say that a column of four in front, whose rear required an hour to arrive at the spot where the head started out, performed the same distance in three-quarters of an hour if it filed with six in front, and half an hour if it filed with eight in front.

Jarry stated that 'experience has taught us, that in roads considered as bad, infantry [could] march at a rate of 3000 paces in an hour; in middling roads 3900; in an even good road they [could] advance as much as 4800 steps in an hour, which is at the rate of about 80 steps per minute, and should be considered as the utmost rapidity with which infantry are capable of advancing.'

The length of the step of which Jarry spoke was 30 inches. With that he calculated:

$$3000 \text{ steps} = 2500 \text{ yds} = 1.42 \text{ mph } (2.3 \text{ kph})$$
$$3900 \text{ steps} = 3250 \text{ yds} = 1.85 \text{ mph } (3.0 \text{ kph})$$
$$4800 \text{ steps} = 4000 \text{ yds} = 2.27 \text{ mph } (3.6 \text{ kph})$$

Jarry considered the rate of a loaded soldier marching in column to be the same as that of a man free and unencumbered. On very bad roads, marches were greatly retarded by battalion guns, which served to slow the advance of the infantry even though it could march significantly faster.

In describing cavalry, Jarry calculated a horse's pace at 35 inches and its hourly rate of advance when walking (not trotting) on various roads as follows:

Bad roads	3600 steps = 1.88 mph
Medium roads	4800 steps = 2.65 mph
Good roads	5400 steps = 2.98 mph

Similarly, he calculated for artillery the following hourly rates of advance:

Bad roads	2400 steps = 1.32 mph
Medium roads	3000 steps = 1.66 mph
Good roads	3600 steps = 1.99 mph

Escalle, in his work *Des marches dans les armées de Napoléon*, also provides some discussion of French marching rates. He states that cavalry was able to move at a rate of 4800 to 5000 metres (3 to 3.125 miles) per hour and infantry at a rate of 3000 to 3500 metres (1.9 to 2.2 miles) per hour. However, the *Règlement* provides for movements of up to 4000 metres (2.5 miles) per hour. The problem appeared to be the movement of the artillery and other cartage, which could seldom exceed 3000 metres (1.9 miles) per hour because of bad roads. Assuming, therefore, that the march was to be normal, and not a forced march, a speed of approximately 3 kph (2 mph) would be the movement rate of a French mixed-arms force on strategic manoeuvres.

It would appear that on the hour every hour the march would stop for a period of five minutes, and after three-quarters of the day's march a halt of at least a half-hour would occur, depending on how far the march was to be. Of course, as the column elongated there could be, and were, further halts to allow the tail to catch up. When the march stopped the regimental musicians would play.

Jarry stated that when marching in the presence of the enemy, the columns must take care to not become separated by obstacles, which might prevent them from linking up if threatened. This was where reconnaissance became important, as the officer leading must know if his column could clear the obstacle before the enemy might be able to engage it.

In providing an example, Jarry recounts the specifics of a battalion advancing. In his example, a 600-man battalion in three ranks, allowing two feet per man, would be 400 ft or 200 marching paces long. If it were thrown into column of march at a width of 12 men or more, there would be space for the officers without making allowance for them in the calculations. However, if it had a frontage of less than 12 men, an allowance must be made for the officers. If on a front of eight, the file would have 75 ranks which, at six feet per rank, made a column 450 ft long. The addition of 20 mounted officers, marching in pairs that he calculated at 12 ft long, added another 120 ft to the length of the column, making it 570 ft long. Using the same calculations, a battalion marching with a front of four men would make a column of 1020 ft.

Several columns, moving in column in a line, required an interval of about 20 ft between them. With the two regimental guns (drawn by four horses) and their two wagons assigned to each battalion in the column another 160 ft was added. This obliged the battalions in the column to expand the distance between them. This prevented the columns from marching in their exact order of battle, though the battalions could.

Escalle also provides some specific examples. In 1805 three divisions containing 24 battalions, their artillery, train and sappers, or 21,500 men, had a length of 9767 metres (6.1 miles). This gives a strategic marching length of 0.28 miles per 1000 men, or about 75% that of the Austrians and 64% of the Russians. The French could and did, however, march in *serré* or dense columns, which would reduce them to 40% of normal length, or 0.11 miles per 1000 men.

If a lateral march was to be executed by the right or left flank within sight of the enemy, the cannons marched separately on one side of the column, so that the column could be wheeled into order of battle by a mere movement to the right or left, with the proper intervals between each battalion. It was the duty of those who regulated the march to open the necessary passages for both the column and the guns.

Jarry's calculations go on to project that a column of 20 battalions, filing by eights, with their guns and other material, would be 14,600 ft or 5840 marching paces long.

This distance was such that it required 90 minutes for the last eight men to arrive at the point where the head of the column stood.

Jarry felt that the 'most perfect marches' were those that were executed with the same number of columns in the first and second lines. That is to say, that eight columns should be marching with four in the front line and four in the second line. These columns should, preferably, enter by the left of the battlefield. By doing this the troops of the first and second line arrived together upon the ground marked for them.

Jarry noted that the head of the columns which composed the second line were not to march at the same height or parallel with those of the first line, but at a distance of 300 or 400 paces behind. Although it was generally expressed that the heads of columns ought to march at the same height or parallel, it was necessary to understand this only of such columns as composed the same line.

If there was a reserve or third line, and if it marched separately in two columns, the head of those two columns was to be 300 to 400 paces in the rear of the head of the columns of the second line. This was because, in marching, the heads of the columns belonging to the different lines, should preserve the same distance from each other as they would in camp.

Though the marches of separate columns for the first and second lines were considered as the most desirable as the army arrived in order of battle simultaneously, it was an arrangement that was difficult to execute in perpendicular marches. This was because it was difficult to find sufficient numbers of roads moving in a roughly parallel direction to support this movement.

Narrow passages and other constrictions required that the column narrow its frontage from, say, 12 to eight or four files. They also required that the troops remain as close as possible. It was the duty of the assistant quartermasters to mark out to the assistant majors-general (*aides major-généraux*), agreeably to point of view, or of *appui*, indicated by the general, the places where the heads of the columns of the first and second lines ought to turn, in order to enter into the field of battle. The assistant majors-general of the brigade (*aides major-généraux de brigade*) should remain there in person until the whole of the columns had passed.

This service could not be properly executed in an army unless the head of each particular department knew perfectly what was, and what was not, his duty. In case there was not an assistant brigade-major (*aide major de brigade*) with each column, it became the duty of the assistant duty quartermaster[55] to be on the spot where the head of the column was to turn into its new direction.

When the enemy was approached through hollow ways, or by narrow and deep valleys, the assistant quartermasters (*aides maréchaux des logis*) charged to open the route were to take care to provide, on one side of the road, a passage wide enough for a man to pass on horseback. 'Without this precaution, it often happened that those who carry orders are stopped and cannot proceed without greatly difficulty. Under certain circumstances, an order thus delayed could cause great problems.'

When an army marched with the intention of giving battle, and, from the nature of the ground, no more than three or four columns could be formed across the defiles, great difficulties were experienced in correctly combining the march of the heavy artillery with those of the infantry regiments without retarding the latter.

[55] 'The officers of the staff were responsible for the regularity of the troop while they were in march to occupy their battlefield, conforming to the ground which has been marked out for them.'

Jarry states that, if a march was being executed in three or more columns, it should have an advanced guard. He goes on to state that, according to the nature of the battleground, the advanced guard should be followed by a greater or lesser detachment of cavalry at an interval of an hour's march. Once the enemy was discovered, the cavalry was to halt and dismount. Its position was to be marked out by an assistant quartermaster, in the rear of each advanced guard, to the right and left of the road, leaving the passage free.

In addition, during day marches the roads were to have signs posted within sight of each other, to guide the direction of the march. These signs were posted by staff officers, whose duty it was to ensure that they were correct.

A Russian corps

Each Russian regiment was authorised to have 41 wagons and carts. If one assumes that the cart was 10 ft long and that the two pairs of horses were another 20 ft, one can reasonably assume that each wagon and its horses would be 30 ft long. If one allows a five-foot interval between each cart moving in a column, each wagon took up a total distance of 35 ft. The wagon train of a regiment was therefore 1435 ft long.

The regiment would not march in the normal, tight formation. Escalle indicates that the ranks opened up to double the normal distance. A battalion in 1810 had a normal length of 368 ft.[56] At double distance, plus a second battalion for a regiment, the total length of the marching infantry of a Russian regiment was 1472 ft. Adding 1435 ft for the regimental train, the regiment had a marching length of 2907 ft. A six-regiment division was, therefore, 17,442 ft long (3.3 miles). A two-division corps would be 34,884 ft long (6.6 miles).

However, when dealing with a Russian corps of two divisions another 2000 ft must be added for the normal interval between divisions. In addition there would be an artillery brigade with one 12-pdr and two 6-pdr batteries (12 guns and 24 limbers each) for each division. The 12-pdr guns were drawn by six horses and the 20-pdr licornes were drawn by 10. The 6-pdr guns were drawn by four horses and the 10-pdr licornes by six. This provides four 20-pdr licornes (40 horses), 16 12-pdr cannons and 10-pdr licornes (96 horses), 16 6-pdr cannons (64 horses), 36 guns and limbers and 72 caissons, a total of 200 horses and 108 guns, limbers and caissons. At 10 ft for pair of horses, 10 ft for the cartage, and a five-foot interval for each of the 108 vehicles, the total length of the artillery brigade was 2620 ft. With two brigades in the corps that comes to 5240 ft. The corps would be 42,124 ft or 7.97 miles long.

As this hypothetical Russian corps would have a total strength of 17,184 infantry and about 1000 artillerists. The total strength of 18,184 men would be spread over a distance of 42,124 ft (7.97 miles or 12.96 km), giving a strategic marching distance of 2300 ft (0.44 miles) for 1000 men.

An Austrian corps

In the 1809 Austrian army each regiment had 13 four-horse wagons and 26 pack animals. If one assumes three pack animals move abreast and the previous calculations for a two-team wagon, the regimental tail would have been 545 ft long. Selecting

---

[56] Though the battalions of different nations all had different theoretical organisations, on a practical basis, with casualties arising from operations, recruitment variations, etc, for the purposes of this discussion a battalion is treated as a battalion, regardless of its nationality.

Feldzeugmeister Graf H. Colloredo's corps on 10 August 1813 as a typical Austrian corps we have a force with 22 infantry battalions, 12 cavalry squadrons, one horse battery, four brigade batteries, one 6-pdr position battery, and two 12-pdr position batteries. Since the Austrian infantry varied by nationalities, let us assume an average length of 723 ft normal length, doubled for marching to 1,446 ft. There are 10 regiments with a total train length of 5450 ft. Twenty-two battalions would, therefore, be 37,262 ft long. Allocating 2000 ft for intervals between divisions adds 4000 ft.

The cavalry had 168 men per squadron, which marched in columns of threes; allocating 10 ft per horse renders a total length for the 12 squadrons of 6720 ft. The artillery had 14 guns drawn by six horses and 32 drawn by four horses, or 60 two-horse teams, and 138 guns, limbers and caissons, giving a total length of 2670 ft.

The corps, with a total strength of 25,928 men, would be a total of 50,652 ft long (9.6 miles). The strategic marching length of 1000 Austrians was, therefore, 1954 ft or 0.37 miles.

Crossed lines of march

There are numerous accounts of battles being delayed because two corps or divisions accidentally encountered one another on the same road or crossed the paths of one another. When columns encountered one another they were to march on the right side of the road, in the same manner as modern vehicles in most of the world.[57]

If the road was not large enough to permit the simultaneous movement of both columns, one was to stop, permitting the other to pass. The decision of which was to stop was based on their rank in the battle order if the units were in the same corps. Train and equipage always stopped to permit the passage of combat troops. This was for two reasons, the first being the higher priority of the combat troops, and the second being the slower rate of march of the train. Similar actions were taken in crossing situations, except when specific orders obliged a deviation from this process.

Marching armies

The French *Règlement de 1792* directed that an army should march in six columns. Each cavalry wing and each infantry division were to be formed with the senior brigade in the lead, followed by the others of the first line, and subsequently by those of the second, in the order of the first.

There were exceptions where the army could march in four columns. This meant that the cavalry was divided up amongst the four columns. The first line of cavalry of each wing marched with the first and fourth infantry divisions, while the second cavalry line marched with the second and third infantry divisions. The two infantry brigades covered the wings marching with the same column as the first line of cavalry of each wing, but forming the rear guard of the column. The French Revolutionary armies soon abandoned the division of the cavalry on the two wings and divided it up amongst the divisions. Only a weak cavalry force remained unified as a reserve.

Finally, the French army orders of battle lost their rigidity in order to adapt to the terrain over which they had to pass. In addition march dispositions and stations modi-

---

[57] This is in contrast to the British and Japanese practice of driving on the left side of the road and is, apparently, the reason why the rest of the world drives on the right side.

fied the march organisation. Armies frequently marched in three columns, preceded by an advanced guard division. This was an infraction of the *Règlement de 1792*, which directed the division of the army into a number of infantry and cavalry divisions proportioned to the quality of troops of each arm.

The progressive development of Napoleon's army exposed new difficulties which the previous experiences of the French army could only, with difficulty, surmount. Assisted by an imperfect general staff, Napoleon resolved almost all of these problems himself rather than delegate their resolution to his staff. There was some attempt at codification of his procedures, but General Duhesme stated that 'all the regulations, in their successive copings, appear to have been proposed by individuals who had not understood our actual battle directives.' Napoleon's doctrine was, therefore, not documented before the collapse of the First Empire.

The *Règlement de 1809* continued the partitioning of an army into four columns. The wings of cavalry marched with the infantry divisions on the right and left. In 1811 General Préval criticised these regulations, which did not have their origin in the organisation of the Imperial armies, stating that they did not reflect contemporary progress in the art of war and the 'master's irrefutable lessons.'

In the Empire, when the French formed their army to march, they organised four columns and distributed their cavalry between each of them. The cavalry generally served as an advanced guard. The artillery of the divisions marched with its assigned divisions. There was no specific system, as with the cavalry, but it appears to have marched in the order in which it was expected to appear in the division's order of battle. The one exception was the grand park, which generally marched along the 'best road'.

The advanced guards that preceded the columns were not specifically regulated by the various French regulations. During the Revolutionary period they were generally formed from the grenadier battalions of each division. Habitually the division staff advanced with the grenadiers leading the second division from the right. Any attached artillery followed behind the grenadiers.

The *Règlement de 1809* established the idea of permanent advanced guards and this was reiterated by General Préval in 1811. The advanced guards were directed to be one hour's march ahead of the main column. It was also common for the grenadier battalions to be preceded by a number of cavalry at a distance of 450 to 700 *toises* (3000 to 4500 ft). In order to maintain the necessary constant communication between the advanced guard and the main body a chain of men was strung out between them.

According to the *Extrait des règlement provisoire pour le service des troupes en campagne*, when an army marched each wing of cavalry and each infantry division was to be formed as a single column. The senior brigade was to form the head of the column, followed by the other brigades of the first line and then by those of the second line in the same order as those of the first line. If the army was to march in four columns the first line of cavalry of the right wing was to march with the first infantry division and the second line of cavalry was to march with the second infantry division. The first line of the left wing of cavalry was to march with the fourth infantry division and the second line of the left wing of cavalry was to march with the third infantry division. The two infantry brigades covering the wings were to march in the same column as the first line of cavalry on their wing and to form the rearguard of the troops in this column.

The infantry appears to have marched in *colonnes serrées*. Each brigade was preceded by 50 workers or sappers who were charged with repairing or opening the road to allow the passage of the brigade. Each regiment was always preceded by an officer at a distance of 50 paces. His job was to reconnoitre the terrain over which the regiment was to pass and assure that it was suitable or could be made suitable for the regiment's passage.

If the force marched in six columns, the two infantry brigades destined to cover the flanks of the cavalry marched at the head or tail of the cavalry on their wing, according to the nature of the terrain.

The artillery parks attached to the divisions always marched in the train of the division of which they were part. They would be assigned to follow a specific brigade within the divisional column. The bulk of the artillery, however, always moved by the route most suitable for wheeled traffic.

When marching the army should ordinarily be open with amalgamated battalions of grenadiers from each division deployed forward of the divisional column to form an advanced guard. Any artillery assigned to the advanced guard should follow immediately behind the grenadiers.

During the march no-one was allowed to break ranks, whether officers or enlisted men. They were forbidden to congregate at streams to quench their thirsts; it was felt that their canteens should suffice. When passing through villages the officers and NCOs were to close up the unit to ensure that no-one broke ranks.

Though march discipline appears to have been tight, there was no passage of verbal orders. It would appear that the tail simply followed the head. If it was unable to do so a superior officer would take charge and lead it on once it was possible to resume the march. No honours were to be rendered; however, it is reasonable to assume that if Napoleon rode by there would be some notice.

Each company detached a sergeant or corporal under the command of a regimental lieutenant to serve as military police during the march and sweep up any deserters that might attempt to conceal themselves and escape from the regiment. Any and all marauders were to be turned over to the commandant of the *gendarmerie impériale*.

Grand tactical marches

One could begin a review of tactical marches by simply saying that the various regulations state that specific given speeds were mandated, and that these must therefore be realistic. Certainly it would be strange for the military establishment to mandate that a unit should march at a specific cadence, if that cadence was either unattainable, or not intended to be used.

For brevity's sake – though it eliminates considerable explanation – the actual cadences, length of prescribed paces, and velocities are summarised in Table 91.

One does need to take into account the style of march used by these nations. The Russians used a goose-step technique, and any attempt to march in this manner at high speed for an extended period would quickly exhaust the troops. As a result the *udwonyi szag* was not used very often or for very long periods.

By contrast, the French and Prussians marched with a locked knee where the foot was thrust straight forward as if to kick the back of the leg of the man in front. The kick was relatively low and required absolute faith on the part of everyone involved that it would be simultaneous. If it was not, because of the closeness of the ranks,

		Paces per minute	Length of pace (ins)	Feet per minute	Miles per hour
Austrian	*Ordinairschritt*	90–95	25.0	188–98	2.14–2.25
	Geschwindschritt	105	–	217	2.47
	Doublirschritt	120	–	249	2.83
French	*Pas ordinaire*	76	26.0	165	1.88
	Pas de route	85–90	–	184–95	2.10–2.22
	Pas accéléré	100	–	217	2.47
	Pas de manoeuvre	120	–	260	2.95
	Pas de charge	120	–	260	2.95
	Pas de course	250	–	542	6.16
Prussian	*Ordinairschritt*	75	25.0	156	1.77
	Geschwindschritt	108	–	225	2.56
British	Ordinary pace	75	30.0	188	2.14
	Quick pace	108	–	270	3.07
Russian	*Tchyi szag*	60–70	28.0	150–75	1.70–1.99
	Skoryi szag	100–110	–	250–275	2.84–3.13
	Udwonyi szag	140–60	–	350–400	3.98–4.26

Table 91. Comparison of marching cadences.

chaos would reign. However, if the French operated at the *pas de course* the method would change from this 'kick' to a bent-knee run, and the problem ceased to exist. The Prussians and other nations, however, did not have a cadence with this extreme rate, and the table reflects their maximum grand tactical movement rates.

Of course, when considering grand tactical movement one also needs to consider the terrain to be traversed and the load being carried by the soldiers. Maintaining a high speed of march is difficult over broken or mountainous terrain, which would doubtless reduce the speed at which a formation could move if it was marching at either the *pas de course* or the *udwonyi szag*. Slower cadences under 120 paces per minute are not likely to have been affected.

The second issue is the loading of the soldier. The *Extrait des règlement provisoure pour le service des troupes en campagne* provides the only solid information available regarding this question. It expressly states that French soldiers were not to take off their haversacks when preparing for combat. It does, however, state that the manner in which they chose to carry their haversacks was entirely up to them. On the other hand, it is reported that the Russians did take off their haversacks at Austerlitz. This question will probably never be completely resolved.

In the tactical arena, unfortunately, the historical records lack specific movement details, *ie* those of time and distance. The generals and men alike usually had more pressing considerations than timing and measuring marches while under fire. In addition, when subjected to fire one does not tend to straggle. Indeed, there are incentives to move faster and for longer, as well as to absorb a little pain in preference to absorbing a bullet. The spice of fear and a dose of adrenalin can make a soldier's feet and pack much lighter.

With this lack of historical documentation, the question of how fast grand tactical movements could be executed must be left to the regulations, and a final decision based on the logical assumption that anything in the regulation was probably based on experience and practical application in the field. The regulated rates of march for tactical situations, as provided by the various regulations, range from 1.77 to 6.16 mph. It is necessary to accept that the military establishments of the day knew these rates of march to be possible and to have been used on the battlefield.

The question of alignment and organisation are certainly a consideration. There are repeated statements about disorganisation arising from any sustained use of the faster cadences, be they the British quick pace (3.07 mph), the Russian *udwonyi szag* (3.98–4.26 mph) or the French *pas de course* (6.16 mph). But a quick rush to a vital sector, followed by a few minutes for the troops to catch their breath and reorganise themselves, make the use of these cadences completely possible. There are many accounts of the *pas de course* being used between 1792 and 1815. No-one would suggest that this pace could be maintained for very long periods, but certainly the soldiers, who marched across Europe repeatedly, would have been in sufficient condition to hold such a pace for an hour.

Jomini on orders of march and strategy

In his work *Traité des grandes opérations militaires*, Jomini reviews the systems of battle used by both Napoleon and Frederick the Great. He discusses orders of march and holds up Frederick's manoeuvres at Kollin, Rossbach and Leuthen as ideal examples. Here the Prussian army formed each line into a column, breaking right or left by platoons, and marched into position.

Jomini extols this manoeuvre as an ideal system. He states that in this order of march the army can make all of its movements, yet remain united. It did not risk being attacked with its forces scattered, as it had formed just two columns (one being the first line of battle and the other being the second line of battle). Both columns are in easy supporting distance of each other and if attacked both can instantly be employed. Because the columns are close the enemy cannot penetrate between them or isolate any part of the army. And, because it is in column, the army can march to its selected terrain and quickly deploy into line of battle. Jomini says that it is only necessary to protect the army with an advanced guard to ensure the success of this type of manoeuvre.

The precision of this manoeuvre was assured because the two columns marched with only 200 or 300 paces between them. If the terrain required it, Jomini allows that an army could double its line and form four columns. In his study Jomini reviews two situations: that in which the two opposing armies are formed in line of battle parallel to each other; and that where the lead elements of an army in march column is attacked.

In speaking of an advancing army being attacked prior to its being able to deploy, Jomini expresses the necessity of keeping the two supporting columns close enough

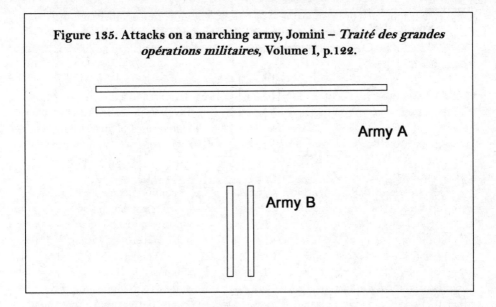

Figure 135. Attacks on a marching army, Jomini – *Traité des grandes opérations militaires*, **Volume I, p.122.**

that neither can be defeated without having had the support of the other. He states that attacking an army while it marches is always advantageous, inasmuch as it allows an army to concentrate its forces against one end of the enemy's line in the same manner as 'crossing the T' in naval warfare allows the same advantage.

In Figure 135, Army A is in the same position as that of Frederick the Great at Rossbach and Army B is in the position of the Allies. Though in the actual battle the Allies were stationary, it has the same effect as if they were marching. This situation allows Army A to destroy the head of Army B's column as well as to outflank it on both sides. Army A can engage all its forces immediately, but Army B is able to engage its forces only successively.

The situation where two advancing armies collide while they are both in march column is shown in Figure 136. Army A, marching in two columns, collides with Army B, also marching in two columns. In this situation the army which is able to deploy in line faster is highly likely to defeat the other. Army A deploys into line C–C and Army B deploys into line D–D. If the deployment takes approximately the same length of time the result is a bloody fight that is decided by the tenacity of the troops and not the skill of the general.

To alleviate this situation Jomini recommended the use of an advanced guard. The advanced guard would deploy into line and face the enemy, be he deployed in line or advancing in column. Jomini states very clearly that this smaller, advanced guard was to fix the main enemy line in position and allow the main army, the instrument of destruction, to manoeuvre against the fixed enemy, be it to take him in the flank or to withdraw if he was too strong.

In Figure 137 the advanced guard (A) forms the head of the column of Army B. If it is attacked by the enemy it deploys to the right or left, according to the direction of the attack, and occupies a position *en potence* relative to the column. This movement is necessary to resist the first effort of the enemy and gain time for the rest of the army to deploy as favourably as possible.

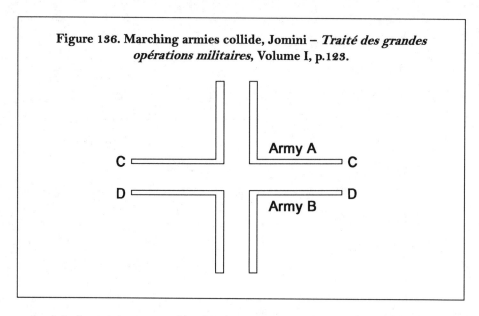

Figure 136. Marching armies collide, Jomini – *Traité des grandes opérations militaires*, Volume I, p.123.

Jomini advocated manoeuvring the remainder of the Army B to one flank or the other of the enemy so as to maximise the chances of victory. By fixing the enemy's army (C) in position with the advanced guard, the remainder of the army can then manoeuvre against a fixed enemy, or at least an enemy who is less able to manoeuvre against it.

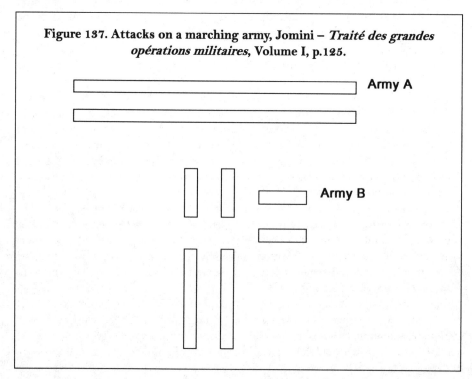

Figure 137. Attacks on a marching army, Jomini – *Traité des grandes opérations militaires*, Volume I, p.125.

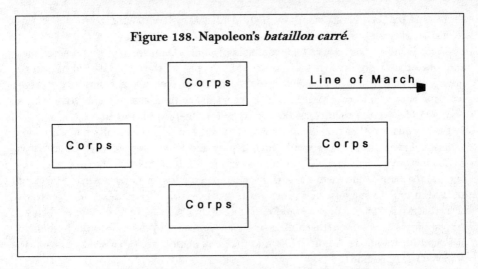

Figure 138. Napoleon's *bataillon carré*.

Napoleon's strategic manoeuvring system

The evolutionary sequence between Jomini's work and the development of Napoleon's strategy is the reverse of how it is presented here. Jomini wrote his *Traité des grandes opérations militaires* as both a refutation of Guibert and as a comparison of Napoleon's generalship to that of Frederick the Great. Jomini discussed the smaller scale manoeuvres of two armies and the use of a small force – the advanced guard – to tie the enemy's forces in place while the rest of the army manoeuvred against his flank.

This is what Napoleon did, but on a far greater scale with what he called the *batallion carré*. This formation was in fact composed on a corps level and ideally had four corps advancing in a roughly diamond-shaped formation. Because Napoleon did it on a larger scale than that which Jomini extolled it was more logical to deal with Jomini before looking at Napoleon's system.

The *bataillon carré* worked on the same principal as Jomini's advanced guard and main body. Once contact was made by one of the four formations the French used their superior staff to re-direct the movement of the other three formations. Their goal was the same as Jomini's – to strike the enemy in his flank. The only difference was that instead of an advanced guard of a few regiments holding the enemy in place, Napoleon used a complete corps.

The corps that established contact would engage in battle and lock the enemy formation in position. Much like a 'tar baby', the smaller force would pin a larger enemy force in position while the other three corps manoeuvred on his flanks or advanced to form a reserve behind the corps already engaged in combat. The most impressive example of this manoeuvre is found in the 1813 spring campaign and led to the Battle of Lützen. Eugène was the point of the diamond formation moving on Leipzig. Ney was on his right flank, the guard, Oudinot and Marmont were to his left, with Bertrand advancing in the rear. Ney's corps contacted the main Allied army south of Leipzig. Eugène swung south from his advance on Leipzig to manoeuvre on the Allied right while Bertrand and Marmont closed on the Allied left. The Imperial Guard, forming the fourth formation, closed behind Ney where it formed a general reserve and eventually executed the *coup de grace* on the Allied centre. If night had not allowed the Allies to slip off the battlefield, the morning would have found them being struck in the centre and on both flanks simultaneously. As it was, when dawn arrived the Russo-Prussian army had vanished eastwards.

Traditionally, other armies had marched onto the battlefield, deployed their armies and, once they were deployed, began to fight. Napoleon's system allowed him to be fully prepared to act as he marched onto the battlefield. He could theoretically concentrate the bulk of his army on the head of the enemy column, crush it, and drive it back on the tail before the enemy had time to completely deploy his forces.

Indications are that the advanced guards would engage one another when major armies collided. Both forces would then deploy and whichever side had other corps advancing onto the battlefield would do so either filling in holes in the line, or crashing into the flank of the enemy. Two prime examples of this are Lützen, where Marmont arrived in time to support Ney's corps as it was beginning to crumble, and Dessaix's arrival at Marengo. Again we could cite Lützen, but we should also recognise Ney's arrival on the Russian northern flank at Eylau, Junot's movement into the battlefield at Valentino-Lubino in August 1812, and the flank manoeuvre proposed by Davout to Napoleon at Borodino.

For the French, this system of moving over different roads served their logistical system because each corps passed over ground that was not shared by any other corps. Each corps consequently had fresh terrain in which to forage, thereby maximising the food available and minimising the need for a formalised supply system.

Though, under Napoleon, the French made more use of this system and were far better coordinated when they did it, the various members of the coalitions against the French also occasionally manoeuvred their armies in several independent corps and army-sized columns down roughly parallel tracks.

The principal reason for French superiority and their ability to execute these strategic manoeuvres was their highly developed staff corps. It was during the 1813 campaign that French superiority began to wane. This was not only because the Allies had learned to execute this type of manoeuvre any better, or because their staffs were becoming better organised, but was also because the French had lost their light cavalry. When this cavalry was gone, or was badly outnumbered, its ability to screen the French lines and protect their couriers faded perceptibly. During the 1813 and 1814 campaign the French regularly suffered from a high percentage of intercepted messages. With this communication breakdown came inability to coordinate manoeuvres and to maximise the effectiveness of their forces on the battlefield.

Select Bibliography

Barber, Captain, *Instructions for the Formation and Exercise of Volunteer Sharpshooters*, London (1804).

Belhomme, Lieutenant-Colonel V.L.J.F., *Histoire de l'Infanterie en France*, Vol. V, *1792–1815*, Paris (1899).

B'eskrovnij, L.G., *Ot'ecestv'ennaja Vojna 1812 Goda (Patriotic War of 1812)*, Moscow (1962).

Bonie, General T., *Tactique francaise, cavalerie au combat*, Paris (1887).

Bujac, E., *L'Armée Russe, son histoire, son organization actuelle*, Paris (1894).

Carnot, M., *De la défense des places fortes*, Paris (1810).

Chandler, D., *The Campaigns of Napoleon*, New York (1966).

Colin, J., *La tactique et la discipline dans les armées de la révolution; correspondance du général Schauenbourg du 4 avril au 2 août 1793*, Paris (1902).

Cooper, T.H., *A Practical Guide for the Light Infantry Officer*, London (1806).

Dedon Sr., Chef de brigade, *Précis Historique des Campagnes de l'Armée de Rhin et Moselle, Pendant l'An IV et l'An V Contenant le récit de tout les opérations de cette armée, sous le commandement du général Moreau, depuis la rupture de l'armistice conclu à la fin de l'An III, jusqu'a la signature des prémliminaires de la paix à Léoben*, Paris (1803), which contains *Dissertation sur l'Ordonnace de l'Infanterie*.

Duffy, C., *Austerlitz*, Hamden, Conn (1977).

Duhesme, P.G., *Essai historique sur l'infanterie légère*, Paris (1864).

Dundas, *Principals of Military Movements Chiefly Applied to Infantry Illustrated by Manoeuvres of the Prussian Troops and an Outline of the British Campaigns in Germany during the War of 1757*, London (1795).

Durova, N., *The Cavalry Maiden, Journals of a Female Russian Officer in the Napoleonic Wars*, London (1988).

Escalle,C.P., *Des marches dans les armées de Napoléon*, Paris (1912).

Favé, Capitaine, *Emperor Napoleon's New System of Field Artillery*, London (1854).

Fletcher, I., *Craufurd's Light Division, The Life of Robert Craufurd and his Command of the Light Division*, Tunbridge Wells (1991).

Foucart, P.J., *Bautzen (une bataille de deux jours) 20–21 mai 1813*, Paris (1897).

von der Goltz, C., *Von Rossbach bis Jena*, Berlin (1906).

German Grosser Generalstab, (Jany), *Urkundliche Beiträge und Forsuchungen zur Geschichte des Preussischen Herres*, Heft 14/15: *Die Preussische Artillerie von ihrer neuformation 1809 bis zum Jahre 1816*, Heft 21–25: *Das Preussische Heer im Jahre 1812*, Berlin (1909).

German Grosser Generalstab Kriegsgeschichteliche Abteilung II Deutschland, *1806, Das Preussische Offizierkorps und die Untersuchung der Kriegsereignisse*, Berlin (1906).

Hughes, Major-General B.P., *British Smooth-Bore Artillery, The Muzzle Loading Artillery of the 18th and 19th Centuries*, London (1969).

———, *Firepower: Weapons Effectiveness on the Battlefield, 1630–1850*, London (1974).

Jarry, General A.A.G., *Treatise on the Marches and Movements of Armies*, trans. by R. Rochfort, London (1807).

Jomini, A.H., *Traité des grand opérations militaires contenant l'histoire critique des campagnes de Fréderic II comparées à celles de l'empereur Napoléon avec un recueil des principes généraux de l'art de la guerre*, Paris (1811).

Keegan, J., *The Face of War*, New York (1976).

Kosciusko, General T., *Manoeuvres of Horse Artillery*, New York (1808).

Lauerma, M., *L'Artillerie de campagne francaise pendant les guerres de la révolution*, Helsinki (1956).

Lünsmann, F.O., *Die westfälische Armee*, Hanover (1934).

Lynn, J.A., *The Bayonets of the Republic*, Chicago (1984).

McCelland, Captain G.B., *Report of the Secretary of War*, Washington (1957).

Magueron, L.J., *Campagne de Russie*, Paris (1897–1906).

Meunier, Baron, *Evolutions par brigade ou instruction servant de developement aux manoeuvres de ligne indiques par les règlements*, Paris (1814).

de Morla, T., *Tratado de Artillerie Para el Uso de la Academia de Caballeros Cadetes del Real Cuerpo de Artilleria, Dividido en Tres Tomos y Otro de Laminas, Que tratan de las Principales funciones de los Oficiales de este Cuerpo en pas y en guerra*, Segovia (1816).

Müller, H., *Die Entwicklung der Feld-Artillerie in Bezug auf Material, Organization und Taktik, von 1815 bis 1870*, Berlin (1873).

Nafziger, G.F. *The Bavarian and Westphalian Armies, 1799–1815*, (1981).

———, *The Russian Army, 1800–1815*, Cambridge, Ontario (1983).

———, *Napoleon's 1812 Invasion of Russia*, Novato, CA (1988).

———, *The French Army, 1788–1815*, Leeds (1988).

———, *Lutzen and Bautzen*, Chicago (1993).

———, *Napoleon at Dresden, The Battles of August 1814*, Chicago (1994).

———, and Park, J., *The British Military; Its System and Organization, 1803–1815*, Cambridge, Ontario (1983).

Ney, M., *Memoirs of Marshal Ney*, London (1833).

Oman, C.W.C., *Wellington's Army 1809–1814*, New York (1913).

———, *A History of the Peninsular War*, Oxford (1980).

von Quistorp, B., *Geschichte der Nord Armee im Jahre 1813*, Berlin (1894).

Roberts, J., *The Hand-Book of Artillery for the Service of the United States, (Army and Militia) with the Manual of Heavy Artillery, Including that of the New Iron Carriage*, New York (1863).

de Rogniat, Baron, *Considerations sur l'art de la guerre*, Paris (1816).

Rottemberg, H., *Regulations for the Exercise and Conduct of Rifles and Light Infantry on Parade and in the Field*, Whitehall (1798).

Rouquerol, G., *L'artillerie au début des guerres de la révolution*, Paris (1898).

Russian Army General Staff, *La Guerre nationale de 1812*, Paris (1912).

Scott, Major-General W., *Infantry Tactics; or, Rules for the Exercise and Manoeuvers of the United States' Infantry*, New York (1861).

du Seruzier, Baron, *Memoires militaires du Baron Seruzier, colonel d'artillerie légère*, Paris (nd).

Smirke, R., *Review of a Battalion of Infantry including the 18 Manoeuvres*, London (1810).

Tanski, J., *Tableau statistique, politique, et moral du système militaire de la Russie*, Paris (1833).

d'Urtubie, T.B.S.D., *Manuel de l'artilleur, contenant tous les objects dont la conaissance est nécessaire aux officiers et sous officiers d'artillerie suivant l'approbation de Gribeauval*, Paris (1795).

Valentini, *Abhandlung über den Kleinen Krieg und über den Gebrach der leichten Truppen*, Leipzig (1820).

Zweguintzov, W., *L'Armee russe*, 4th Part: 1801–25, Paris (1969).

Drill regulations

Austria

Auszug aus dem Abrichtungs-Reglement der K.K. Infanterie Zum Begrachte für die Landwehre in den K. öst Provinzen, Brunn (1808).

Exercir-Reglement für die Kaiserlich-königlich Infanterie, Vienna (1807).

Exercir-Reglement für die Kaiserlich-königlich Kavallerie, Vienna (1808).

Bavaria

Allegemine Verordungen über das Aufgeboten der mobilen Legionen und die Errichtung eines National-Chevauxlegers-Regiments, Munich (1813).

Exerzierreglement für das Bürger-Militair im Königreich Baiern, Bergen (1809).

Britain

Instructions and Regulations for the Formations and Movements of the Cavalry, Whitehall (1813).

Manual and Platoon Exercises, etc., etc., London (1804).

Regulations for the Exercise and Control of Rifles and Light Infantry on Parade and in the Field, London (1798).

Rules and Regulations for the Manual and Platoon Exercise and Formations and Field Exercise for His Majesty's Forces for use of the Non-Commissioned Officers of the British Army, London (1807).

Rules and Regulations for the Manual and Platoon Exercises, Formations, Field Exercise and Movements of His Majesty's Forces, London (1808).

France

Aide memoire à l'usage des officiers d'artillerie de France, Paris (1801).

Ecole du cavalier à pied par demands et par réponses, Paris (1803).

Extrait du règlement provisoire pour le service des troupes en campagne, Paris (1813).

French Minister of War for the Instruction of Students at St Cyr, *Manual d'infanterie ou resumé de tous les règlements, décrets, usages, et renseignements propres aux sous-officiers de cette armée*, Paris (1813).

Instruction concernant les manoeuvres de la cavalerie légère, Paris (Year VII).

Instruction concernant les manoeuvres de l'infanterie donné par l'Inspecteur général de l'infanterie de l'armée du Rhin, Strasbourg (1809).

Instruction destinee au troupes légère et aux officiers, (*c* 1805–8).

Instruction destinee aux troupes légères et aux officiers qui servant dans les avant-postes, rédigée sur un instruction de Frederic II a ses officiers de cavalerie, 4th edition, Paris (nd).

Instruction pour le service et les Manoeuvres de l'Infanterie légère, Paris (*c* 1805–8).

Instruction pour les gardes nationales arrêtée par le comité militaire, Paris (1791).

Instruction theoretique d'apres l'ordonnance de 1788, Paris (Year IX).

Manoeuvres des batteries de campagne pour l'artillerie de la garde impériale, Paris (1812).

Manual des sous-officiers de cavalerie extrait des règlements militaires, Hamburg (1812).

Règlement concernant la manoeuvre de l'Infanterie de 1er Août 1791, Paris (1811).

Manuel du garde nationale, ou recueil de tout ce qu'il est indispensable à tout officier, sous-officier et garde national de savoir, Paris (1814).

Ordonnance provisoire sur l'exercice et les manoeuvres de la cavallerie rédigée par order du ministre de la guerre du 1er Vendémiaire an XIII, Paris (1810).

Petit manual du cannonier, Paris (1810).

Project de règlement sur les manoeuvres de l'artillerie, Paris (1825).

Hesse-Darmstadt

Exerzier-Reglement für die Landgräflich Hessische Leichte Infanterie, Darmstadt (1805).

Hesse-Kassel

Exerzir-Reglement für Cürassiers, Dragoners und Husaren, Kassel (1796).

Exerzir-Reglement für die Infanterie der Kurhessischen Armee, Kassel (1814).

Instructions for samtliche Infanterie-Regimenter und das Fusilier-Bataillon, handwritten document, Kassel (1797).

Hanover

Haushalts Reglement für die Chur-Braunschweig-Lüneburgische Infanterie in Friedens auch Krieges-Zeiten, Hanover (1786).

Prussia

Exerzir-Reglement für die Artillerie der Königlich Preussischen Armee, Berlin (1812).

Exerzir-Reglement für die Infanterie der Königlich Preussischen Armee, Berlin (1812).

Exerzir-Reglement für die Kavallerie der Königlich Preussischen Armee, Berlin (1812).

Reglement für die Husaren-Regimenter und für das Regiment Bosniacken der Königlich-Preussischen Armee, Berlin (1796).

Reglement für die Königl. Preuss. leichte Infanterie, Berlin (1788).

Regulations for the Prussian Infantry, London (1759).

Saxony

Auszug aus dem Reglement für die Königlich Sächsische Infanterie zu den Ubungen in geschlossener Ordnung, Dresden (1826).

Exercir Reglement für die Königlich Sächsische Cavalerie, Dresden (1810).

Fragen über Stellung und Bewegung einen Compagnie und eines Bataillon nach dem Königlich Sachsischen Exercir-Reglement für Junge Personen entworfen, welche sich zu Officieren bilden wollen, Dresden (1809).

Reglement zu den Ubungen für die Königlich Sächsische leichte Infanterie, Dresden (1822).

Sweden

Exercitie-Reglemente för Cavaleriet, Griefswald (1806).

Exercitie-Reglemente för Cavaleriet, Stockholm (1808).

Kongl. Maj:ts Förnyade Nadiga Förordning Och Reglement för Regementerne til Fot. Dat. den 29 April 1794, Stockholm (1794).

Kongl. Maj:ts Nadiga Förängdringar Och Tilläggningar Uti Infanterie-Exercitie-Reglementet 1806, Stockholm (1807).

Kongl. Maj:ts Nadiga Förordning Och Reglement för Regementerne til Fot. Dat. den 10 Feb. 1813, Stockholm (1813).

Reglemente för Akande Artilleriets Tjenstgöring Och Exercice, Stockholm (1808).

Reglemente för Kongl. Maj:ts Tunga och Latta Cavalerie, Stockholm (1793).

Reglemente för Kongl. Maj:ts Tunga och Lätta Cavalerie, Stockholm (1795).

Sammandrag af Exercitie-Reglemente för Cavalerie, Stockholm (1807).

Stycke-Reglemente för Kongl. Maj:ts Artillerie Reglemente, Stockholm (1788).

Tillagg Utgi Infanterie Exercitie Reglementet; Af Kongl. Maj:t til iakttagande i Nader anbefalt, Stockholm (1812).

Russia

Réglement de sa majesté impériale concernant le service de l'infanterie, St Petersburg (1798).

Voinse Ostav' o P'khotnoe Sdozh'b , Kniga I, Stroevoe Sdozh'b, Chassh' III, St Petersburg (1837).

Index

A HISTORY OF
THE PENINSULAR WAR

THE
NAPOLEONIC LIBRARY
Published by Greenhill Books

The Campaign of 1812 in Russia
by General Carl von Clausewitz
Introduction by George F. Nafziger

The Campaign of Waterloo
by the Hon. Sir John Fortescue
History of the Waterloo Campaign
by Captain William Siborne

In the Peninsula with a French Hussar:
Memoirs of the War of the French in Spain
by Albert Jean Michel de Rocca

Journal of the Waterloo Campaign
by General Cavalié Mercer

Life in Napoleon's Army:
The Memoirs of Captain Elzéar Blaze
Commentary by Lt. Gen. Charles Napier
Introduction by Philip Haythornthwaite

Memoirs of a French Napoleonic Officer:
Jean-Baptiste Barrès, Chasseur of the Imperial Guard
Edited by Maurice Barrès

The Memoirs of Baron de Marbot, volume 1
The Memoirs of Baron de Marbot, volume 2

Napoleon and Iberia: The Twin Sieges of
Ciudad Rodrigo and Almeida, 1810
by Donald D. Horward

Napoleon and Waterloo: The Emperor's Campaign
with the Armée du Nord, 1815
by A. F. Becke

Napoleon's Army:
The Military Memoirs of Charles Parquin
Translated and edited by B. T. Jones

The Notebooks of Captain Coignet
by Captain Jean-Roche Coignet

The Peninsular Journal, 1808–1817
by Major-General Sir Benjamin D'Urban

Twenty-Five Years in the Rifle Brigade
by William Surtees. Introduction by Ian Fletcher

Waterloo Letters
Edited by Major-General H. T. Siborne

With the Guns in the Peninsula:
The Peninsular War Journal of
Captain William Webber
Edited by Richard Henry Wollocombe

OTHER
NAPOLEONIC BOOKS
Published by Greenhill Books

Greenhill Books

Dictionary of the Napoleonic Wars
by David G. Chandler

The Eagle's Last Triumph:
Napoleon's Victory at Ligny, June 1815
by Andrew Uffindell

1812: The March on Moscow
by Paul Britten Austin
Introduction by David G. Chandler

1812: Napoleon in Moscow
by Paul Britten Austin

1812: The Great Retreat
by Paul Britten Austin

The Illustrated Napoleon
by David G. Chandler

Imperial Bayonets: Tactics of the
Napoleonic Battery, Battalion and Brigade
as Found in Contemporary Regulations
by George Nafziger

Military Maxims of Napoleon
Edited and with Introduction and Commentary
by David G. Chandler

On the Fields of Glory:
The Battlefields of the 1815 Campaign
by Andrew Uffindell and Michael Corum

On the Napoleonic Wars: Collected Essays
by David G. Chandler

With Eagles to Glory:
Napoleon and his German Allies in the
1809 Campaign
by John H. Gill